"David Congdon and I grew up together theologically. It has been my privilege to watch his penetrating insight grow and develop into a creative theological program. Rumors of dialectical theology's demise have been greatly exaggerated. If you are interested in a glimpse of what a fresh dialectical theology for the twenty-first century looks like—and you should be!—you need look no further."

"While the idea of universal salvation has long been a minority report in the Christian tradition, it has found an increasing number of advocates in recent times. This volume provides a rigorous, creative, and comprehensive dogmatic account of this belief from one of the brightest young scholars at work today. Even those who are not in agreement with Congdon's line of argument and conclusions will be challenged and enriched by the detail and scope of his engaging theological vision."

"Congdon has authored a sophisticated and ambitious, dogmatic essay, full of insight and bristling with provocation. He invites us to join him in a sustained experiment in radically soterio-centric thinking: what if the work of the God of the gospel on the cross were truly the Archimedean point from which all things are moved and so saved? Congdon's aim is to limn the revolution in Christian theology that should follow when Christian imagination and intelligence are animated and disciplined anew by faith in the God whose very being is at stake in his advent 'for us and for our salvation.' *The God Who Saves* is an important intervention in contemporary doctrinal debate."

"This is a bold, clear, and stimulating articulation of the Good News. While few will follow Congdon at every point, his account of eschatological theo-actualized universalism provokes in the places where it matters most, and reminds us again why the advent of Jesus Christ is the first article of faith, and the ground that makes Christian dogmatics possible, intelligible, and profoundly hopeful. Dorothee Sölle once insisted that 'when we ask ourselves what God is like, we must answer first by looking at what God does.' This essay takes up that momentous task admirably."

—JASON GORONCY
Senior Lecturer in Systematic Theology, Whitley College, University of Divinity, Australia

"A powerful and provocative work. In prose that is simultaneously critical, polemical, and constructive, Congdon articulates in outline a distinctive theological vision of the apocalyptic gospel of God's gracious salvation. Though many will disagree with the proposals found herein, none can afford to ignore the searching questions that Congdon puts to contemporary theological discussions. To do so would impoverish our discourse and impair our witness to the expansiveness of God's embrace."

—CHRISTIAN T. COLLINS WINN
Professor of Historical and Systematic Theology, Bethel University

The God Who Saves

The God Who Saves

A Dogmatic Sketch

DAVID W. CONGDON

▲ CASCADE *Books* • Eugene, Oregon

THE GOD WHO SAVES
A Dogmatic Sketch

Cascade Books
An Imprint of Wipf and Stock Publishers
199 W. 8th Ave., Suite 3
Eugene, OR 97401

www.wipfandstock.com

PAPERBACK ISBN: 978-1-60899-827-2
HARDCOVER ISBN: 978-1-4982-8539-1
EBOOK ISBN: 978-1-5326-0849-0

Cataloguing-in-Publication data:

Names: Congdon, David W.

Title: The God who saves : a dogmatic sketch / David W. Congdon.

Description: Eugene, OR: Cascade Books, 2016 | Includes bibliographical references and indexes.

Identifiers: ISBN 978-1-60899-827-2 (paperback) | ISBN 978-1-4982-8539-1 (hardcover) | ISBN 978-1-5326-0849-0 (ebook)

Subjects: LCSH: Salvation—Christianity | Universalism | Eschatology | Apocalyptic literature

Classification: BX9941 C23 2016 (print edition) | BX9941 (ebook)

Manufactured in the U.S.A.   09/27/16

For Mark Husbands and Bruce L. McCormack
who taught me to think theologically

Hope in *God* is the essence of hope in the resurrection. This hope is hope in salvation only to the extent that it is directed toward the God who saves.

—EBERHARD JÜNGEL, *TOD*

Contents

Prologue
How My Mind Has Changed

This is not the book I initially set out to write. For that reason, some biographical context is necessary.

This book had its genesis in 2006, when I came to the realization that universal salvation was the only account of Christianity I could find credible. The reasons for this are varied and I will not go into them here. Suffice it to say that everything I studied since has only confirmed those initial intuitions, even if my explanatory account has dramatically changed. At the time I was still a theological neophyte, a seminarian discovering the diversity of the Christian tradition. I was under two main influences. The first was my complicated, often antagonistic, relationship with my evangelical heritage. I was raised within the context of conservative American evangelicalism and was a sixth-generation Wheaton College graduate—my evangelical credentials were second to none. But my experience at Wheaton left me disillusioned with this community and I sought to expand my theological horizons. Following graduation I matriculated at Princeton Theological Seminary in fall 2005 to study under Bruce McCormack, who had lectured at Wheaton on the doctrine of justification in 2003. The year 2006 was also important because that year Gregory MacDonald published *The Evangelical Universalist*. As I was seeking to flee my evangelical identity in favor of universalism, MacDonald's work came along to show how to have one's cake and eat it too. While I never shared MacDonald's particular view on the matter, it arrived at a most opportune time and convinced me I was on the right path, albeit a different one.

Naturally, as a Princeton Seminary student, the second influence was my study of Karl Barth. From Barth I appropriated a strong sense of Jesus Christ's centrality to faith and theology. But even more importantly, Barth taught me to see Christ's saving work as the *actuality* of salvation and not merely its *possibility*. In those early years of seminary I was still in the mode of deconstructing my evangelical upbringing, a process that began the summer between my freshman and sophomore years of college. Barth provided me with the tools to leave evangelical theology behind where soteriology was concerned. Evangelicalism, especially in North America, has always placed a premium on the personal decision of faith. Salvation occurs when a person consciously commits to follow Jesus. Such a person, some say, is now "born again." Many have criticized this evangelical paradigm for making salvation contingent upon being born in a context in which one is likely to hear the gospel and be able to respond to it—hence the perennial question, "What about those who have never heard?" Barth taught me to reject this paradigm for a more basic theological reason, namely, that it made the human person, rather than God in Christ, sovereign over my eternal place before God. If Christ alone actualizes our reconciliation to God, then the only question is whether Christ represents all people or only a select few. On that point I had no doubts—the former! I was never a Calvinist—and despite what I tried telling myself in 2006 and 2007, I was never Reformed either. Things then took a surprising turn in 2008.

Like many seminary graduates, I thought my theological perspective was more or less settled. But in the autumn of 2008 I began the PhD program in theology with an independent study on Rudolf Bultmann under the tutelage of James F. Kay. Reading Bultmann threw open the windows of my mind and let a fresh wind blow through me. In that independent study I read Bultmann's 1959 response to Barth's essay, *Christ and Adam,* in which Bultmann objects, among other things, to the clearly universalistic thrust of Barth's piece.[1] This was initially quite a shock. I recognized all the key elements of Barth's dialectical theology in Bultmann's writings, so I naturally expected the latter to reach the same soteriological conclusions. The fact that he did not—and demurred emphatically—took me months, even years, to process. In a way unlike any theologian I had encountered, Bultmann emphasized the problem and significance of our *historicity* (*Geschichtlichkeit*), referring to the fact that our existence, including our thinking and speaking, occurs within a particular historical location. For Bultmann any theological claim has to concern us in our historicity. The problem with universalism—as well as any notion of pretemporal election—is that it makes a judgment about the individual without regard for her particular historicity and is only, at best, indirectly related to personal existence. Reading Bultmann thus validated an instinct I had inherited from my evangelical upbringing. Bultmann (perhaps ironically, perhaps not) helped me to recover my evangelicalism!

---

1. See Bultmann, "Adam and Christ," 158.

During the following years, with assistance from further study of Barth and the writings of Eberhard Jüngel, I would gradually internalize Bultmann's insights into the historical nature of both God and appropriate talk of God. But my basic intuitions about universal salvation remained unshakeable. The result was a deep internal tension—a tension between a Bultmannian methodological starting point and a Barthian soteriological conclusion. My dissertation, which I began to formulate in 2010, was an attempt to reconcile Barth and Bultmann at the methodological level. The received wisdom is that the Bultmann who formulated the program of demythologizing had abandoned the dialectical theology he once shared with Barth in the 1920s. Before I could tackle the question of soteriology I first had to overturn that widely held assumption. The research I conducted revealed that Barth and Bultmann shared a core dialectical thesis from beginning to end, and it was *Barth*, rather than Bultmann, who departed from the original version of this thesis in response to various theological and political pressures. Because the shared thesis is soteriological in nature, their disagreement was also soteriological. Essentially, dialectical theology is "an eschatological-christological soteriology, in which the saving event of the transcendent God that occurs in Jesus Christ remains beyond every immanent situation," but "one can either develop this soteriology consistently to the end (as in Bultmann), or one can reinterpret it protologically (as in Barth)."[2] The difference between Barth and Bultmann is "a difference in soteriology, but both soteriologies remain dialectical in nature. Both establish the nongivenness of God, but the one does so in terms of an eschatologically-grounded time-eternity dialectic in the event of revelation, while the other does so in terms of a protologically-grounded divine-human dialectic in the person of Christ."[3]

I am getting ahead of myself. It took me until at least 2012 before I had the details of Barth and Bultmann's relationship worked out, which was also around the time I was figuring out what my own position would be. The virtue of studying the Barth-Bultmann debate is that it forces one to become a systematic theologian, since their dispute touches on the core matters of Christian doctrine. But in 2010 I had not yet gone through that theological gauntlet. On January 5, 2010, Robin Parry contacted me about the idea of writing a "systematic theology on universalism." I had attempted something

2. Congdon, *Mission*, 233.

3. Ibid., 290. See ibid., 281n112: "Bultmann, by remaining consistent with the soteriology of the early Barth, remains consistently dialectical in his theology. Barth's change in soteriology does not mean he abandons dialectical thinking altogether, but it does mean that he adopts a new *kind* of dialectical theology. . . . By shifting the center of gravity to protology Barth broke away from the dialectical movement he inaugurated."

along these lines back in 2006, when I wrote a series of posts for my weblog called, "Why I Am a Universalist: A Dogmatic Sketch." The outline hews closely to the pattern of Barth's *Church Dogmatics*, with some modifications borrowed from Eberhard Jüngel, whom I was avidly reading at the time:

1. Prolegomena

2. The Doctrine of God, Part 1: Introduction

3. The Doctrine of God, Part 2: *Deus pro nobis*

4. The Doctrine of God, Part 3: The Attributes of God

    4.1. God's complexity and simplicity as the "one who loves in freedom"

    4.2. Grace

5. The Doctrine of God, Part 4: The Doctrine of Election

    5.1. A summary of Barth's doctrine of election

    5.2. Jesus Christ, electing and elected

    5.3. Jesus Christ, divine election, and predestination

    5.4. The election of the individual

6. Jesus Christ, the Judge Judged in Our Place

7. The Doctrine of Justification

    7.1. Introduction to the doctrine of justification

    7.2. *Solus Christus*

    7.3. *Sola gratia*

    7.4. *Solo verbo*

    7.5. *Sola fide*

8. The Doctrine of the Atonement

    8.1. Introduction to the doctrine of the atonement

    8.2. Models of the atonement

    8.3. Foundations for a doctrine of the atonement

    8.4. Parameters for a doctrine of the atonement

        8.4.1. Triune

        8.4.2. Concretely christocentric

        8.4.3. Substitutionary

        8.4.4. Actualized

The work reached nearly 40,000 words before I called a halt to the series after four months. The posts garnered a surprising amount of attention. I regularly received emails from people around the world expressing appreciation for defending universalism. I was even invited to speak at a Christian Universalist Association meeting (which I declined due to scheduling conflicts). I became tired of explaining to people why the series ended so abruptly. Two years later, on November 12, 2010, I left a note on my blog explaining why I abandoned the project:

> Because some people have asked, I want to make it clear that (a) I will not finish this series and (b) I no longer agree with some of the theological claims I make in these posts. That's not to say I now reject the "universal scope" of God's grace. Rather, I reject a number of the theological moves and concepts that I employ in order to articulate this grace. I am currently working on a book (to appear in a few years) that will clarify my thinking on these matters.

This brings me back to the email from Robin. In January 2010 I was still very much in a period of transition. My theology was no longer what it was when I wrote the 2006 series, but it had not yet matured into something more firmly rooted. I responded to Robin the same day, agreeing to the project in principle and offering a tentative outline of the project I had in mind.

1. Dare We Hope? Dogmatic Theology, Evangelicalism, and the Question of Universalism

2. The God Who Saves: YHWH, Yeshua, and Divine Love

3. God's Decision to Save: Christology and Election

4. Humanity's Decision to Receive: Pneumatology and Faith

5. The Communion of Saints: Ecclesiology and the Mission of God

6. "All Things New": Eschatology and the Glory of God

7. God is Victor!

This outline operates within the same theological framework as my 2006 series. Like Barth's dogmatics, it not only begins with the doctrine of God, but it also moves from the objective side of soteriology (christology and election) to the subjective side of soteriology (pneumatology and ecclesiology). The language of decision is also indebted to Barth and makes the human participation in reconciliation a matter of conscious response. Robin contacted me again in May to discuss the project further and solicit a formal proposal, which I submitted on May 20. In the proposal version of the outline, I added a chapter after "God's Decision to Save: Christology and Election" on "God's Saving Action: Christology and Atonement." I also added a discussion of sin in the pneumatology chapter. These seemed only to reinforce the connection between my proposed study and Barth's work.

At the same time, the chapter descriptions in the proposal revealed my nascent attempt to grapple with Bultmann's challenge to Barth. In the chapter on election, for instance, I wrote: "I put forward a pneumatological reworking of Barth's doctrine of election. Briefly, I argue that Barth tends to make election a one-time decision in pretemporal eternity, which abstracts election both from the lived historicity of Jesus Christ and the lived historicities of human persons here and now." In the chapter on atonement I proposed to "construe the atonement as an eschatological word-event in which the cry of dereliction becomes the divine-human event of reconciliation." I stated my intent "to develop a nonmetaphysical conception of the atoning work of Christ, which means that the ancient substance ontology is done away with entirely." The pneumatology chapter would criticize Barth's "christocentric universalism" for "remain[ing] mired in a metaphysical logic that [Barth] never successfully extirpated from his theology despite his best efforts." I wanted to develop an account of participation that "does not require recourse to a substantival 'logic of assumption.'" All of this material would eventually find its way into the final version of the work. What changed after 2010 was my recognition that the *content* I envisioned required a commensurate *form*. It was not sufficient to animadvert against the metaphysical logic underpinning Barth's theology while retaining the structure of his dogmatics. I would have to reconstruct the whole on a different methodological basis.[4]

4. Another important part of this story took place in 2012. I was invited to speak at the 2012 Karl Barth Conference held annually at Princeton Theological Seminary. The theme was the fiftieth anniversary of Barth's trip to America, where he gave the lectures that became *Evangelical Theology: An Introduction.* I spoke on Barth's engagement with

The answer finally came in 2011. After trying and failing to make my new approach to soteriology work within a Barthian framework, I finally realized the problem: the starting point had to be the saving event itself rather than God, and this saving event had to be simultaneously objective and subjective, or rather it had to dispense with the distinction between objective and subjective altogether. On July 3 I sent Travis McMaken a draft of the opening pages of my new chapter titled "Soteriocentrism." While it would take many more years to realize the full consequences of this decision, all the essential pieces were now in place. Unfortunately, I had to shelve the project in order to work on my dissertation, which consumed my attention between the fall of 2011 and the fall of 2013. I returned to *The God Who Saves* in earnest only in the spring of 2014.

Toward the end of my dissertation, which was published by Fortress Press in 2015 as *The Mission of Demythologizing: Rudolf Bultmann's Dialectical Theology*, I sketched my new approach to theology and soteriology:

> Theology is not merely christocentric but always *soteriocentric*. It is God-talk ordered by the eschatological saving event in which God and human beings are concretely related in Christ. This, of course, has profound implications for numerous doctrinal *loci*. Given that soteriology is the permanent starting point for future dogmatic theology after Bultmann, a theology of demythologizing must begin there. . . . Among other things, the missionary

---

existentialism in those lectures and the way he sought to be *more* existentialist than the existentialists by grounding existence eternally in the being of God (see Congdon, "Theology"). Later that same summer I wrote an article responding to Oliver Crisp's criticism of Barth's inconsistency regarding universalism (see Congdon, "*Apokatastasis*"). My work on Barth's engagement with existentialism gave me a new appreciation for his response to universalism. Theology for Barth is not merely describing what is "objectively" true, as if the theological facts need only to be recounted in print. He instead affirms the existentialist insight that theology always speaks existentially—speaking of God is also speaking of ourselves. This connection between objective reality and subjective encounter has implications for what he is able to say soteriologically. We are not finished with soteriology once we affirm that all human beings are objectively reconciled in Christ. For Barth our election in Christ is not an election to *objective* reconciliation but an election to *subjective* witness. We have only adequately described Christian salvation once we have accounted for each person's participation in the missionary act of proclaiming the gospel. The error of universalism, as Barth understands it, is that it collapses subjective witness into objective reconciliation. It thus runs roughshod over the historicity of each person. We cannot speak in general and in the abstract about the particular histories of those who are included objectively in Christ. My own work is an attempt to take seriously Barth's existential insights. The problem is Barth's sharp distinction between the objective and subjective, which is what leads to interpretations of inconsistency and perpetuates the metaphysical notion that reconciliation applies to us even though it does not concern us existentially. I developed *The God Who Saves* in response to this problem.

account of the kerygma . . . denies the metaphysical differentiation between "objective" and "subjective" soteriology. Reconciliation is not first a transaction or change that occurs "above us," so to speak, in relation to some general human substance (a universal *humanum*) in which we all participate; it is always only a contingent event within each person's concrete history.[5]

I wrote this with *The God Who Saves* in mind, where I was concurrently fleshing out these ideas. The challenge, of course, was how to conceive a universal salvation within these parameters. How does salvation include all persons without a universal human nature? The start of an answer gradually formed during the months I was writing my dissertation and combined two ideas I had encountered as early as 2010: the concept of repetition (developed by Kierkegaard) and the concept of unconscious Christianity (developed by Dietrich Bonhoeffer). By conceiving the saving event as an unconscious act that is repeated in each person, it became possible to see how salvation could be universal while still located in the concrete historicity of each person.[6] Later I translated this conception of faith into an existential and es-

---

5. Congdon, *Mission*, 833–34.

6. In a way my attempt to answer this problem serves as my constructive counterproposal to Schubert Ogden's *Christ without Myth*. In this fine but flawed study, Ogden argues that there is a structural inconsistency in Bultmann's demythologizing program insofar as it consists of two contradictory claims: (1) "Christian faith is to be interpreted exhaustively and without remainder as man's original possibility of authentic historical (*geschichtlich*) existence as this is more or less adequately clarified and conceptualized by an appropriate philosophical analysis"; (2) "Christian faith is actually realizable, or is a 'possibility in fact,' only because of the particular historical (*historisch*) event Jesus of Nazareth" (*Christ*, 112). Ogden finds in Bultmann "the self-contradictory assertion that Christian existence is a historical (*geschichtlich*) possibility open to man as such and yet first *becomes* possible for him because of a particular historical (*historisch*) event" (ibid., 117). Ogden's interpretation rests on his use of Bultmann's distinction between faith as an ontological "possibility in principle" (which is universal) and faith as an ontic "possibility in fact" (which is only available to those who have faith in Jesus as the Christ). The key to Ogden's argument is that Bultmann, he claims, understands human beings as responsible before God for not realizing the authentic existence that is ontologically possible in principle (ibid., 141–42). But if the historical occurrence of Jesus is the exclusive means for accessing authentic existence, then those who could not have known Jesus—such as those who lived before Jesus—cannot be held responsible for a lack of faith. Either authentic existence is possible outside of faith in Jesus or people are not actually free and responsible before God.

Ogden's reading of Bultmann is flawed. Among other things, Bultmann does *not* think faith can be interpreted *exhaustively* as the original human possibility; Ogden mistakenly interprets demythologizing as a reduction of theology to philosophy. Nor does Bultmann make the natural person guilty before God for not realizing faith—a notion based largely on Ogden's own reading of Paul and his misreading of Bultmann on "natural revelation"—but instead human beings are sinful because they actualize their

chatological register with the help especially of Eberhard Jüngel and J. Louis Martyn. All of this formed the basis for the new soteriological norm around which the rest of my dogmatic sketch would be constructed: the apocalypse as an unconscious event of being placed outside oneself in participation in the crucified Christ. The pieces came together in chapter 3, "The Act of Salvation," which constitutes the heart of this book. The other chapters then explore what christology, pneumatology, ecclesiology, creation, and trinity look like when reinterpreted according to this norm.

The order of these chapters is integral to their content. Soteriocentrism is an inherently *actualistic* approach to theology, and for this reason we must treat the *act* of salvation prior to the *agent*. We only know the agent in light of the act. But since the act is inseparable from the agent, there is already a substantial amount of christology in chapter 3. The discussion of the agent in chapter 4 focuses specifically on the question of the divine person who is defined by this saving act, but since the act is simultaneously past and present, the agent is not Christ or the Spirit in isolation but only the Christ-Spirit. Christology and pneumatology are two perspectives on the same divine activity. The discussion of ecclesiology is not a comprehensive account of the church but an interpretation of the community of faith as defined by the soteriological norm of the apocalypse. Many important topics, such as sacramentology, are largely ignored. Chapter 5, in other words, is an account of the *being* of the church as constituted by the saving event; it is an exercise in ecclesial ontology. Only after those doctrines have been covered do I then look at the doctrine of creation. A soteriocentric approach reverses the creed: it integrates the second and third articles and then treats

---

existential inauthenticity by boasting of their deeds and living ungratefully (Bultmann, "New Testament," 28–29). But we can set aside the interpretive issues because it is clear that Ogden is using Bultmann to raise a fundamental issue within Christianity. The "structural inconsistency" is not unique to Bultmann but arises out of a dilemma basic to Christian theology: is it possible to affirm (a) the freedom and responsibility of the human person before God *and* (b) the exclusive uniqueness of Jesus Christ? Liberal theologians like Ogden deny the second proposition, while those in the Augustinian-Reformed tradition deny the first. Many modern evangelicals and Bultmann ironically belong together insofar as they seek to uphold both propositions, albeit in different ways. The point here is that Ogden is driven to his position in part because of his observation—one that I share—that the authentic existence of faith is clearly manifest among people who do not have faith in Christ. His solution is not only to reject the exclusivity of Christ, something he thinks is necessary on the basis of the NT itself (*Christ*, 144), but he also says "it is arguable that 'salvation' and all it implies must be meaningless to the modern man" (ibid., 136). The present book is my attempt to address Ogden's classic dilemma in a way that affirms the truth of his position—namely, that authentic existence is found outside of *explicit* faith in Christ—while still upholding the exclusivity of Christ in agreement with Bultmann. In doing so I hope to demonstrate the ongoing relevance of talk of "salvation."

them first before turning to the first article. Taking this approach means that creation is seen strictly in terms of the new creation—in terms of what Barth would call the covenant of grace—but more importantly it means the doctrine of creation is primarily anthropology and only indirectly concerned with cosmology. Finally, the work ends with the trinity as the appropriate conclusion—or *Schluss*, according to Friedrich Schleiermacher—to Christian dogmatics. We only know the *God* of salvation in the *act* of salvation. God defines God's being as Christ, Spirit, and Creator in the event of the apocalypse.

This work is not a complete systematic theology—it is a "dogmatic sketch" for a reason. I was commissioned by Parry to explore what systematic theology would look like if one took a universalist perspective. But in order to do so I had to solve a problem: how to affirm the universal scope of God's saving grace within the existential, historical parameters of hermeneutical theology. *The God Who Saves* is my answer to this problem. The answer has meant I could not simply tack on universalism to an otherwise traditional Protestant theology. I could no longer view a universalist variation on Barth as sufficient. Instead, I had to rethink the very nature of salvation—even the meaning of the word—from the ground up. So while I engage in systematic theological reflection, I do so in order to explain what makes my answer to this question cogent and coherent. *The God Who Saves* is the beating heart of my systematic theology but not the full realization of it. Whether I tackle a complete systematics, and how my mind may change should that day come, only time will tell.

The God Who Saves is not only my attempt to solve this soteriological problem, however. It is also an attempt to demonstrate that a genuinely *dialectical* systematic theology is possible—dialectical in the consistently actualistic sense represented by a synthetic reading of *inter alia* Barth, Bultmann, Ebeling, Gollwitzer, and Jüngel. It is an attempt, in order words, to construct a dogmatic theology according to a demythologizing hermeneutic that recognizes the absolute transcendence of God, the historicity of revelation, the contextual nature of God-talk, and the existential significance of faith.[7] Much more still needs to be done. Hopefully many others will take up the mantle.

David W. Congdon
Pentecost 2016

---

7. Insofar as dialectical theology is both exegetically grounded and existentially concerned, it is also the realization of genuinely *evangelical* theology.

Acknowledgments

I would not have attempted such a project had Robin Parry not asked me about it in 2010. A good editor is able to discern what someone can and should write even if she or he does not know it yet, and Robin is one of the best. Writing this book has been personally rewarding beyond anything I anticipated. I am grateful to him for his confidence in my ability to carry it out, as well as for his patience as the project stretched well past the original deadline.

The ideas behind this book were first explored on my blog, *The Fire and the Rose*. I am thankful to the many readers who interacted with me over the years on that site and pressed me to test, refine, and expand my thoughts. The blog may be in semi-retirement now, but I will always be grateful to the online community for helping me to discover my own voice and perspective. It takes a village to raise a theologian!

It also takes a family—and I have been especially blessed to have such a supportive and forgiving spouse in Amy, as well as children who give me boundless grace when my mind is lost in the world of dogmatics instead of the worlds of Minecraft and dollhouses.

Thanks to the many friends and colleagues who have been gracious dialogue partners on the topics of soteriology, apocalyptic theology, and systematic theology: Samuel Adams, Sigurd Baark, Christian Collins Winn, Oliver Crisp, John Drury, Kait Dugan, John Flett, Douglas Harink, Nathan Kerr, R. David Nelson, Paul Nimmo, Ry Siggelkow, Shannon Smythe, Sarah Stewart-Kroeker, and Philip Ziegler. A very special word of thanks (as always!) to W. Travis McMaken for his willingness to read through the whole manuscript and offer extensive invaluable feedback—all in the space of a week! It would be impossible to list all the ways in which my theology has been formed in conversation with Travis. I am fortunate to have him as a friend.

I have had two of the best teachers in systematic theology one could ask for. At Wheaton College in fall 2003 I had my first taste of systematic theology under the guidance of Mark Husbands. In that course I encountered many of the ideas and appropriated many of the theological instincts that continue to guide me today. Prof. Husbands introduced me to the Lutheran "theology of the cross" for the first time in that course, which was a revelation to me then and remains normative for my thought now. In spring 2006 I enrolled in the first of two semesters of systematic theology at Princeton Theological Seminary. The course covered the doctrines of God and creation and was cotaught by Bruce L. McCormack. His mastery of the history of doctrine showed me that to become a good systematician, one needed to become a good historian. Constructive theology that lacks historical consciousness is an exercise in futility. Prof. McCormack's scholarly rigor and personal interest in my well-being modeled what it looks like to *live* one's theology. In 2010, while a PhD student under Prof. McCormack, I was privileged to be a teaching fellow in his systematic theology course, which was as educational for me as it was for the seminary students. I am eternally grateful to both Mark Husbands and Bruce McCormack. I dedicate this work to them as a small token of my appreciation.

Abbreviations

BSLK	Deutscher Evangelischer Kirchenausschuss, *Die Bekenntnisschriften der evangelisch-lutherischen Kirche*
CD	Karl Barth, *Church Dogmatics*
GuV	Rudolf Bultmann, *Glauben und Verstehen*
KD	Karl Barth, *Die kirchliche Dogmatik*
LW	Martin Luther, *Luther's Works*
NT	New Testament
OT	Old Testament
ST	Thomas Aquinas, *Summa Theologica*
WA	Martin Luther, *D. Martin Luthers Werke* (*Weimar Ausgabe*)

I

Introduction

The Problem of Christian Universalism

And now, O Lord, what do I wait for? My hope is in you.

PSALM 39:7

DARE WE HOPE? CAN WE KNOW?

For what may we hope? The question is not just an eschatological adden-
dum. It is the primal question of faith, the "burning bush" at the center
of Christian existence (R. S. Thomas). The question, when asked by faith,
does not concern *what* will happen in the chronological future, but rather
who we are in the eschatological now. Can we live—right now—as creatures
of hope? This is the question of our identity and mission in light of our true
end (*telos*) as constituted and revealed in Jesus Christ through his Spirit.
In asking it here, we thus mean something very different from Immanuel
Kant's asking of the same question in his third *Critique*. Theological eschatology is qualitatively different from philosophical teleology. And this is
because eschatology is wholly and simultaneously a matter of soteriology,
christology, and the doctrine of God. In other words, it is not merely one
part of a larger system of doctrine; it is instead the heart of the Christian

1

life. As Karl Barth famously put it, "Christianity that is not completely and utterly eschatology has completely and utterly nothing to do with *Christ*."[1]

Today, however, the recognition of the centrality of eschatological hope is insufficient. We hear about "hope" everywhere we go. What ought to be a decisive word of divine grace and new possibilities too often seems to be a way of skirting the radical implications of God's revelation in Christ. The confidence that belongs to the hope of *faith* is often confused with the ambivalence that belongs to merely worldly hope. The Psalmist declares, "And now, O Lord, what do I wait for? My hope is in you" (Ps 39:7). How different this is from the trivial remarks we hear every day: "I hope I get a new bike for my birthday" or "I hope I get chosen for this new position at work." Even theologians often speak about eschatological hope in a way that sounds more like one's hope for a new bike than the Psalmist's paradoxically *confident* and *certain* hope in the loving-kindness of God. In his response to T. F. Torrance's claim that "at the very best universalism could only be concerned with a hope, with a possibility,"[2] John A. T. Robinson remains profoundly correct in his judgment that to speak about eschatological "possibilities" may sound humble but "is in fact that most subtly unbiblical. For the New Testament never says that God *may* be all in all, that Christ *may* draw all men unto himself, but that he *will*. And to assert that he will is not human dogmatism, but to hold fast to the fundamental declaration of the gospel of the effective election of all men in Christ."[3] To ask with Hans Urs von Balthasar, "Dare we *hope* that all will be saved?"[4] does not preclude asking, "Can we *know* that all will be saved?" To affirm the former's hope does not compete with the latter's certainty. If it is truly *Christian* hope, then such confidence is not only possible but in fact necessary. Anything less would contradict the faith attested by Paul before Agrippa: "I stand here on trial on account of my *hope* in the *promise* made by God to our ancestors" (Acts 26:6; emphasis mine). Christian faith is *confident hope* in the *effective promise* of God.

The purpose of this book is to develop a Christian dogmatics in light of the universality of God's saving grace in Jesus Christ. If the redemptive promise of God is indeed universal in scope, then what must we say about God, the world, and ourselves in light of this?[5] This dogmatic sketch

1. Barth, *Der Römerbrief*, 430. Originally translated in Barth, *Epistle*, 314.

2. Torrance, "Universalism," 313.

3. Robinson, *In the End*, 96.

4. See Balthasar, *Dare We Hope*.

5. I will not argue in this work for the "orthodoxy" of universal salvation, simply because, as many others have already demonstrated, it was never condemned as heretical in the first place. Gregory MacDonald, commenting on the well-known anathemas

examines what it means to think systematically according to the revelation that *God is the one who saves*—that is, the one who saves *all*. Before we can properly turn to that dogmatic project, however, it is first necessary to do some introductory ground-clearing by (a) defining what we mean by "Christian universalism" and (b) presenting the two main problems that a doctrine of universal salvation must overcome.

DEFINING UNIVERSALISM: A TYPOLOGY

Universalism is an ambiguous concept that requires clarification. Since this is a work of Christian theology, I do not use this word with any of its philosophical connotations. I do not have in mind anything related to the metaphysical problem of universals, nor do I use it as an antonym of relativism. Instead, the word as employed here pertains to the theological debate over the nature and scope of salvation. Universalism refers to an account of the God-world relationship that includes all creatures within the scope of God's reconciling grace—though precisely how we should understand the nature of this grace and the way it includes every creature is what I will explore in later chapters.

What follows is a brief typology of universalisms, drawing on the work of Robin Parry and Christopher Partridge.[6] Because every typology trades in abstract categories and ideal types, there is the persistent threat of doing violence to the uncategorizable complexities of history. The typology on offer here is therefore little more than a heuristic device to orient our analysis. No claim is made to comprehensiveness, nor is each category necessarily

---

of the fifth ecumenical council of 553, observes that "in anathemas I and XV the concern is with *apokatastasis* as linked with the idea of the pre-existence of souls and an eschatology that sees a simple return of souls to an original unity. In anathema XIV it is *apokatastasis* as associated with an immaterial, pantheistic eschatology. But this is not a condemnation of universalism *as such*" ("Introduction," 8). Despite the council's reference to Origen, it is questionable whether the anathemas even apply to Origen's own position. Ilaria Ramelli speaks for many when she says that Origen's "thought is grounded in the Bible first and in Plato after" (*Christian Doctrine*, 137–221, here 214). As both Ramelli and MacDonald demonstrate in their respective works, there are a host of Christian theologians who develop accounts of universal salvation that do not depend upon the metaphysical schema condemned in 553. See MacDonald, *All Shall*; on Origen's universalism see also Greggs, *Barth*. The other reason for not arguing over universalism's orthodoxy is that I do not accept the assumption that the ecumenical councils determine what counts as authentically "Christian." The councils and creeds are only authoritative insofar as they embody and bear witness to the norm of the gospel that stands always beyond them.

6. See Parry and Partridge, "Introduction," xv–xix.

exclusive of the others. But this typology provides a basic roadmap by which to navigate complex theological waters.

Multiethnic Universalism

A certain kind of multiethnic universalism[7] is basic to Christianity, in the sense that God calls people from every nation or people group (in Greek, *ethnos*) to become followers of Jesus Christ and participants in the community of faith. People from "every tribe and language and people and nation" (Rev 5:9) are included within the family of God. The experience of the early church at Pentecost, as recorded in the Acts of the Apostles, is decisive: whereas salvation under the old law entailed becoming part of a specific people group (viz., Israel), the new community of the Spirit is one that affirms the presence of God equally within each ethnicity and social context. Salvation no longer involves becoming part of Israel, and the mission of God is no longer the diffusion of a specific social and cultural framework. While there are debates over how radically to understand the multiethnicity of Christianity, some account of it is a *sine qua non* for Christian faith and thus not a matter of serious dispute within theology.

Potential Universalism

"Potential universalism" claims that all people *can* be saved, but not necessarily that all people *will* be saved. It affirms that the salvation of all people is a *possibility*, not an *actuality*. God's saving work in Christ is potentially effective for all but not actually effective. It only *becomes* effective when an individual responds to the gospel in faith. This form of universalism finds its scriptural warrant in 1 Timothy 2:3b–4: "God our Savior . . . desires everyone to be saved and to come to the knowledge of the truth." While potential universalism takes seriously the description of God's universal desire, it assumes that God's will regarding the salvation of all is not efficacious. God can will something to be the case without causing it to be so. The causal "moment" that effects one's reconciled status before God occurs in a conscious act of the human will.

Parry and Partridge refer to this position as "Arminian universalism" because of the Arminian emphasis on human free will as the basis for individual salvation. The adjective "Arminian" is of course defined in

---

7. Parry and Partridge describe this as "multiracial universalism," but I prefer to use the language of ethnicity.

contraposition to "Calvinist," which emphasizes God's absolute sovereignty over all creaturely matters. Calvinism, according to this typology, is any position that (a) denies the human will's capacity to effect one's salvation and (b) denies that all people will be saved. The result is therefore double predestination: God's determination in pretemporal eternity that some will be saved and others will be damned. Both "Arminian" and "Calvinist" soteriologies deny universal salvation: the former by virtue of the fact that some freely reject the gospel, and the latter by virtue of the fact that God freely determines that some will not be saved. The Arminian position is thus a *potential universalism*, while Calvinism is an *actual nonuniversalism*. What unites both positions is their experiential starting point: they begin with the empirical fact that some people believe and other people do not. On that basis they draw two diametrically opposed positions: the "Arminian" position claims that salvation must depend upon the will of the individual human person, while the "Calvinist" position claims that God must have determined in advance that only some would believe.

I have chosen in my analysis to replace the language of Arminian and Calvinist with the language of potential and actual for the following two reasons. First, the Calvinist-Arminian typology often loses contact with the actual writings of Calvin and Arminius. While it is not inaccurate to see Calvin as a proto-Calvinist or Arminius as a proto-Arminian, it is nevertheless problematic to abstract from their respective writings by creating an ahistorical either-or that has questionable historical merit. Recall that Calvin and Arminius were not contemporaries and consequently never engaged in direct debate. Arminius was a student of Theodore Beza, one of Calvin's protégés, and one can only understand his work against the background of the infralapsarian-supralapsarian debate that led to the Synod of Dort. Arminianism, for that matter, is more associated with those influenced by his theology—especially the Methodist movement as it developed in North America—rather than with Arminius himself and the Remonstrants. Isolating the issue of free will from the rest of the Remonstrant articles distorts the larger theological context within which the controversy over Arminius's teachings occurred—a decisively *Reformed* theological context. Since the issue in question lies at the heart of all Christian theology, we are better served by using terms not derived from a highly specific moment in Protestant church history.

Actual Universalism

The third type of universalism refers broadly to those positions most people associate with the term. These are soteriologies that entail the *actual salvation of all people*. Parry and Partridge call this "strong universalism," referring to those positions that "agree with the Arminian universalists that God does indeed desire to save all individuals," but which "go on to add that *God will achieve his purposes*. Thus all individuals will in fact be saved."[8] They further subdivide this category as: (a) non-Christian universalism, (b) pluralist universalism, and (c) Christian universalism. The first is irrelevant to the present essay. With regard to the second, we will simply note the seminal work of John Hick, who wrestled with the theological challenge of religious pluralism.[9] Though his approach is a theological dead-end, we cannot simply dismiss the questions he raised or the honesty and integrity with which he sought to answer them. On the contrary, it is essential for Christian theology to deal with the pluralistic question seriously and responsibly. We must, in our own way, venture a theological proposal that does not disregard but *integrates* the problem of pluralism into an account of Christian theology that does not lessen in any way the uniqueness of Jesus. This will be the task of subsequent chapters. Having set aside the first two of the three versions of "actual" or "strong" universalism, we turn to an analysis of "Christian" universalism.

The category of Christian universalism is itself too vague to be helpful. Parry and Partridge acknowledge a long list of questions over which Christian universalists disagree, but they refuse to specify further categories. Any attempt at a comprehensive typology capable of accounting for every one of these contentious issues would quickly become tedious and pointless. At the same time, leaving off at "Christian universalism" fails to account for the differences that really matter to people, the ones that are especially decisive for the current debates. What follows is a description of the two most significant divides within Christian universalism.

The Who of the Actualization: Individual or God

At the most basic level, Christian theology splits over the question: Where is the locus of salvation? Are we to locate a person's salvation in the agency of the human individual, or in the agency of God? Putting it this way is, of course, a false contrast. No theologian who repudiates the pelagian heresy

8. Parry and Partridge, "Introduction," xvi–xvii.

9. See, in particular, Hick, *God*; Hick, *Death*; Hick, *Metaphor*; Hick, *Evil*.

would permit the individual to be pitted against God, as if salvation were a matter of pulling oneself up by one's own bootstraps, so to speak. Such a notion does not even apply to ancient Israel, whose "covenantal nomism" understands adherence to Torah to be a way of life that follows from one's inclusion in the covenant that YHWH has sovereignly and graciously established with Israel.[10]

The question therefore needs to be specified more exactly. Let us put it this way: is the "objective status" of the individual before God actualized by something that occurs "in" the individual, or is it actualized by God entirely outside of and apart from—even in spite of—the individual without her being aware of it? By placing scare-quotes around "objective status" and "in," I mean to indicate that there is still much more unpacking that needs to take place regarding the concepts of objectivity and subjectivity as they pertain to soteriology. The present concern is to note that there are Christian universalists on both sides of this question. For lack of better terminology, we will refer to these two groups as "evangelical universalists" and "Barthian universalists."

The term "evangelical universalist" comes from the 2006 work of the same name by Gregory MacDonald. This work presents an exegetical case for a version of Christian universalism. The introduction presents an imaginary representative of the position named Anastasia:

> Anastasia is an evangelical Christian. She believes in the inspiration and authority of the Bible. She believes in all those crucial Christian doctrines such as Trinity, creation, sin, atonement, the return of Christ, salvation through Christ alone, by grace alone, through faith alone. In fact, on most things you'd be hard pressed to tell her apart from any other evangelical. Contrary to what we may suspect, she even believes in the eschatological wrath of God—in hell. She differs most obviously in two unusual beliefs. First, she believes that one's eternal destiny is not *fixed* at death and, consequently, that those in hell can repent and throw themselves upon the mercy of God in Christ and thus

---

10. This insight into the nature of Judaism is a constitutive element in what is called the "New Perspective on Paul" (NPP). In stating my agreement on the question of Israel and Torah, I do *not* mean to imply that I thereby agree with NPP's reconstruction of Pauline theology, especially with regard to the doctrine of justification. Scholars in the NPP movement seem to think that the former necessarily entails the latter, but this is a judgment I strongly dispute. However, I do not thereby side with the conservative evangelical and Reformed critics of NPP, who blindly adhere to a Protestant orthodox theology over against any challenges from modern theological and historical scholarship.

be saved. Second, she also believes that *in the end* everyone will
do this.[11]

We will return to the eschatological focus of this passage below. The important thing to notice here is the assumption that one's "eternal destiny"
is determined by an individual's conscious decision to place one's trust in
Christ. This assumption above all is what makes this version of universalism
distinctively *evangelical*.

It is worth noting that this version of universal salvation stands in
basic continuity with the account of "potential universalism" noted above.
The only real difference between potential universalism and evangelical
universalism is that the former places a limit for conversion at the time
of death, while the latter rejects such a limit—the dubious basis for such
a limit being the ambiguous passage in Hebrews 9:27. Potential universalism opposes actual universalism not on the grounds of a divine decision
to condemn certain persons, but because of the various contingent factors
related to the brevity of human life. The problem with this position, as many
have pointed out, is that it effectively condemns the majority of humankind
due to nothing more than the sheer fact (one might say, "bad luck") of being born in one place rather than another. Some will simply never hear the
gospel; others will only hear a gospel distorted through ideological perver-
sion; still others will be unable to hear the gospel because the lives of those
who proclaim it are fraught with violence, greed, lust, pride, and other vices,
often toward the very ones who are the intended recipients of the message.
Denying universalism implies that God's favor belongs especially to those
who just happen to be born in traditionally Christian cultures to traditionally Christian families. Once one learns about the mutual entanglement of
religion and politics throughout the history of the church, it is impossible
to overlook the fact that the opposition to some form of actual universalism
goes hand-in-hand with the affirmation of the imperial and colonial powers
of the western world as the mediators of divine grace. This is a problem
for both potential universalism (i.e., "Arminianism") and actual nonuniversalism (i.e., "Calvinism"). The difference between them is that potential
universalism places the blame for these failures on the Christian church,
while predestinarianism or actual nonuniversalism places the "blame" upon
God—though without there being any real blame, since it is all a confirmation of God's justice in the face of human depravity. The consequences of
each position are catastrophic. The former lays an evangelistic burden upon
the church at least as heavy—if not infinitely heavier—than anything Luther
faced in his experience of *Anfechtung*. The church's mission becomes purely

11. MacDonald, *The Evangelical Universalist*, 6.

one of law, not of gospel. No wonder the so-called "good news" often sounds like a threat rather than a promise. The latter, by contrast, is quite freeing for the church, but only at the expense of turning God into the devil.[12]

The alternative position is what we will call "Barthian universalism." This term appears to be an oxymoron since Barth himself rejected universalism. I have argued elsewhere that Barth's denial of universalism has nothing to do with a denial of the universal scope of God's saving work in Christ and everything to do with his consistent denial of doctrinal worldviews that speak in the abstract about humanity. It is the "ism" and not the "universal" that is most problematic for Barth—or, put differently, it is universal understood as something general and not universal understood as inclusive of all that worries Barth.[13] The concept of "Barthian universalism" seeks to highlight his radically Protestant and rigorously christocentric approach to soteriology. Barth developed a theological method that sought to cut the nerve of nineteenth-century liberal theology, which was characterized by a kind of anthropocentrism, even egocentrism, that made the individual believer the norm and center of Christian faith. He contended that Friedrich Schleiermacher was the primary culprit, and he identified (rightly or wrongly) contemporaries like Adolf von Harnack, Emanuel Hirsch, Emil Brunner, and Rudolf Bultmann as carrying on this anthropocentric tradition in theology. Barth saw the specter of this liberalism almost everywhere: in Roman Catholicism, European pietism, American evangelicalism, German missiology, and existentialist theology, among others. Each was found to be an instance of "natural theology," and thus found wanting. In their place Barth stressed the "wholly otherness" of God, the sovereignty and freedom of divine grace. He later corrected the *totaliter aliter* conception of God in favor of emphasizing God's humanity and nearness to the world, but this alteration preserved—even radicalized—his understanding of reconciliation

---

12. Terry Eagleton observes that "the biblical name for God as judge or accuser is Satan, which literally means 'adversary.' Satan is a way of seeing God as a great big bully" (*Reason*, 20).

13. See Congdon, "*Apokatastasis*," 464–80. Cf. Greggs, "Jesus," 196–212. I am all too aware that many evangelicals have dismissed Barth on the grounds that he is a universalist, while defenders of Barth have been quick to deny the validity of this charge, arguing that Barth is not at all a universalist. The irony is that these people have sought to rescue Barth's reputation among conservative evangelicals by saddling him with a deplorable theology. This is the very definition of a *sacrificium intellectus*. The proper response to these evangelical critics is not to make Barth into an evangelical, but rather to demonstrate both the validity of universalism and the erroneous basis for the claim that nonuniversalism is the only "biblical" and "orthodox" position. Bruce McCormack's defense of Barth takes a mediating position: he still denies that Barth was a universalist, but he spends the bulk of his time arguing for the possibility of universal salvation as a valid Christian position. See McCormack, "So That He May."

and salvation as an act solely effected by God in Christ.[14] What occurs in
Christ, according to Barth, is not the mere possibility of reconciliation but
its *actuality*. To be sure, the event of salvation is always actualized *for* the
human person (*pro nobis*), but the person does not contribute to this event
in any way except as a *witness* to it in the world. Faith is not the condition for
one's reconciled status before God. This status is determined in advance in
Christ. Faith is rather the condition for one's correspondence to this status,
to the truth of our being in Christ. Faith recognizes and responds to what
has already been accomplished, in its full efficacy, on our behalf. We could
avoid the thicket of Barth interpretation by calling this position simply "objective universalism."[15] It refers to a saving relation to God exclusively and
efficaciously established by God alone.

At the risk of over-jargonization, we might describe these two positions
on the "who" of salvation as "anthropo-actualized" and "theo-actualized"
universalism. The former refers to a salvation whose establishment occurs
through an act of the individual human being. The latter refers to a salvation
whose establishment occurs through an act of God alone in Jesus Christ.

The When of the Actualization: Protology or Eschatology

Closely related to the first differentiation regarding the "who" is a second
differentiation regarding the "when." We can identify the two options here
as "protological actualization" and "eschatological actualization." Protology
is the study of the first things (*prota*), while eschatology is the study of the
last things (*eschata*). The concept of protology refers, in this context, to that
which precedes human history, to what theologians call pretemporal eternity, though it is not properly used in reference to the debate over human
origins. It is a theological term referring to the *ground* of human history,
not a scientific term referring to the *beginning* of history. The concept of eschatology, by contrast, refers not only to that which follows human history
(i.e., to posttemporal eternity), but also to world history itself as understood
in light of its proper end. The New Testament understands the eschaton
to begin with the arrival (παρουσία) of the Messiah—"the coming of our
Lord Jesus Christ" (1 Thess 5:23). Paul clearly thought himself to be living

14. See Barth, "Humanity," 37–65.

15. Travis McMaken refers to Barth's position as "soteriological objectivism" (*Sign*,
4). Later he comments: "Rather than understanding the salvation Christ achieves as
requiring application to the individual at a later time in order to become effective, Barth
understands the reconciliation between God and humanity enacted by and in Christ as
complete *per se*. Salvation is something that is complete and effective for all here and
now because Jesus Christ accomplished it once and for all there and then" (ibid., 86).

in the "last days." While the early community's expectation of the imminent parousia proved to be misguided, their theological interpretation of present history remains necessary, at least in some form. The distinction between protology and eschatology in the context of Christian universalism comes down to this: is the salvation of all people a reality that has already occurred in the past (protology), or is it a reality that is occurring or will occur in the future (eschatology)?

Already it should be clear that the protological-eschatological differentiation is closely connected to the individual-God differentiation. The evangelical or anthropo-actualized universalism is necessarily an eschatological universalism. Since one's salvation is only possible by virtue of the individual's conscious conversion to faith in Christ, that salvation cannot be protological in nature. It can only be a salvation that occurs (ideally) *within* human history or (if necessary) *after* human history, as a conversion to God that happens while one is experiencing the divine wrath of hell.[16] By contrast, the Barthian or theo-actualized universalism is necessarily a protological universalism. Barth grounds salvation in the protological election of God, that is to say, in God's pretemporal decision to reconcile the world to Godself in the Son. To be sure, this decision is only efficaciously actualized in Jesus Christ's history. The electing decision of God is made *in anticipation of* this historical occurrence; it is a "stop-gap" for the man Jesus himself in his lived history.[17] Barth's grounding of this event in an eternal decision by God has the intended effect of precluding every human attempt to lay a special claim upon God. Salvation is something that is *already* actualized; it precedes each person as a fact to be acknowledged. It does not meet us as a potentiality to be realized by our decision of faith. What happens in the present and the future is only the recognition and manifestation of what is already true about us on the basis of what Christ has done for us in his life of obedience.

There is, however, a third option irreducible to Barthian protology and evangelical eschatology. The third way would be a universalism effected by God, but effected *eschatologically*. This would entail locating the sovereign and gracious work of God in the present tense and/or the future tense, as

16. Some accounts, particularly those that argue for some kind of "anonymous Christianity," place the moment of conversion at the moment of death, or in that liminal space between life and death. I see this as a variation on the category of "within human history."

17. *CD* 2.2:96. We must not make the mistake of some early critics of Barth (e.g., Emil Brunner), who claimed that, for Barth, Christ was merely a manifestation of something antecedently actualized in pretemporal eternity. In truth, history is not a mere reflection of eternity, but rather the content of eternity is constituted by what happens *in* history.

opposed to the past tense. It would also entail giving greater attention to the subjective or personal dimension as playing some kind of role. It cannot be a conscious and constitutive role, or else we would have the evangelical account of universalism noted above. But neither can it be a totally passive role, or else we have God possessing human beings against their will. There is a variety of possible ways of articulating an *eschatological theo-actualized universalism* between these extremes. The present essay offers just such an account. Barth himself actually comes very close to some version of this position, though he demurs for reasons that we will need to explore in depth. For now, it will suffice to note the types of Christian universalism that we have identified:

   a. protological theo-actualized (or Barthian) universalism;

   b. eschatological anthropo-actualized (or evangelical) universalism; and

   c. eschatological theo-actualized universalism.

THE PROBLEM OF UNIVERSALISM

Having mapped the universalist terrain, we must now take stock of the problems that confront any credible account of Christian universalism. Typically, of course, universal salvation is ruled out in principle on the grounds that it is unbiblical and heterodox (if not heretical). This common, knee-jerk dismissal of the idea is a thoroughly anti-intellectual response because it has little interest in actually investigating the traditions and texts in question. Universalism is a threat to a certain account of ecclesial power, and those who feel threatened end up making blanket appeals to authority (e.g., orthodoxy and proof-texts) in order to shore up both their faith and their power over the faith of others. In the end, such objections are false objections, and they are false because they presuppose precisely what must be interrogated, namely, what it means to be "orthodox" and "biblical." To conduct this interrogation is to enter the field of hermeneutics, which we will treat in the next chapter.

There are, however, two serious objections to universal salvation: (a) the freedom of God and (b) the historicity of the individual believer. We will address them initially here, though the only way to respond adequately is by engaging in constructive theological reflection, which we will do in later chapters.

The Freedom of God

The standard objection to universal salvation from those in the Augustinian-Reformed tradition is that it compromises the sovereignty and freedom of God. A classic prooftext for this position is Romans 9:18–21:

> So then [God] has mercy on whomever he chooses, and he hardens the heart of whomever he chooses. You will say to me then, "Why then does he still find fault? For who can resist his will?" But who indeed are you, a human being, to argue with God? Will what is molded say to the one who molds it, "Why have you made me like this?" Has the potter no right over the clay, to make out of the same lump one object for special use and another for ordinary use?

Those who appeal to divine freedom on the basis of passages like this generally assume that God wills, or at least willingly permits, the damnation of most people. God's freedom is a *freedom to condemn*. The doctrine of universalism thus appears as an idea that expressly contravenes the divine will. Those who propose universalism are seen as setting up an abstract principle to which God is necessarily bound: God *must* save everyone, against God's own will as described in scripture. Universalism, so this line of thinking argues, ties God's hands and forces God to act graciously toward all people.

Outside of fundamentalist Reformed circles, Barth is often seen as the most prominent proponent of this objection in recent theology. In a conversation with members of Princeton Theological Seminary in 1962, Barth responded to a question about universal salvation with the following: "[By] universal salvation I understand what Origen has told people, in the end all will be good, all will be saved, even the Devil is coming home. . . . And if we proclaim, well, we are all saved, we all will end in a pleasant way, *then we take away God's freedom to do it*."[18] Barth made the same point more famously in *Church Dogmatics* 4.3:

> To the man who persistently tries to change the truth into untruth, God does not owe eternal patience and therefore deliverance any more than He does those provisional manifestations. We should be denying or disarming that evil attempt and our own participation in it if, in relation to ourselves or others or all men, we were to permit ourselves to postulate a withdrawal of that threat and in this sense to expect or maintain an *apokatastasis* or universal reconciliation as the goal and end of all things. No such postulate can be made even though we appeal to the

18. Barth, *Gespräche 1959–1962*, 503. Emphasis mine.

cross and resurrection of Jesus Christ. Even though theological consistency might seem to lead our thoughts and utterances
most clearly in this direction, we must not arrogate to ourselves
that which can be given and received only as a free gift.[19]

The point is clear: to posit universal salvation or *apokatastasis* is to deny
God's divine prerogative to bestow mercy and grace as a "free gift." Universalism *obligates* God to be gracious, which of course contradicts the very nature of grace. Salvation is not something we are given but something we are
owed. Effectively, then, to posit this doctrine is to attempt to save ourselves.

The problem is that this objection presupposes we already know that
God's will is a will to condemn sinners to eternal damnation. In other
words, it is an exercise in begging the question. If God has determined to
send some people to hell, then of course any doctrine that proclaims the
salvation of all would be an infringement on God's freedom. There is, of
course, a very simple response to this problem, namely, to reject the original
premise. Nothing prevents us from saying that God saves all people because
God *wills* to save all—precisely *as* an exercise of God's sovereign freedom.[20]
Election does not need to be double predestination; it could also simply be
an election of all people to salvation. God cannot compromise God's own
freedom. If God determines that something must take place, this is a genuinely sovereign act of God. And God could just as well determine that all
people belong in reconciled fellowship with God.

Whether this is the right way to think about God's saving purposes is
another question, but the point here is simply that universalism need not
contradict divine freedom; it can instead be the natural expression of it. I
would argue that this is Barth's actual position, though he refuses to call it
universalism because of the problematic connotations of the word. Indeed,
and as I have argued elsewhere, Barth's real problem with universalism has
to do not with the freedom of God but with the *historicity* of the believer.[21]

19. *CD* 4.3:477.

20. Ironically, those who argue that God is only true free if God is able to condemn
certain individuals to an eternal hell are in fact the ones placing external limitations
on God's freedom. The real problem people have with universal salvation is that most
people do not want a God of such boundless mercy. They cannot stomach a God who
might forgive evildoers and display infinite hospitality to those who denied such hospitality to others. And so they end up creating a God in their own image who *must*
condemn and *must* exclude. Of course, this is itself a denial of hospitality.

21. See Congdon, "*Apokatastasis*," 464–80.

The Historicity of the Believer

Most objections—and also the most serious objections—to universal salvation focus instead on the freedom of the individual believer. A classic prooftext in this case is from Romans 10:9: "If you confess with your lips that Jesus is Lord and believe in your heart that God raised him from the dead, you will be saved." This approach does not deny that salvation is a gift of grace, but it insists, on good biblical grounds, that this gift necessarily includes the decision of the human recipient. Those who advocate this view also oppose the doctrine of double predestination for precisely the same reason. From this perspective, double predestination and universalism both operate according to the same logic of an abstract, overriding divine decision that nullifies the significance of human agency.

This argument is typically framed as a matter of human freedom. Supporters of this view often draw an analogy to the relation of love between two persons, where the free response of each person is necessary in order for a relationship of love to exist.[22] But this raises serious problems when

22. The assumption behind this way of thinking about the divine-human relation is the notion that God is a "personal" God. Evangelicals, in particular, are fond of speaking about faith as a "personal relationship" with Jesus. If by "personal" we mean the kind of relationship that I have with another human person, then such language is clearly being used metaphorically, all personal delusions to the contrary notwithstanding. God is not *a* person, as Paul Tillich rightly stressed in his writings. What then is the meaning of such talk? In the best sense, it affirms that God is not an impersonal thing, an object lying at our disposal, which we are free either to use or ignore. A "personal" God is a living *subject* that confronts us and unsettles us. To say that faith is a "personal" relationship with God is to say that faith is a personally transformative event wherein we encounter the active reality of God. That much we can and must affirm. But to go beyond this and construe God in anthropomorphic terms as a supernatural person is to leave the realm of faith and enter the world of mythology and fantasy.

While it is rarely discussed, the mythological conception of God as a personal deity is substantially based on passages from the Old Testament, particularly the covenant texts that describe the relation between YHWH and Israel in terms taken from the suzerainty treaties of the ancient Near East (ANE). We thus read in Deuteronomy, which is based on such ANE documents, that YHWH "maintains covenant loyalty with those who love him and keep his commandments" (Deut 7:9). Here is a clear expression of the divine-human relationship that takes a human-human relationship as its *analogans* and template. Those who operate on a model of biblical authority that believes whatever is in the Bible was divinely ordained to be there—once again assuming that God is a person, much the way I am personally authoring this book—are forced to conclude that this account of God as a heavenly suzerain (or king) testifies authoritatively to the nature of God. This would imply either that YHWH selected the suzerainty treaty as the model for the treaty/covenant with Israel or that the ANE culture was superintended by God to develop suzerainty treaties so that the Israelite people could come along later and use the format to describe a treaty/covenant with their national deity, named YHWH.

applied to the divine-human relationship. The analogy implies that divine agency and human agency occur on the same ontological plane: God relates to me the way my friend does, except what I receive from God is not merely affection but salvation. Within this single order of being, we only have two options: another person can either *elicit* my love through persuasion or *effect* my love through coercion. The elicitation of love suggests a *cooperative* relationship in which the human person supplements and completes a relation that God merely initiates and makes possible. By contrast, the external effectuation of love implies a *competitive* relationship in which the sovereignty of God comes at the expense of my own free agency. The freedom of God and the freedom of the individual exist in a zero-sum game, and in that game, God always wins—and violently so. Given this ontological presupposition, and the binary opposition it entails, it is no wonder that many people simply opt for the synergistic account of divine-human cooperation. Mutual reciprocity is obviously superior to divine abuse. When set within this kind of framework, universalism (along with double predestination) appears to be spiritually pernicious, much less theologically and exegetically doubtful. As Barth stated on another occasion in 1962, this time in a conversation with a group from the World Student Christian Federation: "What do we mean by *apokatastasis*? It is the theory that finally and ultimately all men, and possibly the Devil too, will be saved, *whether they wish it or not.*"[23]

The problem, as those in the Reformed tradition are often quick to point out, is that this appeal to human freedom misunderstands the Reformed understanding of divine sovereignty because it fails to see the

---

The sheer mythology of all this aside, trying to give such notions a divine sanction is a misguided attempt to escape the historicity of the biblical text. We must not sacrifice our intellect in this manner. We must instead face the fact that the scriptures are thoroughly historical documents of their time. There is nothing directly divine or inspired about the suzerainty treaty; it was simply what the Hebrew tribes knew as part of their cultural context. We must not ascribe any intrinsic theological significance to it. With Barth we can instead affirm that the "spiritual horizon [of the prophets and apostles] was as limited as—and in an important respect much more limited than—our own," and that "their natural science, their world-picture, and to a great extent even their morality cannot be authoritative for us. . . . They were with few exceptions not remarkable theologians." See Barth, "Die Autorität," 6. We see this most clearly in the way the Hebrew scriptures project an ANE conception of the suzerain-vassal relation onto the YHWH-Israel covenantal relation. We must not take this view of God as definitive in any way for theology today. These texts *become* authoritative and meaningful for Christian theology only when interpreted retrospectively from the normative reality of Jesus. Seen from that perspective, God does not relate to us as a cosmic suzerain but as a crucified prophet.

23. Barth, *Gespräche 1959–1962*, 431; emphasis mine. Barth certainly does not share the univocal ontological framework, but his comment nicely captures the basic objection.

significance of God's absolute transcendence. Once we recognize that divine agency operates on a qualitatively different ontological order, we no longer need to worry about a competition between God and the human person, and thus we no longer need to resort to a cooperative account of the divine-human relation. Indeed, both cooperation and competition trade on a fundamentally mythological and metaphysical understanding of God as one causal agent among others within the cosmos. If divine agency does not conflict with any creaturely agency—being of a wholly different order— then a universal divine decision to elect all human beings in Jesus Christ need not compete with the free decision of individual persons.[24] There are various ways of explaining how this is possible, some being more satisfactory than others. At this point I am not advocating for any of the typical Protestant options. I am only interested in demonstrating that a responsible account of divine being and agency makes it possible to hold together a strongly monergistic doctrine of divine sovereignty with an equally strong doctrine of human freedom. Indeed, if freedom is not defined negatively as freedom *from* limitation—which is the doctrine of freedom underpinning modern capitalist ideology—but rather *positively* as freedom *for* the good, and if this good is understood theologically in terms of the liberating justice of Jesus Christ, then the only genuine human freedom is the one established and preserved by the Spirit of God. True human freedom occurs only *within* the space opened up by divine action, not alongside or apart from it.

My point here is not to dismiss the appeal to human freedom by those who are (often justifiably) put off by the Reformed tradition. Instead, I wish to reframe the problem in order to discern the actual issue at stake. The real issue is not one of freedom but of *historicity*. The problem of historicity arose in the nineteenth century as people began to recognize as never before that human beings are situated within a particular moment of history, and that every idea, text, and event is inseparable from its historical location—including those religious texts that are invested with normative authority.[25] The problem of historicity is thus the problem of hermeneutics, which we will take up in the following chapter. But it is also the problem of existence, of our being-in-the-world. To be a historical person is to be one who is "caught up with the world in constant change," and who thereby

24. The argument works for the traditional Reformed doctrine of double predestination, which is generally the context in which such debates play out. I am, of course, only interested in the way that this understanding of divine agency impinges on the possibility of universal salvation. I will treat questions of divine and human agency more fully and constructively in later chapters.

25. The best account of the problem of historicity and its significance for the church can be found in Ebeling, *Problem*, esp. 3–33.

constantly places oneself in relation to one's past and future.[26] The historicity of a person, like that of a text, means that a person is never static, never
a fixed entity; each person is always in the process of understanding herself
(and being understood by others) ever anew. This means that true humanity
is *historical*. There is nothing behind or above one's history. Put another way,
to accept the problem of historicity is to reject the Platonic ontology that
posits an eternal form or essence behind historical phenomena. Each person is a historical being whose being is thus only ever in becoming. People
are inseparable from the historical moments in which they exist in relation
to God, the world, and themselves.

The problem with most versions of universalism—especially those
that ground salvation in God's sovereign will—is that they run roughshod
over the question of historicity. This is a problem, in fact, for any soteriology that rejects the evangelical emphasis on the individual human person
as the site for the actualization of salvation (e.g., double predestination or
Barthian objectivism). If a person's nature is historical—that is, if there is
no human essence behind one's concrete actions and decisions—then *the
question of salvation cannot be decided apart from the particular moment in
which a person realizes her historical existence*. Salvation is meaningless if
it ignores or bypasses a person's historicity, since that would mean ignor-
ing or bypassing the person altogether. Unfortunately, many doctrines of
salvation are guilty of doing precisely that, and perhaps none more so than
the doctrine of universalism. Indeed, universalism—particularly its theo-
actualized instantiation—almost by definition trades on an abstract and
ahistorical conception of salvation.

Does this mean we are left with evangelical soteriology as the only
credible option? Must we accept that the individual believer consciously
and willingly actualizes her salvation, as Romans 10:9 might suggest? In
doing so we face a dilemma. If we insist with the tradition that such faith is
a gift from God, then we are still left with double predestination, where God
determines who will have saving faith and who will not. If we hold, by contrast, that this faith is a purely human magnitude, such that we contribute
decisively to our own salvation out of our own resources, then we end up
abandoning what is arguably the central claim of the entire New Testament
witness, namely, that we are dead in our transgressions and only the resur-
recting work of God can make us alive again. We who belong to the old age
would be unable to participate in the new were it not for God's apocalyptic
intervention in Christ. Sixteenth-century Lutherans could therefore rightly
say that "in spiritual and divine matters . . . the human being is like a pillar

26. Ibid., 25, 38.

of salt, like Lot's wife, indeed like a block of wood or a stone, like a lifeless statue."[27] Similarly, according to Barth, "Fallen human beings are surely
dead. But for the wonder of their awakening from the dead, which they
need, and in which their reconciliation with God consists, it is necessary
that they should still be there as corpses, as human corpses."[28] The dead
cannot save themselves. Only the miracle of new life can rescue them from
their desperate situation. Such is the grace that confronts us and elicits our
response. To be sure, we are speaking here in a naively traditional idiom,
and we will have occasion later to rethink what it means to speak of sin
and grace. The point is that we cannot ascribe salvific significance to our
actions—understood as purely natural, human deeds—and still remain
connected to the truth that comes to expression in the Christian kerygma.
Indeed, if we had to reduce Christianity to a single idea, we could plausibly,
and I would argue correctly, identify this idea with the claim that we achieve
authentic existence "by grace alone" (*sola gratia*).[29]

We thus find ourselves in a theological conundrum. On the one hand,
a credible soteriology, especially if it is universalistic, has to take the historicity of the believer seriously. On the other hand, we must avoid any soteriology that makes salvation a cooperative effort between God and the human
person. But in rejecting soteriological synergism we must also preserve
divine freedom. There is indeed a way out of this conundrum—or rather
through it—which we have named above as "eschatological theo-actualized
universalism." It protects divine freedom because it is actualized by God,

27. Formula of Concord, Solid Declaration II.20 in Kolb and Wengert, *Book of Concord*. The quoted material is culled from several of Martin Luther's own writings and
attributed to him as a quote.

28. *KD* 4.1:535. Cf. *CD* 4.1:481.

29. In effect, I am denying in principle the central tenet of evangelical soteriology,
namely, that a person is saved by the response of faith—and according to this soteriology salvation means being saved from reprobation. I will readily admit that this tenet
appears to have biblical support, but that is an insufficient criterion for theology. Many
positions can be supported from scripture that we have good reason to reject, both
ethical (e.g., slavery and the subordination of women) and theological (e.g., binitarianism, dispensationalism, and supersessionism). The question is whether this soteriology
makes coherent sense of God and the gospel, and here I must render a negative verdict.
The aporias are simply too great to overcome. I will discuss this more in chapter 3, but
a few points can be noted here. Evangelical soteriology proclaims a sovereign God of
grace who is capable of rescuing people from damnation (and desires to do so), and
yet God requires that each individual make a response of faith in order to carry this
out—unless this faith is a divine gift, in which case we have predestination again. On
this account, when a person dies who has not responded in faith, God's hands are supposedly tied. Such a God may be personal, but at the expense of being impotent.

and it protects the historicity of the believer because it is eschatological. What this might look like will be explored in the chapters to come.

TOWARD A UNIVERSALISM WITHOUT METAPHYSICS

The task of the present work is to develop an account of universalism that addresses the aforementioned challenges. We can name this a "universalism without metaphysics." We will say more about metaphysics in the next chapter, but we can define it here as a mode of thinking that constrains rational inquiry from the outset with abstract, ahistorical presuppositions. For instance, attention to human historicity might be constrained by an idea that determines human nature as such in advance (e.g., body-soul dualism), and divine freedom might be constrained by an idea that determines the nature of divine action in advance (e.g., the notion that God's salvific will is constrained by human response). An account of universalism will avoid metaphysics by defining each concretely and historically in accordance with the following conditions:

1. Salvation is freely actualized by God in history.

2. Salvation relates to each person in concrete historicity; it is situated but not synergistic.

3. Salvation is not a once-for-all ontological transformation of nature but an ongoing ontic transformation of existence.

Sketching a version of universalism that meets these conditions is the task of the subsequent chapters.

2

Soteriocentrism
Prolegomena to a Dogmatic Sketch

For the sake of your tradition, you make void the word of God.

MATTHEW 15:6

For the law of the Spirit of life in Christ Jesus has set you free.

ROMANS 8:2

EXORDIUM TO A SOTERIOCENTRIC THEOLOGY

Theology is traditionally understood as the science of God—the *logos* of *theos*. Like every other science, theology operates under a variety of presuppositions. Not all of the presuppositions are shared by every theologian, hence the many intractable conundrums and the apparent incommensurability between various parties. The initial task of a systematic theology is to come clean about one's presuppositions for the sake of clarity and mutual understanding. Achieving such prolegomenous clarity will be the goal of this chapter.

In the case of discussions of soteriology—and especially such a contested issue as universal salvation—the presuppositions are numerous, decisive, and often hidden from view. This is largely because it is hard for us to
imagine others thinking differently about something so basic and essential
to the faith. It is easy to think that one's view of salvation is self-evidently
"biblical" or that it is the obvious position to hold in light of one's confessional tradition. Of all the doctrinal *loci*, soteriology is perhaps the one
most determined by latent presuppositions, in part because the scriptural
texts and doctrinal traditions are so ambiguous, even at times contradictory. Moreover, there has never been an official dogma regarding salvation.
The consequence has been a diverse multiplicity of positions, even within
a single confessional tradition. There are almost as many soteriologies as
there are theologians to espouse them. In such a situation, it is crucial that
one's methodological assumptions are made evident for the sake of promoting a dialogue that will edify the communion of the saints.

What follows in this chapter is an all-too-brief discussion of how I
define the task of theology. In order to define this task, however, I must already engage in theological reflection. There is an ineluctable circularity in
theological prolegomena. One cannot speak *about* theology without already
doing theology. One's methodological presuppositions, if they are not to
unjustly prejudice one's understanding of the subject matter, must in some
sense be determined by, or at least derived from, the object of one's inquiry.
In other words, the presuppositions for the theological task are determined
by the object of theology—God—and thus they themselves already presuppose some level of theological analysis. The way in which one speaks about
God is conditioned from the beginning by one's understanding of God. And
this understanding is not a private conversation constructed by the individual monad; it is conditioned by one's confessional tradition, historical
situation, and social relations.

We find ourselves in the midst of an ongoing dialogue about God. We
are not the originators of this conversation, nor will we bring it to a close.
This does not mean we are constrained by the parameters of past generations, only that we cannot isolate our theological reflection from this wider
social and historical context. To put it another way, there is no neutral, ahistorical, and universally-acceptable starting point for theology. We approach
the task of thinking and speaking about God from a particular location
within history, under various personal limitations and social conditions.
But this is as it should be, since our concern is not with a general, ahistorical
concept of deity, but rather with the God of Abraham, Isaac, and Jacob, who
is revealed to us in the concrete person of Jesus and who encounters us in the
particularities of our present situation. A *God* who is within history—whose

very *being* is, as Eberhard Jüngel puts it, "historical being"[1]—can therefore only be approached appropriately from within history. The triune God of Christian faith is one who embraces the radical contingency of worldly existence. Any attempt to speak faithfully of this God will similarly have to acknowledge and affirm the historical contingency and cultural plurality that characterizes our creaturely relation to God.

All this is simply to say up front that what follows has no pretensions of providing a universally valid description of the theological task. Every theology is written in and for a specific location within history. I follow Rudolf Bultmann in the view that "there is neither a definitive form of Christian kerygma nor a definitive expression of Christian self-understanding, but both must always appear in an ever new form contingently upon each historical situation."[2] This work seeks to be nothing more than just such a contingent form of Christian self-understanding, a modest yet systematic treatment of what the Christian gospel compels us to proclaim boldly in the present moment.

This chapter is divided into four main parts, each of which is a key facet of theological inquiry. The order of presentation does not indicate priority. Each is an equally essential aspect. I begin with a brief discussion of theology as a *science*. This will strike some as both problematic and somewhat dated. The scientific (i.e., *wissenschaftlich*) nature of theology is a German tradition going back to Schleiermacher and given new life by Karl Barth. By employing the notion here, I consciously place myself in that tradition of thought, though I also seek to break it open from within in recognition of its limitations. Certain insights are lost by giving up the language of theology as a science, but retaining it requires careful qualifications. I thus follow by treating theology as an exercise in *hermeneutics*. Theology is an act of interpretation; it seeks to understand what it means to speak of God today. It is an attempt to understand who we are in light of the church's missionary proclamation of the gospel news about Jesus. The third facet connects the scientific and hermeneutical dimensions of theology to its concrete, bodily instantiation within particular sociopolitical situations. Theology is always necessarily *praxis*, a mode of embodied action. The theological task is irreducibly communal, ethical, and political in nature.

Theology is scientific, hermeneutical, and praxical. The fourth and decisive section brings these three elements together by speaking of theology as *soteriology*. Here I lay my cards on the table in terms of how I approach the topic at hand. This work radicalizes the "christocentric turn" in theology

1. Jüngel, *God's Being*, 109.
2. Bultmann, "Theology," 64–65.

inaugurated by Barth. Following Jüngel's lead, I claim that theology must be *soteriocentric*.[3] The position of soteriocentrism is not meant as a contrast to christocentrism but rather as a postmetaphysical radicalization of it. A soteriocentric approach to theological inquiry affirms that the person of Christ is defined in terms of his saving work and, therefore, the being of God is defined in terms of God's trinitarian economy of grace. It is not the being of God as an isolated metaphysical entity in itself (which does not exist) but rather the concrete being of God *for us* (which is deity as such) that is the topic of Christian theology. Clarifying this starting point will set us on the right path for evaluating the dogmatic basis for answering the question of universal salvation. The problem of universalism is not a secondary and dispensable issue. It thrusts us deep into the heart of the doctrine of God, and it can only be properly analyzed from that perspective.

A concluding section will draw out the implications of these methodological points for the problem of theological unity and diversity. The topic of universal salvation has long raised questions about what counts as "orthodox" and whether universalism is a "heresy." This chapter will propose jettisoning the dichotomy between orthodoxy and heterodoxy by speaking instead of an *orthoheterodoxy*, defined as "speaking differently but in the right way." A soteriocentric theology radicalizes the path of the reformers not only by refusing to take any received tradition as a norm to which one is bound, but also by refusing to participate altogether in the ongoing attempt to "normalize" the faith by identifying a particular creaturely artifact (e.g., scriptural text or creedal formula) with God's revelation. The pursuit of an abstract and authoritative "Christian worldview" undermines the hermeneutical and practical character of theological discourse, and it cuts the very nerve of the gospel as a word that absolutely resists all attempts to turn it into propaganda. The good news that God saves eternally subtracts itself from and continually subverts all attempts to convert it into a religioideological superstructure. It is instead a word that announces every day the true *freedom* of a Christian, as Luther rightly saw. Theology is therefore an eminently *free* discourse. Its orthoheterodox multivocality is not opposed to the gospel but rather takes place within the very space opened up by God's word of grace in Jesus Christ.

---

3. The term "soteriocentric" is most widely associated with Paul Knitter's pluralistic, liberationist theology of religions. In *One Earth Many Religions*, he rejects his previous "theocentric" position for a "soteriocentric" understanding of religions, which finds a common soteriological concern at the heart of all religions, though this concern for "salvation" is normed differently within particular faiths (*One Earth*, 17). I use the term "soteriocentric" somewhat differently here, though I do see it as having a similar relevance for interfaith dialogue.

THEOLOGY AS SCIENCE

Theology is the science of God. Science is here understood as a mode of rational inquiry appropriate to its object. The method of its inquiry is determined by the particular characteristics of the object under investigation. If, as Rudolf Bultmann claims, "the object of theology is that which constitutes what is Christian," we must ask what precisely is the nature of this object if we are going to understand what kind of science theology actually is.[4]

Theology throughout history has vacillated between two main objects of reflection: the *fides quae creditur* ("the faith *that* is believed") and the *fides qua creditur* ("the faith *by which* it is believed"). The distinction itself originates with Augustine, who says in *De trinitate* that "what is believed is one thing, the faith it is believed with is another."[5] It was later developed by Peter Lombard, Philipp Melanchthon, and Johann Gerhard. In essence, the *fides quae* refers to the received content (i.e., orthodox doctrine or *regula fidei*) to which one relates, while the *fides qua* refers to the faith of the human subject that relates to God. The tradition of orthodoxy, particularly in its late medieval and post-reformational forms, placed the emphasis on the received dogmas and doctrines of the faith, on the *fides quae creditur* understood as something passed on unchanged from one generation to the next. Christian faith was primarily the intellectual assent to the truth of these theological propositions.

The simplicity of this account was challenged in the modern era with the recognition that the human subject does not passively receive content from the world around her but actively contributes to the production of knowledge. The rise of historical consciousness radicalized this insight, as people became ever more aware of the historical conditions of our thinking and speaking—that is to say, of the contingency and historicity of our knowledge. As a result, the tradition of liberal theology established by Friedrich Schleiermacher shifted the emphasis to the consciousness and experience of the believer. If the divine being—the theological *Ding an sich*, so to speak—was no longer accessible as an object in itself apart from the consciousness of the subject, then it seemed to follow that theology ought to inquire instead into the nature of this consciousness. Theology shifted its object to the *fides qua creditur*; its concern was no longer God as such but now God as experienced and believed by a person or community. Schleiermacher thus defined theology in 1811 as a "positive science" (*positive Wissenschaft*), in which the various parts form a "cohesive whole only through

---

4. Bultmann, *What Is Theology?*, 32.
5. Augustine, *The Trinity*, 13.5, 345.

their common relation to a particular mode of faith."[6] Unlike a "speculative science," theology eschews metaphysical speculation and concerns itself with a "practical task."[7]

While the definition of theology as a "positive science" remains valid in its broad strokes, Bultmann judged that, in the modern era, theology "lost its object." And that is because "this object, clearly, is God, in some sense or other."[8] In the final analysis, both orthodoxy and liberalism speak of God, but they do not have God as their object. The former makes scriptural texts, church dogma, and logical propositions the object; the latter makes personal experience and historical research the object of theology. In either case, one ends up only with a science of *religion*, not a science of *God*.[9] Each position assumes that the divine is directly accessible or given within the immanent nexus of the world. This givenness can take the form of officially approved structures and practices (e.g., scripture, church teaching, sacraments, etc.), or it can take the form of structures and practices that are either generally accessible (historical analysis) or generally inaccessible (experience). Both positions assume a static conception of God as something fixed and stable. What neither contemplates is a God who *acts*, who actually *does* something in the world. Neither the *fides quae* nor the *fides qua* in isolation relates to the God who is an object only *in actu*. God does not act in the mythical-supernatural sense of effecting miraculous occurrences, but in the noncompetitive sense of being actively present in worldly occurrences, all of which have a so-called "natural" cause.[10] The God who acts

6. Schleiermacher, *Brief Outline*, §1, 1.

7. Ibid., §1, 2. According to Clifford Anderson's analysis of Schleiermacher, "theology is more akin to engineering or medicine than to physics or biology. Strictly speaking, theology does not produce scientific knowledge, but puts knowledge from other sciences to a particular use" ("Crisis," 145–46).

8. Bultmann, *What Is Theology?* 45.

9. Regarding liberal theology, Bultmann writes: "As a matter of fact, in the course of the nineteenth century and by the beginning of the twentieth, theology became essentially the science of religion. The biblical sciences became branches of the history of religion, and the same was true of church history insofar as it did not become simply profane history. Systematic theology became the philosophy or psychology of religion (Ernst Troeltsch and Rudolf Otto), and practical theology was now simply religious folklore, psychology of religion, and education" (Bultmann, "Theology," 51).

10. We will continue to clarify talk of divine action throughout the course of this book, since to speak meaningfully of such action requires that we understand the agent. For now we will simply observe that talk of divine action is metaphorical and analogous talk. I can talk about God as agent the way I talk about my love for another person. In each case, this talking-about is an objectification of the reality itself and so inadequate if taken literally or in isolation. The idea of God as agent only truly makes sense in the event of this action. The aim of this book is to clarify the nature of this event, and thus

is the eschatological God who annuls the world *within* the world and who establishes the new creation *within* the old creation. This is the paradox of the Christian faith: the Word becomes flesh without ceasing to be Word; the eschatological becomes the historical without ceasing to be eschatological.[11] In other words, *the God who is not an object of science becomes an object of science without ceasing to be the God who is not an object of science.* This event, whereby God acts in a decisive and paradoxical way, is what theology seeks to comprehend and clarify, while always recognizing that its object is beyond comprehension and precludes any final clarification. All of this means two things: (1) if God is an object of thought, God is unlike any other object we know; and (2) the object that is God is only accessible to a certain kind of subject, namely, the faithful subject who is confronted with the paradoxical presence of God in the world.

We can therefore agree with orthodoxy that the *fides quae creditur*, rightly understood, is the object of faith. There is indeed a reality *that* we believe, which stands outside of ourselves and to which we are responsible. But because this reality is utterly *sui generis*—being pure noncompetitive activity in the world available to faith alone—the *fides quae creditur* is inaccessible apart from the *fides qua creditur*. The object of theology is the unity of the *fides quae* and the *fides qua*; subjective reception is included within the object itself. Unlike the objects of the general sciences, the object of theology is not available for empirical observation and investigation by any human person. While the knowing subject is never irrelevant to the general sciences—since every knower is personally involved in the production of knowledge—the general sciences do not restrict knowledge to a certain

to clarify the nature of the divine.

11. The Chalcedonian point, of course, is that the flesh remains flesh and the historical remains historical. This is already implied in the statement that the word remains word and the eschatological remains eschatological, but it is worth making it explicit, not only to indicate my continuity with the tradition, but also to reinforce the *non-miraculous* nature of divine action in the world. A miracle is, by definition, non-paradoxical: the water actually becomes wine, and the blind person actually receives sight. But this is precisely what cannot be the case christologically, on the grounds of orthodoxy itself, since the entire basis of Christianity depends on the claim that divinity and humanity—however we understand these terms—remain unchanged in the event of their union in Christ. Each dimension of Christ remains unimpaired in its integrity. This is not to deny the unity and mutual participation of divinity and humanity, but only to point out that such participation cannot lose the paradoxicality of the Christ-event without losing Jesus Christ altogether. It is thus more accurate to speak of a *paradoxical identity* of divinity and humanity in this event. Traditional accounts of theology want to make the Christ-event an exception to the way God acts elsewhere in the world. Here I take a radically christocentric approach and argue that God acts elsewhere *only* in the way God acts in Christ, since the Christ-event is definitive, even constitutive, of who God is and how God acts.

kind of subject.[12] The general sciences only care about the *that* of the subject, not the *how* of the subject. Theology is of a different order altogether. Theology's object is qualitatively different from every other scientific object, since its object stands over against the knower as an uncontrollable *subject*, and therefore theology is qualitatively different from every other science. Because theology's object is a divine subject, it demands a certain kind of human subject as its knower and restricts knowledge of itself to this particular subject. The *how* of the theological subject is essential to the encounter with the theological object. Objectivity within theology is irreducibly and simultaneously subjectivity. In other words, the object determines the means by which it comes to objectivity—encounter, thought, and speech. The faithful human subject of theological inquiry comes into existence, so to speak, in the event of the object's coming to speech. *Theology is thus the science that reflects on the coming-to-speech of the object, which is at the same time the coming-into-existence of the subject.*

The upshot of this is that "[theology's] object is found in no other science than in theology."[13] Apologetics as the attempt to defend Christianity according to extratheological criteria is consequently ruled out in principle. If God is only perceptible to faith, then theology does not investigate

---

12. Some theologians have tried to appeal to the likes of Michael Polanyi, with his account of "personal knowledge" (see *Personal Knowledge*), because they think this allows them to *deny* the distinction between the general sciences and theology. The claim is that post-critical, post-Kantian philosophy of science shows that there is no pure objectivity, since every scientific inquiry is shaped by the person engaged in this inquiry. As true as this may be, such theologians attempt to use this insight to claim that theology's statements are no less "objective" than those of chemistry or biology, as if the admission of a subjective dimension suddenly means that theology and the natural sciences are operating at the same level of discourse. This position fails to start by considering the true nature of the *object* of theological inquiry. Doing so quickly reveals that theology speaks of a qualitatively different kind of object, which leads to a qualitatively different kind of subject. Subjective or personal involvement in the sciences is an insufficiently formal analysis. In the end, appeals to such ideas almost inevitably serve crude apologetic ends that end up falsifying the content of Christian faith. The aim here is really to secure the validity of Christianity by defending the scientific rationality of a bodily resurrection, and they try to do so by undermining the objectivity of the natural sciences. The result of this failed procedure is a gross misunderstanding of both theology and the natural sciences.

13. Bultmann, *What Is Theology?*, 45. The full context of this statement reads: "The question, What is theology? is itself a theological question, or can only be treated theologically. It is not to be answered apart from knowledge of the object of theology, which cannot be known apart from theology. . . . To say what theology is, it would itself have to be theology. Theology, therefore, can be defined only on the basis of its object, and its object is found in no other science than in theology. This object, clearly, is God, in some sense or other. . . . Thus to deal with the question, What is theology? already means to do theology."

evidence accessible to any neutral observer. There is no extratheological access to the reality of God. Theology does not conform to the standard scientific parameters of verification and falsifiability, because God is not a datum like other data capable of being verified or falsified according to general criteria. God is not a self-evident axiom, a fact of history, a specimen of nature, or the conclusion to a logical syllogism. God is only known in the faithful encounter with the kerygmatic word of Jesus Christ, that is to say, only in the divine act whereby God gives Godself to be known. Christian theology is thus possible only when and where God makes it possible. The theologian *responds* to a divine *act* that calls forth her responsible inquiry and disciplined speech. God calls us children, commands our attention, and commissions our proclamation.

Theology is a science whose very scientificity is exploded from within by the singularity and eventfulness of a God who "does not stand still and does not put up with being made an object of observation."[14] Christian faith concerns a God who is both radically transcendent and radically immanent, both intimately subjective and gloriously objective, who is "nearer to me than I am to myself" and yet is "radically removed from me" as the one who "distances us from ourselves."[15] God sublates—in the Hegelian double sense of both preserving and abolishing—the distinction between subjective and objective as an *event* that is, at one and the same time, "more inward than my most inward part"[16] and more real than any purported reality. Theology is therefore the science in which to know God is to know *ourselves* anew, since it is not so much God who is known as *we* who are known by God: "you have come to know God, or rather to be known by God" (Gal 4:9). Put another way, "all knowledge of God is included in the being-known-by-God."[17]

In sum, the nature of theology as the science of God requires that we attend equally to the human subject who speaks of God. To understand God is to understand the historical situation in which God-talk takes place. For this reason, the science of God is an intrinsically *hermeneutical* science.

THEOLOGY AS HERMENEUTICS

"Hermeneutics is necessary, because the truth is elusive. What is normal, commonplace, and apparently self-evident largely reveals what is false

---

14. Bultmann, "Science and Existence," 144.

15. Jüngel, *God as the Mystery*, 182–83.

16. Augustine, *Confessions*, 3.6.11, 43.

17. Stoevesandt, "Basel—Marburg," 109.

and conceals what is true."[18] Heinrich Balz's axiom regarding the necessity of hermeneutics is, on the surface, merely a description of life within
the world. We are fallible creatures within a bewildering environment: the
world is a thoroughly ambiguous place, and what we try to make of it—the
things we see, think, and do—often has very little connection with the truth.
On a certain level, then, Balz's statement is simply a fact of life. We can
no more escape the problem of hermeneutics than we can escape our very
creatureliness.[19]

The apparent obviousness of the hermeneutical problem is deceiv-
ing. The very fact that we can now take for granted the elusiveness of truth
is a sign of our historical location. For precisely the opposite assumption
prevailed throughout most of western history, dominated religiously by a
Christianity concerned with precluding all ambiguity and uncertainty and
philosophically by a naïve realism that took for granted the correspondence
between our language and the world. The two coincided as part of the medieval synthesis of Christianity and Aristotelian philosophy. Hilary Putnam
refers to this scholastic metaphysical position as the belief in a "ready-
made world with a wholly precise structure and a determinate relation of
correspondence."[20] To believe in the "metaphysical fantasy" of a "ready-
made world" is "to think that a sign-relation is *built into nature*," which is
"to revert to medieval essentialism, to the idea that there are 'self-identifying
objects' and 'species' out there. . . . Such an idea made sense in the context of
a medieval world view, which had not only an elaborate ontology . . . to back
it up, but also an elaborate psychology . . . and an elaborate correspondence
between the two."[21] We need not examine the details of correspondentist
metaphysics. The point is that the medieval metaphysical belief in a ready-
made world took for granted the direct connection between language and
reality, because the rational explanation for the world was thought to be
"built into" the world. The *conceptual understanding* of the world was seen
as being just as self-evident and unambiguous as the world itself. In other

18. Balz, "Hermeneutik," 206.

19. On this point I agree with James K. A. Smith in his rejection of those "who
consider hermeneutics to be a result of the Fall and who understand interpretation
as somehow fallen. . . . These thinkers express the confident hope of overcoming and
escaping human finitude" (*Fall*, 18). My agreement with Smith on the *problem* should
not be taken to imply an agreement with him on the *solution*. Indeed, my own work is
diametrically opposed to his "creational hermeneutic" and the cultural-liturgical conception of Christianity that follows from it.

20. Putnam, *Realism*, 278. Putnam provides the argument against this premodern
metaphysics in his essay, "Why There Isn't a Ready-Made World," in ibid., 205–28.

21. Ibid., xii–xiii.

words, the metaphysical belief in a ready-made world was the absolutization of a culturally specific idea, which obscured its historicity and contingency.

The philosophical position that Putnam describes was at the same time a theological position. The "medieval world view," with its ontology and psychology, was the worldview of medieval Christianity. The philosophical belief in the self-evidentness of the ready-made world was inseparable from the theological conviction that Christian orthodoxy was a universal truth that alone made sense of reality. The truth of Christianity was believed to be just as objective as the structure of the ready-made world, precisely because a certain kind of Judeo-Christian theism was the "sign-relation" that they believed to be "built into nature." Scholastic theologians built their entire apologetic edifice on this foundation, with proofs for the existence of God based, for example, on worldly causality—as if the "sign-relation" of God were an objective feature of the world.

This metaphysical-theological fantasy of the ready-made world was not merely an epistemological position. Like its religious predecessors, ancient and medieval Christianity posited an all-encompassing teleological cosmology, which ordered every entity within a cosmic hierarchy and understood the world to be the unfolding of an overarching divine plan determined in advance.

> Just as the contents of a play are established beforehand in the major and minor roles which appear in it, so too the events of this history are given in advance in the "spiritual substances of all the orders," which "are united in the Church as a mystical body, which extends from the Trinity and the angels which are nearest to Them [*sic*] down to the beggar at the church door and to the serf who kneels humbly in the obscurest corner of the church to receive the sacrifice of the Mass." But this interpretation of history as a kingdom of metaphysical essences or substances, motivated teleologically within itself and comprising the whole world within this teleology, allows no historical significance to precisely that which we regard as the actual historical process, namely the vital personal experiences of particular individuals in their particular characters and responsibilities. This loses its historical significance because history anticipates it by taking place within the framework of those metaphysical beings. And it is only in so far as they enter into this metaphysical framework that man's life and its events have a place in the history which unfolds there.[22]

22. Gogarten, *Demythologizing*, 22–23. Gogarten is here quoting from Wilhelm Dilthey.

As Friedrich Gogarten observes, the metaphysical framework of medieval Christianity involved much more than a normative epistemology; it was a comprehensive ontology that placed every detail of life within a divine order. In other words, the ready-made world was a ready-made *culture*. We can start to see the intrinsic connection between the great medieval synthesis and the church's constantinian collusion with imperial power.

The point is that today's problem of hermeneutics was simply not a problem in the medieval context. Ambiguity or uncertainty was, at least in theory, precluded by the ecclesiastical expropriation of all hermeneutical queries. Ambiguity was impossible for people who were supposed to submit to the authoritative interpretation provided by the church—an interpretation that was as authoritative regarding the cosmos as it was regarding salvation. For this reason, Balz's axiom regarding the elusiveness of the truth presupposes a situation in which one can actually recognize the truth to be elusive, in which there are competing claims regarding what is true and false. It therefore assumes the modern crisis of authority, namely, the era in which the old structures of meaning—primarily, the institutional authority of the church as the authoritative interpreter of the scriptures and thus the arbiter of what counts as true or meaningful—are no longer taken for granted. There are numerous persons and events that contributed to this situation: the Cartesian pursuit of rational certainty, the Pascalian wager, the Kantian turn to the subject (i.e., the so-called "Copernican Revolution" in philosophy), the rise of the empirical sciences as a competing norm for what is real and true, the fragmentation of the church itself due to the Reformation, the imperial and colonial efforts of European Christendom, the rise of the nation-state, and various other developments that, in time, placed the traditional orders and narratives into question, or at least led to a disillusionment with those orders.

At the heart of all these developments is the rise of what scholars refer to as "historical consciousness." The rise of historical consciousness names the replacement of the old metaphysical and teleological interpretation of the world and our existence in it with a historical interpretation. The word "historical" here means dynamic, evolving, contingent, spatiotemporally located, socially constructed, political, and open to ongoing criticism and interrogation. Whereas a metaphysical interpretation understands God, the world, and human existence in terms of an eternally fixed and unchangeable order, a historical interpretation understands them in terms of a historically situated and ever-changing nexus of forces. Whereas a metaphysical interpretation posits timeless essences underneath the contingencies and complexities on the surface of history, a historical interpretation denies that there is anything behind or beneath the historical that could stabilize and secure human existence in advance. *Metaphysics*, as the term is used here, is simply any conceptual schema that secures the object of its inquiry (e.g., the being of God or the nature of human existence) apart from and prior to the historical situation. By contrast, *hermeneutics* is the project that understands its object in terms of its radical historicity, which means understanding it as subject to constant reinterpretation and renegotiation.

For our purposes, the rise of historical consciousness is what defines modernity. Modernity is the age in which the metaphysical understanding of history was called into question thoroughly and irrevocably. It was thus in the modern era that human beings became aware of the elusiveness of truth and the necessity of hermeneutical inquiry. "Only with the collapse of traditional Western metaphysics, i.e., with the loss of its self-evident character, did people become fully aware of the historic character of existence," out of which arose "the freedom, but also the sheer necessity, to regard historical events in their pure historicity."[23] No longer was the hierarchical "chain of being" taken for granted. No longer was the ecclesiastical tale of our given place in God's order accepted on faith. It was no longer assumed that the old stories exhaustively narrate each person's identity. Modernity initiated a turn to human subjectivity as people sought to make sense of their existence.[24] For those institutions and ideologies that depend on this authority,

23. Ebeling, "Significance," 46.

24. It has become increasingly fashionable over the past century—especially over the past fifty years—for theologians to disparage modernity and the so-called "turn to the subject" initiated by thinkers like Descartes and Immanuel Kant. Oswald Bayer, for instance, refers to the post-Kantian concern with subjectivity as a "modern narcissism," in which "subjectivity no longer has a counterbalance in a cosmic piety. Rather cosmic piety is absorbed into subjectivity." See Bayer, *Gott*, 74. Cf. Bayer, "Modern Narcissus." Defenders of modernism observe that the turn to subjectivity in modern thought has nothing to do with solipsistic inwardness and vicious individualism. It is rather a recognition that human beings are not merely passive observers but active participants in the pursuit of meaning and identity. Kevin Hector calls this pursuit of meaningful identity the modern project of "mineness" (see *Theological Project*). Of course, for the reactionary enforcers of orthodoxy this is precisely the problem: human beings should not actively make sense of their existence but rather receive the meaning given to it by God. Not only does this require a *sacrificium intellectus*, but it also serves to reinforce a particular sociocultural worldview as divinely authorized and so necessarily imposed upon human beings as the only appropriate framework for interpreting the meaningfulness of one's life. Such an approach is at odds not only with the Reformation but also with the missionary principle of recipiency, according to which the recipients of the gospel message determine what counts as a faithful translation of the message. Translation is thus "surrender to the terms of the target culture" and has more to do "with their self-understanding than with literalness and accuracy. . . . To ignore this fact is to concede the idea of mission as foreign imperialism" (Sanneh, *Translating*, 237–38). Those who cast stones on modernity need to be careful lest they inadvertently find themselves on the side of colonialist missions.

new strategies were devised to shore up faith: for example, Roman Catholics put forward the doctrine of papal infallibility in the early 1870s, while
Reformed Protestants formulated the doctrine of biblical inerrancy with
renewed vigor in the early 1880s. Both sides were certainly able to claim that
such views were held long before they were codified in these forms. And
yet it is significant that this codification occurred at precisely this moment.
Their very formulation indicates that the traditional "plausibility structures"
were no longer taken for granted.[25] The end of metaphysics ushered in an
era of fear in the face of the unknown. Proliferation of theologies of fear
designed to safeguard Christians from the hermeneutical problem was a
predictable result. Today's culture wars are simply the long death rattle of
an antiquated version of Christianity trying to maintain some vestige of
metaphysical security.

The church can no longer afford to ignore the problem of hermeneutics. Theology that engages in metaphysical thinking today is an exercise
in pretending that the curtain has not been pulled back to reveal the man
posturing as a wizard.[26] We ignore the elusiveness and ambiguity of truth

25. See Berger, *Heretical Imperative*.

26. The reference to the story of *The Wonderful Wizard of Oz* is quite intentional.
As many have observed, the original 1900 novel, made famous by the 1939 film *The
Wizard of Oz*, can be read quite persuasively as a parable about the disillusionment with
Christianity and the rise of secularism. There are numerous religious parallels, with the
Emerald City bearing no small resemblance to the New Jerusalem in John's Apocalypse;
there is even a yellow-brick road in place of streets of gold. And the need for brains
(faith), courage (hope), and heart (love) represent the classic theological virtues, for
which traditional Christian theology believed one needed the infused gift of God's
Spirit. In the story, God—or at least the metaphysical notion of God—is represented
by the wizard, whom they discover is just an ordinary old man playing a trick on the
people. The pseudo-wizard still gives each of them something, but they are useless objects that they invest with "power" through their own belief. The message is clear: God
cannot save us, but we can save ourselves if we simply believe in ourselves. We can see
in this story a parable of the transition from religion to psychotherapy that was taking
place concurrently in the work of Sigmund Freud and others.

What is perhaps even more remarkable as a commentary on our culture is the 2013
film, *Oz the Great and Powerful*. Serving as a kind of prequel to *The Wizard of Oz*, this
film tells the story of how Oscar "Oz" Diggs ends up in the Land of Oz and eventually
has to pretend to be a great wizard in order to save the people from the wicked witch. In
effect, the story is the reverse of the 1939 film. Here we begin with the knowledge that
Oz is a fraud with no powers, but the film concludes with Oz becoming a great wizard
(i.e., "God") thanks to the collective belief of the people. As an audience, we are led to
believe that, even though it is fake and meaningless in itself, corporate religion is necessary to achieve certain social ends. The main characters in the story all know the truth
but keep it a secret so that the people of Oz have something to motivate them. And
so Oz, played by James Franco, declares rather remarkably: "Oscar Diggs died so that
the Wizard of Oz could live. When those witches come back, and they will come back,
we're going to need everyone to believe." Here we have an all-too-obvious Jesus-figure,

at our peril, because to do so is to ignore our own historicity, that is, our situatedness within a particular cultural context. Such an account faces an immediate objection from Christian orthodoxy, insofar as we appear to be privileging a nontheological or extrabiblical starting point, viz. the modern-western historical context. The fact is that the theological significance of this modern context—in the sense of its radical historical consciousness—is itself theologically grounded. We can substantiate this in three primary ways, in conversation especially with the work of Gerhard Ebeling.

First, Christianity "stands or falls with the tie that binds it to its unique historical origin."[27] Christianity is rooted in a concrete historical event. More precisely, Christianity identifies a particular historical event as revelation, as God's unique self-disclosure to humankind. In a certain basic sense, therefore, the contingencies and complexities of history are *internal* to Christian faith because they are internal to the very identity of God. This is the beating heart of Christianity's rejection of docetism. It keeps the church open to the contingencies of history, and thus continually exposes the church's teaching to critical analysis in light of the present situation. Of course, Christianity was quick to betray this orientation to history through numerous attempts at securing ahistorical or permanent points of access to revelation, which allow people to bypass the hermeneutical problem altogether as nonexistent. As Ebeling points out, this occurred in a number of ways, including

---

though in a crude Tillichian sense wherein Jesus dies so that the Christ may live in and through the community of faith. It is strongly reminiscent of Philip Pullman's provocative retelling of the Gospel narrative, *The Good Man Jesus and the Scoundrel Christ* (2010), in which Christ, the brother of Jesus, fabricates the story of Jesus's resurrection in order to create a religious force for good in the world.

If the 1939 film captures the twentieth century's "death of God," the 2013 film captures, among other things, the return and proliferation of gods and religions in the twenty-first century, as well as the apologetic entrenchment of conservative evangelicalism. And this is why I brought the story up. Since the 1970s we have seen a reaction against historical consciousness and the hermeneutical problem throughout North American Christianity, both evangelical and mainline. Metaphysics is on the rise in multiple forms. We need to name this return to metaphysics for what it is: a naïve belief in the power of a pseudo-wizard. Of course, the unfortunate truth is that many people today, as the 2013 film accurately portrays, no longer care if the "God" of religion is a fake. Just as Oz and his friends in *Oz the Great and Powerful* supported the myth of his greatness in order to mobilize the people, so too people support traditional religion because it "works." We see this, for example, in apologetic arguments that appeal to psychological studies about the personal benefits of religion and prayer—as if this somehow proves that God is real or that we were created by God. And while many people actually believe the religious myths on a literal level, they are unconcerned about matters of veracity and historicity, because at the end of the day, religion *helps* them. For this reason, genuine Christian theologians may find that outspoken atheists are actually their strongest and closest allies in the pursuit of truth.

27. Ebeling, "Significance," 28.

the use of metaphysical and metahistorical concepts in the formulation of christological dogma, the interpretation of scripture as a "sacred history" (*historia sacra*) through the doctrine of verbal inspiration, the whole system of sacraments and relics designed to grant immediate and objective access to salvation, and finally the very institution of the church itself as the prolongation of the incarnation that possesses the "deposit of faith" (*depositum fidei*).[28] Together these serve "to secure for the event of revelation its place in the world and its history, but on the other hand to isolate it at the same time from the world and its history."[29] If the Reformation served only one purpose, it served to call into question the entire ecclesiastical attempt to secure revelation, either *for* us or *from* the world.

Hence, second, the present essay takes for granted the reformational commitment to the doctrine of justification—*sola fide, sola gratia, solus Christus*—which is fundamentally a "de-securing" of revelation.[30] Setting aside the question of the reformers' interpretation of Paul, the doctrine of justification is a theological position that is faithful to the scandalous nature of the originating Christ-event. The heart of this doctrine is the *sola fide*, "by faith alone," which is set against the "works of the law." Revelation is therefore present exclusively to faith, and thus exclusively within the concrete historicity of human existence.

> The *sola fide* of the Reformation is directed not only against justification by works and thereby against a legalistic exposition of scripture, not only against mysticism and against multiplication of the revealing reality in the form of saints and against materialization of the revealing reality in the form of sacred objects. But the *sola fide* has undoubtedly also an anti-sacramental and an anti-clerical point. To the *sola fide* there corresponds *solus Christus*. Revelation and the present are separated from each other in such a way that only one bridge remains: the Word alone—and indeed, lest any misunderstanding should arise, the Word interpreted as salvation *sola gratia, sola fide*. All other bridges have been broken up. . . . There is no such thing as a simple, matter-of-fact presence of revelation.[31]

Sola fide thus rejects every means of controlling our access to revelation—whether conceptual, sacramental, or institutional. The only available means

---

28. See ibid., 30–35.

29. Ibid., 30.

30. See Eberhard Jüngel's view that the "certainty of faith" is a "de-securing" (*Entsicherung*) of oneself in *Gott als Geheimnis*, 227.

31. Ebeling, "Significance," 35–36.

is entirely outside of our control, namely, a personal encounter with God's present word within our historicity. The reformational rejection of both justification by works and the *opus operatum* of the sacrament leads to "the shattering of all historical assurances that supposedly render the decision of faith superfluous. . . . The *sola fide* destroys all secretly docetic views of revelation which evade the historicalness of revelation by making it a history *sui generis*, a sacred area from which the critical historical method must be anxiously debarred."[32]

For this reason Ebeling argues that the doctrine of justification laid the foundation for the rise of the historical-critical method. To be sure, the reformers did not themselves adopt a historical-critical perspective, and Ebeling is quick to point out that the reformers had their own means of securing revelation in ways counter to their own central insights. Nevertheless, what emerged in the Reformation was the necessity of the hermeneutical problem for theology.[33] The Reformation destroyed the ideal of a *theologia perennis*, a perennial or permanent theology safe from the hermeneutical queries of the present situation. As a consequence, there can be no "archaizing repetition of 'pure doctrine,'" but only a fresh encounter with the word of God.[34] This does not mean, of course, that everyone who championed the historical-critical method was thereby faithful to the Reformation by default. "But what it certainly does mean is, that wherever they made way for the critical historical method and, however grievous their errors, took it seriously as their task, there, if certainly often in a very paradoxical way, they were really asserting the fundamental principle of the reformers in the intellectual situation of the modern age."[35]

A third and final reason why the modern historical consciousness is theologically grounded follows closely from the former point. *Sola fide* not only entails the radical dependence of human beings upon the gracious action of God, but it simultaneously entails the radical transcendence and unavailability of God. The axiom of divine transcendence is the ontological correlate of the reformational axiom of justification by faith alone without the works of the law. To acknowledge that justification is outside of our grasp is to acknowledge that *God* is outside of our grasp. This point has significant hermeneutical implications. Balz's claim about the necessity of hermeneutics in general is thus especially applicable to theology. Hermeneutics is uniquely necessary within theology because the truth about God

32. Ibid., 56.
33. Ibid., 42.
34. Ibid., 41.
35. Ibid., 55.

is uniquely elusive. Whereas general truths are *relatively* hidden within the ambiguities of history, the truth about God is *absolutely* hidden by virtue of the fact that God absolutely transcends the world. The event of revelation does not change this situation. Revelation is not a datum that grants immediate and self-evident access to eternal truth; instead, revelation is always God's *self*-revelation. For this reason, divine revelation is not only inseparable from but also coincides with divine hiddenness. Put another way, revelation demands the patient work of interpretation. Revelation actually *creates*, rather than solves, the problem of hermeneutics.

We can summarize as follows: *Theology is hermeneutical, because theology is historical. And theology is historical, because it reflects on the God of history—the God who is a "historical being."*[36] The God revealed in Jesus Christ unsettles our assumptions about what is self-evident and disrupts our self-assured attempts to secure our existence. As the apocalyptic agent of new creation, the God of the gospel is perpetually problematizing the world and our place within it. For this reason, a theological science faithful to this God can only ever take the form of hermeneutics.

> The nature of theology as a whole is hermeneutical. . . . It is a matter of understanding Biblical texts, of understanding the subject matter that comes to expression in them, and ultimately of the understandability of the witness to this subject matter in each present situation. He who inquires as to the nature and the program of theology cannot avoid the problem of understanding, the hermeneutical problem. . . . What used to be treated in the system of orthodox dogmatics in the opening chapters entitled "De Theologia" and "De Scriptura Sacra" must be discussed today under the title of the hermeneutical problem.[37]

The problem of hermeneutics, as Heinrich Ott observes, is foundational to systematic theology. It is thus appropriate that I treat it here in the prolegomenal chapter. Everything else flows from this.

What form will such a theological hermeneutics take? We have already alluded to the answer: it will take the form of a *critical* hermeneutic, one that is both historical and theological in its critique. Such a hermeneutic will critically interrogate the text or tradition in question in light of its twofold historicity as both a past artifact and a present event. The dialectical theologians of the twentieth century gave this hermeneutic the name of *Sachkritik*, meaning a criticism according to the content or subject matter (*Sache*).[38] A

36. Jüngel, *God's Being*, 109.
37. Ott, "What Is Systematic Theology?," 78–79.
38. Barth initiated this approach in the preface to the second edition of his Romans

program of *Sachkritik* differentiates between "what is said" and "what is meant," and it tests what is said against the criterion of what is meant.[39] Of course, we only access what is meant through what is said, which means that interpretation is an ongoing process as we continually discern the word that is being spoken to us today in this text. Ott calls this ongoing process the "hermeneutical arch." With this image he means to convey the continuity that persists between artifact and event in the midst of the plurality of historical situations and interpretive encounters. The unity of the hermeneutical process, he says, lies in the *kerygma* or what I have called the *Sache*: "A single arch stretches from the Biblical texts to the contemporary preaching of the church. It is the arch of the kerygma and of the understanding of the kerygma."[40] The kerygma is the divine word-event that unites past and present, there and here, then and now. It is an event pregnant with infinite possibilities of meaning, which presses us ever onward toward the open future, compelling the community of those who hear this word to understand its contemporary significance in surprising new ways.

As a program for discerning the possibilities of meaning available to the present moment, *Sachkritik* is not concerned with separating husk and kernel—since there is no textual "canon within the canon," no set of

commentary, where he writes: "I must push forward to the point where I virtually only confront the riddle of the *subject matter* [*Sache*], and no longer merely the riddle of the *document* [*Urkunde*] as such, where I thus virtually forget that I am not the author, where I have understood him so well that I let him speak in my name and can myself speak in his name." He adds later: "I must confess that I am concerned now . . . more with the *real* than with the so-called *whole* gospel, because I can see no way to the *whole* gospel than by grasping the *real* gospel." See Barth, *Der Römerbrief*, 14, 20.

39. Bultmann, "Problem," 239. Gregory MacDonald argues *against Sachkritik* in his argument for universalism: "This observation [regarding the affirmation of God's justice and love together] serves to undercut the common objection that universalists practice *Sachkritik*—criticizing and rejecting one part of the Bible on the basis of another. Thus, it is said, universalists make much of the biblical texts about God's love but use them to reject the many texts about God's justice and fierce punishments. This is a fair criticism of some contemporary Christian universalists; but, as it stands, this objection does not apply to the argument in this book" (*Evangelical Universalist*, 164). MacDonald associates *Sachkritik* with a crude husk-kernel approach that simply disregards certain texts. A more sophisticated approach as seen in the work of Bultmann *interprets all texts* in light of the norm that stands *beyond* every text. Certain texts certainly correspond more faithfully to the norm than other texts, but every passage has to be read and interpreted anew. No verse is directly identical with the *Sache*. That being said, *Sachkritik* freely criticizes the Bible where appropriate and does not take every passage as equally authoritative. These judgments are based on an ever-new hermeneutical inquiry. The process of testing our interpretations in light of the dialogue between kerygma and context is always ongoing and must not be halted through appeals to the timeless infallibility of the text or authority of the tradition.

40. Ott, "What Is Systematic Theology?," 79.

texts and traditions that escapes hermeneutical criticism—but rather with understanding the whole text as an event for the hearer(s) of this word today.[41] For this reason, "textual interpretation cannot be separated from

---

41. I agree in part here with the hermeneutical program of Elisabeth Schüssler Fiorenza. In *Bread Not Stone* she presents three hermeneutical models: (1) the doctrinal model, (2) the historical-factual model, and (3) the dialogical-pluralistic model. The doctrinal model "subscribes fully to the archetypal understanding of the Bible, especially in literal interpretations, and conceives of biblical revelation as verbal inspiration." The historical-factual model "identifies biblical truth and authority with historical or textual factualness." The dialogical-pluralistic model "seeks to recover *all* canonical texts and traditions and to understand them as theological responses to their historical-communal situations." Because it acknowledges the multiple contexts and forms within the canon, the dialogical-pluralistic model "must establish a 'canon within the canon,' a theological criterion and measuring rod with which to assess the truth and authority of the various biblical texts and traditions" (*Bread*, 11–12). There are two basic versions of this third model. What Schüssler Fiorenza calls the "neo-orthodox model" identifies certain texts and traditions as normative. This textual/traditional canon can be historical-factual (e.g., historical Jesus), doctrinal (e.g., justification by faith alone), or philosophical (e.g., universal revelation or liberating truth). Schüssler Fiorenza associates the neo-orthodox model with figures like Rudolf Bultmann and Rosemary Radford Ruether (ibid., 12). Her own alternative version of this third model "derives this canon [within the canon], *not* from the biblical writings, but from the contemporary struggle of women against racism, sexism, and poverty as oppressive systems of patriarchy and from its systematic explorations in feminist theory" (ibid., 14). She therefore locates the normative "canon within the canon" outside of the biblical canon altogether. "In doing so this mode of interpretation subjects the Bible to a critical feminist scrutiny and to the theological authority of the church of women, an authority that seeks to assess the oppressive or liberating dynamics of all biblical texts" (ibid., 13). The Bible "no longer functions as authoritative source but as a *resource* for women's struggle for liberation" (ibid., 14). Schüssler Fiorenza further develops her analysis in *But She Said*, where she criticizes the "logic of identity" that looks "for a unifying center of Scripture" (*But She Said*, 141). In contrast, she says that "inspiration—the life-giving breath and power of Sophia-Spirit—does not reside in texts: It dwells among people" (ibid., 156).

While Schüssler Fiorenza does not make this observation, the two versions of her third hermeneutical model essentially divide along Protestant and Roman Catholic lines. A Protestant critical hermeneutic locates the theological norm in some essence that is connected to the text, even if it lies beyond or outside of it. A Roman Catholic critical hermeneutic locates the theological norm in the community of faith—which for Schüssler Fiorenza is "women-church." She claims that the "Protestant" versions of a critical hermeneutic ultimately posit an abstract, idealized unity that remains trapped within the logic of the patriarchal West. For instance, regarding Bultmann's demythologizing program, she writes: "Yet such a reduction of particular biblical texts to a theological principle, theological essence, or ethical norm not only cuts down the rich pluriformity of biblical discourse to abstract principle and norm, it then goes on to claim that such a theological principle is the inspired and revealed Word of G-d" (ibid., 142). She elsewhere clarifies that "I share Bultmann's program of *Sachkritik*, [but] I do not share his neo-orthodox existentialist position or his method of demythologization" (*Bread*, 184n22). I would dispute her reading of Bultmann on three counts. First, a demythologizing or existential *Sachkritik* does not reduce texts to a principle but *tests* the

self-interpretation," and since "a specific self-interpretation underlies every exegesis, no exegesis is neutral."[42] Every genuine interpretation is an existential encounter with a reality that confronts and claims us in and through this text. And "it is not the letter of the Bible but the One who is proclaimed by it that makes it a divine address to us, the bearer of all promise."[43] The task of the exegete is thus to hear that message and see the text in its light. Consequently, "no exegesis is able to simply reproduce the wording of the text, but tries somehow to say what is meant."[44] In some cases, this meaning—which is always for today—will require that we interpret the text *against* the text, since what is said actually obscures or even contradicts the meaning. We cannot shy away from criticizing scripture. In many instances, *only* such critique will enable us to hear the kerygmatic word that God means for us to hear in the text. The question for us as exegetes is whether we are existentially *alive* to this word, whether we are ready and willing to hear its demand upon our existence.

THEOLOGY AS PRAXIS

Thus far we have defined theology in terms of science and hermeneutics—in other words, in terms of its *epistemology*. That is crucial, of course, since theology must be, in some sense, a way of knowing and talking about something. But we have also seen that theology's distinct mode of God-talk is one that *concerns* the human subject in a unique way. Indeed, if knowledge of God is always a knowledge of ourselves—since it is not so much we who

---

text against the material norm of the kerygma. Second, Bultmann does not then identify this principle or this reduced text with some "inspired and revealed Word," which is a concept he entirely rejects. Third, it is not clear to me that her reconstruction of women-church is any less abstract or more pluriform than Bultmann's reconstruction of the kerygma. The ultimate issue at stake is whether we understand revelation to be a transcendent divine act (Bultmann) or an immanent historical community (Schüssler Fiorenza), but even this proves to be a false binary, since Bultmann's divine act is a paradoxical event that occurs simultaneously and noncompetitively in the historical community of faith, wherever this genuinely occurs. Perhaps the main difference between the Protestant Bultmann and the Catholic Schüssler Fiorenza is that, for Bultmann, we cannot point to a place in the world and say definitively and securely "this is revelation" or "this is the people of God," whereas it would seem that, for Schüssler Fiorenza, we can indeed do so. Both, I argue, would point to the same community—the discipleship of equals—as the site where the kerygma takes bodily form, but Bultmann would make a *paradoxical or indirect identification* of this site with revelation, whereas Schüssler Fiorenza would make a *direct identification*.

42. Bultmann, "Problem," 253, 243.

43. Käsemann, *On Being a Disciple*, 139.

44. Bultmann, "Problem," 243.

know God but God who knows us—then to engage in theological inquiry is
to interrogate our life in the world. And since our life involves the totality of
our bodily existence, theology is fundamentally concerned with *praxis*, that
is, with the question of creaturely agency and action. Scientific and hermeneutical theology is essentially *praxical* theology.

The intrinsic link between hermeneutics and praxis comes to expression most clearly in the intercultural hermeneutics of Theo Sundermeier.[45]
Born in 1935, Sundermeier has been a professor of religious studies and
mission studies at the University of Heidelberg since 1983. His work operates at the generative intersection of missiology, hermeneutics, and inter-
religious studies, which has led him to his central project of "intercultural
understanding."[46] The term "intercultural" refers to the broad range of issues addressed by missiology and (inter)religious studies, where people
who are cultural-religious strangers must learn to communicate and share
life together.[47] The term "understanding" refers to the discipline of hermeneutics, which is the science of understanding. Sundermeier's key insight is
that mission is fundamentally hermeneutical, and conversely, hermeneutics
is fundamentally missionary. Each involves the interpretation and affirmation of the other precisely in his or her otherness. His term for this coexistence with the other is convivence (*Konvivenz*), which he takes from the
word *convivencia* used by Latin American liberation theologians. The word
literally means "living-with," and sharing life with those who are culturally
different from oneself is precisely what he deems to be the goal of mission.
For this reason, if theology is fundamentally concerned with the mission of
God, and if this mission is concerned with understanding and embracing
the stranger, then theology is necessarily *practical* or *praxical* in nature.[48]

45. What follows draws upon Congdon, "Emancipatory Intercultural Hermeneutics."

46. See Sundermeier, "Erwägungen," 87–101.

47. There is a debate within the German academy over whether "missiology" or
"mission studies" (*Missionswissenschaft*) ought to be replaced by the term "intercultural
theology" (*Interkulturelle Theologie*). The proposal to make this change was formulated
in 2005 by the Wissenschaftliche Gesellschaft für Theologie and Deutsche Gesellschaft
für Missionswissenschaft. See their document, "Mission Studies as Intercultural Theology." For the German original, see http://www.dgmw.org/Missionswissenschaft.pdf. As
part of this change, the Deutsche Gesellschaft für Missionswissenschaft changed the
name of their scholarly journal from *Zeitschrift für Mission* to *Interkulturelle Theologie:
Zeitschrift für Missionswissenschaft*. Though Sundermeier uses the term "intercultural"
in his writings, he disagrees with this attempt to remove talk of mission from the theological academy, as if mission were reducible to its imperialistic and colonialistic legacy.

48. For those accustomed to associating mission with evangelism, the definition of
mission as intercultural understanding will doubtless seem strange. The shared point
of origin is the definition of mission as sending (Latin, *missio*), which implies a sending towards one who is strange and other. Mission is thus concerned with the relation

Sundermeier differentiates himself from the modern western herme-neutical tradition stretching from Schleiermacher to Gadamer. He affirms this tradition in its emphasis upon one's given preunderstanding (*Vorver-ständnis*) as integral to the interpretation and understanding of the subject matter of a text. He further recognizes that this tradition rightly makes praxis part of the interpretive process, in the sense that "the obedience of faith precedes the understanding of faith."[49] But he criticizes western herme-neutics for its overly individualistic conception of understanding:

> It is remarkable that in western hermeneutics, particularly in existentialist interpretation, it is always an understanding of myself. It is not the understanding of other persons, of strange texts, but rather of my new self-understanding, produced by the encounter with the text. The other, the stranger, is already in Hegel a roundabout path to myself. . . . The conversation that seeks understanding is, in the end, a conversation with oneself [*Selbstgespräch*, i.e., a monologue].[50]

Sundermeier charges most western hermeneutics with an egocentric version of interpretation that makes *self*-understanding the goal of understanding as such.[51] The other, the stranger, is merely an ancillary for the primary task of understanding oneself. He names the basic form of this hermeneutical approach a "hermeneutic of absorption" (*Vereinnahmungshermeneutik*), in which the reader seeks "to make the strange text his or her own."[52] A varia-tion on this tradition is Hans-Georg Gadamer's "hermeneutic of fusion" (*Verschmelzungshermeneutik*), which concerns "not only the understanding of texts but also the understanding of persons." On this view, "understand-ing has ideally reached its goal if the different perspectives become identical and the horizons fuse together."[53] While fusion is preferable to absorption, the end result is still the same: the amalgamation of stranger and self and

---

between gospel and culture, between the divine norm and human norms. Whereas much missionary theory in the past assumed that the gospel colonizes culture, inter-cultural theologians, like Sundermeier, argue instead that the gospel understands and dialogues with culture. I discuss the question of mission further in chapter 5.

49. Sundermeier, "Erwägungen," 90.

50. Ibid., 90–91.

51. I argue in *The Mission of Demythologizing* that Sundermeier's critique does not apply to the hermeneutics of Rudolf Bultmann, despite the centrality of the concept of self-understanding in the latter's hermeneutical program. See Congdon, *Mission*, 511–16.

52. Sundermeier, *Den Fremden verstehen*, 12–13.

53. Ibid., 13.

thus the reduction of the other to the same. Neither approach affirms and preserves the otherness of the other in the process of understanding.

The result is that the question of praxis only enters into the picture as a *presupposition* for interpretation and not as the *goal*. In other words, the question of agency and action is relevant only in terms of identifying the individual interpreter's historical situation, which functions as a *condition* for understanding; praxis is not thematized as essential to the act of understanding itself. Classical hermeneutics, according to Sundermeier, reaches its goal in the interpretation of the text, while "the application of the text is a secondary act."[54] By contrast, an intercultural hermeneutic includes the practical application *within* the hermeneutical process. The process of coming to understand strange texts cannot be separated from the process of learning to live with strangers, which means learning to understand the stranger precisely in her strangeness and not conforming her into a familiar cultural mold. For this reason, Sundermeier identifies his approach as a "hermeneutic of difference" (*Differenzhermeneutik*), which "teaches how to understand what is different without absorbing it, which offers practical help in practicing the proximity of life together, while at the same time preserving the proper distance, by respecting both the identity of the stranger and the human dignity common to us all."[55] He also names his approach a "xenological hermeneutic."[56] His program is a hermeneutic of difference or strangeness, in which the object of the interpretation is "the strange counterpart," the cultural other who stands before us, with whom we must constructively coexist.[57]

Sundermeier's interpretive method consists of a four-step process. Each of these four steps involves a subjective attitude, an objective assessment, and an action. The first step is the *level of phenomena*. Its subjective attitude is "*epoché*," an ancient Greek term for the suspension of judgment, which was later taken up by Descartes and Edmund Husserl. Here it simply means setting aside prior assumptions and ideas so that the stranger can encounter me on her or his own terms. The objective assessment is thus "descriptive analysis" and the action is "perception at a distance."[58] One has to *see* the other for who she or he is before genuine understanding can take place. The second step is the *level of sign* (*Zeichen*). After perception and description, the second step seeks to understand what the phenomenal level

54. Ibid., 189.
55. Ibid., 13.
56. Ibid., 9, 13.
57. Ibid., 155.
58. Ibid.

indicates about the stranger and her situation. Here the subjective attitude is "sympathy," the objective assessment is "contextualization," and the action is "participatory observation."[59] Having perceived the other, the task now is to situate and observe the other in her or his otherness, that is, to learn "to understand others in their context."[60] To sympathize with the other is to "feel-with" (*sun-pathos*) her or him, to bring myself alongside that person. Sundermeier cautions against moving too quickly past this stage:

> The signs must first be read in their own context and must not be hastily translated into our own and incorporated with our *logos*. Whoever wants to understand the stranger must get involved in the other culture and religion, in order to learn what their signs mean for them and what they want to say to outsiders. . . . In order to understand [the stranger], one must enter into the other culture.[61]

The third step is the *level of symbol*. The subjective attitude at this stage is "empathy," the objective assessment is "comparative interpretation," and the action is "(partial) identification."[62] The move from sign to symbol indicates a deeper level of participation and engagement with the stranger, which also entails greater complexity. "While the sign is unique and must say precisely what it wants to say (cf. road signs), symbols oscillate, are ambiguous, and can be perceived and interpreted differently by different observers."[63] Given this ambiguity, true understanding requires that we empathetically "*identify* with the strange culture and religion."[64] The goal here is to "feel-in" (*en-pathos*) the stranger, so that I identify her situation as my own. But such identification must not become absorption or fusion. Empathy means that "the stranger must be endured as strange."[65] Despite the empathetic identification, "there will always be a wall between [oneself] and the stranger" that we cannot and should not remove.[66] The process of hermeneutical understanding of the other involves a dialectic of agreement and difference, unity and separation, convergence and divergence. It is within this complex dialectical encounter with the stranger that we are able to move to the fourth stage of convivence.

59. Ibid.
60. Ibid., 161.
61. Ibid., 162.
62. Ibid., 155.
63. Ibid., 166–67.
64. Ibid., 168–69.
65. Ibid., 170.
66. Ibid., 169.

Sundermeier calls the fourth step the "level of relevance" and the "level of pure action."[67] This is where interpretation and praxis coincide. The subjective attitude at this stage is "respect," the objective assessment is "translation," and the action is "convivence," the act of living together with others.[68] This fourth level is the level of relevance, he says, because it is "directly relevant in dealing with strange neighbors, the upstairs tenant who is identified as culturally other. The goal of an intercultural hermeneutic is a successful living-together, in which each one can remain, no one is co-opted, and yet there still occurs an exchange that respects and strengthens the dignity of others."[69] Interpretation thus reaches its goal when people learn to understand and respect each other. The end of the hermeneutical process is communal praxis.

While an intercultural hermeneutic provides a helpful framework for understanding the praxical nature of theology, we must further explore the nature of this praxis. The concept of convivence—a respectful coexistence with others—is helpful but vague. We need to say more about what is entailed in situations where systems of oppression and injustice threaten this convivence. What does coexistence with a stranger look like when that stranger is systematically marginalized in ways that may even work to one's benefit? Following Mary Jane Collier and others, we need to develop not only an intercultural hermeneutic but an "intercultural praxis," which recognizes that cultures are "complex, complicated, contradictory, multiple, and multileveled locations of speaking/acting/producing/distributing and consuming."[70] Cultures include "spaces of struggle and contested spaces of relation," and thus to enter into an empathetic relation with the marginalized cultural other necessarily means entering into her struggle for recognition and liberation.[71] The factors involved in the relation between person A and person B are not merely local and interpersonal; they are also global and social. It is not enough to see the visible phenomenon of the stranger. We must also learn to see the invisible nexus of socioeconomic forces and neoliberal ideologies that perpetuate violent regimes of terror and suppression. Sympathy and empathy for one another means recognizing the ways we have been conscripted into this regime as agents of oppression, while the level of "pure action" means generating "counterdiscursive practices" that restore agency to those who have been marginalized and silenced by

67. Ibid., 183.
68. Ibid., 155.
69. Ibid., 183.
70. Collier, "Critical Community Engagement," 8.
71. Ibid., 9.

imperial power.[72] Intercultural understanding today must therefore take the form of an emancipatory praxis—a praxis which "seeks to disrupt relationships of domination by developing new forms of internationalist understanding and communication."[73] In short, hermeneutics is always praxical, but praxis is also always hermeneutical.

In the end, the praxical nature of Christian theology means that doctrine is primarily concerned with existence, with concrete forms of life. I therefore concur with the criterion that Charles Finney puts forward in his *Lectures on Revivals of Religion*: "The proper end of all doctrine is practice. Any thing brought forward as doctrine, which cannot be made use of as practical, is not preaching the gospel."[74] Whereas Finney understood this usefulness in terms of its effectiveness in winning converts to Christianity, today we can understand such effectiveness in terms of the emancipatory mission of the gospel to bring freedom to the captives and justice to the oppressed. The point is that the truth of the gospel is not a theory but a concrete mode of existence: "Truth is not taught and then accepted, but lived and practiced."[75]

Now that we have examined the building blocks of theology as science, hermeneutics, and praxis, we are in a position to bring these elements together in our reflection on the material, soteriological norm of theological discourse.

THEOLOGY AS SOTERIOLOGY

Our discussion of theology as science, hermeneutics, and praxis brings us to the realization that theology is essentially soteriology. Following Ebeling, we can say that "talk of God is as such soteriological, i.e., it communicates salvation. ... For the doctrine of God and the doctrine of salvation are identical."[76]

72. "Social justice includes a vision of the equitable distribution of resources where social actors experience agency with and responsibility for others" (Sorrells, *Intercultural Communication*, 228).

73. Heaney, "Prospects," 31.

74. Finney, *Lectures*, 184.

75. Sölle, *Political Theology*, 72.

76. Ebeling, "Theologische Erwägungen," 429–30. Gerhard Ebeling pulls back from this identification of theology with soteriology in his dogmatics. There he admits that one could indeed frame the whole of dogmatics as soteriology according to the analytical method of old Protestant orthodoxy, but that this would have to be regarded as an "extreme stretch in the use of language" (Ebeling, *Dogmatik*, 2:13). Ebeling thus restricts soteriology to a subordinate role in his dogmatics, located in the second and

Each of the three foregoing aspects of theology has led us to this conclusion. In our discussion of theology as science, we observed that theology
is reflection on the object of faith. But this object is only available to a certain
kind of subject that is called into existence in relation to this object. The God
who is not-an-object becomes an object while remaining not-an-object, and
this is possible because God is only an object to the faithful subject in the
moment of faithful obedience. That is to say, God is only an object in the
particular event whereby certain persons hear themselves addressed from
the beyond and are called outside of themselves. God's objectivity resides in
the very moment that the human being becomes a new subject—namely, a
child of God. The event of God's revelatory self-disclosure is thus the event
of salvation. Since theology is the scientific reflection on this event, it follows that theology is soteriology.

We turned next to the topic of hermeneutics. The inescapable correlation between object and subject means that talk of God is always talk of
what God *does* in history. The object of theology is an object *in actu*. God is
only known in the event wherein God comes on the scene—and only *as* the
one who comes on the scene. Theology thus cannot speak about being apart
from becoming. Truth is only known in its historicity and ambiguity. Even
apart from other considerations, this in itself already nullifies the medieval
metaphysical framework that trades on timeless essences that are ahistorical
and thus prehermeneutical. Such a framework purports to be universally
valid (i.e., "ready-made"), since the divine object is supposedly available for
investigation by any rational person. But this object—however cogent and
persuasive the argumentation that supports it—is not *God*. Talk of God is
always talk of an act within history. And since this act always occurs to and
for a particular person, talk of God is always also talk of the human subject
and her historical situation. Interpretation of God's word is always *self*-in-
terpretation, since this word is a word that concerns our existence. In other
words, God-talk is hermeneutical for the same reason it is soteriological.

Finally, if theology is praxis, we still have to know what *norms* this
praxis. What grounds and funds the process of understanding the stranger?
As a theologian and missiologist, Sundermeier appeals to a trinitarian
theology of strangeness. God in God's first mode of being is the "strange
God," whose strangeness is the divine holiness "that is not absorbed into
our categories of experience, but rather prepares people for the new and

---

especially the third volumes. I regard this as a crucial error. It is only a stretching of
language if one tries to pack all of the traditional dogmatic content under the merely
formal label of soteriology. But if one lets soteriology reinterpret all of the other doctrinal themes, then there is no stretching—only hermeneutical reconstruction. And as
a hermeneutical theologian, that would seem to be what Ebeling is striving for anyway.

unexpected."[77] The truly new event appears in Christ, who is the "strange guest," the one who came to his own, as the Gospel of John puts it, but was not recognized and accepted (John 1:10–11). "Jesus is the strange guest in the house of the tax collector," according to the Gospel of Luke (Luke 19:1–10). The Gospel of Matthew even identifies Jesus with the strangers of the world (Matt 25:31–46), so that "the stranger is indeed the *Christus praesens*."[78] It is this "deep, abiding strangeness of Jesus" that "Paul summarizes in the idea of *kenosis*" (Phil 2:5–8).[79] Christ the stranger welcomes all strangers as his friends. The gospel is essentially concerned with hospitality (in German, *Gastfreundschaft*, lit. "friendship with guests"), with a community of strangers who are the friends of God and thus of each other.[80] Sundermeier connects this to the Pauline concept of justification, which is always *justitia aliena*, an alien or strange righteousness that, like the strange guest of Christ himself, identifies all people in their estrangement from God as new friends. To be declared righteous is to be recognized and affirmed as God's friend and neighbor. "The gospel declares to people who are estranged from God and from their fellow human beings . . . that they have a right to live, and grants them a space to live."[81] The Holy Spirit is the one who "makes the strangeness of different people understandable. . . . The Spirit wants diversity. The Spirit makes it possible to accept the strangeness of others, to understand strange languages."[82] Sundermeier draws on a pneumatology of Pentecost in which the Spirit is the "holy and life-giving Spirit" (*Spiritum sanctum vivificantem*) that generates a "creative pluralism" where "everyone hears and freely responds to the word of reconciliation in their own language, in their horizon of thought, and in their social condition."[83] The Spirit thus enables and empowers the communal space of hospitality and diversity that characterizes the people of God. All of this points to the fact

77. Sundermeier, *Den Fremden verstehen*, 207.

78. Ibid., 209.

79. Ibid., 208.

80. Ibid., 209.

81. Ibid., 210. Unfortunately, Sundermeier goes on to say that "this space is the church, the *Christus prolongatus*, the community of believers" (ibid.). Having just rejected the Roman Catholic understanding of justification and righteousness, it is ironic that he now appeals to a Catholic ecclesiology, which understands the church as a prolongation of the incarnation. If we accept the Protestant account of justification as alien righteousness, as we do here, then we cannot accept any account of the church that conflates it with the person of Christ. Such a position undermines our confession of the strange God, Jesus the strange guest, and the Spirit who guides us in our dealings with strangers.

82. Ibid., 211.

83. Sundermeier, *Mission*, 29.

that a certain soteriology—that is, a kenotic, christocentric, pentecostal, and justifying understanding of salvation—grounds an emancipatory praxis.

Our prolegomenous reflections lead us to the single conclusion that *Christian theology reflects on the saving action of God*. God's saving action is the origin, object, and norm of theological discourse. The single divine act that elects, justifies, reconciles, redeems, and reveals makes theology *possible* by bringing human beings into an encounter with God, makes theology *meaningful* by providing the material content for scientific reflection, and makes theology *orderly* and *critical* by supplying the criteria for authentic God-talk. This is by no means a break with the tradition. In a way we are merely drawing out the implications of Melanchthon's famous axiom: "To know Christ means to know his benefits."[84] Or as Calvin states in the opening of his *Institutes*, the knowledge of God is the knowledge of ourselves and vice versa.[85] As we have argued above, theology has no access to a divine in-itself—a theological *Ding an sich*—apart from the human subject on whom God acts.[86] To speak of God means to speak of God's acting upon us—that is, to speak of ourselves as acted upon by God. In the words of Bultmann, therefore, "there is knowledge of God only as existential knowing."[87] The following statement by Gerhard Ebeling thus serves as a dogmatic axiom: "Theology is not metaphysics or metahistory, but rather *metanoia*, a conversion in conformity to Christ."[88]

With respect to both method and material content, Christian theology is necessarily *soteriocentric*. Methodologically, every theological claim and doctrinal decision has to be tested critically against the norm of God's saving action. Materially, every theological locus or theme derives from the saving event; each doctrine reflects a dimension of the soteriological center of Christian faith. When we speak about any theological topic, whether trinity or ecclesiology or eschatology, we have to (re)construct this doctrine soteriologically. In a certain sense this is what the Christian tradition has tried to do, insofar as theology from the beginning was an attempt to understand what it means to confess that Jesus is Lord. But the tradition has rarely, if ever, been consistently soteriocentric. It has frequently wandered off into

84. Melanchthon and Bucer, *Melanchthon and Bucer*, 21.

85. See Calvin, *Institutes*, 1.1.

86. The epistemological claim is also ontological: the event of revelation is God's self-determining self-revelation. In other words, we only have *access* to a God who acts upon us, because God simply *is* the God who acts upon us. God's being *is* the act of salvation. There is no theological *Ding an sich*. We will develop this claim and its implications throughout the course of this book.

87. Bultmann, "Theology," 50.

88. Ebeling, "Erwägungen zur Eschatologie," 447.

abstract speculation (e.g., the notion of an immanent trinity apart from the economy), pointless conundrums regarding problems like predestination and free will, apologetic exercises, and the like. There have been innumerable futile debates all based on the idea that the entire text of scripture is infallible, such that every statement must be reconcilable with every other statement. And there have been innumerable other debates trying to find loopholes in this logic. The history of Christian theology is largely a story of missing the (kerygmatic, soteriological) forest for the (biblical, confessional, scholastic) trees. Our present task, therefore, is to adhere rigorously to the soteriological and soteriocentric nature of theological discourse that seeks to understand the God revealed in Jesus Christ. Doing so will result in a theology that is scientific, hermeneutical, and practical. And, conversely, we might say, a theology that is scientific, hermeneutical, and practical will necessarily be soteriocentric.

We should point out that soteriocentrism need not compete with Barth's christocentrism or evangelical crucicentrism.[89] The fact that many assume it does compete with them indicates a problem with these other concepts that we must expose and interrogate. The term christocentrism is a perfectly valid and useful term in itself, one that we will use here on occasion, but it is also overused and overly vague. Almost any exercise in Christian theology can claim to be christocentric by virtue of giving Christ some kind of centrality. But we must inquire about both the nature of this centrality and the nature of Christ. The centrality could be merely narratival, in which Jesus is the climax of salvation history; it could also be merely instrumental, in which Jesus is the means toward an end not itself determined by him. And the christology could be highly metaphysical, with a strong emphasis on the eternal Logos as definitive of Christ's identity. The point is that the term christocentrism in itself tells us very little about the theology. By defining christocentrism in terms of soteriocentrism, we clarify what it is about Christ that makes him the center of theological discourse.

If the term christocentrism is too broad, the term crucicentrism is too narrow. This concept has the virtue of at least focusing our attention upon the soteriological heart of christology (viz. the cross), but in doing so it goes too far by zeroing in on the doctrine of atonement—and specifically a (penal) substitutionary atonement. In the orthodox tradition, something literally *happens* in the crucifixion—a debt is paid, a ransom is offered, Satan is defeated. The whole doctrine rests on the ancient belief succinctly expressed in the letter to the Hebrews: "Indeed, under the law almost everything is purified with blood, and without the shedding of blood there is

89. On "crucicentrism," see Bebbington, *Evangelicalism*, 14–17.

no forgiveness of sins" (Heb 9:22). Crucicentrism, in the sense in which it is applied to classical evangelical theology, is premised on the ancient near eastern belief in the efficacy of animal sacrifice in propitiating the gods and purifying the people. This magical-mythological belief forms the bedrock assumption within Israelite religion,[90] and it is only against the background of this belief that the New Testament makes sense. Jesus is the ultimate and final sacrifice who thereby brings the sacrificial system to an end. Christian religion is originally a cultic practice whereby individuals share in the atoning sacrifice of Jesus. The rites of baptism and Lord's Supper—along with private prayer, public witness, martyrdom, and other acts—become the effective means whereby one's sin is removed and a person is made pure. Modern evangelicals have other rituals, such as the altar call and the so-called "sinner's prayer," but the basic logic remains the same. And at the heart of this logic is the notion that the shedding of blood results in the forgiveness of sins. In short, evangelical crucicentrism depends on a host of culturally conditioned assumptions that the hermeneutical approach put forward above must criticize and finally reject.

If we are going to salvage christocentrism and crucicentrism, then these terms will have to be soteriocentrically reconstructed in the scientific, hermeneutical, and practical sense outlined above. Christocentrism cannot

90. There are many kinds of rituals and offerings, but the Day of Atonement ritual is representative of the overall religious framework of ancient Israel. According to Patrick Miller, "There were two dimensions to the ritual centering around two goats, one 'for the Lord' and the other 'for Azazel' (Lev 16:8–10; cf. v. 26). The goat on which the lot fell 'for the Lord' was slaughtered as a *ḥaṭṭā't* offering and its blood sprinkled in the sanctuary to purge it of impurities. As for the other goat, the priest would lay hands on it and confess the 'iniquities,' that is, the deliberate sins and transgressions of the people. Having been confessed, they were now transferred to the goat who was sent away into the wilderness 'for Azazel' (Lev. 16:10, 20–22). Verse 16 (cf. vv. 21–22) identifies the dual purpose of the ritual, the removal of impurities and the removal of sins: 'Thus he shall make atonement for the sanctuary, because of the uncleannesses of the people of Israel, and because of their transgressions, all their sins.' . . . Purification and elimination rites were common in the ancient Near East, though not necessarily joined as they are in this instance." See Miller, *Religion*, 115–16.

The term "magic" comes from Dorothee Sölle's analysis in *Christ the Representative*, where she speaks of the "magical interpretation" of representation in ancient religion. While we find this primarily in ancient near eastern cultures, it applies to the Hebrew scriptures as well: "The concept of the scapegoat does not go beyond the circle of imitative magic. Sin is presented as something physical. The priest identifies the sin of the people with the goat by laying his hands on its head and confessing over it all the sins of the people. The goat, a domestic animal and as such belonging to and closely associated with man, suffers in place of man. Instead of the sinful people, who deserve the punishment, it is the goat which is driven into the desert, into the desolate, unclean, unholy place. The sin can no longer defile the people. . . . Representation is accordingly understood in magical terms as a transfer and removal" (*Christ*, 64–65).

mean elevating the person of Christ apart from his saving work, or locating his identity in a realm above and anterior to his historical existence. Likewise, crucicentrism cannot mean that the crucifixion in itself "does" something—whether to God or to ourselves. It is not some divine instrument for redeeming the world from sin, any more than slaughtering a goat is really capable of cleansing people from impurity. Such notions may have made sense within an ancient cultural context, but we cannot universalize them as normative for theology in every time and place. And since theology is for today and only for today, we need to think creatively about what salvation means in a world without animal sacrifice. At this point, of course, I am only setting forth the methodology for this study. The precise contours of my soteriocentric program will only become clear in the course of expounding the nature of the saving act itself. For now it must suffice to observe that a soteriocentric theology will *also* be christocentric and crucicentric, but it will be both of these only insofar as they are critically interpreted and reconstructed for the contemporary situation.

ORTHOHETERODOXY: IN DEFENSE OF THE FREEDOM OF THEOLOGY

I have argued that Christian faith confesses a God who saves. Theology is the conceptual interpretation and clarification of this axiom of faith. It is a scientific, hermeneutical, and practical discipline that humbly and rigorously reflects on the relation between God and humanity in the light of God's reconciling self-revelation in Jesus Christ. But what does it mean for God to save? What does it mean for us to be saved? These questions—which lie at the very heart of Christian self-understanding—elude easy answers and must be asked anew by every generation. The difficulty of reaching any kind of agreement is only compounded by the fact that there has never been a dogma of the atonement. No ecumenical conciliar statement about the meaning of salvation exists. The ecumenical councils were content with clarifying the nature of Christ's person without clarifying the nature of his saving work and how we participate in it. This has left the church with "an inherited heap of proposals" and little agreement about how to evaluate them.[91]

The following chapters attempt to offer a systematic theological account of salvation, a soteriological *dogmatica minora*. That is to say, they seek to articulate various doctrines of the Christian faith in terms of the economy of grace. Christology, pneumatology, ecclesiology, and creation—these and

91. Jenson, "On the Doctrine," 100.

other doctrines will be explicated in light of the saving event that Christian faith confesses has taken place in Christ. This project is thus the consistent application of Melanchthon's axiom ("to know Christ means to know his benefits") to the whole of Christian theology. *To know God is to know the God who saves.* Theology is only properly Christian theology when it interprets the subject matter of theology—the material content of dogmatics—in terms of its salvific significance for us.

The implication is that, as Eberhard Jüngel puts it, "you are not teaching the *matter* properly if you do not at the same time think of its use."[92] Jüngel cites a passage from Martin Luther regarding the work of the Spirit that is worth quoting in full:

> He gives utterance not only to things, but also to the use which things are to be put to. For many preach Christ, but in such a way that they neither recognize nor express his ways and his miracles . . . as do most of those preachers who only preach the stories of Christ, when they are preaching at their best. But it is not Christian preaching when you preach Christ only from a historical point of view; that is not proclaiming the glory of God. But *this* is: when you teach that Christ's story refers to its usefulness for us as believers unto righteousness and salvation. That is [then], that he accomplished all not for himself, but for us by the will of God the Father, so that we may know that everything that is in Christ belongs to us.[93]

Similarly, see also the following passage from Luther's commentary on the so-called "Catholic Epistles":

> Through the Gospel we are told who Christ is, in order that we may learn to know that He is our Savior, that He delivers us from sin and death, helps us out of all misfortune, reconciles us to the Father, and makes us pious and saves us without our works. *He who does not learn to know Christ in this way must go wrong.* For even though you know that He is God's Son, that He died and rose again, and that He sits at the right hand of the Father, you have not yet learned to know Christ aright, and this knowledge still does not help you. You must also know and believe that He did all this for your sake, in order to help you.[94]

To adapt Luther, unless we learn to know God in this way (i.e., soteriologically), we necessarily go wrong. Unless theology speaks of a reality that is

92. Jüngel, *Justification*, 29.

93. Ibid. Cf. Luther, *Operationes in Psalmos* (1519–21) in *WA* 5:543.13–21.

94. *LW*, 30:29–30. Quoted in Lohse, *Martin Luther's Theology*, 223; emphasis mine.

"useful for us as believers," that "helps us," it speaks in vain. To borrow an image from Wittgenstein, theology that is not determined by soteriology is language "idling," that is, not "doing work."[95] If any doctrinal statement is irrelevant to the question of salvation, then it is highly questionable whether it has a place in a distinctively *Christian* articulation of faith. To paraphrase Luther, it is not Christian theology when you explicate doctrines from a historical or metaphysical point of view; they must be interpreted in terms of their usefulness and significance for us as believers.

A commonly expressed concern is that this kind of practical, soteriological criterion may well lead to theological accounts that depart from the "orthodox" tradition. But that is precisely the point. We must take a long hard look at the assumption that protecting and perpetuating a purported orthodoxy (lit. "right thinking") is some kind of Christian virtue. We certainly see this view in the New Testament. The epistles of Jude, 2 Peter, and 2 John are particularly paranoid about differentiating between true Christians and false teachers. Jude speaks about "the faith that was once for all entrusted to the saints" (Jude 3) as if "the faith" were an object, a deposit, that one could possess and pass along to someone else. The author of 2 Peter draws on Jude in presenting a vituperative attack against "false prophets" who bring "destructive opinions," "licentious ways," and "deceptive words" (2 Pet 2:1–3). These people "are like irrational animals, mere creatures of instinct, born to be caught and killed" (2 Pet 2:12).[96] The author even says that "it would have been better for them never to have known the way of righteousness than, after knowing it, to turn back from the holy commandment that was passed on to them" (2 Pet 2:21). Finally, 2 John speaks about "deceivers" who teach a docetic view of Christ. Such a person "is the deceiver and the antichrist," since that person "does not abide in the teaching of Christ, but goes beyond it" (2 John 7, 9). What we see in these ancient Christian texts is a community deeply concerned about protecting its authority. Here we see a magisterium in the making—the early seeds of a church that binds the Holy Spirit to its institutional office. We are thus led to echo Ernst Käsemann's sharp rebuke to these texts when he asks:

> What have we to say about an eschatology, which . . . is concerned only with the hope of the triumphal entry of believers into the eternal kingdom and with the destruction of the ungodly? . . . What have we to say about a Church, which is so

---

95. Wittgenstein, *Philosophical Investigations*, ¶132.

96. Unfortunately, the long history of violent Christian rhetoric finds scriptural authorization in passages like this. It is morally imperative, for the health of the church, to reject the posture of fear underpinning this passage as inauthentically Christian.

concerned to defend herself against heretics, that she no longer
distinguishes between Spirit and letter; that she identifies the
Gospel with her own tradition and, further, with a particular
religious world-view; that she regulates exegesis according to
her system of teaching authority and makes faith into a mere
assent to the dogmas of orthodoxy?[97]

But on what basis can we reject these texts, given that they are part of
the New Testament canon? As we argued above, the hermeneutical nature
of theology demands that we engage in faithful criticism of scripture in the
light of its genuine subject matter. The New Testament as a whole bears
witness to a soteriological-christological truth that provides a criterion for
evaluating the authority of particular passages. To be sure, the apostle Paul
could at times speak like the author of Jude or 2 John: "if anyone proclaims
to you a gospel contrary to what you received, let that one be accursed!"
(Gal 1:9). While this could lend itself to an exclusivist and defensive posture
on the part of the church—depending on how we define "gospel"—Paul also
provides ample resources for a rather different approach. In Galatians 3,
he speaks of the coming of faith, but unlike later generations that identify
"the faith" with a set of orthodox doctrines, Paul identifies the faith with
Christ himself, indicated by the parallel phrases, "before faith came . . .
until Christ came," and "now that faith has come . . . for in Christ Jesus"
(Gal 3:23–26). Paul everywhere makes the saving event of Christ the center
and norm for our faith and practice, represented by the repeated use of the
technical phrase "in Christ" (see Rom 8:1–2; Gal 2:19–20). Moreover, his
first letter to the Corinthians provides the closest thing to a hermeneutical
principle: "For I decided to know nothing among you except Jesus Christ,
and him crucified" (1 Cor 2:2; cf. 1:23). It is the soteriocentric christocen-
tricity of Paul's thought that grounds his message of freedom from the law,
from works, from every kind of slavery, but also a freedom from boasting,
from anxiety, from the need to control every detail and know every fact.
Christians are to be neither slaves nor masters, since the entire master-slave
dynamic has been shattered by the coming of Christ—"for all of you are one
in Christ Jesus" (Gal 3:28). The only law that remains in force is the "law of
the Spirit of life in Christ Jesus" (Rom 8:2), but we know from Paul that "if
you are led by the Spirit, you are not subject to the law" (Gal 5:18). So the
law of Christ's Spirit is, paradoxically, the total nullification of the law as we
know it, and thus the death of the law *as* law. Paul can therefore declare: "For
freedom Christ has set us free" (Gal 5:1).[98]

97. Käsemann, *Essays*, 195.

98. It is no accident that the event that marks the church's break with the law (the

There is therefore something deeply perverse about the way the early Christian community quickly retreated into a fortress mentality in an attempt to lock down the truth in a new law of doctrine. When the church became the guardian of orthodoxy, it reinstated the very master-slave dynamic that Christ, according to Paul, came to abolish. Whereas the old dynamic was a largely covenantal and ethical relation, the new dynamic is now intellectual and doctrinal. The master is no longer the law but the right teaching, the pure doctrine, the deposit of faith. And it is apparent that many in the church did not see the irony in teaching Paul's message of justification apart from the works of the law while enforcing a justification according to the teachings of the doctrinal law. But that does not mean we are forbidden from seeing the problem today and addressing it.

A solution is only possible when we demythologize the binary opposition between orthodoxy and heterodoxy, between saints and deceivers, between Christians and antichrists. This dichotomizing logic forces a false decision upon the church, as if doctrine is either true or false—and self-evidently one or the other. Against this "myth of the two ways," I propose here a hybridized alternative, which I call *orthoheterodoxy* or *heteroorthodoxy*. Orthoheterodoxy would entail "believing differently" (*hetero*-doxy) but "in the right way" (*ortho*-doxy), while heteroorthodoxy would entail "believing rightly in a different way." Either way the result is the same, namely, a theological approach that simultaneously preserves both normativity and difference. Indeed, we can even say that difference is *internal* to the norm of the gospel; the norm generates its own diversity. It can do so because the norm is not a fixed set of propositional claims but rather an event irrupting into each new situation, calling forth new modes of thinking and speaking about God. Every proposition or doctrine is thus a mode of God-talk situated within a specific historical context to which the kerygmatic norm—being the active presence of the wholly other God—is not bound.

Such a notion is not entirely alien to the biblical witness. The Pentecost narrative in the Acts of the Apostles is a powerful metaphor and catalyst for this dialectic of normative singularity and contextual multiplicity. In the event of Pentecost, God pours out Christ's Spirit "upon all flesh" (Acts 2:17), which coincides with the followers of Jesus speaking "in other languages," and with "Jews from every nation under heaven" hearing them speak "in the native language of each" (Acts 2:4–6). Pentecost is not the overturning

---

Jerusalem council of Acts 15) is the same event wherein the apostles appeal to the Holy Spirit (Acts 15:8, 28). The break in question is not with the law as such but with the law as an absolute and transcultural norm. The coming of the Spirit coincides with the church's recognition that the law is a relative and culturally specific authority subject to the freedom of God.

of Babel, as is sometimes alleged, but rather the *consecration* of Babel. The multiplicity of cultures and languages is seen as a blessing and no longer as a curse. The gospel that Peter proclaims encounters each person as a message native to her situation, as a truth transposable to every new context. The pouring out of the Spirit is thus an event of intercultural understanding in which the irreducible differences between people are affirmed *within* the singular truth of Christ. Insofar as heterodoxy is primarily the consequence of cultural difference, a program of orthoheterodoxy is a theological method and hermeneutic concerned with contextualizing the kerygma within particular cultural moments. The "rightness" of such belief is located not at the level of fixed propositional claims about God and the world, but rather at the level of the pentecostal outpouring of the Spirit upon all flesh. Such faith is "orthodox" insofar as it is a genuine encounter with and empowerment by the Spirit of Christ. But since this Spirit embraces cultural plurality and enjoins the community of faith to migrate to new contexts, orthodoxy includes a creative and unanticipatable heterodoxy within it. Heterodoxy is intrinsic to Christian faith. It is an essential dimension of the freedom for which Christ has set us free.

In conclusion, theology is an eminently *free* science. It is both free *from* the past—that is, from past traditions and interpretations that would bind the kerygmatic norm to a particular culture—and free *for* the future—that is, for new situations where the norm can be authentically encountered and expressed in ways that may be unrecognizable to others. All of this means that the event of salvation that constitutes theology's normative center is "infinitely translatable,"[99] and so unreservedly open to the multiplicity of contexts. To adhere to this norm is to live "without guarantees,"[100] to abandon the pursuit of theological and ecclesial security in order to find oneself sustained in God alone, for "they alone find security who let all security go, who—to speak with Luther—are ready to enter into inner darkness."[101]

99. Bevans and Schroeder, *Constants*, 2.

100. Kraidy, *Hybridity*, 148.

101. Bultmann, "Zum Problem," 207.

3

The Act of Salvation
Apocalypse

For I am not ashamed of the gospel; it is the power of God for salvation to everyone who has faith, to the Jew first and also to the Greek. For in it the righteousness of God is apocalypsed through faith for faith.

ROMANS 1:16–17A

I have been crucified with Christ; and I no longer live, but Christ lives in me. And the life I now live in the flesh I live by faith in the Son of God, who loved me and gave himself for me.

GALATIANS 2:19B–20

Now is the judgment of this world; now the ruler of this world will be driven out.

JOHN 12:31

SOTERIOLOGICAL MULTIVALENCE AND THE
HERMENEUTICAL PROBLEM

Qui propter nos homines et propter nostram salutem—for us human beings and for our salvation.[1] With these words from the Niceno-Constantinopolitan Creed the church confesses the saving significance of Jesus Christ. But what is the *salutis*, the *soteria*, the salvation? Even though salvation—understood in its fullness as the reconciling self-revelation of God—is the material norm of everything we say about God, there is little agreement about what this norm actually is or how we should understand it.

The paradox of soteriology is that there is no dogmatic clarity about the very essence of Christian faith. Christians confess that Jesus has saving significance, but there is no consensus about what this significance actually is. What exactly does Jesus save *from* and save *for*? And *how* does he save? Should we understand salvation as election, new citizenship, regeneration, justification, reconciliation, healing, deification, perfection, liberation from oppression, all of the above, or something else altogether? Christians traditionally understand Jesus to be of central importance to this saving work, but which aspect is the decisive factor—incarnation, sinless life, passion and death, or resurrection? If we choose just the death of Jesus, for instance, how are we to understand its significance? Is it a ransom, a satisfaction of divine honor, a substitutionary sacrifice, a final scapegoating, a divine victory over evil, or something else? And how does one come to participate in this salvation—through faith, moral obedience, ascetic self-discipline, sacramental participation, or some other way?[2] On these and other soteriological questions, we find a baffling proliferation of different answers from Christians throughout history. The whole matter quickly becomes bewildering in its scope and complexity. Rather than finding such complexity an embarrassment, however, this work seeks to articulate a theological vision that can embrace this soteriological multivalence, while also offering at certain points a critical clarification of it.

We can trace the source of this confusion primarily to the multiple forms and images of salvation in the biblical canon. As we have already indicated, the biblical texts do not know a single account of salvation, not even a single account of the saving significance of the cross. Mark Baker and Joel Green highlight this fact well:

---

1. *BSLK*, 26.12–13.

2. The point is not that these are mutually exclusive, but that these indicate different points of emphasis that reveal distinct theological judgments and traditions. And in some cases they are indeed mutually exclusive.

The idea that the Bible or the classical Christian tradition has "one" view of the atonement is unfounded. In the New Testament, the saving effect of Jesus's death is represented primarily through five constellations of images, each of which is borrowed from the public life of the ancient Mediterranean world: the court of law (e.g., justification), the world of commerce (e.g., redemption), personal relationships (e.g., reconciliation), worship (e.g., sacrifice), and the battleground (e.g., triumph over evil). Within these categories are clusters of terms, leading us to the conclusion that the significance of Jesus's death could not be represented without remainder by any one concept or theory of metaphor.[3]

Brenda Colijn underscores the multiplicity of soteriologies in the Bible in her work on *Images of Salvation in the New Testament*. She discusses election, justification, adoption, inheritance, glorification, deliverance, and many others. As she says in the introduction, "the variety of images attests to the complexity of both the human problem and its solution. No single picture is adequate to express the whole."[4] Colijn, like Green and Baker, argues that we need a plurality of images and concepts to understand salvation. Green calls his position the "kaleidoscopic view," which denies that any single theory or image is more important than any other.[5] Like Colijn, he says that "no one model or metaphor will do when it comes to the task of articulating and proclaiming that significance [of the cross] in the world today."[6]

As attractive as this kaleidoscopic approach may be, it fails to take seriously the hermeneutical problem posed by the historicity of both text and reader. While this approach acknowledges the cultural-historical diversity within the text, it places the multiplicity of images and concepts within the safe confines of a canonical narrative that renders each image equally authoritative and obscures the need for clarity and consistency in our understanding of salvation. This is ironic, since Baker and Green elsewhere do an admirable job of highlighting the hermeneutical problem in their analysis: "Many of us have been content merely to repeat the words of the New Testament itself, as though those words were themselves self-interpreting, as though they were not tied to one of several ways of articulating a narrative context for grasping the meaning of Jesus's death on a Roman cross."[7]

---

3. Baker and Green, *Recovering the Scandal*, 41.

4. Colijn, *Images*, 14.

5. See Green, "Kaleidoscopic View," 157–85.

6. Ibid., 157.

7. Baker and Green, *Recovering the Scandal*, 36.

They even connect interpretation of this narrative plurality to the problem
of crosscultural understanding:

> As is often the case in our use of the New Testament, our use
> of tradition frequently falters because, rather than learn how
> the theological task has been undertaken and exemplified, we
> attempt instead to carry over into our own lives and pronounce-
> ments models and metaphors that belong to another age and
> that are dead to us. Metaphors work within cultures where a
> shared encyclopedia, or cultural narrative, can be assumed.
> Crossing cultures sometimes requires new idioms, working
> with fresh ways of conceptualizing and communicating.[8]

Baker and Green have perfectly articulated the need for hermeneutical
translation and the critical reconstruction of the message of the text within
a new situation. If some metaphors are "dead to us," then hermeneutical
inquiry requires that we discern new metaphors and concepts to make sense
of the biblical text for the present moment. And yet, rather than present an
argument for *Sachkritik*, Green withdraws from the challenge posed by history. After acknowledging that the language of sacrifice belongs to a foreign
context, Green suggests that "a more fruitful strategy is to induct Christians
fully into the narrative world of Scripture that they will be so transformed
by their encounter with this 'full, perfect, and sufficient sacrifice for the sins
of the whole world' that they will embody his life as their own."[9] In other
words, instead of recognizing that some metaphors are culturally dead and
can be discarded, Green suggests that we somehow need to enter the alien
cultural world of the ancient biblical narrative.

This response to the hermeneutical problem is distinctively postliberal
in the sense defined by George Lindbeck, according to his famous line: "It
is the text, so to speak, which absorbs the world, rather than the world the
text."[10] Lindbeck uses this statement to oppose all hermeneutical translation
as the faithless attempt to allow the "extrascriptural" world to absorb the
text. By contrast, he advocates an "intratextual theology" that makes the
narrative world of the text absolute and untranslatable. Green similarly says
that scripture "promotes a narrative structure by which to comprehend the
world."[11] Postliberalism finally locates the saving significance of the cross in
this function of scripture as a *narrative worldview*. According to Green, in a
remarkable juxtaposition, the narrative revelation of scripture "promot[es]

---

8. Ibid., 38.

9. Green, "Kaleidoscopic View," 178.

10. Lindbeck, *Nature of Doctrine*, 104.

11. Green, "Kaleidoscopic View," 180.

a real change in how people construe the whole of God's creation and make their homes in it. 'See, everything has become new!'"[12] Everything is ostensibly new in the sense that the text absorbs the world within its totalizing gaze.

The conclusion we are led to draw is that the *biblical narrative* saves. That is to say, Jesus saves *through the text*. Above all, the text saves us from the problem of historicity. But this text did not simply fall from heaven; it is a product of the community's traditioning process. To believe the narrative is to believe the church. Lindbeck can thus say that his intratextual method is "a hermeneutics of intratextual social or ecclesial embodiment."[13] Intratextual reading of Scripture occurs through the social construction of reality in the form of the church. If the text is supposed to absorb the world, and if this absorption into the text takes the form of ecclesial embodiment, then biblical interpretation is properly the construction of an ecclesial culture—that is, Christendom. A kaleidoscopic view is finally an *ecclesiocentric view*. It is only to be expected that the postliberal escape from the hermeneutical problem involves the elevation of the church's received tradition as the authoritative norm for theology. Green concludes his essay by stating that all interpretations of the cross "that counter the narrative of Scripture as this is understood within the classical faith (see the ecumenical creeds of the early church and their precursors in the 'rule of faith') should be left aside."[14]

Green is entirely correct to point out that "interpretations of Jesus's death are tied to particular cultures and times, so that no interpretation can be regarded as the only authentic or definitive one."[15] But it will not do to establish an ahistorical, prehermeneutical *regula fidei* ("rule of faith") as the criterion for what counts as an authentic interpretation of Jesus's death. The *regula fidei* itself is tied to a particular culture and time; it too is an interpretation of what occurred in Jesus, albeit one that gained conciliar (and imperial) endorsement. But that must not mean the so-called "classical faith" is beyond historical and theological scrutiny. A kaleidoscope is of no benefit if it finally requires a sacrifice of the intellect—indeed, a sacrifice of one's critical faculties to the world-absorbing totality of ecclesial orthodoxy.

Neither will it suffice to posit a so-called "unified" theory of the atonement—namely, a master theory that melds the main concepts into a new doctrinal creation—which leads to dogmatic monstrosities like "triune

12. Ibid., 184.
13. Lindbeck, "Atonement," 226.
14. Green, "Kaleidoscopic View," 185.
15. Ibid., 170.

covenantal mediation."[16] Theological unity at the expense of hermeneutical understanding is a pyrrhic victory at best. We cannot bandy about concepts and metaphors without interrogating the underlying mythological and metaphysical logics involved in their use. For example, speaking of sacrifice involves one in the ancient near eastern zero-sum logic that requires the death of one creature in order to gain life for another. Within this cultural framework, blood-shedding has the capacity to propitiate a deity. To borrow from Baker and Green, such an idea belongs to another age and is now dead to us. Baker and Green make this point strongly with respect to Anselm's atonement theory, but the insight equally applies to many of the concepts contained within the Bible itself and the so-called "rule of faith."[17]

A way forward begins to emerge in Colijn's comment that the variety of atonement images "reflects the diversity of New Testament writers and their concerns, as well as the diversity of their audiences and their needs. It also results from the *missional orientation of the New Testament*—the need to proclaim the gospel in different terms to reach different contexts."[18] If the soteriological plurality and multivalence within the New Testament is a consequence of the missionary concern to contextualize the kerygma for particular situations, then we have a twofold hermeneutical task for thinking about salvation today. We must inquire after the kerygma that comes to contextual expression in the New Testament, and then reflect on how this kerygma may appropriately come to expression in our contemporary situation.

SALVATION AS APOCALYPSE: INTERROGATING NEW TESTAMENT SOTERIOLOGY

In order to discern what salvation-talk might mean for us today, we need to forget the received meanings associated with the term and investigate the matter anew. Toward that end, I will develop the following thesis throughout the course of this chapter: *salvation in the New Testament is fundamentally a matter of eschatology, wherein one is saved through the inbreaking apocalypse of God.* Salvation is an apocalyptic event. The ambiguity associated with the notion of apocalypse is the basis for the ambiguity associated with the

16. See Vanhoozer, "Atonement," 175–202, here 201.

17. "It will not do for us simply to borrow Anselm's theory, as though it could be read into our lives with any significance resembling that of his own world. He has located Jesus's death in a cultural narrative that most of us in the West simply do not share" (Baker and Green, *Recovering the Scandal*, 40).

18. Colijn, *Images*, 14. Emphasis mine.

notion of salvation. For this reason, we need to interrogate the problem of eschatology in order to clarify the problem of soteriology.

Christianity was born within the contested arena of Second Temple Judaism. Indeed, Christianity is best understood originally as a Jewish sect sharing, in broad contours, the apocalyptic beliefs of this fertile context. There is, of course, no single theology of Second Temple Judaism. We are dealing instead with "diverse and competing theologies" in this period, ranging from Zadokite and Enochic Judaism to the Sadducees and Essenes.[19] What distinguishes the theology of this postexilic period, however, is its highly eschatological or messianic consciousness: "The facts that the Jews were dispersed among the nations during the Second Temple period, Israel was often under foreign occupation, and the temple fell short of the glory of its predecessor—all these heightened the messianic tension within Judaism."[20] As David Flusser notes, "A survey of the relevant sources indicates that the concept of a new Jerusalem and an eschatological temple developed in the wake of the destruction of the first temple and the return of the Babylonian exiles."[21] The radically eschatological vision of this period is a direct reaction to the experience of homelessness, exile, oppression, and suffering. Salvation, in this period, was therefore understood as a restoration of all those living in the diaspora. To be saved is to return to one's true home, to live once again within the blessing promised by God to one's ancestors. The various sects within this period interpreted this salvation differently, some with a cosmic scope and others focused on a select remnant, along with differing views on the relation of divine and human agency. But however it was understood, the essential elements were the rebuilding of the temple and the ingathering of the elect people of God.[22] The saving apocalypse of God proclaimed by the prophets is here identified with the establishment of Zion, the new Jerusalem, at which point Israel will be free from the threat of oppression because YHWH will rule all the nations of the world.

19. Boccaccini, "Inner-Jewish Debate," 10.

20. Flusser, *Judaism*, 2:29. According to Jacob Taubes, "the Jewish situation is the ideal climate for the spiritual state of apocalypticism. The apocalypses and the messianic expectations come about at this time of great divisive tension. The oppression of Antiochus Epiphanes gives rise to the Apocalypse of Daniel. It is under the yoke of Roman rule that the Apocalypses of Baruch and the Fourth Book of Ezra emerge. The Johanine [*sic*] Apocalypse is written by a martyr for martyrs. The Christian Church has always preserved the connection between the coming of Jesus and its occurrence *sub Pontio Pilato*. The messianic tide in Israel from Jesus, Menahem, Bar Kochba to Molcho, Sabbatai Zvi, and Frank is closely related to the 'horrors of devastation'" (*Occidental Eschatology*, 24).

21. Flusser, *Judaism*, 1:208.

22. Ibid., 2:132.

Christianity arose within this context as the belief in Jesus as the Messiah proclaimed by the prophets. This belief in the messiahship of Jesus is connected in the New Testament to the conviction that Jesus was resurrected from the dead. Belief in resurrection was already a prominent feature of the apocalyptic literature in Second Temple Judaism, as seen especially in 1 Enoch, Daniel, and the Wisdom of Solomon.[23] What occurred among the followers of Jesus was the belief that this resurrection had occurred already in him, which indicated that the long-expected apocalypse of God was already present—the kingdom of God was truly *near*, as Jesus himself proclaimed. But the nearness of this kingdom was qualitatively different than the nearness hoped for by the Hebrew prophets. Christian belief in the apocalypse was no longer the belief in a political kingdom on earth, which would supplant the evil empires of the world with the global reign of YHWH from Zion. What differentiated Christianity from Judaism was the belief in the *spiritualization* of salvation: "Christian messianism emphasized, almost from the start, the spiritual aspect of redemption, while Judaism kept the political, worldly dimension of messianic redemption at the forefront."[24] Bultmann calls this the "dehistoricizing" of salvation. For Judaism, the hope of salvation "is historicized," for it "expects a king from the house of David."[25] But with the rise of apocalyptic thought, this hope was transferred to a coming age that would arrive only with the end of history. "The end of the world is the goal of history" within later Judaism and especially early Christianity, a position that Bultmann calls the "dehistoricizing of history."[26]

23. "The reason for such an interest in resurrection may have been due to the marginalization of the Jews by other nations in the period. Belief in resurrection may have provided the only real hope for Jewry in dire circumstances. In *1 Enoch*, for example, after all of Israel's enemies are destroyed, once-despised Israel gathers together to rebuild the temple. After the completion of this new temple the resurrection comes" (Anderson, *Internal Diversification*, 193). For more on resurrection and Second Temple Judaism, see Avery-Peck, Neusner, and Chilton, *Judaism*, vol. 4; Novakovic, *Raised*.

24. Flusser, *Judaism*, 2:277.

25. Bultmann, *History*, 28–29; cf. Bultmann, *Geschichte*, 30.

26. Bultmann, *Geschichte*, 35. The foregoing explains why the Easter-experience has its necessary counterpart in the Pentecost-experience. Easter is the event in which the community recognizes the man Jesus as the promised Messiah, and thus as the one who inaugurates the eschatological age within the present age. Pentecost is the event in which the community actually enters into and participates in the eschatological age here and now. Easter is the objective side of Pentecost; Pentecost is the subjective side of Easter. The two narratives within the New Testament are descriptions from two different perspectives of what is, in essence, one and the same event. In the following chapter I will develop this historical insight dogmatically as I turn to my soteriocentric reconstruction of christology and pneumatology. For now, it is important to understand that talk of the apocalypse in Jesus is not something exclusive of the Spirit and pneumatology. On the contrary, the apocalyptic approach to salvation that I am developing here is

We see the spiritualization of salvation especially in the Gospel narratives—largely composed during or after the first Jewish-Roman war in 66–73 CE—which portray Jesus as emphasizing the otherness of his kingdom in contrast to the worldly nature of Roman and Jewish expectations. Jesus repeatedly emphasizes that the kingdom of God must be sought where people least expect to find it, and that it will arrive at the most surprising moment in an unpredictable way (see, e.g., Mark 4:1–32; Luke 17:20–37; Matt 25:1–13). The kingdom comes near, then, in ways that break with all prior expectations. Across the Synoptics, particularly in the parables, Jesus includes the poor and humble among the citizens of God's kingdom and excludes the wealthy and religious authorities. This eschatological ethic, the transvaluation of all values, is determined by Jesus's understanding of the kingdom as an imminent apocalypse (cf. Matt 10:23), which does not become one worldly reign among others but rather brings the world as such to an end. This apocalyptic expectation is precisely the meaning of salvation: "The kingdom of God is salvation for human beings, and indeed the eschatological salvation that brings an end to all earthly being."[27] The kingdom, according to Jesus, belongs to those who have the proper spiritual relationship to this imminent apocalypse, a relation of expectancy and receptivity. It belongs to people who have already left the present world behind, or who have been left behind by it.[28] The proclamation of the kingdom is not a zealous call to arms but a prophetic call to faith and obedience, since what is proclaimed is not the restoration of an earthly hope but the arrival of the world's end and a corresponding freedom from the need to worry about earthly principalities and powers.[29] The apocalyptic speeches of Jesus in the

---

one that necessarily unites Christ and Spirit in a single event.

27. Bultmann, *Jesus*, 28.

28. I am grateful to Travis McMaken for this insight.

29. This does not mean that those of us who live on this side of the failed parousia—who cannot hope for the end of history but must instead discover the eschatological *within* the historical—cannot translate the apocalyptic proclamation of Jesus into a sociopolitical message of shalom as a way of enacting an anticipation of the eschatological event within the present historical situation. The point is that, for the original community of Jesus, the idea of the believing community being itself the site of political action was incomprehensible because the community's only reason for existing was to proclaim the news of the kingdom's imminent arrival. To be sure, this proclamation was political in the sense of invalidating the political status of the Roman empire. But there was no "church" in the sense of a constructive, sociocultural community. That only arose in later generations as the imminent expectation was shattered. The initial options were either participation in Jewish zealotry or the expectation of a coming apocalypse, and the Christian community rejected the former in favor of the latter. They soon had to leave the latter behind as well, and with that came the emergence of the church as we now know it. But the emergence of the church was also the emergence

Synoptics further indicate to their recipients during this period of oppression ("let the reader understand," Mark 13:14) that the kingdom proclaimed by Jesus is a freedom from worldly and political struggles. The Gospel of Mark speaks of the "Son of Man" coming to gather the elect to heaven— a kind of heavenly, spiritual Jerusalem no longer subject to the whims of imperial power (Mark 13:26–27). Luke even refers to the elect as those who "have the strength to escape all these things" (Luke 21:36). The Gospel of John, written well after the desolation of Jerusalem, makes explicit the spiritual and otherworldly nature of Jesus's kingdom, with his well-known statement before Pilate, "My kingdom is not from this world" (John 18:36).

Though the imminent expectation of the messianic kingdom was initially a defining feature of the Christian community, it did not last long. "We have to state clearly and without evasion that this hope proved to be a delusion," observes Käsemann.[30] The messianic Son of God did not appear within their lifetimes as expected. And with the evaporation of their hope in the imminent apocalypse of God, the fledgling community of Jesus followers sought to find new ways of understanding the saving event in Christ. One way was to reconcile imminent expectation with the expectation of an apocalypse in the distant future, such as the pious bromide that "with the Lord one day is like a thousand years" (2 Pet 3:8). This approach allowed the early community to retain the literal view of Christ's future coming.[31] This is the conservative position of church orthodoxy, and it is no accident that 2 Peter is an epistle concerned with denouncing heretics and propping up the teaching authority of the church.[32]

---

of anti-Judaism within Christianity, for now the followers of Jesus were no longer simply Jews who expected God's reign in the immediate future. Now they were a historical entity with their own rites and laws, doctrines and practices, standing in competition with other religious communities, struggling for recognition and survival. The task today is to recover a historicized version of the eschatological consciousness that the early Christians were compelled to abandon—not for the purpose of returning to some original form of Christianity but in order to construct a contemporary translation of the apostolate.

30. Käsemann, *New Testament Questions*, 106.

31. Some appeal to Jesus's statement in the Gospel of Mark—that "about that day or hour no one knows, neither the angels in heaven, nor the Son, but only the Father" (Mark 13:32)—as evidence that the early church kerygma was not bound up with the imminent expectation of the apocalypse. Even if we discount the hypothesis that this is a later ecclesiastical redaction, it would still fail to neutralize the imminent apocalyptic eschatology of the text. As Joel Marcus observes, "many Jewish apocalyptic texts seamlessly combine the idea that knowledge of the 'hour' is restricted to God with the conviction of that hour's imminence" (*Mark 8–16*, 918). Marcus points to passages in the Psalms of Solomon, 4 Ezra, and 2 Baruch.

32. See Käsemann, *Essays*, 169–95.

Another option was to reinterpret the apocalypse itself. Resources for doing so were already abundant in the writings of Paul, who speaks of the eschatological justice (or righteousness) of God as a present reality: "But now, apart from law, the righteousness of God [δικαιοσύνη θεοῦ] has been disclosed" (Rom 3:21). Indeed, in the gospel (εὐαγγέλιον) of salvation, "the righteousness of God is revealed [or apocalypsed, ἀποκαλύπτεται] through faith for faith" (Rom 1:16–17). For Paul, the apocalypse of God has already occurred and is already present for faith. "God already pronounces God's eschatological verdict (over the person of faith) in the present; the eschatological event is already present reality, or, rather, is beginning in the present."[33] And so Paul can say "we are justified [δικαιωθέντες] by faith" (Rom 5:1) and, again, that "we have been justified [δικαιωθέντες] by his blood" (Rom 5:9). By speaking of God's δικαιοσύνη—God's eschatologically rectifying justice—as already effective here and now, Paul has relocated the essence of the apocalyptic event expected in the near future and placed it in the past and present of the believer. In this way Paul was carrying on Jesus's own proclamation of God's nearness at hand (Phil 4:5).[34] He hammers this point home by repeatedly using the aorist tense when speaking about justification and reconciliation (καταλλαγή). The final verdict that determines our standing before God has already been determined. Given that the eschatological judgment is the heart of what Christianity expects from the coming messianic parousia, if this judgment has already taken place, if it is already available now, then the need for an imminent cosmic apocalypse has certainly been lessened, if not abrogated altogether.

---

33. Bultmann, *Theology*, 276, rev.

34. Käsemann claims that Jesus's proclamation of the nearness of God indicates that he was nonapocalyptic, which leads him to think that the primitive community's belief in the presence of the Spirit is an "enthusiasm" that Paul opposes by asserting Christian apocalyptic, with its notions of a final eschatological judgment. See Käsemann, *New Testament Questions*, 82–107. There are numerous problems with Käsemann's account, which many others have analyzed. For helpful overviews of some major critiques, see Gillespie, *First Theologians*, 10–17; Kuck, *Judgment*, 7–16. I agree here with Ulrich Luz that Paul does not advocate all forms of apocalyptic, nor does he reject all enthusiasm (see Luz, *Geschichtsverständnis*, 301–17). I would instead suggest seeing the enthusiasm, which has a pejorative connotation, as a kind of "present apocalyptic," one that remains in continuity with Jesus's own proclamation, albeit in a radicalized post-Easter form. This present apocalyptic is a genuine aspect of early Christian theology, which finds its most substantial support in Paul's letter to the Galatians. I would argue that the imminent expectation that Käsemann identifies with early Christian apocalyptic is itself an enthusiastic variation on Second Temple Judaism that quickly dies away with the Jewish-Roman War and the loss of hope in the coming of the Messiah. Käsemann thus misidentifies what is actually essential to Christian theology.

Along with this turn to a present eschatology, Paul also further spiri-
tualizes or existentializes salvation. In his earliest letter, Paul describes the
"hope of salvation" as consisting in the confidence that, whether "awake or
asleep," we will "live with [Christ]" (1 Thess 5:8-10). But later, in his letter
to the Galatian community, we read that salvation (as justification) consists
in the faith that the Messiah "lives in me" (Gal 2:20). This is a far cry from
the Jewish expectation of a messiah who will liberate the people from oppression and gather the people to Jerusalem. Following the interpretation
of J. Louis Martyn, we can still call this an apocalyptic eschatology in the
sense that there is a radical disjunction between the old and new ages—except now the apocalypse is no longer cosmological and future but rather
existential and present.[35] The transition from old to new occurs insofar as I
am justified by faith in Jesus as the Christ, insofar as "it is no longer I who
live, but it is Christ who lives in me" (Gal 2:20).[36] According to Käsemann,
justification is apocalyptic since it proclaims the truth "that God is only 'for
us' when God shatters our illusions and characterizes the new obedience of
those who set aside their own authority in order to await [erwarten] their
salvation from God alone. . . . The dying Christ becomes the creator of a
new humanity by liberating us both from the attempt to follow the way of
the law and from the despair of the rebel."[37] The expectation (Erwartung) is
now the expectation of God's present liberation of the believer through the
word of the Christus praesens. To await the kingdom is, in a sense, to await
the gift of freedom here and now.

To be sure, Paul still believes in the arrival of a future cosmic kingdom where Christ will rule the nations; he does not abandon this belief
entirely.[38] But he augments this belief with the conviction that, contrary to

35. See Martyn, Galatians, 97-105; Martyn, Theological Issues, 111-23; Martyn,
"Apocalyptic Gospel," 246-66. Cf. Congdon, "Eschatologizing Apocalyptic," 118-36.

36. I have retained the traditional phrase, "justified by faith in Christ," as opposed to
the more fashionable, "justified by the faith(fulness) of Christ," or even, "rectified by the
faith(fulness) of Christ." I do not dispute the arguments in favor of the subjective genitive, nor do I intend my use of the objective genitive to exclude the subjective. I do wish
to register my concern that emphasis on the "faith of Christ" runs the risk of turning
into a new kind of metaphysical christology, one that essentializes and objectifies Jesus
not on the level of nature but on the level of narrative. The faithfulness of Christ is only
meaningful if it occurs simultaneously with faith in Christ. The subjective and objective
genitives must take place together.

37. Käsemann, Paulinische Perspektiven, 77-78.

38. This is perhaps most apparent in Rom 5:9-10. The first half of each verse
speaks of justification and reconciliation, respectively, as an already-completed reality, while the second half speaks of salvation (σῴζω/σωτηρία) as something still future.
The emphasis on a future liberation of the cosmos from its present sufferings (Rom
8), along with the restoration of Israel (Rom 9-11), is an important theme in Romans,

Judaism, the Messiah has already arrived and his reign is already effective for the faithful. Moreover, his theology, especially in his later letters, decidedly shifts the emphasis to the present existence of the believer in the community of faith. But whereas the enthusiasts at Corinth believed in the *undialectical* presence of the Spirit, Paul insists on a *dialectical* presence, which understands the reign of Christ and the new aeon of the Spirit to be invisible apart from faith and thus at a certain eschatological remove from present existence.[39] What will change in the future, according to Paul, is not the arrival of a kingdom that has yet to arrive but the full manifestation of a kingdom that has already come in power through the justifying event of the gospel.

The Gospel of John was written well after the hope in the imminent advent of Christ had been shattered and takes this present eschatology even further. John also makes it clear that the eschatological judgment is already a present reality: "Now is the judgment of this world; now the ruler of this world will be driven out" (John 12:31). But unlike Paul, who pairs talk of a past and present apocalypse with talk of a still-future salvation, John presents the whole of salvation as already present: "Very truly, I tell you, anyone who hears my word and believes him who sent me has eternal life, and does not come under judgment, but has passed from death to life" (John 5:24). The decision of faith itself is the eschatological event; what Paul still hopes for in the future is now already present to believers. Faith is the ultimate apocalypse—ultimate both in the sense of fundamental and final. In the event of faith, Christ's apocalyptic invasion of the world is really present in its full actuality. We need not posit an ecclesiastical redactor to see that John's eschatology is predominantly present tense in nature.[40] The last remnants of traditional Jewish-Christian apocalyptic have now been either

and it reveals how thoroughly his thought resides within its Second Temple context. Nevertheless, there are important motifs in his letters that indicate another side to his theology.

39. As Bultmann puts it, "by his thesis that *righteousness is a present reality* Paul, nevertheless, does not rob it of its *forensic-eschatological meaning*" (*Theology*, 276).

40. Even if we judge Bultmann's argument for ecclesiastical redaction in the Johannine literature to be speculative, we can readily acknowledge its reasonableness. From a historical perspective, the present eschatology in John makes logical sense, given that the community by this point in time would have been searching for ways to reconcile their faith in Jesus with the nonoccurrence of the parousia. At the same time, the church was growing rapidly and beginning to form an inchoate institutional structure, and that process of establishing a fixed orthodoxy and orthopraxy necessarily came with the need to make their sacred texts consistent in order to shore up any doubts among their followers. It is by no means far-fetched to imagine an official church redactor adjusting, adding, and reordering statements to bring it more in line with the other Gospels and epistles.

expunged or transformed into an existential account of abiding in Christ: "Abide in me as I abide in you" (John 15:4). Both Paul and John replace the kingdom that is near at hand with the Christ who "lives in me" or "abides in me." In this way, they interpret the message of the gospel in a way that no longer depends upon a literal return of the Messiah. *The truth of the gospel is that the Messiah is already here with me and you today.*

Salvation within Second Temple Judaism, as we have seen, is essentially a matter of eschatology. Christianity arose within this context as an alternative account of the eschaton and thus as an alternative account of salvation itself. The heart of Christian soteriology is the belief that the eschatological judgment has, in a decisive sense, already been rendered. The messianic judge—whom the disciples quickly identified with Jesus of Nazareth in light of their Easter faith—has already come. This resulted in a spiritualization of salvation insofar as salvation could be actual and effective without any external or empirical evidence. Salvation is essentially *paradoxical*, in that it must be believed against all appearances to the contrary. This paradox runs like a red thread throughout the whole of Christian faith, from the paradox of a Jewish man who is simultaneously the presence of God, to the paradox of the Messiah's presence in the elements of bread and wine, to the paradox of justification that is true and effective apart from any external proof. We find in this paradox the decisive point of distinction between Judaism and Christianity.

The main divergence within Christianity is over whether this paradox must eventually resolve into a nonparadoxical, objective verification of the gospel. In other words, has the ultimate apocalypse already occurred, or is it still outstanding?[41] Is it essential that Christ return as the universally recognizable Lord of creation? Must the reign of Christ become a visible, sociopolitical reality in some distant future, given that the early church's imminent expectation has been shattered? The dominant tradition has always insisted that it must. The saving event cannot always remain spiritualized; it has to assert its supremacy at some point in the future. Many theologians in the modern period have thought otherwise, however, and Eberhard Jüngel has recently argued that we should reject both a definitive "yes" and a definitive "no" to a future advent. It is to his alternative approach that I now turn.

---

41. "Today it is commonly accepted that the reign of God which Jesus proclaimed is the eschatological reign. The only point in dispute is whether Jesus thought that the reign of God was immediately imminent, indeed already dawning in his exorcisms, or whether he thought that it was already present in his person—what today is called 'realised eschatology'" (Bultmann, *History*, 31).

SALVATION AS EMBARRASSMENT: EBERHARD
JÜNGEL'S ECCENTRIC ESCHATOLOGY

As a student of Ernst Fuchs, Jüngel cut his theological teeth within the field of New Testament studies. He was trained at a time when people were dealing with Barth's and Bultmann's complicated and controversial legacies, especially the latter's. The central question was eschatology. While most everyone agreed with Bultmann (and the early Barth) that eschatology was at the heart of the Christian kerygma, there was sharp disagreement over the nature of that eschatology. Ernst Käsemann insisted that it was an apocalyptic eschatology (i.e., one determined by the imminent expectation of the Son of God), while Bultmann, Fuchs, and Gerhard Ebeling denied this claim. Though Jüngel did not weigh in on that debate directly, his 1962 dissertation on the relation of Paul and Jesus, which argues for a material connection between them rooted in eschatology, indicated his fidelity to Fuchs's position and the Bultmannian school.[42] Jüngel came under the strong influence of Barth in subsequent years, however, the result of which was his remarkable "paraphrase" of Barth's theology in the *Church Dogmatics*.[43] But

---

42. The dissertation was originally titled *Das Verhältnis der paulinischen Rechtfertigungslehre zur Verkündigung Jesu* and published as *Paulus und Jesus*. Jüngel argues that Paul's doctrine of justification is grounded in Jesus's proclamation of God's reign, which he supports through a novel approach to the parables of Jesus and a rethinking of the relation between history and eschatology. The debate between Bultmann's "eschatology" and Käsemann's "apocalyptic" was a debate between whether the Christian message of the kingdom was primarily anthropological (Bultmann) or theological (Käsemann), that is, whether it was about the salvation of the human person or the exaltation and enthronement of the Messiah. Jüngel rejects the terms of this debate, which associates anthropology/eschatology with the nonoccurrence of the coming parousia and theology/apocalyptic with the imminent expectation of the parousia. He argues instead that *"the concept of eschatology is not an anthropological but rather an eminently theological concept,"* because "the so-called imminent expectation [*Naherwartung*]" is a "secondary eschatological phenomenon." The primary element in eschatology is not expectation but a "being-determined by the eschaton," and it is this determination by the eschaton that Jesus's proclamation of the kingdom "brings to speech" (Jüngel, *Paulus und Jesus*, 265). Jüngel thereby takes Bultmann's side in this dispute by reinterpreting the latter's position in a way that nullifies Käsemann's objections. Eschatology, Jüngel says, is not the expectation of an event that is near or imminent (*Naherwartung*), but rather "the event of the nearness of God to history" (ibid., 288). Moreover, "the place of the nearness of God is the word. The event of God's nearness is the coming-to-speech of God" (ibid., 289). It is precisely this coming-to-speech of God that Jesus actualized in his proclamation and which continues in the proclamation of God's justification of the ungodly, according to Paul. Jüngel has thus unified the anthropological and the theological within a new eschatology. We will return to this eschatology later since it encapsulates, in essence, the position I elaborate in this chapter.

43. See Jüngel, *Gottes Sein*; ET, Jüngel, *God's Being*.

Barth was also a strong proponent of a future advent, though his doctrine of the "threefold parousia" is admittedly a creative blending of the two sides insofar as the future coming of Christ does not inaugurate anything new in terms of content. For Barth, Easter, Pentecost, and eschatological Advent are "a single event" in three forms.[44] So while Barth was certainly closer to Bultmann at this point than Käsemann, he still insisted on the necessity of a future advent as integral to the salvific reality of Christ as the goal of history.[45]

Jüngel took up this debate again many years later, in an essay published in a Festschrift for Eilert Herms. The article in question is the third in a series of three essays of theses on the Holy Spirit, which together form a mini-dogmatics oriented around the theme of freedom.[46] The first two examine the Holy Spirit as the Spirit of truth (justification) and love (sanctification), respectively. The third focuses on the Spirit of hope (eschatology).[47] He begins this set of theses by immediately wading into the issue of the parousia's delay. The experience of the "not yet" should not be understood as the experience of a lack, but rather as "the promise of future consummation."[48] Eschatology concerns "a *definite* future already guaranteed now in the being of Jesus Christ, but still pending."[49] He even goes on later to say that "hope leads with material necessity to the expectation that the arrival of

44. *CD* 4.3:293.

45. To be sure, Barth's insistence on a future advent was a highly minimalist one in that he nowhere engages in speculation about what this future advent will entail. While he insists on it as essential to the gospel, he often seems to treat the notion as an instance of limit language—something beyond which we must not go. His denial of a literal existence beyond death seems to suggest that we should deliteralize the future advent as well. In his doctrine of creation, Barth says that the end-time will be a "*present without a future*" in the same way that the creation was a "present without a past." The final eschatological moment will be "the 'eternalizing' of our *ending* life," and "*nothing* further will follow this happening." There is no "continuing into an unending future." *This* particular historical existence will "put on incorruption and immortality." "Our *past* life, which we lived in our limited time, which did not begin before its time and does not continue beyond it, our *real* but also our *only* life," will participate in the eternal life of God. To speculate about or desire anything more than this is to pursue "pagan dreams of all kinds of good times after death" (*CD* 3.2:624–25, rev.). For more on this see the epilogue of this book.

46. See Congdon, "Spirit of Freedom," 13–27. Like Ebeling before him, Jüngel loves to write in the form of thesis statements, and he is a master of the form.

47. The fact that Jüngel develops the question of parousia and future advent within the context of pneumatology only further confirms my earlier and ongoing thesis that, when it comes to the apocalypse of salvation, christology and pneumatology are simply two ways of describing a single event.

48. Jüngel, "Der Geist," 306 (thesis 2).

49. Ibid. (thesis 2.1).

Jesus Christ in glory . . . is *near at hand*."[50] All of this strongly suggests that Jüngel sides with Barth over against Bultmann regarding the necessity of a future advent. So has he simply changed his mind in the years since his dissertation? Has Jüngel abandoned the Bultmann school in favor of the Barthian position?

As if to address this very question, Jüngel goes on to reject the notion that the nonoccurrence of the parousia undermines all future eschatology, not because the parousia will actually arrive in some distant future but because a literal, chronological understanding of the parousia misunderstands the function of imminent expectation for the life of faith. Jüngel thus states the following in theses 4.31 and 4.32:

> 4.31 The negative explanation of early Christian imminent expectation [*Naherwartung*] (cf. 1 Thess 4.15; 1 Cor 15.51; Rom 13.11f.; Mark 13.24ff.; Matt 24.3, etc.) as a mistake discrediting all future eschatology misses the essence of imminent expectation just as much as any positive explanation of the delay of the parousia (cf. 2 Pet 3.4ff.; Matt 25.5; Luke 12.45; 1 Clem 23.3; 2 Clem 11.2f.), which eliminates, through the positivity of its explanation, *the embarrassment* that the problem of imminent expectation poses and must pose.

> 4.32 In contrast to the imminent expectation attested in both Old Testament prophecy and Jewish apocalyptic and the question raised by them (cf. Isa 5.19; Ezek 12.12; Dan 8.13, 12.5ff.; 4 Ezra 4.33f., 6.59; 2 Bar. 26, 81.3; 1 En. 97.3–5, 104.3, *passim*), early Christian imminent expectation presents a case that is *sui generis*, insofar as it does not expect something unprecedentedly new, but rather expects the new coming of the one who has already come [*neue Kommen des schon Gekommenen*].[51]

The juxtaposition of these two theses is illuminating. Taken on its own, thesis 4.32 reads like a standard Barthian eschatology, according to which the future advent is identical in content with the past advent of Christ. The only difference would be the universal recognizability of the coming parousia.[52]

But Jüngel does not want to affirm a future advent any more than he wants to deny it. As the previous thesis indicates, both affirmation and denial "miss the essence of imminent expectation." So what is this essence? According to Jüngel, it is *embarrassment*. To be sure, there is embarrassment in the fact that an expected parousia does not occur, as many a fundamentalist

50. Ibid., 312 (thesis 4.3).
51. Ibid., 312–13.
52. For a version of this, see Kreck, *Die Zukunft*.

cult could confirm. But Jüngel's point goes deeper than that. He seems to suggest that the expectation of Christ's imminent arrival is an intrinsically unsettling hope, one that fills us with mounting unease and discontent. The doctrine of imminent expectation is not a problem that demands a definitive solution, either through rejection or affirmation, but instead a belief whose purpose is to *problematize the believer*. Ironically, therefore, the nonoccurrence of the parousia actually *fulfills* the purpose of this expectant hope insofar as it compounds the embarrassment and thereby actualizes the essence of Christian eschatology. It naturally follows that Jüngel rejects both Bultmann and Barth on this question: "In contrast to a negative (Rudolf Bultmann) or positive (Karl Barth) way of explaining the problem of imminent expectation and the delay of the parousia, *it is dogmatically essential to keep alive the theological embarrassment that is given with this problem*."[53] The removal of this embarrassment, he says, is just as problematic as a "chronological fixing" of the parousia.[54] The certainty that comes with either denying or affirming the coming advent leads to the comfortable domestication of the kerygma. To prevent this, the embarrassment "must remain . . . a lively embarrassment," so that we never experience ourselves as settled and secure.[55]

We can now return to the question of what it means for the one-who-has-already-come to come anew. If the essence of imminent expectation is its embarrassment—if the parousia is fulfilled precisely in its delay, in the unresolvable dissonance with the present moment—then the hope in a "definite future" and the expectation that the glorified Christ is "near at hand" cannot mean a hope in some literal, public occurrence in the distant future. But that does not mean a definite future is mere wishful thinking or that Christ is not, in fact, near at hand. It means that we must rethink the nature of the promised future and of Christ's nearness—not to lessen in any way the embarrassment of the parousia's nonoccurrence, but to understand how this nonoccurrence can itself be the fulfillment of Christ's promise.[56] If Christ is near at hand in his very disruption of our propensity toward

53. Jüngel, "Der Geist," 313 (thesis 4.322). Emphasis mine.

54. Ibid. (thesis 4.324).

55. Ibid. (thesis 4.323).

56. Jüngel walks a fine line here. In truth, his position is a variation on Bultmann's position, but it is a variation that seeks to lay the emphasis on the existential discomfort with the nonarrival of Christ. This discomfort is lost in Bultmann insofar as it is dismissed as part of the mythical world-picture. Jüngel does not deny that it is mythical, but he finds more truth in the myth than Bultmann does—a truth that he argues lives on even in the rejection of the world-picture that once gave validity to this mythical notion.

easy solutions and self-security, then his parousia occurs in the event of the word of justification that disturbs our illusions of peace and safety and thereby places us outside ourselves (*extra nos*). And this disturbing word from the eschatological beyond, this *verbum externum*, would indeed be the "new coming of the one who has already come," since the essence of Christ's initial presence was the proclamation of this same unsettling eschatological word. I call this existential account of the apocalypse an *eccentric eschatology*; it is a soteriology determined by the ex-centricity that defines the being of the person who belongs to the new age of faith, who is a justified creature before God.[57]

We are thus led, by way of Jüngel's theses on eschatology, back to his first work, *Paulus und Jesus*, where he establishes continuity between the proclamation of Jesus and the doctrine of justification on the grounds that both are "speech-events" that bring the eschaton—the reign of God—to speech.[58] The theme of justification (i.e., δικαιοσύνη θεοῦ) and the theme of Jesus's preaching (i.e., βασιλεία θεοῦ) speak in different ways about the eschatological reality of God's righteousness. They each proclaim, and thus actualize, the event of God's reign and righteousness within history, "which elucidates the being of human persons as *nos extra nos esse* [our being outside ourselves]. In that Paul and Jesus address human persons with their message *extra se*, they grant them a new being *extra se*."[59] In other words, Jesus's message of the coming kingdom and Paul's message of God's justifying righteousness are both different ways of proclaiming the message of a reality that resides outside of ourselves, a reality that, when we encounter it as a word *pro me*, places us outside of ourselves as well. The eschatological word makes us eschatological creatures. The eschaton, the apocalypse of salvation, comes near to us as we become distanced from ourselves. "God is only *near* to us in that God *distances* us from ourselves."[60] And God dis-

---

57. An eccentric eschatology is simply the historical-hermeneutical reconstruction of the reformational particles: *solus Christus, sola gratia, sola fide, solo verbo*—by Christ, grace, faith, and the word alone. These particles amount to one simple claim: *the truth of our existence lies outside of ourselves*. By reconstructing soteriology in light of the eschatological context of early Christianity, I have defined that which is "outside ourselves"—what the reformers identified as Christ, grace, faith, and the word—in terms of the *future*.

58. Jüngel, *Paulus und Jesus*, 267. As a member of the New Hermeneutic school associated with Fuchs and Ebeling, especially, Jüngel develops the idea that Jesus's parables do not merely speak *about* the kingdom of God but actually make the kingdom a reality for his hearers. The parables bring the kingdom to speech, that is to say, they actualize the kingdom through language. See ibid., 87–174.

59. Ibid., 266.

60. Jüngel, *Gott als Geheimnis*, 246.

tances us from ourselves precisely by coming near (*nah*) to us in the expectation (*Erwartung*) of Christ's imminent arrival in the word that justifies the ungodly. Stated simply, the proclamation of the kerygma in the present situation *is* the parousia of Christ, the expected future, the new coming of the one who has already come. The justifying word of the cross is an event that problematizes our very existence as the futile exercise of the "works of the law" (ἔργα νόμου), and so keeps alive the embarrassment of our inability to justify ourselves and our corresponding dependence upon the eschatological inbreaking of forgiveness.

Let us step back now to survey the argument thus far and press ahead toward our conclusion. I have argued that Christian soteriology was, from the start, a function of eschatology. Christian faith arose as a variation on the apocalyptic expectations of Second Temple Judaism. Initially, the community expected a salvation to come within their lifetimes, when the messianic Son of God would appear to bring the present age to an end and inaugurate the reign of God on earth. When this did not occur, the early Christian community turned to a more realized, present-tense eschatology, drawing on resources already available on the basis of their Easter belief in Jesus as the promised Messiah and the pentecostal belief in the presence and power of God's Spirit. This present or realized eschatology took two forms. Initially, as in Paul and John, the eschaton was identified with Jesus Christ and in his Spirit already bestowed upon the people of faith; it was a highly *christological* and *pneumatological* eschatology. But very soon, indeed already with Paul's disciples (see Ephesians, Colossians), the eschaton was located primarily in the *community* of Jesus Christ, with its doctrine and liturgy. Christ and his Spirit were collapsed into the institution that carried the message *about* Christ and his Spirit. The result is that eschatology quickly became an *ecclesiological* eschatology.[61] The church saw itself as the guardian and steward of the eschatological salvation promised in Christ. To belong to the church was to belong to the new age, to be "saved."

Whether construed christo-/pneumatocentrically or ecclesiocentrically, the point is that salvation was relocated from the imminent future to the past and present. For many centuries the ecclesiocentric account dominated. Even where the christological or pneumatological was emphasized, it was generally conflated with the ecclesiological, particularly with the church's cultic-liturgical practices. The Reformation differentiated these trajectories in an unprecedented way, thus opening the door to the rediscovery of a christological eschatology not determined from the outset by

61. See Käsemann, *Paulinische Perspektiven*, 178–210. Cf. Bultmann, "Transformation," 73–81.

the ecclesiastical tradition. The rise of the modern era soon complicated matters further by splitting eschatology and christology: the eschatological was co-opted by and conflated with the political and so used to support the colonialist policies of western Europe;[62] the christological, having been separated from an eschatology that was rejected by modern theology, collapsed back into a new ecclesiology, one shaped by European culture and bourgeois-colonialist politics (e.g., Harnack's "brotherhood of man").

It was with the onset of dialectical theology in the twentieth century that a genuine christological eschatology was rediscovered—though now under the conditions of a modern, rather than mythical, world-picture. But dialectical theology split over whether to lay emphasis on the continuity with New Testament eschatology (Barth) or on the context of the modern world-picture (Bultmann). Jüngel offers a third way that identifies continuity with the New Testament precisely in the modern incredulity toward the imminent advent of Christ. The parousia occurs *in* the existential apprehension of its embarrassing otherness, which is ultimately the otherness of God. To encounter the parousia in all its disorienting and scandalous strangeness—that is to say, to be placed outside ourselves—is to participate in the salvific event of Christ, with whom one is crucified in the existential apocalypse of faith.[63]

SALVATION AS COCRUCIFIXION: THE PARTICIPATORY EVENT OF THE APOCALYPSE

I have argued, on the basis of the eschatological kerygma of the early Christian community, that the apocalypse of salvation, the revelation of true life, occurs when a person is placed outside of herself. "Our theology is sure," states Martin Luther in his 1531 lectures on Galatians, "because it places us outside ourselves [*ponit nos extra nos*]."[64] To be saved is to be eschatological-

62. See the postcolonial analysis of the influence of Joachimite apocalyptic on modern colonialism in Collins Winn and Yong, "Apocalypse," 139–51.

63. I agree here with Friedrich Gogarten, who argues that, according to ancient, non-Christian eschatologies, "the old world is replaced by a new world," but the world still constitutes the reality that "encloses" human existence. "New Testament eschatology, however, sees the essential significance of the world-historical change, occurring at that time, in that the world ceases to be man's all-enclosing reality. The old which comes to an end is here not actually the world but its enclosure of man.... New Testament eschatology does, therefore, not contain an expectation of an actually new world. ... Rather, the expectation of New Testament eschatology concerns a radically new relationship to God" (*Despair*, 129).

64. *WA* 40.1:589.8; *LW* 26:387.

ly *extra se*. Salvation is not salvation from suffering, from oppression, from the final judgment, from eternal torment, from annihilation, from the devil, from mortality—from any of the traditional threats. It is a salvation *from ourselves*. Not salvation from the sinful "old self," as in the classic religious paradigm, but from the illusion that we belong to ourselves, from the anxious attempt to secure ourselves, from the desire to possess our identity and thus our future, from the struggle to assert our freedom and authority.[65] To use traditional Lutheran terminology, it is salvation from being "curved in upon ourselves" (*incurvatus in se*), from having a heart viciously and solipsistically turned in upon its own twisted concern for self-preservation and self-aggrandizement. The apocalypse of salvation is, in a sense, *our death*— the death of the existentially secure world that we build around ourselves.

Paul proclaims this existential death-to-ourselves to be a participation in the world-transfiguring death of Christ. In his letter to the Galatians— which, as Luther understood, is the beating heart of the biblical witness— Paul finds himself in an apocalyptic struggle for the ἀλήθεια τοῦ εὐαγγελίου, the "truth of the gospel" (Gal 2:5, 14). This kerygmatic truth is the startling revelation of "God's unconditional grace in Christ for all who believe . . . and thus, concretely, the freedom of Gentile believers in Antioch from the imposition of the law."[66] That this struggle is apocalyptic in nature, and thus concerns the very being and existence of the cosmos itself, is indicated already in the opening greeting, where Paul announces that Christ gave himself up to death to liberate[67] us "from the present evil age," which is a "distinctly apocalyptic expression."[68] Paul reiterates this point in his summary of the gospel in chapter 4. We were "enslaved to the elemental spirits [στοιχεῖα] of the world," he says, using another apocalyptic expression, "but when the fullness of time had come, God sent his Son, born of a woman, born under

65. I would argue, however, that this freedom from ourselves *is* the very salvation that earlier Christians spoke of in terms of the devil, eternal torment, annihilation, etc. Those mythical ideas were ways of translating this existential liberation into a narrative framework that made sense to them. The concept of "the satan" entered Judaism subsequent to its contact with Persian religious culture; it was a way of contextualizing their beliefs within a new context. The same is true for other mythical concepts. It no longer makes sense to speak and think in these terms, so a new way of understanding salvation is necessary, one that retains the essential content but within a new cultural and conceptual framework.

66. Boer, *Galatians*, 136.

67. The word is ἐξέληται ("to deliver, rescue"), the root verb of which (ἐξαιρεω) is used in the LXX to translate the Hebrew word נצל, which is the standard term for deliverance, used especially with reference to YHWH's liberation of the Hebrews from slavery to Pharaoh and the Egyptians. See Acts 7:34.

68. Martyn, *Galatians*, 97.

the law, in order to redeem those who were under the law, so that we might receive adoption as children" (Gal 4:3–5). The advent of Christ, which for Paul is entirely concentrated in his self-giving unto death, is the eschatological event that brings to an end the present age enslaved under the elemental powers of the cosmos in order to bring into existence the "new creation" (Gal 6:15; 2 Cor 5:17), wherein creatures are liberated for lives of genuine freedom (Gal 5:1).

Paul's reinterpretation of the apocalypse as something that *has already happened* means that it is utterly unlike the apocalypse expected by his Jewish contemporaries. For one thing, it is a new age ushered in not by brute strength, nor with ceremonial fanfare, but through the ignoble execution of a (wrongly) convicted criminal. Paul makes much of this point in his first letter to the Corinthian community as part of his effort to temper their triumphant enthusiasm (see 1 Cor 1:27). Here in Galatians, Paul faces the opposite problem: a community that is not confident enough in the radicality of divine grace. In both cases, however, his response is the same: a reminder that the apocalypse has actually happened, but it has happened *in death*, even death on a cross. Consequently, the incursion of this emancipatory grace is not self-evident; it cannot be treated as a given or observed with the innate faculties that belong to us as creatures of the present age. "God's invasive action . . . is not visible, demonstrable, or provable in the categories and with the means of perception native to 'everyday' existence."[69] The apocalypse can only be believed in against appearances. It has only truly happened, therefore, for the one who is able to see "both the evil age and the new creation simultaneously," who thus shares in both everyday and eschatological existence. The implication is that one cannot belong to the eschatological age without becoming an eschatological person, that is to say, without participating in the apocalypse itself.

For Paul, this can only mean one thing: *salvation occurs through co-crucifixion*. He thus declares, in what I would identify as the kerygmatic norm—the only potential "canon within the canon"—for all Christian soteriology: Χριστῷ συνεσταύρωμαι, ζῶ δὲ οὐκέτι ἐγώ, ζῇ δὲ ἐν ἐμοὶ Χριστός—"I have been crucified with Christ; and I no longer live, but Christ lives in me" (Gal 2:19–20; my translation). It is important to see, first of all, that "Paul's perception of Christ's crucifixion is thoroughly apocalyptic, in that it is both this-worldly and other-worldly."[70] While the crucifixion is a historical event involving tangible elements of wood and iron, blood and bone, it is at the same time, for Paul, "the cosmic event that cannot be truly seen by

69. Ibid., 104.
70. Ibid., 277.

those who look" only with their native means of perception and thereby fail to see that this event is an apocalyptic conflict with the powers of death.[71] Insofar as cocrucifixion is a salvific event—and does not refer to the literal crucifixion of other men alongside Jesus (Matt 27:44; Mark 15:32; John 19:32)—it pertains only to the latter, apocalyptic dimension. To be crucified with Christ is not to be physically nailed to a wooden cross but to share in the cosmos-rupturing incursion that took place in the death of Jesus.

Paul uses the word in this sense in Romans, where he says that "our old self was crucified with him so that the body of sin might be destroyed" (Rom 6:6). He speaks metaphorically of a "body of sin" as a way of connecting it to the literal body of Jesus. Our participation in Christ's death, which Paul ties to baptism (Rom 6:4), involves the death of our old self, that is to say, our old self-understanding, while our corresponding participation in his resurrection involves a new life and freedom from our enslavement to sin (Rom 6:4, 6), which we can call a new self-understanding. This transition from the old to the new self-understanding is a thoroughly *apocalyptic* event. It involves the death of one world and the inauguration of a new one. Martyn comments in this regard: "the crucifixion is *the* apocalyptic, cosmic event in which God confronts the powers that hold all of humanity in subjection," and therefore Paul's participation in this event means that "Paul was torn away from the cosmos in which he had lived, and it was torn away from him."[72]

The distinctive aspect of cocrucifixion in Galatians is the connection Paul makes there to justification.[73] Here we need to see Galatians 2:19–20 in light of its context. In the verses prior to this passage, Paul presents his distinction between two forms of justification: "by faith in Christ (or the faith[fulness] of Christ)" and "by the works of the law" (Gal 2:16).[74] The truth of the gospel, he says, is that the former actually justifies, while the latter does not. The eschatological event of justification thus involves the

71. Ibid., 278.

72. Ibid., 279–80.

73. Regarding this connection, see the work of Michael Gorman in *Inhabiting*, 40–104.

74. I will not explore the *pistis Christou* debate here. Elsewhere I have argued in support of that reading in Galatians (see Congdon, "Trinitarian Shape"), though I would now offer a more cautious and dialectical interpretation. I worry that the subjective genitive reading—in which the faith in question is Christ's own faith, rather than our faith in him—trades on a certain substitutionary ontology that I would want to subject to hermeneutical critique. I do not question whether it is the more accurate reading of Paul's text, only whether it is a position we should adopt within theology today. I would argue that we need to overcome the subject-object binary altogether, and the existential apocalypse that I am developing in this chapter is one way of doing so.

death of an old way of life (by the law) and the arrival of a new way of life (by faith). Paul then explains this transition using the literary device of parallelism, a common form within Hebrew poetry in which two parallel lines reinforce each other through symmetry and repetition. This occurs in 2:19–20:

> 2:19a (a) For through the law I died to the law,
> (b) so that I might live to God.
> 2:19b–20a (a) I have been crucified with Christ; and I no longer live,
> (b) but Christ lives in me.[75]

The two sentences parallel each other, so that dying to the law is identified with being crucified with Christ,[76] while living to God is identified with Christ living in me. What this indicates is that "Paul is clearly not speaking about some experience *subsequent* to justification but is speaking of justification itself, understood now as occurring by co-crucifixion instead of Law-keeping."[77]

The observation that cocrucifixion and justification are identical thus brings us full circle, for we have already seen that cocrucifixion is identical with the apocalyptic event of Christ's incursion in the world, and we have also seen, thanks to Jüngel, that this apocalyptic event is itself identical to justification. The point is that apocalypse, justification, and cocrucifixion are all speaking about one and the same reality: the singular event whereby God eschatologically interrupts our existence and places us outside ourselves, thus making us wholly insecure in ourselves but wholly secure in God. We should therefore understand salvation as a *participatory* occurrence: to be saved is to participate existentially in the death of Christ, understood as the eschatological judgment of the world, and this existential participation occurs insofar as we die to our old way of existence and experience ourselves anew: "Those who in faith know the mystery of Jesus Christ, who are thus placed outside themselves, find their existential location 'in Christ' (2 Cor 5:17)."[78] It is important to prevent a psychological reduction of this event to the sentimental Jesusolatry of the sort that happens year after year in

---

75. This analysis bears some resemblance to, and is partially inspired by, the analysis in Gorman, *Inhabiting*, 66. Gorman's point is slightly different, in that he is trying to show how Gal 2:19b–20a flesh out the parallel in 2:19a.

76. The English translation obscures the fact that, in the Greek, the first parts of each sentence are both exactly six words long, similar line length being a feature of Hebrew parallelism.

77. Gorman, *Inhabiting*, 66–67.

78. Jüngel, "Die Wahrheit," 55.

churches around Good Friday, where well-meaning Christians feel a deep
inward connection to Jesus as they contemplate his death on the cross for
an hour in a dimly lit room. Nor must we permit a dogmatic reduction of
this event to metaphysical claims regarding Christ's assumption of human
nature in his incarnation and the "objectivity" of his atoning work on the
cross for the sins of the world. The one reduces the Christ-event to a pious
subjectivism, while the other reduces it to an abstract objectivism. Neither
appreciates the apocalyptic nature of Christ's death as we have developed
it here. If, however, this singular historical occurrence is an *eschatological*
event that involves us existentially, it is not so much *we* who must discover
our connection to the past, whether through psychological or dogmatic
means—as if what is savingly significant is a past datum of world history—
as it is that the past *discovers us* and continues to discover us anew.[79]

We must resist the easy explanation of NT soteriology through the
one-size-fits-all formula of "already but not yet."[80] To be sure, Paul in particular tends to differentiate in his incipient soteriology between a past-tense
justification or reconciliation and a future-tense salvation. Romans 5:9–10
is the *locus classicus* for this distinction. In these verses he puts the verbs "to
justify" and "to reconcile" in the aorist, while "to save" is put in the future:

> 9 Much more surely then, now that we have been justified
> [δικαιωθέντες] by his blood, will we be saved [σωθησόμεθα]
> through him from the wrath of God. 10 For if while we were
> enemies, we were reconciled [κατηλλάγημεν] to God through
> the death of his Son, much more surely, having been reconciled
> [καταλλαγέντες], will we be saved [σωθησόμεθα] by his life.[81]

It would be easy to conclude from this that we ought to split between an
objective reconciliation that has already happened in Christ and a future
redemption that is yet to come in the now-distant future. In truth this approach fails to grapple with the context of early Christian apocalyptic with

79. According to Ronald Gregor Smith, to identify the life and death of Jesus as
an eschatological reality means that "we in our present lives may be confronted by his
reality in such a way that we may enter into a new life" (*Secular Christianity*, 99).

80. Of course, it all depends on what we understand to have come "already" and
what it still "not yet." The flexibility of these terms means that we can mold it to apply in
almost any theological scheme. My point here is simply that it was first introduced into
New Testament studies in the mid-twentieth century as a way of offering a facile both-
and that allowed one to escape the historical and hermeneutical problems presented
by the text.

81. Each of these verbs, it is worth noting, is also in the passive, which captures well
Paul's understanding of grace as something that *happens to us*, as an event whereby God
acts upon us.

sufficient seriousness. Like many of his fellow Jewish believers, Paul believed in the imminent arrival of the Messiah who would usher in the reign of YHWH. His radical Christian idea was that, in some decisive way, this Messiah had already arrived. In other words, his belief in Jesus as the Messiah was dependent upon, and was a variation of, the more basic belief in the imminent apocalypse that he largely took for granted. It is not as if Paul only posited a future salvation in light of the apparent fact that Jesus did not complete the work expected of him. What this means is that, given the shattering of the mythical hope in the imminent reign of God, one cannot simply push that advent out into the indefinite future and so keep the formal structure suggested by Paul's letters. We cannot and need not sustain belief in a literal cosmic apocalypse in the chronological future, what Catherine Keller calls a "retroapocalypse."[82] We must instead come to grips with the historical nature of Paul's soteriology and reconstruct the whole on a different footing.

The proper starting point is to see the apocalyptic event in Christ as simultaneously and paradoxically *both* a past occurrence in Jesus *and* a present encounter in the believer—and because present, also a future event. The apocalypse *has arrived*, and yet it is also *still coming* always anew. The saving apocalypse cannot be split in any way between past and future, as if it were partially realized and still partially unrealized, or realized in the past but only manifest in the future. Rather we must say that the apocalypse is *wholly* past, *wholly* present, and *wholly* future. The apocalypse was already fully realized and manifest in Christ's death-and-resurrection, and we must not expect it to be any different in the present or future. The apocalypse is necessarily existential and paradoxical, visible only to those who are able to see by faith both the evil age and the new creation simultaneously. It occurred in its fullness for the Christian community at Easter and Pentecost, and it occurs in its fullness for us today as the kerygmatic apocalypse encounters us in our historicity and we come to participate in the apocalypse through our cocrucifixion in faith. We can be confident that it will occur tomorrow in the same way it occurred yesterday and today (Heb 13:8).

If the saving event of the apocalypse involves a participation in the death of Christ, which is kerygmatically present to us, then we have to inquire further into the precise nature of this death. And what we learn from the Synoptic accounts is that this death is not merely apocalyptic and saving, but it is apocalyptic and saving *because it is a death in God-abandonment.* At the heart of the Markan passion narrative is the cry of abandonment, "My

---

82. Keller, *Apocalypse*, 7.

God, my God, why have you forsaken me?" (Mark 15:34; cf. Matt 27:46).[83] Attempts to lessen the force of this cry by appealing to abstract ontological claims about the unity of the godhead or to the full text of Psalm 22—the two appeals always go hand-in-hand, since Psalm 22 is simply used to provide the requisite "biblical support" for a presupposed trinitarian position—is a paradigmatic instance of metaphysical grotesquerie, which insists on protecting its philosophical commitments by smothering the word of God in Christ.

The dogmatic sanitizing of Jesus's cry of abandonment fails especially to contend with its apocalyptic character. The Gospel of Mark initially conveys the apocalyptic nature of Jesus's death by placing it on an appropriately cosmic stage: from the sixth to the ninth hour, "the whole earth"[84] was covered in darkness (Mark 15:33, my translation), which seems to echo the description of the eschatological day of judgment in Amos 8:9–10.[85] Several verses later, as Jesus breathes his last in a "loud cry" (Mark 15:37)—seemingly a supernatural, veil-rending exhalation,[86] which leads the centurion to confess that this man was "a son of God"[87]—the text records that "the curtain of the temple was torn in two, from top to bottom" (Mark 15:38).[88]

---

83. We can leave to one side here the disputed question of Mark's relationship to Paul, though the close affinity between Markan and Pauline christologies—exemplified in their unflinching emphasis on the crucified one—suggests, at least to me, that the author of Mark was indeed a disciple of Paul. With respect to the cry of abandonment, Marcus speaks, correctly in my view, of "Mark's Pauline soteriology" (*Mark 8–16*, 1064).

84. The NRSV puts the translation of "earth" (as opposed to "land") in footnotes, and I follow Joel Marcus and others in seeing this as the preferable translation, given that the Greek phrase is generally used to refer to the whole earth unless specifically referring to the land of Egypt. See ibid., 1053.

85. See ibid., 1062.

86. Gundry, *Mark*, 950.

87. Virtually all English translations choose to render this as "God's Son" or "the Son of God," despite the absence of a definite article, but Mark's rather adoptionist christology suggests that the less dogmatically-biased, theologically-sanitized translation is the more accurate version.

88. The author of the Gospel of Matthew apparently wanted to lay extra stress on the apocalyptic nature of this event, so between the tearing of the temple curtain and the confession of the centurion, Matthew has inserted into Mark's account a mythical-apocalyptic description of an end-of-history scenario: "At that moment the curtain of the temple was torn in two, from top to bottom. The earth shook, and the rocks were split. The tombs also were opened, and many bodies of the saints who had fallen asleep were raised. After his resurrection they came out of the tombs and entered the holy city and appeared to many" (Matt 27:51–53). Part of the explanation for this bizarre addition to the narrative is that it hearkens back to the Olivet discourse (i.e., the "little apocalypse") found originally in Mark 13, and repeated in Matthew 24 and Luke 21. There Jesus says that one of the signs of the end of the age will be "earthquakes in

Framed within this context, the cry of abandonment, almost certainly the same cry described in v. 37 as his final breath, marks the climactic moment of the apocalypse itself, the event of God's eschatological judgment.[89] Given the disjunction between the eschatological age and the present evil age, this climax is not readily visible to all. But "for those with eyes to see ... the fearful trek of the befuddled, bedraggled little band of disciples *is* the return of Israel to Zion, and Jesus's suffering and death there *are* the prophesied apocalyptic victory of the divine warrior."[90]

In both 15:34 and 15:37, Jesus's cry is described as being in a "loud voice" (φωνῇ μεγάλῃ). This description is distinctive and it appears in only two other places in Mark, both of them exorcisms. The first occurrence is in the very first act of Jesus's ministry following the calling of the disciples (Mark 1:23–27). After Jesus rebukes the unclean spirit, it shakes the man violently and comes out crying "with a loud voice" (Mark 1:26). The other appearance of the phrase occurs when Jesus heals the demon-possessed Gerasene. There again, after Jesus calls out the unclean spirit, the man shouts at him "with a loud voice" (Mark 5:7, my translation). The connection between exorcism and crucifixion is further reinforced in Mark 9,

---

various places" (Mark 13:8; cf. Matt 24:7). The point of Matthew's addition is not, of course, to describe something that actually happened, but rather to clarify the fact that what occurred in the death of Jesus was nothing less than the final eschatological event, the end of the old age and the dawning of the new. Apparently Matthew did not think Mark's account was sufficiently clear on this point, so he decided to make it plain to his readers what was really going on here. The paradoxical nature of Pauline, Markan, and Johannine christology is more or less abandoned by Matthew and Luke.

89. Marcus, *Mark 8–16*, 1056. The apocalyptic character of Jesus's cry is made all the stronger if we connect it to the notion of the "second death" in the Apocalypse of John (Rev 2:11; 20:6, 14; 21:8). Karl Barth suggests a connection along these lines in his *Church Dogmatics*. In his doctrine of creation, we read: "In the judgment of God man is in fact a sinner and debtor, and therefore by divine sentence subject to death, i.e., to death in the harsher sense, the 'second death.' And Jesus Christ has actually gone in our place to death, to death in this second sense, in this absolutely negative sense of the term. It is actually the case that we cannot see or describe in any other way but as the second death the end of human existence and what death means for man. ... We know the end of our temporal existence, our death, only as it overshadowed by His death" (*CD* 3.2:628). Jesus "did not submit to a blind fate or chance, but to the judgment of God," and for this reason his "being in death becomes punishment, torment, outer darkness, the worm, the flame" (*CD* 3.2:603). For this reason, according to Barth, "the incarnation, the taking of the *forma servi*, means not only God's becoming a creature, becoming a man ... but it means his giving himself up to the contradiction of man against him, his placing himself under the judgment under which man has fallen in this contradiction, under the curse of death which rests upon him. The meaning of the incarnation is plainly revealed in the question of Jesus on the cross: 'My God, my God, why hast thou forsaken me?'" (*CD* 4.1:185).

90. Marcus, *Way*, 36.

where Jesus heals a boy with a spirit that makes him unable to speak. After
the spirit convulses and cries out, it leaves the boy, who "was like a corpse"
(Mark 9:26). But then Jesus took him by the hand and "raised him" (Mark
9:27, my translation), the same word (ἐγείρω) we find used with reference to
Jesus's resurrection at the end of the Gospel (Mark 16:6, 14). Marcus rightly
sees a connection here between Jesus's apocalyptic battle against demonic
powers and his own crucifixion: "Jesus's word of command . . . is not just
a piece of magic, but a weapon in God's cosmic, eschatological war against
Satan. . . . Within the Markan Gospel, this apocalyptic victory is tied up
with Jesus's death and resurrection."[91] Given these narratival clues, we can
be even more specific: Jesus's death is a death under the sway of demon
possession, and as such a death in God-abandonment. According to Mark,
Jesus's entire ministry is essentially a confrontation with demonic powers;
it is one long eschatological battle with the principalities and powers, which
concludes with him personally entering into the heart of this satanic darkness and defeating it from within. At last, "through Jesus's exorcistic death
on the cross, a blessed, apocalyptic paradox comes into being, in which the
radiance of the new age breaks forth out of the depths of human weakness
and pain, and a suffering *man* is revealed to be the Son of *God*."[92] Jesus's
victory over the demonic powers of death occurs paradoxically *in* the act
of his own death in demon-possessed God-abandonment. His defeat of the
cosmic powers thus occurs in his own dereliction. In the event wherein he
experiences the abyss of apocalyptic desolation—the ultimate, eschatological going-outside-of-oneself—Jesus exorcises the *world*.[93]

The promise of justification by cocrucifixion is that, like the disciples,
we "are not barred from participating in Jesus's communication of the
liberative power of God into a demon-possessed world."[94] To be sure, the
human person does not participate in the full apocalyptic significance of
Christ's death in God-abandonment; cocrucifixion is not coredemption.
Cocrucifixion occurs where and when our existence corresponds to the cruciform existence of Jesus. Insofar as we are driven out of ourselves and made
cocombatants in the eschatological struggle against death and oppression,

91. Marcus, *Mark 8–16*, 664.

92. Ibid., 1068.

93. Consequently, Jesus is "the eschatological man, in whom the eschatological
pattern of suffering-vindication, tribulation-salvation must play itself out. Therefore
in fulfilling the prophets and their ancient oracles of doom and consolation, Jesus is
humiliated and exalted, surrounded by saints and ringed by sinners, clothed with light
and yet wrapped in a garment of darkness" (Davies and Allison, *Critical and Exegetical
Commentary*, 2:706).

94. Marcus, *Mark 8–16*, 660.

we share in the exorcising apocalypse of the gospel, which is "the power of God for salvation" (Rom 1:16). The grace of God that invades the world "points them away from self, frightens them out of themselves, deprives them of any root or soil or country in themselves."[95] We are thrust out of ourselves and into the hands of God, only to find ourselves commissioned for a new existence within the world. To be cocrucified is to be given eyes to see the old world in a thoroughly new way—to see the world "bifocally," as J. Louis Martyn calls it[96]—and with this new vision to see each person as the neighbor in need. Salvation as cocrucifixion is not simply a going outside of ourselves. The event of grace is not exhausted by mere self-displacement. Cocrucifixion is a movement *extra nos* for the sake of being *pro alio*, for another.

The historicity of salvation is, as we have been arguing, inseparable from praxis. Ernst Käsemann captures this especially well in his reflections on Galatians 2:11–21. For those who live in the comfortable affluence of modern, white society, to participate in the apocalyptic event of Christ's crucifixion is to be displaced from the security and contentment that comes with being "respectable" citizens:

> If we look to the churches of the white race and to the life we Christians normally lead in our land, scarcely anything is less understandable or credible [than being crucified with Christ]. It is generally expected of disciples of Jesus that they be brave, peaceful, and friendly citizens, good fathers or faithful mothers, reliable comrades and resolute defenders of discipline, duty, and order. . . . We must keep in mind how scandalous this word of the apostle is. He does not direct us first of all to our place in society or admonish us to behave appropriately there. He calls us instead to Golgotha, for every pious Jew an unclean place, where revolutionaries were hanged and Gentiles carried out their executions of evildoers. The shrieks of pain, hate, and blasphemy were loud there, nor was there anything resembling order, mercy, or humanity. If Paul speaks of our being "crucified with," he must be assuming that at least from time to time Jesus's disciples may be removed from their middle-class circumstances and at last be forced to see the world from Golgotha.[97]

95. *CD* 1.2:393.

96. Martyn, *Galatians*, 104.

97. Käsemann, *On Being a Disciple*, 92.

UNCONSCIOUS APOCALYPSE: ". . . YOU DID IT TO ME"

If salvation takes place where we are placed outside ourselves—that is to say, if being-outside-ourselves simply *is* what it means to have a saving faith—then we are finally in a position to see how one might reconcile the hermeneutical emphasis on our historicity with the soteriological conviction of universal salvation. In fidelity to both the biblical text and the historical context, we must say that salvation is both universal (for all) and particular (for each person), both generally effective and existentially located. And yet we can neither locate salvation in an abstract, general humanity (whether ontological or liturgical), nor can we locate it in the conscious, reflective action of the human individual. In the opening chapter I identified the solution to this dilemma as "eschatological theo-actualized universalism," and we can now see what that position might look like. It entails locating the saving event of divine action in a prereflective present-tense moment—namely, in the *unconscious*.

Dietrich Bonhoeffer gestures in this direction in *Act and Being*. In this important early work of his from 1930, Bonhoeffer develops a distinction between *actus directus* and *actus reflexus*, that is, between a direct act of consciousness and the consciousness of subsequent reflection: "In the former, consciousness is purely 'outwardly directed,' whereas in the latter, consciousness has the power to become its own object of attention, conscious of its own self in reflection."[98] The two terms, which he takes from the work of Franz Delitzsch, derive from a distinction in Protestant scholasticism between *fides directa* and *fides reflexa*. The former refers to an act of faith that takes place in the consciousness without being consciously reflected upon, while the latter is a conscious reflection upon this act of faith:

> Classical Protestant dogmatics spoke of *fides directa* to describe the act of faith which, even though completed within a person's consciousness, could not be reflected in it. . . . Clinging to Christ need not become self-conscious; rather, it is wholly taken up by completion of the act itself. Human beings are in Christ, and as there is no sin and death in Christ, human beings do not see their sin or death, nor do they see themselves or their own faith. They see only Christ and their Lord and God.[99]

98. Bonhoeffer, *Act and Being*, 28.

99. Ibid., 158. Bonhoeffer grounds this position in the nonobjectifiability of God, namely, the fact that God is not an objective entity within the world. To reflect on the act of faith is to objectify it, and thus to objectify God; the direct act of faith is a nonobjectifying act precisely because it does not involve conscious reflection. He writes:

Within *fides directa*, the being of the person is inseparable from its act, so that conscious reflection, which presupposes a separation between essence and existence, is impossible. "It is not as if the act offers no material to reflection, only that reflection cannot 'find' the act," since the act cannot be isolated from the totality of the person's being.[100] Bonhoeffer connects *fides directa* with infant baptism, to the child whose existence is entirely dependent upon the act of God, while *fides reflexa* belongs to the adult whose conscious faith reflects upon the child's *fides directa*. *Fides reflexa* is the reflective act of a believing adult, while *fides directa* is the nonreflective act of the child whose being is wholly outside itself. Infant baptism is *actus directus* insofar as revelation occurs "without the reflexive answer of consciousness."[101] Bonhoeffer then places this distinction between *actus directus* and *actus reflexus* in a temporal perspective. The child whose being is located in the *actus directus* is defined or "directed" by the *future*,[102] whereas those "who are mature . . . desire to be defined by the present" and thereby "fall subject to the past, to themselves, death and guilt," since "it is only out of the future that the present can be lived."[103] The future here is not the chronological but the *theological* future, that is, the *eschatological* future, which becomes present in the *actus directus* and so "determines the present." To receive or share in the *actus directus* is thus "to-let-oneself-be-defined by means of the future," that is, to participate in the eschatological event of Christ.[104] All of this is a

---

"Faith, being effected by God, is only in the act and never something one just comes across. But from that it follows that the I of faith, which is to be God's as well as mine, also can never be something one just comes across but is something that acts only in each act of faith. Whether I do or do not believe is something that no reflection on my religious acts can determine; it is equally impossible for me, in the process of believing, to focus on my faith, so that I would have to believe in my faith. Faith is never directed towards itself but always towards Christ, toward that which comes from outside. Thus, only in faith in Christ do I know that I believe (which is to say that here I do not know it), and in reflection on faith in Christ I know nothing. From the nonobjectivity of God follows necessarily the nonobjectivity of the I which knows God—and this implies that revelation should be the nonobjectivity of faith" (ibid., 93–94).

100. Ibid., 28.

101. Ibid., 159. In a 1942 report on baptism, Bonhoeffer writes: "Unlike the pietistic concept of faith, the Reformation concept is defined not psychologically but theologically. . . . The later Lutheran differentiation between fides directa and reflexiva [*sic*], immediata and mediata, exists for a theologically good reason, and protects against any psychologizing and law-oriented distortions of the concept of faith" (*Conspiracy and Imprisonment*, 562).

102. Bonhoeffer, *Act and Being*, 160.

103. Ibid., 159.

104. Ibid.

way of saying, with Paul, that we do not come to faith but rather faith comes to us.[105]

Twenty years later, Bultmann made similar remarks in a clarification of his hermeneutical program. One of the central areas of confusion regarding this program is the notion that Bultmann reduces faith to certain timeless truths that are known to existentialist philosophy. He combats this by differentiating between the *existentialist understanding of human being* that is indeed accessible to philosophy and the *existential self-understanding* that is known to faith alone. The former is a general, ontological description of our being-in-the-world, while the latter is a concrete, ontic event that occurs in one's personal existence; the former pertains to our *historical being*, while the latter pertains to our *eschatological identity*, that is, to our "free openness for the future."[106] Faith concerns the latter, and there, at least, philosophy is absolutely barred from gaining access. Bultmann then adds: "It goes without saying that this existential self-understanding need not be raised to the level of consciousness." This new self-understanding of faith guides my existence "in a hidden way." Much like Bonhoeffer, he then illustrates it by referring to the example of the child: "The child who understands itself as a child and understands its begetters as its parents is already sustained by such a self-understanding—in its love, its trust, its feeling of security, its gratitude, its respect, and its obedience."[107] As if to clarify that this existential self-understanding is not some generic spirituality without connection to the God who judges and saves, he says elsewhere, in the context of discussing Christian faith in God's saving action, that "such faith can be actualized genuinely only when I understand myself existentially here and now as God's creature, *which naturally need not come to consciousness as reflective knowledge*." Indeed, faith in God's creating and saving power "can be actualized only existentially by subjecting myself to the power of God that subdues me here and now, which, again, *need not be raised to the level of explicit consciousness*."[108] Genuine faith in God can be as incognito as Christ himself was.

Unlike Bultmann, however, Bonhoeffer makes the connection between the eschatological *actus directus*, which takes place as a new, albeit unconscious, self-understanding, and the possibility of universal salvation: "Our discussion of the *actus directus*—as something that can never be

---

105. "The person only comes to faith insofar as faith comes to the person. Faith is essentially *fides adventitia* (Gal 3.23–25)" (Jüngel, "Zur Lehre," 110).

106. Bultmann, "On the Problem," 117.

107. Ibid., 116.

108. Ibid., 112. Emphasis mine.

captured in reflection (I cannot capture the act in myself, not to mention in someone else) . . . allows a perspective to open up in which not all roads appear blocked to the eschatology of apocatastasis [sic]."[109] Bonhoeffer speaks with an appropriate hesitancy and tentativeness here, and he does not explore the idea further at this stage. Nearly fifteen years after *Act and Being*, while sitting in the Tegel military prison, Bonhoeffer returned to these ideas,[110] this time connecting the distinction between the two forms of faith to a new concept, that of "unconscious Christianity."[111] A letter to Eberhard Bethge postmarked July 27, 1944, has the following remark: "The question how there can be a 'natural' piety is at the same time the question about 'unconscious Christianity' [*unbewußten Christentum*] that preoccupies me more and more. The Lutheran dogmatists distinguished a *fides directa* from a *fides reflexa*."[112] The idea of unconscious Christianity possibly first appears in a marginal note at the end of the *Ethics* manuscript, "Ultimate and Penultimate Things," written in November 1940, though it may have been added later.[113] According to the editors of the collected edition, Bonhoeffer wrote: "unconscious Christianity. Balzac. People of the Antichrist."[114] These are some of Bonhoeffer's most enigmatic comments. He seems to be suggesting that it is possible to conceive of a faith that one has without being consciously aware of it. Bonhoeffer's remark about the *fides directa* is perhaps our best clue. If the *actus directus* consists, as he says in *Act and*

---

109. Bonhoeffer, *Act and Being*, 160.

110. In truth, the *actus directus/actus reflexus* remains central to Bonhoeffer's thinking from beginning to end, as the German editor of *Akt und Sein* in the Dietrich Bonhoeffer Works series, Hans-Richard Reuter, observes: "The constant in the development of Bonhoeffer's theology remains—as his subsequent writings bear out—the understanding of faith as *actus directus*, as immediate, intentional orientation. The differentiation of the *actus directus* from the *actus reflexus* manifests itself from now on as a structural principle rich with consequences, which Bonhoeffer retains, albeit in changing terminological instrumentation." Reuter notes the idea of "simple obedience" in *Discipleship* and the person with the "undivided heart" in the *Ethics*. See ibid., 181.

111. For a comparison of Bonhoeffer's "unconscious Christianity" and Karl Rahner's concept of "anonymous Christianity," see Kelly, "Unconscious Christianity."

112. Bonhoeffer, *Letters and Papers*, 489.

113. Bonhoeffer, *Ethics*, 443. The concept of "unconscious Christianity" does not originate with Bonhoeffer, but rather goes back to an 1867 article by Richard Rothe. Martin Rade gave a lecture in Berlin on November 22, 1904, in conversation with Rothe's essay, which Rade published under the title *Unbewußtes Christentum*. The lecture begins: "Unconscious Christianity is a Christianity that one does not know one has." He then differentiates it from "undogmatic Christianity," "unchurchly Christianity," "modern Christianity," and the *fides implicita* of Roman Catholicism. See Rade, *Unbewußtes Christentum*, 4.

114. Bonhoeffer, *Ethics*, 170n111.

Being, in being wholly "defined by means of the future," existing in an immediate relation to the eschatological reality of Christ, then we can draw the conclusion that whoever shares in the existential posture of the child is an unconscious Christian. What might this look like? We find a further clue in a note from Tegel prison written sometime in July–August 1944: "Unconscious Christianity: Left hand doesn't know what the right hand is doing. Matt. 25."[115]

The reference to the parable of the final judgment in Matthew 25 provides an important additional piece in the hermeneutical reconstruction of soteriology. While Bonhoeffer himself does not develop the significance of this passage with respect to unconscious Christianity, Rudolf Bultmann actually picks up where Bonhoeffer leaves off. On April 26, 1959, Bultmann gave a sermon at the Hendricks Chapel in Syracuse, New York, on Matthew 25:31–46. He focuses his interpretation of this passage on the fact that the righteous seem unaware that they did anything to merit the kingdom:

> Then the righteous will answer him, "Lord, when was it that we saw you hungry and gave you food, or thirsty and gave you something to drink? And when was it that we saw you a stranger and welcomed you, or naked and gave you clothing? And when was it that we saw you sick or in prison and visited you?" And the king will answer them, "Truly I tell you, just as you did it to one of the least of these who are members of my family, you did it to me." (Matt 25:37–40)

And, conversely, the condemned are not aware they did anything to merit eternal punishment. In both cases, the "Son of Man" takes their actions toward "the least of these" as actions toward himself. Bultmann discovers in this parable the counterintuitive truth that, where our relation to the reign of Christ is concerned, the unconscious has theological priority over the conscious:

> The people to the right are not conscious of the fact, that their deeds were done for the Lord, that the Lord encountered them again and again, just as the people at the left were unaware that they had failed to recognize the encounters of the Lord. If we wish to give a title to our text, it must be this: The importance of our unconscious behaviour. ... Don't be grieved, don't be troubled, for the judgment of the Lord does not depend on your conscious working, but on your unconscious behaviour, and his eyes see, what you have done without the conscious effort to fulfill his commandments, what you have done without reflection.

115. Bonhoeffer, *Letters and Papers*, 491.

> We can formulate the truth of Jesus's words as follows: The es-
> sential requirement is not the doing of men, but the being; in
> other words: the essential requirement is not what we do, but
> what we are.[116]

Bultmann does not mean in the least that there are two different orders of
people—good people and bad people—and that our unconscious deeds are
merely a reflection of what we are by nature. As he clarifies later, the words
of Jesus "open our eyes to a deeper dimension of life" beyond the realm of
the law, with its rules and regulations, its duties and responsibilities. We
discover this deeper dimension in our "encounters with Christ" that are "always unexpected" and "cannot be planned or prearranged and . . . are often
disturbing. . . . Thus we are asked: Will we pay attention to those unexpected
moments in our daily life?"[117] We are asked, in other words, "to examine
ourselves" to see whether our life is guided by the power of love.[118]

Bultmann speaks here to people who are already *conscious* Christians,
as we would expect in a sermon. As such he focuses his interpretation on
the moral point of the parable, namely, Jesus's admonition to show love to
the marginalized and estranged—namely, to become like the child who is
unconsciously Christian. But there is a still *deeper* dimension to the text
that demands our attention. At the same time that he identifies as an unconscious disciple the person who shows such love, Jesus identifies himself with
those to whom this love is shown. Resounding at the heart of this parable,
then, is the ontologically explosive claim: "you did it to me" (Matt 25:40).
Statements of identity like this are generally held in high regard: "this is
my body" (Mark 14:22) and "whoever listens to you listens to me" (Luke
10:16).[119] If we take Matthew 25 with equal seriousness, we must conclude
that the original and primary mode of unconscious Christianity is found
among the outcasts, the strangers, the hungry, and the imprisoned. Jesus
identifies himself with them; they are "unconscious Christians" by virtue
of God's preferential option for the poor, God's eternal decision to be the
God of the oppressed.[120] None of this should come as any surprise. If indeed

116. Bultmann, "Sermon," 48.

117. Ibid., 50.

118. Ibid., 51.

119. These passages are taken more seriously because they connect Jesus to the
church and reinforce ecclesial authority. A passage like Matthew 25, which relates Jesus
to those outside the church, can be seen as a threat to religious power.

120. Many scholars today interpret "the least of these brothers and sisters of
mine" (Matt 25:40 NIV) as a reference to followers of Jesus, since the "least" or "small-
est" (ἐλάχιστος) echoes earlier passages referring to "these little ones who believe in
me" (Matt 18:6). This interpretation only invalidates the claims about unconscious

the apocalypse of God occurs in Jesus's cry of abandonment, and if we participate in this apocalypse through our being-outside-ourselves, then God's saving action is to be found first and foremost among those abandoned by the world, forsaken by the powers of this age, and handed over to death. The eschatological promises belong to those to whom God has identified Godself in God's own forsakenness. Like Jesus, their being is wholly outside themselves, wholly at the mercy of God—a being-in-receptivity. It is entirely appropriate to the kerygma of Christ's eschatological reign that God would be present to them before and above all others. They participate in Christ's crucifixion in a manner that bears witness to revelation for those whose eyes are open to the deeper dimension of life. They, like the child who lives from the future, are "the greatest in the kingdom of heaven" (Matt 18:4).

The words of Jesus—and Bultmann—are then directed toward those who, in their conscious faith, seek to participate in this eschatological existence that belongs to the child and the marginalized, the stranger and the oppressed. If salvation involves participating in the crucified Christ, then salvation is to be found by participating in the existence of those with whom Christ has identified himself. They who "become like children" (Matt 18:3) and inhabit an unconscious, eccentric faith are the ones who share in the kingdom. They must demonstrate an unconscious love for others and thereby let the future determine their existence, as opposed to having a conscious, reflective faith that seeks security in knowing salvation as an object of one's past. Conscious Christianity is a turning in upon oneself in care for one's own spiritual health and relationship with God. Conscious faith, in other words, is not genuine faith, but rather the objectifying gaze of religion, which turns divine action into a datum of the past, that is, into an idol.[121] Reflection petrifies the apocalyptic power of God's word, fixing

---

Christianity if we presuppose what it means to "believe" in Jesus. But if faith is an act of participating in the crucified Christ, and if this participation occurs in those who are placed outside themselves, then this apparently more exclusivist interpretation can still be understood in a universalistic way—indeed, that is the thesis of this entire work, namely, that universal salvation can be affirmed within the limits of exclusive faith in Jesus. Moreover, this approach finds support in Matthew 25, since "both sheep and goats claim that they did not know that their actions were directed toward Jesus. . . . They have helped, or failed to help, not a Jesus recognized in his representatives, but a Jesus incognito." R. T. France concludes that "the least of these" actually "seem closer to what some modern theologians call 'anonymous Christians'" (*Gospel*, 959). In other words, even if we accept the exclusivist reading of "the least of these," the rest of the parable makes the matter effectively irrelevant.

121. David Kangas's fine analysis of Kierkegaard's understanding of consciousness as repetition in *Johannes Climacus* is worth quoting at length: "Reality is simultaneously gained and lost in its repetition. As repetition, consciousness itself interjects duplicity into reality by opening the distinction between appearing and being. As repetition,

the eschaton in its migratory path through the contingencies of history. The call of Jesus is to follow the eschaton—that is, to follow himself as the kerygmatic Christ—into the historicity of the moment by becoming *consciously unconscious*: becoming children in adulthood, becoming eccentric while remaining ourselves, becoming eschatological within the world. In this way "the paradox of Christian existence corresponds to the *paradox of the 'Word became flesh.'*"[122] The constant threat to Christian existence is the temptation to resolve this paradox by becoming wholly adult, worldly, reflective, by becoming egocentric rather than eccentric. The eschatological paradox that characterizes faith-as-cocrucifixion, however, continually calls into question the pursuit of reflective control and worldly security; it is a radically *dereflecting* and *desecuring* mode of existence.

The truth of the gospel is that the apocalypse occurs in the unconscious *actus directus* of being placed outside ourselves. The normative instance of this apocalypse is Christ's self-dispossessing life-act in obedience to God, concentrated climactically in his kenotic death in God-abandonment. Participation in this apocalyptic life-act occurs where human existence corresponds to the eccentric existence of Christ. This correspondence obtains where people are existentially and unconsciously placed outside themselves—unconsciously since conscious reflection counteracts this eccentricity by placing us again within ourselves. The eschatological event of salvation thus belongs to those who are placed outside themselves by the powers and principalities of the world—that is, to the poor, the imprisoned, the socially invisible, the culturally foreign, those who are vulnerable and disposable. Salvation belongs to them irrespective of their acknowledgment of Christ or their participation in conscious Christian faith. And while the unconscious participation in the apocalypse belongs to them first, we can be confident, based on the logic of the kerygma, that every person has been or will be an unconscious Christian. For some, unconscious faith might only occur in a moment of literal unconsciousness—at birth or at death, where we are

---

consciousness is not a domain of certainty and identity, but rather of duplicity. For as soon as there is consciousness, a gap has already been opened up between reality as reality (immediacy), and reality as expressed (mediation): more simply, between reality and its repetition. . . . It is precisely in terms of this originary duplicity, inseparable from the function of consciousness itself, that doubt finds its general possibility" (Kangas, *Kierkegaard's Instant*, 83). "Consciousness is produced by and produces duplicity. . . . Consciousness is thus, from the beginning, not at one with itself—it is, in this sense, basically 'untrue'" (ibid., 86). "Consciousness is the relation between the expression and the reality lost in that very expression. It is between the sayable and the unsayable. . . . The possibility of doubt, in other words, is inseparable from the very possibility of consciousness" (ibid., 87).

122. Bultmann, "Das Befremdliche," 204.

placed wholly outside ourselves. Others will encounter eschatological existence in moments of pure being-for-others, such as at the birth of a child, in
the ecstasy (*ek-stasis*, lit. "standing outside oneself") of love, or in the ethical
encounter with a neighbor in need. Still others will be placed outside themselves through the aesthetic experience of the beautiful, which constitutes
"an *elemental interruption* of our framework of reality" that allows us to "see
anew" our worldly context by giving it "a direction to the future, to a future
that makes whole."[123] These unconscious elemental interruptions occur in
those "fleeting instants scattered throughout our lives when all at once, our
defenses momentarily relaxed, we find ourselves brought to a pause by a
sudden unanticipated sense of the utter uncanniness of the reality we inhabit. . . . When it comes, it is a moment of alienation from the ordinary."[124] To
be elementally interrupted is, according to Laurie Zoloth, "to acknowledge
the power of the other over your being, to see the interrupting, messy, needy
other as entitled to your full attention."[125] In our estrangement from the
world and our own existence, we gain a new understanding of ourselves and
the other. However it occurs, each person will, at some moment, participate
in the authentic existence promised by and actualized in the eschatological
kerygma. Insofar as they are placed outside themselves, faith recognizes that
it is *Christ himself* in whom they are placed.[126]

123. Jüngel, "Auch das Schöne," 392, 382. In the famous closing words of Rainer
Maria Rilke's poem, "Archaic Torso of Apollo," a genuine encounter with art leads to the
epiphanic realization: "You must change your life."

124. Hart, *Experience*, 88.

125. Zoloth, "Interrupting," 11. In her 2014 AAR Presidential Address, Zoloth develops an ethics of interruption as a way of addressing a world in crisis, especially the
crisis of climate change. She describes our modern existence as "living in the illusion of
a life that is a continuous, busy process. We are committed to continuity, to historicity,
to plans and prospects, to the order of things, their repetitions, patterns, and sequences.
. . . To be interrupted is to be broken-in-to. It is to have one's view blocked by something
one does not want to see—say the beggar, say the warming air, the acidifying ocean.
. . . Into our lives, and utterly out of our control or our will, comes the complete otherness of interruption" (ibid., 6). Interruption can be "a moment of justice, of beauty, or
compassion, or grace, in such an unjust world" (ibid., 8). Theologically understood,
this interruption is "the insistent call of God, and when we respond rightly, it is prayer,
it is action for the widow and the orphan, it is standing and saying—*hineni*, I am here"
(ibid., 7).

126. Theological discussions of salvation have often asked whether salvation can
be lost or whether salvation is permanent. In Reformed theology this is known as the
"perseverance of the saints." In the apocalyptic account of salvation developed here, salvation is not a quality we possess and thus it cannot be lost or preserved. To be "saved"
is to participate in Christ, and this participation is enacted by God in the event of our
being-outside-ourselves. It is a divine act in the ephemeral moment; its impermanence
is the temporal clay jar that shows that this divine power belongs to God and not to us

If salvation belongs to each person unconsciously, then what advantage is there, if any, in becoming a conscious Christian, an explicit follower of Jesus? The advantage is twofold. First, the unconscious Christianity that belongs, at some point, to each person is contingent and accidental, momentary and short-lived. Each person quickly falls back into the pattern of egocentric reflection that characterizes our creaturely existence. While this happens for each person on a regular basis, only the reflective believer *recognizes* that it is happening. Conscious Christianity may be, by nature, an exercise in idolatrous unbelief, but it is at least conscious of its idolatry, and so it cries out anew each day: "help my unbelief!" (Mark 9:24). By continually hearing the message of Christ crucified in God-abandonment—that is, by encountering the interruptive word of grace in the kerygma of Christ's eschatological advent—conscious Christian faith becomes the site where Christ himself again and again decenters and disrupts our existence,[127] and thereby enables us to acknowledge our native tendency to pursue individual security at the expense of the other as "the law of sin" that dwells within our flesh (Rom 7:25). Communal Christian existence, when and where it truly occurs, provides space for people to be placed outside themselves—that is to say, space for ongoing cocrucifixion with Christ, for participating again and again in authentic eschatological existence. True faith, as I have argued, is the faith of the child, which is an existential relation to the future. Insofar as faith becomes the reflective, self-conscious faith of the adult, it is always in danger of becoming sin, insofar as the focus is on the past (*homo incurvatus in se*). The task of church proclamation is repeatedly to unsettle the community out of its *fides reflexa* in order to discover anew its *fides directa*. Christians thus gather for the sole purpose of being interrupted and displaced by Christ so that their lives may correspond to his ever anew. If there is a place to use the concept of virtue, it is here, so long as it is shorn of its association with natural human capacities and the notion of an aggregate increase in virtue. To be virtuous is to be a person who places herself again and again before the unsettling "word of the cross" (1 Cor 1:18, my translation).

Second, conscious Christianity gives us the "bifocal vision" to see the apocalypse, the eschatological mode of existence, manifest itself unconsciously in the world around us. Adult, reflective faith does not change or affect the *reality* of our participation in Christ, but it changes our *perception* of this reality, our *knowledge* and *understanding* of it. Indeed, apart from this consciousness one could not know that one's existence was in fact a

---

(2 Cor 4:7).

127. "Jesus is actually present in the kerygma, [and] it is *his* word which meets the hearer in the kerygma" (Bultmann, *Das Verhältnis*, 27).

participation in Christ; conscious Christianity is the condition for recognizing this reality as *Christian*. In other words, if the unconscious *actus directus*
concerns the event of salvation, the conscious *actus reflexus* concerns the
event of revelation, which opens our eyes to the fact that "the kingdom
of God has come near" (Mark 1:15) and that "now is the day of salvation"
(2 Cor 6:2). Conscious Christianity—which expresses itself primarily in
missionary proclamation and doxological praise—makes possible the discipline of theology as critical reflection on our unconscious participation in
the apocalypse of Christ. But it is crucial to see that conscious Christianity is
a reflection on the unconscious Christianity that exists invisibly—invisibly
apart from reflective faith, at least—throughout history, and as such it is not
a reflection on the practices and doctrines of the church itself, as if salvation
were found exclusively within the bounds of conscious Christianity.[128] The
claim here is rather that the eschatological event of salvation belongs *outside*
the bounds of conscious Christianity, and that those who are consciously
Christian are commissioned for a life of *solidarity* with the unconscious
Christians of the world—those cast off by the world and its religions and
into the weak but open arms of the crucified Nazarene.

The mission of conscious Christianity is therefore *not* to make unconscious Christians conscious. One is called, instead, to share in their
unconsciousness, to participate in their cruciform existence, and thereby to
participate in the crucified one himself. In the second edition of his commentary on Romans, Karl Barth declares:

> The children of the world, the unholy, the unbelievers in all
> their naked shame, perhaps even in all their free serenity, are
> *not* objects of our preaching and pastoral care, of our evange-
> lization, mission, apologetics, and rescue activities, *not* objects
> of our "love," because they have been sought and found by the
> mercy *of God* long before we arose to show them mercy; they
> stand already in the light of the righteousness of God, already
> partaking of forgiveness, already participating in the power of
> the resurrection and the power of obedience, already terrified of
> eternity and already hoping for it, already existentially thrown
> onto God![129]

* * * * *

---

128. The practices and doctrines of the church may be first-order theology, but they
are conscious, second-order reflections on the truly first-order reality that belongs to
the unconscious Christian, to the child determined by the future.

129. Barth, *Der Römerbrief*, 494.

In closing it is worth looking briefly at another parable from Matthew 25, this time the parable of the wise and foolish bridesmaids, where Jesus says:

> Then the kingdom of heaven will be like this. Ten bridesmaids took their lamps and went to meet the bridegroom. Five of them were foolish, and five were wise. When the foolish took their lamps, they took no oil with them; but the wise took flasks of oil with their lamps. As the bridegroom was delayed, all of them became drowsy and slept. But at midnight there was a shout, "Look! Here is the bridegroom! Come out to meet him." Then all those bridesmaids got up and trimmed their lamps. The foolish said to the wise, "Give us some of your oil, for our lamps are going out." But the wise replied, "No! there will not be enough for you and for us; you had better go to the dealers and buy some for yourselves." And while they went to buy it, the bridegroom came, and those who were ready went with him into the wedding banquet; and the door was shut. Later the other bridesmaids came also, saying, "Lord, lord, open to us." But he replied, "Truly I tell you, I do not know you." Keep awake therefore, for you know neither the day nor the hour. (Matt 25:1–13)

On its own the parable is an unremarkable example of the prophetic-eschatological sayings of Jesus, which emphasize the imminent arrival of God's reign. I bring it up here to highlight the creative midrashic version of this parable by Philip Pullman, the novelist and outspoken atheist, in his book *The Good Man Jesus and the Scoundrel Christ*. Pullman retells the story, but with some key twists. First, in his version, two of the wise bridesmaids share their oil with two of the foolish ones, and all four were admitted. But the remaining four—the two wise girls who did not share and the other two foolish girls—were all shut out. Then one of the admitted wise bridesmaids tells the bridegroom that "the least of us" have come to celebrate the wedding, so she would rather stay with her sisters outside the wedding than be admitted while others are shut out. So the bridegroom "opened the doors of the banquet and admitted them all." Then Pullman has Jesus add a final, staggering twist: "Now, where was the Kingdom of heaven? Inside the bridegroom's house? Is that what you think? No, it was outside in the dark with the wise girl and her sisters, even when the last of her oil was gone."[130]

Pullman's parable is worthy of the Gospel itself. He leads readers to think that he is correcting Matthew's version by offering a universalist retelling of the story, in which both the wise and foolish bridesmaids are allowed to enter the kingdom. But just when liberal-minded readers are

---

130. Pullman, *Good Man Jesus*, 142.

feeling comfortable and secure about their settled views, he implies, though he does not state it outright, that some of the bridesmaids refused to accept the invitation and remained out in the darkness, and more surprising still, that the kingdom of heaven was with *them*, "outside in the dark," rather than within the house. Pullman may not realize it—he may even think this is a subversive critique of the Bible—but his parable is in fact more faithful to the actual content of the eschatological kerygma of the New Testament than Matthew's own version. He has accessed what Karl Barth calls the "*real* gospel," and thereby has found his way (unconsciously!) to the "*whole* gospel."[131]

The "real gospel," so to speak, is *not* that God's saving apocalypse is available to those who consciously believe, to those who enter the wedding banquet, but rather that the inbreaking of Christ's reign is a reality for those excluded from every banquet and feast, and only because of this can we be confident that it is a reality also for each of us in the eccentricity of our unconscious self-understanding, our unreflective being-outside-ourselves. In this unconscious existence, "our very being is revealed," says Bultmann. And what is revealed there is that "love . . . is the power by which the human being gains his [or her] real value." And "the secret of this power is that it works in unconsciousness."[132] The wise bridesmaid revealed her true being when she gave up her place at the wedding banquet and stayed with her sisters in the dark, outside the doors of the banquet, where the kingdom remained with them until the end, even when their oil was gone. It was by this same secret power of love that Jesus "suffered outside the city gate" (Heb 13:12), and so, even when our lives come to an end and the world seems to have lost all meaning, we can say in truth that, in him, the kingdom of God has come near.

131. Barth, *Der Römerbrief*, 20.
132. Bultmann, "Sermon," 51.

4

The Agent of Salvation
Christ-Spirit

For you did not receive a spirit of slavery to fall back into fear, but you have received the Spirit of adoption. When we cry, "Abba! Father!" it is that very Spirit bearing witness with our spirit that we are children of God.

ROMANS 8:15–16

I will ask the Father, and he will give you another Advocate, to be with you forever.

JOHN 14:16

When the Advocate comes, whom I will send to you from the Father, the Spirit of truth who comes from the Father, he will testify on my behalf.

JOHN 15:26

SOTERIOLOGY AND CHRISTOLOGY

Gerhard Ebeling ventures into the territory of christology in the second volume of his magisterial three-volume dogmatics, *Dogmatik
des christlichen Glaubens*. His opening section is titled "Soteriology and
Christology," which binds the two terms together and places them in their
proper order. As he rightly states, "Jesus Christ cannot be spoken of without
speaking of the salvation of the world. And the salvation of the world cannot
be spoken of, at least not in the sense of Christian faith, without speaking
of Jesus Christ."[1] While Ebeling appeals, as I did in the previous chapter,
to the Niceno-Constantinopolitan Creed's "for us and for our salvation" to
support the inner connection between Jesus and salvation, it remains the
case that the classical conciliar reflection on Christ's two natures was not
always governed by soteriology. Talk of Christ was too often determined by
assumptions about divine immortality and impassibility, and where soteriological concerns did manifest themselves, the salvation in question was
conceptualized as deification—the human participation in the immortal
and impassible nature of the godhead. In other words, soteriology was constrained by extratheological presuppositions regarding both God and the
human person, which allowed talk of Christ and talk of salvation to carry
on independently of each other.

If, as Ebeling claims, to say "Jesus Christ" is to say "salvation of the
world," then the gospel's message of salvation—the apocalyptic interruption of existence—must determine what we think and say about the Christ,
the agent of this salvation. It is not enough to say that Christ *has* saving
significance, as if we can talk about his person independent of his work. We
need to say that Jesus, the Christ, *is* his saving significance—indeed, that
he is his *universal* saving significance. The being of Christ is his identity as
the agent of the universal being-outside-of-ourselves that defines salvation.
But since the saving event is an existential encounter with the kerygma, it
is both christological and *pneumatological*—though, as we will see, it is the
latter because it is the former. And therefore we also have to understand
and articulate the ontological identity of the Holy Spirit as intrinsic to this
singular salvific agency. The saving agent that is Christ is also the Spirit. Our
task now is to reconstruct christology and pneumatology together from the
ground up as the doctrine of the bipartite agent of the salvation of all people.

1. Ebeling, *Dogmatik*, 2:5.

PERSON BEFORE WORK:
THE INTERNAL INCOHERENCE OF
CHALCEDONIAN CHRISTOLOGY

Over a millennium and a half later, the Chalcedonian Definition of 451 CE continues to set the terms for the conversation about the person of Christ. Any attempt to construct a christology for our time has to reckon with the Chalcedonian legacy—both its promise and its problems.[2] According to this key ecumenical document, the church recognizes "one and the same Christ, Son, Lord, Only-begotten, in two natures, without confusion, without change, without division, without separation" (ἕνα καὶ τὸν αὐτὸν Χριστὸν, Υἱὸν, Κύριον μονογενῆ, ἐν δύο φύσεσιν ἀσυγχύτως, ἀτρέπτως, ἀδιαιρέτως, ἀχωρίστως). Jesus Christ is here understood as having "two natures" (δύο φύσεις) in "one person" (ἓν πρόσωπον) or "one subsistence" (μία ὑπόστασις). As with all the ecumenical creeds, the Chalcedonian statement is designed to oppose "heretical" ideas, in this case the twin errors of Eutychianism (a confusion of the natures), also known as monophysitism, and Nestorianism (a separation of the natures). While it was not simply a compromise document, because it sided decisively with Cyril of Alexandria's single subject christology, Chalcedon is nevertheless a fundamentally *negative* document.[3]

Contrary to those critics who want a more definite and fixed statement about Christ,[4] Dietrich Bonhoeffer locates the theological truth of the Chalcedonian Definition precisely in its negativity. In his 1933 lectures on christology, Bonhoeffer says that the four negative particles of the Chalcedonian formula mean *"that all options for thinking all of this together and in juxtaposition are represented as impossible and forbidden options."* Consequently,

2. My analysis of Chalcedon is indebted to the work of my *Doktorvater*, Bruce McCormack, whose own theological work is a rigorous and creative attempt at thinking with and beyond the Chalcedonian tradition.

3. I agree with John McGuckin that the Chalcedonian Definition is thoroughly Cyrillian: three out of the four terms in the Chalcedonian Definition derive from Cyril's writings. See Cyril's *First Letter to Succensus* ¶6, quoted in McGuckin, *Saint Cyril*, 354: "And so, we unite the Word of God the Father to the holy flesh endowed with a rational soul, in an ineffable way that transcends understanding, without confusion, without change, and without alteration." Chalcedon made other changes as well. Whereas Cyril speaks somewhat ambiguously of "one incarnate nature" formed "out of two natures" (ἐκ δύο φύσεων), Chalcedon speaks instead of "one *hypostasis*" being "in two natures" (ἐν δύο φύσεων). Cyril's "one incarnate nature" was not an affirmation of what was later called monophysitism, though it was later taken in that direction. He simply did not have the concept of *hypostasis* available to him. Hans van Loon rightly speaks of Cyril's dyophysite christology. See Loon, *Dyophysite Christology*.

4. For example, Millard Erickson writes: "The Chalcedonian conclusion, unfortunately, is essentially negative" (*Introducing*, 237).

"there is no longer any positive assertion that can be made about what happens in Jesus Christ. . . . Thus the matter itself is left as a mystery."[5] The conceptual tension within this definition means that, in effect, "Chalcedon cancels itself out. . . . It works with the concepts regarding the natures and demonstrates that these concepts are inappropriate and heretical forms."[6] Rather than see this as a defeat of our knowledge of Christ, Bonhoeffer instead sees it as protecting an essential truth, namely, the inability to objectify Christ. We are no longer able "to talk about the human and divine natures of Jesus Christ as about things or facts."[7] In other words, Bonhoeffer interprets Chalcedon as subverting the dominant approach to christology within the church, which sought to explain Christ's person in terms of natures and substances. As he says later, "in the Chalcedonian formulation, the doctrine of the two natures has itself been surmounted. We must carry on in this Chalcedonian sense."[8] To follow in the tradition of Chalcedon thus means to abandon attempts to explain *what* Christ is and instead talk about *who* Christ is as the one who reveals God in the flesh. Bonhoeffer takes up this challenge by replacing the classical discussion of divine and human natures with the modern discussion of Jesus as both humiliated and exalted.[9]

There is much to appreciate in Bonhoeffer's christology, especially his emphasis on who Christ is in his revelatory and saving actions within history, which foreshadows Barth's later christology, and Bonhoeffer's opposition to all objectifying modes of God-talk. I will take up these same concerns later in my own positive exploration of christology. But we must question the coherence of his interpretation of Chalcedon. In his attempt to oppose liberal theologians like Albrecht Ritschl and Adolf von Harnack, who criticized the role of Hellenistic metaphysics in the early church, Bonhoeffer ends up claiming that "nothing is further from being a product of Greek thinking than the Chalcedonian formula."[10] Bonhoeffer seems to derive this notion purely from his observation that the four negative concepts at the heart of the definition appear to contradict themselves. But this paradoxical aspect of the formula hardly means that Chalcedon is not a product of Hellenistic thinking. In fact, just the opposite is the case: Chalcedon ends up canceling itself out *precisely because* it is the product of Hellenistic metaphysics. What Bonhoeffer fails to see is that the Chalcedonian Definition's opposition to

5. Bonhoeffer, *Berlin*, 342.

6. Ibid., 343.

7. Ibid., 342.

8. Ibid., 350.

9. Ibid., 356.

10. Ibid., 352.

the objectification of Christ is, in fact, self-defeating. For the statement opposes objectifying thinking only by engaging in objectifying thinking! While the four negative terms at the heart of the definition—unconfused, unchanged, undivided, unseparated—demarcate the space within which one can develop a responsible christology, we cannot separate these terms from their immediate context, where we find the concepts of "nature" and "person." The *negative* terms are thus parasitic on a *positive* metaphysic. The nonobjectifying limit-language of Chalcedon trades on a prior conception of what counts as "human nature," "divine nature," and the "one person." But this means that we must already objectify Christ before denouncing all objectification. Chalcedon does not use the negative terms to defeat the positive metaphysic; rather, it presupposes the validity of the positive metaphysic and thus finds itself forced to use these negative terms.

Still more problematic is the fact that this positive metaphysic is internally incoherent. In order, on the one hand, to avoid confusing or mixing the natures (out of a need to protect the axiom of divine impassibility), and, on the other hand, to avoid dividing or separating the natures (out of a need to protect their soteriology of deification), the council appealed to a *tertium quid*—to the one *prosopon* or *hypostasis*—as a way of dealing with (i.e., avoiding) the problems posed on either side. But what exactly *is* this "person"?[11] Presumably, based on the classical patristic conception of God, the one person would have to be ontologically self-identical before and after incarnation, and thus it would have to be identical with the eternal Logos, the second trinitarian mode of being. The person of the Logos does not assume the divine nature but *is* the divine nature. The Chalcedonian fathers took for granted "that the Logos is the operative agent who achieves redemption in and through his human nature."[12] Consequently, whereas the Chalcedonian Definition as stated implies three entities—divine nature, human nature, and the one person—in truth there are only *two* entities, the divine person (since nature and person are ontologically identical) and the human nature assumed by that person in the incarnation. Chalcedon accomplished its delicate balancing act through a clever verbal trick, differentiating linguistically between the "divine nature" and the "one person," even though these are a single ontological reality.

But this then placed those gathered at Chalcedon in an aporetic situation. If they affirmed that the person is identical with the divine nature, then the assumption of flesh would have to result in an *ontological*

11. For a similar exploration of this problem, see McCormack, "Ontological Presuppositions," 350–56; McCormack, *Orthodox*, 203–6. I am indebted to McCormack for helping me to understand this point.

12. McCormack, "Ontological Presuppositions," 355.

change—specifically a change from impassible to passible. They could avoid the problem posed by divine mutability by affirming that God is eternally passible—either by claiming that deity is passible by nature, like panentheism or process theism, or that God is eternally defined by the history of Christ—but this would have been inconceivable to the ancient doctors of the church. The only other alternative, then, was to affirm some kind of Nestorianism, a separation between Christ's deity and humanity, which is precisely what Chalcedon was meant to oppose. Not finding any way out of this bind, the church fathers appealed to their *tertium quid*, which is not a *tertium quid* at all—since that would have been yet another heresy—but rather the illusion of one.

Chalcedon finds itself in this impossible situation due to its metaphysical approach to theology. Recall from chapter 2 that "metaphysics" refers to "any conceptual schema that secures the object of its inquiry (e.g., the being of God or the nature of human existence) apart from and prior to the historical situation." When it comes to orthodox christology, we are dealing with something that is doubly metaphysical, since the object of inquiry is *both* deity and humanity in a single reality. Classical orthodoxy is metaphysical because it presupposes what it means to speak of deity and humanity *prior* to wrestling with the particular reality of Jesus. The object of its inquiry has already been essentially defined before coming to grips with the object itself. Even more problematically, the deity of this object has been defined *in opposition to its humanity*, thus guaranteeing the aporia. We can see why this is so when we ask: how exactly can one define deity apart from revelation, that is, apart from being shown by God what it means to be divine? The ancients had only one option, namely, by defining the divine in distinction from the creature. This distinction can take three forms: the way of causality (*via causalitatis*) identifies God as being the uncaused cause of all creatures; the way of projection (*via eminentiae*) identifies God as being the infinite perfection of the creature (e.g., all-powerful, all-loving, all-knowing, etc.); and the way of negation (*via negationis*) identifies God as being what creatures are not (e.g., immortal, immutable, impassible, etc.).[13] In each case the divine is

13. These three ways are known as the *via triplex* of Dionysius the Areopagite. In *De divinis nominibus*, Dionysius says that we know God "by way of the denial and the transcendence of all things and by way of the cause of all things," referring, respectively, to the *via negationis*, *via eminentiae*, and *via causalitatis*. He goes on to say that "God is therefore known in all things and as distinct from all things." See *The Divine Names*, 872A; Pseudo-Dionysius, *Complete Works*, 108. In *De coelesti hierarchia*, Dionysius identifies the ways of eminence and negation as the "double way" by which revelation uses "humble forms to represent the divine and holy ranks." But the way of causality, as Dionysius describes it throughout his works, is the general metaphysical principle undergirding everything else. See *The Celestial Hierarchy*, 140C–141C; Pseudo-Dionysius,

only "known" as something that *stands over against the human*. God is only "God," according to this view, by being "not-creature." We thus find in the classic tradition what Colin Gunton has rightly called "a relentless concentration on what God is not."[14] And this concentration on what God is not is a direct consequence of having to reach an understanding of deity on the basis of general observations about the creation. The quandaries internal to the Christian tradition are all rooted in this metaphysical structure that assumes we can and must know essence—even if this knowledge, as with God, is purely negative in nature—before addressing existence.

It is not hard to see what problems this might cause for understanding Jesus of Nazareth as both human and divine. The entire debate within the ancient church over christology is one long attempt to figure out how to keep deity and humanity together in one person when deity and humanity have already been defined in opposition to each other. We have to understand that this was not just a logical puzzle they were trying to solve; their very salvation was at stake. And that is because the ancient church defined salvation on the basis of their metaphysical schema. If salvation is to become like God, and God has been defined in advance as not-human, then to be saved is, in some sense, to be "deified," to participate ontologically in certain attributes that belong to God over against the creation (e.g., impassibility). The metaphysical concept of God also has implications for the classical understanding of humanity and human sinfulness. This is perhaps most clearly seen among the theologians of the East, particularly someone like Maximus the Confessor. Maximus believed that humanity was created in a state of impassibility without any physical pleasure or pain, but that upon the immediate use of the senses—that is, in the first moment of creation—the first human being "squandered this spiritual capacity" and fell into sin, namely, into the dialectical tensions of creaturely existence: pleasure and pain, knowledge and ignorance, body and soul, male and female, etc.[15] Here we see the ultimate consequence of this metaphysical schema. Not only is salvation understood as being not-human, but sin is now defined as being not-divine (i.e., being a creature). So long as the essential natures of God and

---

Complete Works, 149–50. Dionysius became famous in the Latin West for his *via triplex* due to Thomas Aquinas, who refers to the three ways in his *Commentary on the Sentences of Peter Lombard* where he says that "ex creaturis tribus modis devenimus in Deum: scilicet per causalitatem, per remotionem, per eminentiam" (from creatures we arrive at God in three ways: namely, by way of causality, by way of removal, by way of eminence). See Thomas Aquinas, *Scriptum super Sententiis*, 1.3.1 pr.

14. Gunton, *Act and Being*, 16.

15. See *Ad Thalassium* 61; Maximus the Confessor, *On the Cosmic Mystery*, 131. Cf. Thunberg, *Microcosm and Mediator*, 95–168; Larchet, "Ancestral Guilt," 26–48.

the creature are defined in opposition to each other, with God understood in advance as whatever the creature is not, we remain inevitably trapped within a binary metaphysical logic that predetermines our entire theology. It ensures that our attempts to understand revelation—namely, what God has done in, with, and for us—will become a metaphysical problem to be solved and not a positive mystery to be understood and proclaimed.[16]

Put simply, the internal incoherence of the Chalcedonian tradition derives from its treatment of the *person* of Christ before the *work* of Christ. In other words, it claims to understand *what* Christ is—divine and human—before understanding *who* Christ is and *how* Christ is. The *whatness* of Christ, the constitution of his "natures" (as the tradition says), is supposedly known already. We ostensibly know *what* deity and humanity are. The problem that Chalcedon tries then to solve is how to make this twofold whatness fit together in one person. The church fathers kept trying different approaches. Apollinaris of Laodicea offered the most straightforward picture, with the divine and human fitting together like jigsaw pieces: the divine supplying (i.e., supplanting) the "soul" and the human supplying the "body." While this was finally rejected for good reason—a person without a human soul is not genuinely human—the conclusion was hardly satisfying. The doctors of the church ended up offering a negative solution ("it's not this or that!"), without saying positively what Christ actually is, appealing instead to a negative notion of mystery as sheer ineffability. Bonhoeffer claims this is a radical rejection of objectifying thinking, but in truth it is the ultimate objectification, since the entire approach is built on a thoroughly metaphysical structure that purports to know both God and the creature prior to attending to the historical event of Jesus.[17] Chalcedon trades on a "ready-made world," within which it then tries to fit Jesus. But Jesus the Christ does not fit into any preconceived philosophical framework. He shatters all such assumptions in his eschatological inbreaking. For this reason, the only way to make sense of christology—indeed, the only way truly to overcome objectifying thinking—is by starting with the saving work and letting this define the person.

16. The term "positive mystery" comes from Eberhard Jüngel. In contrast to a "negative mystery," about which one must be silent at all costs, "the New Testament designates that to be a mystery which must be *said* at all costs and which may under no circumstances be kept silent" (*God as the Mystery*, 250).

17. One can verify whether something is genuinely nonobjectifying by checking whether it supports a *positive* mystery. If it can only permit *negative* mystery, that is a sure sign it is an objectifying (i.e., metaphysical) form of God-talk.

PERSON AS WORK:
TOWARD A SOTERIOCENTRIC CHRISTOLOGY

A soteriocentric reconstruction of Chalcedonian christology is not an entirely novel undertaking, even if it remains insufficiently explored. Resources for pursuing this idea can be found especially in the work of Martin Luther and Rudolf Bultmann.[18] I will examine each of their contributions to christological reflection before turning to my own apocalyptic-soteriocentric proposal.

Martin Luther: Translating Chalcedon

Though he did not know it, Luther stood in the tradition of Cyrilline theology.[19] Like Cyril of Alexandria and Maximus the Confessor before him, Luther grasped the single subjectivity of Jesus Christ with the grip of a bulldog. Nothing was more theologically pernicious than a separation between Christ's deity and humanity, for the very basis of faith depended on this union. Despite this continuity with a certain line of patristic thought, Luther was a pathbreaking figure in Christian history, and at the heart of his theological revolution was a reversal of the metaphysics underpinning Chalcedonian christology.

This reversal of Chalcedon is most clearly stated in some of Luther's later disputations, especially his 1539 *Disputatio de sentencia: Verbum caro factum est* (Disputation on the statement: the Word became flesh).[20] There Luther attacks the philosophical school of the Sorbonne, which he associates with the view that truth is univocal and normed by the canons of general rationality. Against this he argues not only that philosophy is able to make formally correct syllogisms that are theologically erroneous,[21] but

18. Many others could have been mentioned as examples, including Wilhelm Herrmann, Karl Barth, and Hugh Ross Mackintosh.

19. "Luther had almost certainly not read Cyril, whom he would have liked enormously" (Yeago, "Bread of Life," 270n15).

20. *WA* 39/2:1–33; English translation in *LW* 38:235–77.

21. Luther approaches this differentiation between philosophy and theology in terms of two closely-related sets of distinctions. The first and most important is the distinction between the major premise and the minor premise. In the syllogisms that Luther uses as examples, the major premise tends to represent the position of philosophy (i.e., some general statement defining "human being" or "God"), while the minor premise represents theology (e.g., "Christ is a man"). Luther responds to the syllogism by questioning or jettisoning the major premise. Here's an example, from argument 14 (version A): "Whatever existed before creation was not born. Christ existed prior to creation. Therefore, Christ was not born a man. *Response*: The form is valid, but the

also—and more importantly—that theology makes claims that are philosophically impossible. Regarding the latter, he argues that philosophy is incapable of affirming the truth of the claim that the "Word became flesh" (John 1:14): "In theology it is true that the Word was made flesh; in philosophy the statement is simply impossible and absurd."[22] Theology, he suggests, operates with a different account of truthfulness. Luther thus condemns the Sorbonne for teaching "that articles of faith are subject to the judgment of human reason."[23] Luther clarifies this in thesis 10, where he criticizes Aristotelian categories as being unable to account for how God becomes a human being in Christ.

Luther's constructive response to the Sorbonne is that "a philosophical word becomes new in theology."[24] The newness in question here is the new event of God's being-in-flesh. He proffers two theses in support of this claim. The first thesis is: *Deus est homo* (God is a human being). Luther states in version A: "God is a human being. In philosophy it is false to say that he is God and a human being. For this reason we separate these spheres in creation to the furthest extent."[25] In the C version of this argument we read: "God is a human being, which is a simple proposition, not twofold as the Sorbonne has made it. We condemn the latter."[26] Luther goes on to reject the notion that we can equivocate on the word "homo" in order to philosophically accommodate the proposition. God simply *is* a human being, according to theology.

On what basis can Luther make such an ostensibly outrageous statement? For this we turn to his second and most crucial thesis: *extra Christum non est Deus alius* (outside Christ there is no other God).[27] For Luther, theology does not merely claim that God has become human; it claims that there is no other God than the human God, no other divinity than the one completely united with humanity in Jesus. The incarnate Christ is the definitive self-revelation of God: "Luther wants to emphasize that God has

---

conclusion is false. The premises are true; nevertheless, the major premise must be differentiated. It is true in philosophy, not in theology" (*WA* 39/2:20.10–13; *LW* 38:253).

22. "In theologia verum est, verbum esse carnem factum, in philosophia simpliciter impossibile et absurdum." *WA* 39/2:3.3–4; *LW* 38:239.

23. *WA* 39/2:4.2–3 (thesis 6); *LW* 38:239.

24. *WA* 39/2:19.7; *LW* 38:253.

25. *WA* 39/2:16.12–14; *LW* 38:250, rev.

26. *WA* 39/2:17.28–29; *LW* 38:273, rev.

27. *WA* 39/2:25.18; *LW* 38:258. Luther makes almost the same statement in German in his 1528 *Confession Concerning Christ's Supper* in the context of the *genus maiestaticum*: "ausser diesem menschen kein Gott ist" (apart from this human being there is no God). See *WA* 26:332.19–20; *LW* 37:218.

revealed himself in Christ, and only in Christ, so that all other ways to the knowledge of God are radically rejected, because they do not lead to the true God."[28] The problem with philosophy—and here the critique extends to Luther's ancient theological kin, including the bishops at Chalcedon—is that it presumes to have conceptions of divinity and humanity readily available, such that the notion of Christ as the Word-made-flesh is then a problem that has to be explained (e.g., by equivocation). Luther argues that just the opposite is the case for theology since the reality of the Word-made-flesh is our sole starting point, which defines for us what it means to be divine and human. The only deity is therefore a deity-with-humanity, a deity that lives, suffers, and dies in the flesh. Luther objects to speaking theologically about humanity or divinity in itself, that is to say, in the abstract. There is no "separated human being" or "separated God" in theology—a view that he elsewhere ascribes to Nestorius.[29] Luther's God-talk is therefore "free of the dualism which sees divine and human, heavenly and earthly, infinite and finite, impassible and passible, as opposites unreconcilable."[30]

The perennial problem with metaphysics is that it attempts to abstract from the concrete particularity of an object in order to speak about it in a detached and universal way. In christology, this leads to an emphasis on the two *natures* over the one concrete *person*, hence the qualification "according to the human nature." Luther rejects the Aristotelian system on the grounds that it moves from the general to the particular, from genus to species. Theology speaks instead on the basis of the particular and concrete, and this gives its words a new meaning in distinction from philosophy. Luther even describes this new meaning as a new *language*. In the 1539 disputation, he says that theology leaves philosophy "in its own sphere" and learns instead "to speak a new language in the realm of faith."[31] The following year, in his

28. Schmidt, *Christologie*, 252.

29. In his response to Nestorius in *On the Councils and the Church* (*Von den Konziliis und Kirchen*), Luther rejects the notion of the detached or separated God (*der abgesonderte Gott*), since such a God is not united with humanity and therefore cannot suffer and die in Christ—and thus is not the God who saves sinners. See *WA* 50:589; *LW* 41:103. Later, in his 1543 treatise, *The Last Words of David* (*Von den letzten worten Davids*), Luther criticizes Nestorius more directly along these same lines. According to Luther, Nestorius speaks of Christ's divinity and humanity in such a way that God does not actually become human but remains "a person separated from the humanity," while the human Jesus likewise remains "a person separated from God" (*WA* 54:90.27–28). Regarding the problem of treating humanity in the abstract (i.e., apart from God), thesis 32 of Luther's *Disputatio de homine* states that "Paul briefly summarizes the definition of humanity, saying, To be human is to be justified by faith" (*WA* 39/1:176.32–33).

30. Nagel, "Heresy," 47.

31. "Rectius ergo fecerimus, si dialectica seu philosophia in sua sphaera relictis discamus loqui novis linguis in regno fidei extra omnem sphaeram." *WA* 39/2:5.35–36;

Disputation on the Divinity and Humanity of Christ (*Disputatio de divinitate et humanitate Christi*), he states quite provocatively that "the Holy Spirit has its own grammar."[32] This does not mean, of course, that theology follows different linguistic rules from ordinary human speech. The new grammar or language of theology is not a new linguistic form alongside other forms already in existence. Formally speaking, the words of the Bible are the same ones employed by philosophy. The difference is not in the letter but in the spirit, not in the *what* (*Was*) but the *how* (*Wie*). Theology *uses* words in a new way, and in that new use, the words themselves become new, which is to say, they become the vehicle for the inbreaking of the eschatologically new reality of God in Christ. This is what I mean by Luther *translating* Chalcedon: he has transferred the judgments of Chalcedon into a new language and new grammar, thereby redefining our talk of Christ as divine and human. In the apocalyptic freedom of Christ's Spirit, the theologian can declare that "creator and creature is [!] one and the same."[33] In his overturning of the essentialist ontology of classical metaphysics, "Luther pushes further than the prepositions, Cyril's ἐχ and Chalcedon's ἐν, to an *est*."[34] He states this identity of God and humanity in a June 1541 letter on the eucharist and christology: "So I say: this human being is God, this child of Mary is the creator of the world. . . . The human being is God, the human being and God is one thing."[35]

Luther's postmetaphysical christology marks the start of theology's freedom from the classical ontology of the ancient and medieval church, which took for granted certain definitions of deity and humanity as part of its "ready-made world." In truth, then, what Luther inaugurated was not merely a *translation* of Chalcedon but in fact a total *reversal* of it. Whereas the tradition began with a certain picture of God and then tried to figure out how to fit Jesus into this picture, Luther begins with Jesus and figures out what this must mean for speaking of God. Long before Barth, it was Luther who realized that if we are going to bear witness to the God revealed in Christ, we must begin theologically not with the immanent but with the economic trinity:

> While Luther does not explicitly oppose the traditional christology of the church, it is difficult, in considering his ideas of the full significance of Christ's humanity for the sole true knowledge

LW 38:242.

32. "Spiritus sanctus habet suam grammaticam." *WA* 39/2:104.24 (arg. 7).

33. "Ibi creator et creatura unus et idem est." *WA* 39/2:105.6–7 (arg. 7).

34. Nagel, "Heresy," 46.

35. Luther, *Briefwechsel*, 9:444.52–53, 445.73.

of God, to overlook the fact that, to put it mildly, he does not merely set out in a completely different direction, but in some places does not understand the humanity and divinity of Christ in the same way. Of course, both Luther and the theologians of the early church were concerned with the unity of God and man in the one person of Jesus Christ. One can even say of the similarity in their doctrines that both consider this unity within the framework of the doctrine of the Trinity. But it is here, in the understanding of this unity, that the difference begins. The theology of the early church works it out in relation to the immanent Trinity, the Trinity as it exists in itself. Luther understands it in the sense of the Trinity of the economy, the Trinity as it is revealed. . . . If this is so, it follows quite unambiguously that Luther proposes not to understand the humanity of Christ from his divinity, but to understand his divinity from his humanity.[36]

Rudolf Bultmann: Demythologizing Chalcedon

Bultmann approaches christology as a NT scholar and form critic. His interest is not Chalcedon itself but rather the development of early Christian theology, and thus the biblical-historical antecedents to later conciliar christology. Nevertheless, his hermeneutical interrogation of the NT understanding of Jesus leads to theological conclusions that have an important bearing on dogmatic christology and share a strong affinity with the work of Luther.

One has to approach early Christian christology, according to Bultmann, with the eschatological expectations of the time clearly in view. Jesus entered a world that was brimming with eschatological fervor. The period of Second Temple Judaism (530 BCE–70 CE) was a prophetic and apocalyptic age, fueled by exile, oppression, and foreign occupation. The development of apocalyptic literature in the second century BCE gave rise to messianic movements and the widespread expectation of a coming new age, in which God's promises to the Jewish people would be fulfilled. Within this politically tense, eschatologically taut situation, there arose various messianic movements, which "expected the end of the Roman rule and the coming of the Kingdom of God."[37] One such movement formed around a man named John, known as the Baptist, and another formed later around Jesus of Nazareth, who seems to have been one of John's disciples. Jesus

36. Gogarten, Christ, 284–86.
37. Bultmann, Jesus, 22.

"appeared in the consciousness of being commissioned by God to proclaim the eschatological message of the inbreaking kingdom of God and the demanding, but also inviting, will of God."[38] He proclaimed "an *eschatological gospel*" that was "based on the certainty: *the Kingdom of God is beginning, is beginning now!*"[39] The kingdom he proclaimed was not a political, historical ideal, but rather a suprahistorical reality about which "we can say only that it draws near, it comes, it appears."[40] But neither did he proclaim himself to be the fulfillment of God's kingdom.[41] Much like the Christian tradition's understanding of John the Baptist as the herald of Jesus, so too Jesus was but a herald of the coming reign of God.

Thanks, however, to the Easter encounter with Jesus, "*the proclaimer became the proclaimed.*"[42] The one who heralded the coming kingdom was now himself heralded as the Messiah who would return to bring God's kingdom to fulfillment. With this unprecedented turn of events, *Christian* theology was effectively born—at the heart of which was *christology*, the theological understanding of Jesus as the Christ. This revolution was not a complete break with Jesus's teachings, since "Jesus's preaching had a 'kerygmatic' character" and even "implied a christology" insofar as it confronted people with God's eschatological claim in a way that demanded a decision.[43] But now the disciples of Jesus were of the conviction that *Jesus himself* confronts people with a decision, that he himself *is* the eschatological claim of God within the world, and that he presents this claim in the kerygma that proclaims his coming as the ultimate saving event. "Jesus is actually present in the kerygma," and "it is *his* word which meets the hearer in the kerygma."[44] For this reason we can say that "the proclaimed is at the same time present as the proclaimer."[45] He is paradoxically present as the crucified one who truly encounters people today in the message about him, in

38. Bultmann, *Verhältnis*, 11. For the English translation of this essay, see Bultmann, "Primitive Christian Kerygma," 15–42.

39. Bultmann, *Jesus*, 27, 30.

40. Ibid., 38.

41. Between Mark and John we see a transition from a Jesus who does not want people to call him the Messiah (William Wrede's "messianic secret") to a Jesus whose entire message is about himself ("I am . . ."). While the Gospels, as later testimonies of a believing community, focus on the person of Jesus, this transition suggests that the Jesus of history was himself focused on the coming reign of God. He was primarily a prophetic rather than messianic figure.

42. Bultmann, *Theology*, 33.

43. Bultmann, *Verhältnis*, 15–16. Original emphasis removed.

44. Ibid., 27.

45. *GuV*, 3:169. Cf. Kay, *Christus Praesens*, 4.

the gospel of God's gracious final judgment that has come to pass in his person, and who confirms this encounter through the liberating experience of his Spirit. Easter and Pentecost, christology and pneumatology, are thus inseparable. Indeed, "there is no faith in Christ which would not be at the same time . . . faith in the Holy Spirit."[46] This insight will become important in my constructive pneuma-christology below.

The point is that early theological reflection on the person of Christ arose as part of the attempt to understand the saving significance of Jesus. What the early church came to believe is that Jesus Christ crucified "*was* himself the *eschaton.*"[47] The eschatological judge expected within Second Temple Judaism had, in fact, already come, and thus in some sense he had already rendered the decisive judgment.[48] According to the theology of Paul, "God as judge becomes concrete for us in Christ: in him the judge of the world appears as our judge."[49] Similarly, the Gospel of John's statement that the Father "has given all judgment to the Son" (5:22) means that "God exercises his office as Judge *through* the Son," such that "the honour of the Father and the Son is *identical.*"[50] The christological titles thus serve not to describe Jesus's person in isolation—since there is no such thing—but rather serve to confess Jesus as the agent of salvation. His person, his being, *is his activity* as the eschatological judge of the world, which takes place in his preaching and passion. The import of the titles is to connect Jesus with the God of Israel, to proclaim him as being the historical presence of God. Just as God is the judge of the world (Rom 3:5; 1 Thess 3:13), so too Christ is the judge of the world (1 Cor 4:5). Just as God bestows grace (Rom 5:15), so too Christ, the κύριος, bestows grace (2 Cor 8:9). Just as Paul is the servant of God (2 Cor 6:4), so too he is the servant of Christ (1 Cor 3:5). In these and other passages, "κύριος and θεός stand here alongside each other as completely synonymous terms."[51] The purpose of such statements is to proclaim that Jesus himself is the event of salvation, that the saving agency of God is incarnate in him.

If talk of Jesus as the Christ or the Son of God means that the eschatological judgment expected from God has already taken place in this person,

---

46. Bultmann, *Verhältnis*, 26.

47. Fuchs, "Christus," 91.

48. "Jesus looks to the future, to the *coming* kingdom of God—which is coming or dawning *now*. But Paul looks back; *the turning point of the ages has already come.* . . . God *has already* bestowed reconciliation through Christ. . . . The decisive event which Jesus *expects*, has for Paul already taken place" (Bultmann, "Significance," 233).

49. Bultmann, "Christological Confession," 283.

50. Bultmann, *Gospel of John*, 256.

51. Bultmann, "Christological Confession," 281.

then it follows that the christological language of the NT is *soteriological* language. And this means that soteriology is not derived from christology, but rather christology is derived from soteriology. Christ-talk is a species of salvation-talk for the early community of Jesus-followers. Bultmann thus asks the question: "Does he help me because he is God's Son, or is he the Son of God because he helps me?"[52] The answer, at least in terms of a historical analysis of Christ-talk, is clear: "the pronouncements about Jesus's divinity or deity are not, in fact, pronouncements of his nature but seek to give expression to his significance."[53] The implication of this insight is that we cannot have a doctrine of Christ's *person* distinct from a doctrine of his *work*. Talk of the person of Christ has no meaning, historically speaking, except to make sense of faith's confession that Jesus is the bringer of salvation. Accordingly, the point of Pauline and Johannine talk of Christ's preexistence is not to speculate about some existence of Jesus apart from history but to reinforce his saving significance by indicating that *this* particular person transcends his historical horizon and is significant for you and me today: "All this is said [about preexistence] not in order to provide the basis for a speculative Christology, but because his origin is grounded in *what he means for us*. . . . Thus the statement about his equality with God refers to the situation of those who hear and see him, and not to his own metaphysical nature."[54] We must not use talk of preexistence, therefore, as a pretext for isolating the person of Christ from his work as the eschatological judge of the world.

It follows, naturally, that the NT identification of God with a particular historical person is misunderstood if this is taken to mean that we can apply a presupposed conception of deity to Jesus. The fact that "the activity of the Father and the Son is *identical*" does not entail a metaphysicization of Jesus according to preconceived ontological categories, but rather it means that "*the idea of God's activity in his Revealer has been historicised*."[55] Jesus is not metaphysicized; instead, God is historicized. The Christ-event within history becomes the hermeneutical norm for understanding what it means to speak responsibly of God. We learn from the biblical witness that "*God is the God of history* and is thereby *the God who is always coming*."[56] God is "never present as a familiar phenomenon but . . . is always the coming God," that is to say, the God who comes to us from the future bearing the

---

52. Ibid., 280.
53. Ibid.
54. Bultmann, *Gospel of John*, 249.
55. Ibid., 251.
56. *GuV*, 3:165.

eschatological promise of new creation.[57] The God revealed in Christ is as such "the one who acts on us and effects faith and we are seen as those who are thereby drawn into God's action."[58] The scriptural testimony to Jesus teaches us how to understand the reality of God. We begin not with a prior concept of deity but with a particular event in history, for Christian faith, which is "indissolubly connected with an historical fact," confesses that "not the metaphysical, but the historical saves."[59]

Bultmann thus achieves by way of critical exegesis what someone like Barth achieves by way of dogmatic reflection: the God revealed in Christ is a *historical* being, a being-in-historical-action. We must define deity in terms of what God actually *does* for us in Jesus. When it comes to christology, therefore, the categories of nature and substance are woefully inadequate to the task. "Humanity can be interpreted as a φύσις just as little as what we call 'deity' may be."[60] What we need is a new conceptuality.

Saving Chalcedon: One Event in Two Modes

The only way to salvage the Chalcedonian tradition is to translate its judgments into a new soteriocentric conceptuality.[61] The notion of Christ being "two natures in one person" is no longer adequate, if it ever was. Instead, we must reverse the order and place the person first in the orders of knowing and being, and then we must understand divine and human as aspects of this person. But we also need to understand the person in terms of his saving activity within history. The person is an event, an action, a historical happening. This means that deity and humanity are not substances that subsist in him, but rather modes of this singular occurrence. In place of "two natures in one person," we must speak of "one event in two modes" or

---

57. Bultmann, *Jesus Christ*, 23.

58. Bultmann, "Theology," 55.

59. Bultmann, *What Is Theology?*, 91.

60. Bultmann, "Christological Confession," 287.

61. For the distinction between judgments and concepts, and the insight that "the same judgement [sic] can be rendered in [a] variety of conceptual terms," see Yeago, "New Testament," 87–100, here 93.

"one action in two levels of agency"[62] or "one history in bifocal perspective."[63] Or, to borrow a metaphor from John Walton, we might speak of "one cake in two layers," so long as we understand that the layers are two ways of looking at the same historical event and not two substances combined in the same reality.[64] The layer cake, so to speak, is *not* the person of Christ, as if deity and humanity are two "parts" of the one person. The cake is instead the saving event, which can be understood in terms of two categorically different levels of explanation: the historical and the eschatological, human and divine.[65]

62. Here I am referring to the idea of "double agency" in Hunsinger, *How to Read*, 185–224. See ibid., 189: "the coincidence and distinction of divine and human agency in a single event." Travis McMaken replaces Hunsinger's term with "paradoxical identity" in order to avoid the "parallelist picture . . . of two relatively distinct agents collaborating in a rather external way" (McMaken, "Definitive," 103n50). The language of "level" comes from the phrase "levels of explanation," used in literature related to the dialogue between Christianity/theology and science, especially psychology. For example, see Myers, "A Levels-of-Explanation View," 49–78. I have chosen not to speak of "one action with two agents," because of the dangerous potential for Nestorianism in that phrase. There is only one agent, the human person Jesus of Nazareth, but insofar as his action is understood as both human and divine, there is a second "level of agency" in him that remains inaccessible to historical science. One could call this second level the "power of the Holy Spirit," following the Gospel narratives, so long as one does not construe the Spirit mythically as a supernatural person or agent operating somehow behind or apart from Jesus or ourselves.

63. The concept of "bifocal vision" as a way of describing the differentiation between divine and human action comes from Martyn, *Galatians*, 104.

64. In his book, *The Lost World of Genesis One*, Walton contrasts two metaphors for thinking about the relation between theology and science: (a) a pie, in which the size of theology's slice competes with the slice of science, and (b) a layer cake, in which theology and science do not compete because they exist at different layers or levels. According to Walton, "We need to think in terms of a layer cake. In this view the realm of scientific investigation would be represented in the lower layer. This layer represents the whole realm of materialistic or naturalistic causation or processes. It is subject to scientific observation, investigation and explanation. Discovery in this layer does not subtract from God or his works. . . . In contrast, the top layer represents the work of God. It covers the entire bottom layer because everything that science discovers is another step in understanding how God has worked or continues to work through the material world and its naturalistic processes. In this way, the bottom layer might be identified as the layer of secondary natural causation while the top layer is identified as ultimate divine causation. Science, by current definition, cannot explore the top layer. . . . A believer's faith holds that there is a top layer, even though science cannot explore it" (*Lost World*, 114–15).

65. Approaching christology soteriocentrically allows us to transcend (or perhaps sublate) the old distinction between christology "from above" and christology "from below." A christology from above approaches Christ from the presupposition of his deity by viewing his person in light of the dogma of the trinity. A christology from below approaches Christ from the presupposition of his historical existence as a human being

If, as I argued in the previous chapter, the event of salvation is an apocalypse that occurs in the unconscious praxis of historical existence—that is to say, if salvation occurs in the being-outside-ourselves that takes place in our being-for-others—and if we must understand the agent in light of the actual event of salvation, *then what must we say about Christ and his Spirit as the singular divine agent of this eschatological salvation?* This is the question that concerns us here.

---

by viewing his person in light of his concrete historicity, as accessible to scientific historical research. Wolfhart Pannenberg, the most prominent twentieth-century advocate of christology "from below," differentiates the two approaches as follows: "For Christology that begins 'from above,' from the divinity of Jesus, the concept of the incarnation stands in the center. A Christology 'from below,' rising from the historical man Jesus to the recognition of his divinity, is concerned first of all with Jesus's message and fate and arrives only at the end at the concept of the incarnation" (*Jesus*, 33). Pannenberg places most of the ancient church theologians, along with Karl Barth, Emil Brunner, and Heinrich Vogel, on the side of the "from above." Despite his disagreements with them, he places Luther, Schleiermacher, Ritschl, Herrmann, Gogarten, Ebeling, and Bultmann on the side of the "from below" (ibid., 35–37).

While marginally helpful as a heuristic device, it is clear that this binary opposition is easily misleading. Barth, for example, is a complicated figure. His doctrine of analogy "works strictly from above to below" (McCormack, "Historical-Criticism," 219), thereby ruling out all natural theology. But Barth's christological method in his later dogmatics is hardly a straightforward theology "from above," given that he reconstructs traditional christology on the basis of the life-history of Jesus of Nazareth, leading McCormack and others to speak of Barth's "historicized christology" (McCormack, *Orthodox*, 201–33). Barth's christology is thus "difficult to pin down" and "cannot be classified as 'from above' or 'from below,' Alexandrian or Antiochene, or even as flatly Reformed" (Sumner, *Karl Barth*, 2). Luther, too, is quite a complicated figure. He may have freed himself from the confines of the scholastic tradition, but he hardly builds his way *toward* the doctrine of Christ's deity or incarnation from a starting point in the humanity. He rather reconceives deity to be entirely receptive to human existence, thus redefining divinity in terms of Christ's humanity. Finally, Bultmann's christology overcomes this forced distinction between above and below. While Bultmann begins by focusing on the message of Jesus and certainly does not take Jesus's deity or identification with a metaphysical Logos for granted, he also explicitly denies that we can arrive at the knowledge of Christ's deity by first examining the historical data about Jesus. There is no bridge for Bultmann from below to above. The truth of Jesus's divinity is either known in the moment of faith in response to our encounter with the word of God, or it is not known at all. There is no movement from above to below or from below to above, but rather both are held together in paradoxical identity (see McMaken, "Definitive," 102–5). As the previous chapter, in particular, indicates, the approach taken here is in line with Bultmann.

THE INTERRUPTIVE EVENT:
APOCALYPTIC CHRISTOLOGY

The question animating this constructive christological inquiry was articulated best by Hugh Ross Mackintosh in his 1912 work, *The Doctrine of the Person of Jesus Christ*:

> How must we think of [Christ's] intrinsic nature in the light
> of this new conception of His work? Who is Christ, if He thus
> embodies to sinful men the redeeming grace of the Eternal?
> There is one principle, then, countersigned by history, which is
> fundamental to all profitable debate. It is the principle that our
> thought of what Christ has achieved will fix and delimit that
> which we can know of Himself. As the redemption is, so by
> necessity is the Redeemer.[66]

If the redemption is an apocalyptic event of cocrucifixion, then who is the redeemer? Who is Christ, if he is the interrupting agent of the apocalypse? In order to answer this question, we need to look again at the decisive moment of his death.

The history of theology is a history of theologians shrinking from the idea that "God reveals himself in the very humanity of Jesus as the God who he is."[67] Rather than entertain the notion that Christ reveals God precisely and definitively "in the humiliation and shame of the cross,"[68] the church has looked elsewhere—particularly to a speculative ontology of his person as the Logos, reinforced through myths and legends about his miraculous birth and wondrous deeds, which removes him from history and protects God from the scandal of a criminal's death. The reason for this is not hard to find. "If the word of the cross is true," writes Ingolf Dalferth, "then the moral and religious coordinates of good and evil, God and the world, salvation and perdition—these coordinates by which we steer our lives—are inaccurate. This means that our wisdom is foolishness, our search for meaning is meaningless, our good deeds are well intentioned at best, and our religion is organized unbelief."[69] The pursuit of these other interpretations and descriptions of Christ is an attempt to escape from the annihilating power of the message of the cross. If, however, the event of salvation is the determinative norm of theology, then Christ is not divine by virtue of a metaphysical unity with the divine being that preexists his historical existence, nor is he

66. Mackintosh, *Doctrine*, 325.

67. Gogarten, *Christ*, 4.

68. *LW* 31:54.

69. Dalferth, *Crucified*, 40–41.

the representative human being by virtue of a metaphysical unity with the rest of humankind that subsists prior to his historical acts. Both of these classical options depend on the assumption that divinity and humanity are substances that permanently and timelessly possess certain ontological properties that cannot coexist. But as we have already seen, starting from this assumption leads one into insoluble aporias. In order to fulfill the intention of Chalcedon to articulate how Jesus can accomplish salvation as the one who is both divine and human in a single person, we must set aside all metaphysical presuppositions about the nature of divinity and humanity and reconstruct both in terms of the cross as the eschatological event. We must think "[God's] deity out of his self-determination to become human, and his eternity out of his identity with the crucified Jesus of Nazareth."[70]

Why the cross? For one thing, the New Testament demands it. The Gospel narratives are oriented around the death of Jesus as the decisive event in the story of God's relationship with humanity. Paul tells the Corinthians that "we proclaim Christ crucified" (1 Cor 1:23; 2:2) and that we celebrate the eucharistic meal in order to "proclaim the Lord's death" (1 Cor 11:26). In his letter to the Galatians he writes: "May I never boast of anything except the cross of our Lord Jesus Christ, by which the world has been crucified to me, and I to the world" (Gal 6:14). For the early Christian community "the cross itself is the definitive *apokalypsis* of God."[71] But if we press further to the underlying logic behind this crucicentrism, we realize that it is rooted in the early community's post-Easter realization that this death was the event of salvation. Their Easter encounter with the present reality of Christ forced them to interpret the cross within the soteriological logic that was available to them within the Hellenistic context of Second Temple Judaism. Different communities reached for different images and explanations. Based on the New Testament, the dominant interpretive matrix was the ancient Hebrew practice of sacrificing an animal as a sin offering that bears the guilt of the community before YHWH. While this idea depends on a cultural world-picture that no longer has meaning for us, it reinforces the central point that *soteriology* drives early christology. The Christian community has to make sense of how God was "in Christ"—indeed, in a *crucified* Christ—by virtue of their conviction that the suffering and death of Jesus was salvific, that "in Christ God was reconciling the world to himself" (2 Cor 5:19).

In the previous chapter I reinterpreted the cross-event as an elemental interruption of our existence—a view that remains in contact with the soteriocentrism of the early community but no longer relies upon a sacrificial

70. Jüngel, *God as the Mystery*, 193.
71. Rutledge, *Crucifixion*, 353.

mode of thinking. But *why* is the cross still capable of serving as the apocalyptic event of salvation and thus as the basis for a reconstruction of christology, if we dispense with the ancient mythological framework in which the cross originally made sense? I suggest that, when interpreted historically, the cross serves this purpose because it constitutes the definitive *intersection* of God and the world. For both the earliest Christians trying to make sense of their Easter experience and for those of us today seeking a postmetaphysical christology beyond "the myth of the incarnate Son of God,"[72] the death of Jesus, seen in the light of Easter faith, is the event in which the divine is decisively revealed as human. The crucifixion of Jesus, in other words, is *the site where the kerygmatic Christ and the historical Jesus coincide.* Prior to his death, Jesus was an apocalyptic prophet of the coming reign of God. His death was not the arrival of the apocalypse but merely the tragic loss of a great teacher. After "faith came" at Easter (Gal 3:23), however, he was recognized by his followers as the Messiah who brought the kingdom into history through his self-offering upon the cross. Faith confesses that the event of his death is therefore the turning-point of history.

This confession has two crucial theological implications. First, any quest for a so-called "historical Jesus" behind the kerygma of his death and resurrection is a quest for a different Jesus than the one who is the subject of the apocalypse. We either have the Jesus of history in and through the eschatological Christ of the kerygma, or we do not have him at all. The research on Jesus as a prophet of the imminent apocalypse is possible and meaningful only when carried out retrospectively from the revelation that the proclaimer of the apocalypse became and is the apocalypse himself. His prophetic office, so to speak, is a function of his kingly and priestly offices. He proclaims the new creation only as the one who actualizes it in his cruciform descent into the horror of the "present evil age" (Gal 1:4). Second, any quest for a metaphysical deity perfect and self-sufficient apart from the historical occurrence of this man's death is a quest for a different god than the one who is the subject of the apocalypse. We either have God in and through the eschatological death of Jesus as the apocalypse of salvation, or we do not have God at all: "In the death of Jesus God has *identified* Godself with this one. God is identical with this dead person, with the crucified one."[73] As the inbreaking of the eschaton, the suffering of the cross is the "event of the nearness of God to history," the site where God is uniquely

72. Fuchs, "Jesus Christus," 39.
73. Jüngel, "Der Tod," 348.

and definitively *present*.[74] For this reason, "Christian theology is therefore essentially *theologia crucifixi*."[75]

There is, however, a significant complication. As we explored in the previous chapter, the cross is also where God is uniquely and definitively *absent*. The death of Jesus is a *death in God-abandonment*: "My God, my God, why have you forsaken me?" It is precisely the forsakenness of this death that marks it as the eschatological event. In this death Jesus hands himself over to the principalities and powers of this world on behalf of the world. He lives in that moment wholly outside of himself, and so wholly in and from the future. Only in this way is his death the apocalyptic judgment of God in which we are able to participate through our cocrucifixion in faith. If this death is indeed the ontological location of God's being, then we can say with Dietrich Bonhoeffer, that, to put it mythically, "God consents to be pushed out of the world and onto the cross; God is weak and powerless in the world and in precisely this way, and only so, is at our side and helps us."[76] And if we take Jesus's cry of dereliction with any seriousness, we must acknowledge that God is even pushed out of the cross as well. This absence, however, does not contradict but rather confirms God's presence in the crucified Jesus.[77]

The binary opposition between presence and absence is, according to Eberhard Jüngel, a legacy of metaphysical thinking. The tradition of metaphysics conceives of God as an absolutely necessary being (*ens necessarium*), the existence of which is required to make sense of the world and ourselves. Jüngel calls this "hermeneutical necessity" in that "God is necessary in order to understand the world as world."[78] According to medieval scholasticism, the world needs the idea of God as the unmoved mover in order to make sense of its existence, and according to Descartes, the ego needs God in or-

74. Jüngel, *Paulus und Jesus*, 289.

75. Jüngel, "Das Sein," 278.

76. Bonhoeffer, *Letters and Papers*, 479. I say "mythically," because the idea of God being pushed around suggests that God is a being like other creatures in the world, who can be moved from one location to another. That is a classic mark of mythical thinking. Bonhoeffer does not mean the statement literally, of course. He is instead suggesting that God's identification with the crucified one actually affirms and grounds the *secularity* of the world. The fact that God is the crucified God means that the world is free to live "even if there were no God" (*etsi Deus non daretur*). See Jüngel, "Säkularisierung," 288–89.

77. The words of Jürgen Moltmann are worth repeating here: "The cross is the really irreligious thing in Christian faith. It is the suffering of God in Christ, rejected and killed in the absence of God, which qualifies Christian faith as faith, and as something different from the projection of man's desire. The modern criticism of religion can attack the whole world of religious Christianity, but not this unreligious cross" (*Crucified God*, 37).

78. Jüngel, *God as the Mystery*, 30.

der to establish the certainty of its knowledge. A necessary being, however, is pure actuality (*actus purus*). Possibility is a characteristic of the contingent world that depends on a supreme being as its ontological ground. If God is hermeneutically necessary, then it is metaphysically impossible for God to be absent without undermining God's being, and thereby also undermining our capacity to understand the world. This metaphysical starting point requires that we explain away the scandal of the cross by subsuming it within a speculative account of God's ontological presence. Metaphysical thinking cannot permit the possibility of divine revelation occurring in Jesus's death in God-abandonment, and thus it precludes God's self-identification with the abandoned of the world, with those forced to exist outside the city and outside themselves.

With Luther and Bonhoeffer, Jüngel rethinks God beyond the polarity between absence and presence.[79] If God is to be understood in the crucified one, then God's being "can no longer be sought in the alternative of *present* or *absent*."[80] The place where God is most radically absent—namely, the cross—is paradoxically the place where God is most radically present. God is present to Jesus precisely in the moment he experiences the depths of divine abandonment.[81] In his sermons during the Second World War, Helmut Thielicke reflects on the fact that "the cross was God's greatest silence." In Jesus's cry of abandonment, "God had nothing to say." And yet, "the very hour when God answered not a word or syllable was the hour of the great turning point when the veil of the temple was rent and God's heart was laid bare with all its wounds. . . . In [God's] silence, [God] experienced

79. Jüngel is here following a path charted over a decade earlier by Gerhard Ebeling in 1965. Contrary to those who read Luther's distinction between the revealed God (*Deus revelatus*) and the hidden God (*Deus absconditus*) as a separation between two sides of God—a being-for-us in Christ and a mysterious, inaccessible being-in-Godself, from which comes God's inscrutable decisions of providence and election—Ebeling interprets this distinction to mean that God is "not only the present but also the absent God." The *Deus revelatus* and *Deus absconditus* refer to two different experiences of God. The "living God" is at the same time the "dead God"; God's "omnipotence" is at the same time "powerlessness"; God's presence is at the same time God's absence (Ebeling, "Existenz," 282). Ebeling creatively distinguishes between God's *absentia* (*ab-esse*, to be away from), *adsentia* (*ad-esse*, to be towards), and *praesentia* (*prae-esse*, to be before): "The being of God as *absentia* and—if I may put it this way—*adsentia* is, in any case, *praesentia*. Absence and presence lie next to each other as dialectical qualifiers" (ibid., 284). God is *present* as both *absent* and *adsent*.

80. Jüngel, *God as the Mystery*, 54. Cf. ibid., 62: "The being of God is in fact to be thought of as a being which explodes the alternative of presence and absence."

81. If the word of God is, as Paul says, the "word of the cross" (1 Cor 1:18, my translation), then it follows that "God is *present as the one absent* in the word" (ibid., 166).

the fellowship of death and the depths with us."[82] Like Elijah, who heard YHWH in the "sound of sheer silence" (1 Kgs 19:12), we hear God's word of revelation most profoundly in the deafening silence of God at Golgotha. We encounter God in the very lack of encounter. "The Cross is . . . the place of inexperience," writes Jean-Yves Lacoste, and the highest inexperience of God coincides with "the highest knowledge," since "God can be closest to us . . . even though the senses know him only as an absence."[83] The cross reveals that God is not known through conscious experience but through the mystery of unconscious inexperience. If Jesus's death in God-abandonment is the self-determining revelation of God, then this singular event becomes the hermeneutical norm for understanding God's relation to the world more generally. "God is present as the one who is absent in the world," according to Jüngel.[84] In fact, "God is *only* present as the one who is absent, just as the resurrected Christ is *only* among us as the crucified one."[85] What holds true ontologically is also true existentially. In correspondence to the cross of Christ, "God's presence can only be experienced simultaneously with his absence."[86] God is near to us as the one who is other than us, revealed to

---

82. Thielicke, *Silence of God*, 14.

83. Lacoste, *Experience*, 191, 142.

84. Jüngel, *God as the Mystery*, 62. In the words of Bonhoeffer: "The same God who is with us is the God who forsakes us (Mark 15:34!)" (Bonhoeffer, *Letters and Papers*, 478–79).

85. Jüngel, "Anfechtung," 113; emphasis mine. While his position is in continuity with the tradition (e.g., 1 Cor 13:12), we must raise a question at this point regarding Jüngel's claim that this dialectic of absence and presence will cease with the eschaton. The parousia, he says, marks "the end of his indirectness, according to which God is only present as the one who is absent (e.g., in word and sacrament)" (Jüngel, "Der Geist," 315). The suggestion that God's presence-in-absence will become full and direct presence implies that, in the *Endzeit*, the eschatological Christ is no longer the crucified one—that his presence among us as the crucified Christ is confined to (perhaps a concession to) our historical existence. This divide between history and eschatology mirrors the divide between the economic and immanent trinity and is no less problematic. Jüngel's theology elsewhere suggests an alternative approach. As we have already seen in the previous chapter, his theses on the Holy Spirit provide the resources for arguing that the nonoccurrence of the parousia is the fulfillment of the parousia itself, because the purpose of eschatological expectation is the *unsettling* of the believer. If that is the case, then any account of the parousia in which this paradoxical indirectness ceases would contradict the interruptive word of the gospel. For this reason, a future parousia—if we wish to retain such an idea—can only be a *new form* of Christ's indirect presence, not its cessation.

86. Jüngel, *God as the Mystery*, 104. Cf. ibid., 55: "Faith cannot speak of God's presence without conceiving at the same time of God's absence, just as it has never been certain of God's presence without experiencing his hiddenness."

us as the one who is hidden from us. *God is most truly with us in the very moment in which we are without God.*

The paradoxical nature of the cross as the event of God's presence-in-absence is what identifies it as the norm of salvation. God's presence in an executed criminal is a scandalous interruption of our worldly assumptions about both deity and humanity. God's hiddenness in this same death ensures that we have no easy escape from this scandal, that our embarrassment is not coincidental but persistent, that the existential interruption is not accidental but essential to the reality of salvation. God does not will to encounter us without interrupting us, without placing us outside of ourselves.

> God does not come near to us without moving us out of our self-realized nearness to ourselves: "he puts us outside of ourselves" (*ponit nos extra nos*). God is only present to the ego which has been moved outside of itself. . . . God with me is removed from me for the very reason that he comes nearer to me and is nearer to me than I am able to come near to myself. That very thing which *is closest* to me is that which is radically removed from me. It can be experienced only in the ecstatic structure of this "we being outside ourselves" (*nos extra nos esse*). . . . Without a fundamental *extra nos* ("outside ourselves") faith knows of no *deus pro nobis* ("God for us") and certainly no *deus in nobis* ("God in us"). God is only *near* to us in that he distances us from ourselves.[87]

God's presence in the crucified Christ reveals that God is only present to us when we are no longer present to ourselves. The resurrection of the crucified Christ confirms this revelation, since the resurrection is not the *cancellation* of death but rather the ultimate *identification* of God with the dead Jesus. "The resurrection of Jesus from the dead," according to Jüngel, "means that God has identified himself with this dead man. . . . The kerygma of the Resurrected One proclaims the Crucified One as the self-definition of God."[88] The resurrection takes death up into the very life of God. Rather than giving assurance of some escape from or end to the offense of the cross, the resurrection instead *intensifies* the offense by eternalizing it. The resurrection guarantees that wherever and whenever we encounter God, we will always encounter the event of God's own self-distancing in death, which distances us from ourselves and so crucifies us with Christ.

Returning now to our main theme, if Christ is the agent defined by this apocalyptic work of salvation, then *Christ is the event of God's*

87. Ibid., 182–83.
88. Ibid., 363–64.

presence-in-absence. He is in himself simultaneously the interrupting God and the interrupted human person. The one who finds herself *without God* simultaneously finds herself *with Christ.* In his theses on christology from 1969–70, Jüngel says that "the being of Jesus Christ is to be thought as the eschatological unity of God's eternity and Jesus's past, so that the presence of Jesus Christ and the absence of Jesus Christ should be conceived in the unity of the same being."[89] If this is the case, then we can neither quest for a historical Jesus behind his present paradoxicality nor hope for a glorified Christ beyond his paradoxicality. The parousia could no more mark the end of his indirectness and absence than it could mark the end of his humanity. It also means that trying to puzzle out how deity and humanity can coincide in a single person is a false metaphysical dilemma. We cannot speak about deity and humanity as if they are substances or natures that preexist the Christ-event. Christ's deity and humanity are revealed in the singular event of the apocalypse. And thus deity simply *is* his humanity in its eschatologically interruptive mode of existence, and his humanity is only accessible to us in this mode. The deity of Jesus is the *existential meaningfulness* of his humanity, the significance of his singular history. He is divine in the sense that his historical existence has been taken up into eschatological unity with the eternity of God, so that whenever and wherever we encounter the reality of God we simultaneously encounter the history of Jesus. The apocalypse of salvation thus reveals "that Jesus is the Son of God precisely *in* his humanity—not apart from his humanity!—and that the Son of God is the human Jesus precisely *in* the operation of his divine essence—and not in suspension of it! From this there follows a stringent theological prohibition against thinking of Jesus's humanity and Jesus's divinity as quantities which somehow supplement each other."[90] Jesus is divine *as human* and he is human *as divine.* He is the interruption of the world as the one put to death on a cross. In this way we have demythologized and historicized the Chalcedonian Definition—and thereby preserved its true judgments without its objectifying conceptuality.

Naturally, the question remains: how does Christ interrupt the *world* if he is a singular historical event? How does the crucified prophet of the apocalypse interrupt *me*? This question is of basic importance for christology, given our soteriocentric starting point, which compels us to say that Christ's person is not only meaningful *for* our histories but is actually constituted in the encounter *with* our histories. In order to address this issue,

89. Jüngel, "Thesen," 277.
90. Jüngel, "Dogmatic Significance," 115.

and thereby to understand how Jesus of Nazareth becomes the savior of all people, we must turn our attention to his *Spirit*.

THE INTERRUPTIVE AGENT: APOCALYPTIC PNEUMATOLOGY

Theologians have traditionally sought to understand the connection between Jesus and all other human beings through an account of the incarnation as the assumption of human nature. In our soteriocentric reconstruction of christology and pneumatology, the Spirit accomplishes the work ascribed dogmatically to the "assumption of flesh" (*assumptio carnis*). To understand why that is the case we will look at the dispute between Karl Barth and Rudolf Bultmann over Christ and Adam.

Assumptio and *Anhypostasis:* The Question of Being-in-Christ

What is the relation between Jesus Christ and the rest of humankind? In his later dogmatic theology, Barth answered this question with a new doctrine of election in which Jesus Christ is the elect one in whom all other human beings are elect. "It cannot be questioned that the election of God does concern all men, and that in it the will of God is determined concerning all men."[91] But individual human beings, he argues, are not elected *as individuals* but only *in* Christ, which means "in his person, in his will, in his own divine choice, in the basic decision of God which he fulfills over against every man. . . . In that he (as God) wills himself (as man), he also wills them."[92] By 1939 (at the latest)—the year he started lecturing on the doctrine of election—Barth had committed himself to a certain understanding of the Christ-world relationship, one that involved a robust ontological realism. All human beings are truly and ontologically *in* the person of Jesus. They are not in Christ in the sense that they *will* be in him once they respond to the gospel but are only in him now in the sense that God *wants* them to respond. That is the position of traditional Western orthodoxy. For Barth, by contrast, what occurs in Christ is the *actuality* of reconciliation and not merely the possibility. Each person is really reconciled to God in Christ apart from any individual response.

After developing his doctrine of election, which was published in 1942, Barth turned to the doctrine of creation. In *CD* 3.2, he addressed the

91. *CD* 2.2:43.
92. *CD* 2.2:117.

issue of anthropology, and in the course of writing those materials he developed an extended exegesis of Romans 5 as part of a section titled "The Human Person and Humanity." This material was eventually cut from the final manuscript, which was published in 1948, but he published it several years later in 1952 under the title, *Christus und Adam nach Röm. 5* (Christ and Adam according to Romans 5) in conjunction with the publication of his essay on Bultmann, *Rudolf Bultmann: Ein Versuch, ihn zu verstehen* (Rudolf Bultmann: An Attempt to Understand Him). As he said later, he thought that, given the polemical nature of the Bultmann essay, the *Christ and Adam* piece would "supplement and clarify" his views.[93]

Much of *Christ and Adam* repeats material from *CD* 2.2, but it does so in a way that highlights the issue of our being-in-Christ. The point is made early and often. In the opening, before he turns to the exegesis itself, he writes:

> [Jesus Christ] reconciles [the multitude of other people] with God through His death. That means that in His own death He makes their peace with God—before they themselves have decided for this peace and quite apart from that decision. In believing, they are only conforming to the decision about them that has already been made in Him. . . . He is an individual in such a way that others are not only beside Him and along with Him, but . . . they are also and first of all *in* Him.[94]

Barth calls this "the *special* anthropology of Jesus Christ," which refers to the claim that Christ is for all people and all people are in Christ. This is "the *norm* of *all* anthropology."[95] The rest of the essay simply repeats this point from various angles. According to his reading of Romans 5:12–21, "the fact of Christ is here presented as something that dominates and includes all men. The nature of Christ objectively conditions human nature and the work of Christ makes an objective difference to the life and destiny of all men."[96] Barth uses the language of objectivity to emphasize the actuality of reconciliation in Christ as opposed to the mere possibility, and it is a key theme of his debate with Bultmann.

Barth and Bultmann engaged in a vigorous correspondence in 1952 over Barth's polemical essay on understanding Bultmann. But Bultmann did not respond to *Christ and Adam* until 1959, when he wrote a response under the title, "Adam und Christus nach Römer 5." We need not examine

93. Barth, *Zwei theologische Studien*, 5.
94. Barth, *Christ and Adam*, 24–25.
95. Ibid., 26.
96. Ibid., 88.

the details of the dispute. Bultmann basically charges Barth with failing to read Romans 5:12–21 in the context of the epistle as a whole, which means that Barth asks the text to comment on matters foreign to Paul's line of inquiry. "While Paul contrasts two modes of human existence [i.e., Adamic humanity and Christian humanity], Barth questions the text concerning the essence of man as such."[97] But even if it were legitimate to ask Romans 5 to shed light on the essence or nature of humanity, Bultmann argues, we still could not conclude that Christ is the true prototype of Adam, since Paul says the exact opposite and everywhere identifies Adam as the first and Christ as the second as part of his understanding of salvation history. Bultmann claims that when Barth says "what is *Christian* is secretly but fundamentally identical with what is *universally human*,"[98] what is really meant is that "human existence received its essence only as Christian existence, i.e., by faith in the grace of God which has revealed itself in Christ."[99] In other words, Christian existence (or life in Christ) is what it means to be genuinely human. That is the truth in Barth's interpretation. But why this must mean that Adamic humanity is already *ontologically* in Christ, so that every sinful person invisibly participates in and reflects the true humanity of Christ, is something Bultmann finds "incomprehensible" as an interpretation of Romans 5.[100]

To be sure, Barth has drawn conclusions not strictly warranted by the text itself. He posits these same ideas elsewhere without any recourse to Romans, so any impression he gives of simply exegeting the text is a misleading one. Bultmann, of course, has his own presuppositions like every exegete, and this becomes especially clear when it comes to the matter of universal salvation:

> According to logical consequence all men after Christ should receive life. Of course Paul does not mean that; instead all men now face the decision whether they wish to belong to "those who have received," provided that the word of proclamation has already reached them. While Adam, then, brought death to all men after him without a possibility of escape, Christ brought for all the possibility (of life).[101]

Bultmann has various reasons for rejecting Barth's universalist reading of the Adam-Christ parallel. Like traditional evangelicals, Bultmann appeals

97. Bultmann, "Adam and Christ," 163.
98. Barth, *Christ and Adam*, 89.
99. Bultmann, "Adam and Christ," 164.
100. Ibid., 165.
101. Ibid., 158.

to other Pauline passages that emphasize the necessity of faith in Christ; unlike evangelicals, he also appeals to his historical-critical thesis that the Adam-Christ parallel, understood as a division between two different humanities, "is a gnostic idea" that Paul is borrowing to make his point.[102]

But the fundamental presupposition is a theological one. Bultmann approaches the question of salvation from the conviction that salvation involves the faithful response of the individual—there is nothing "behind" that existential decision. Barth approaches the question of salvation from the conviction that divine grace is sovereign and unilateral—grace raises to life an otherwise dead sinner. In short, Bultmann sees salvation in light of the *sola fide*; Barth sees it in light of the *sola gratia*. Where the relation between Adam and Christ is concerned, this means that Bultmann thematizes the existential transition from Adamic existence to Christian existence, from law to gospel. The new presupposes the old in the sense that there can be no new existence without a prior old existence.[103] Barth, on the other hand, thematizes the sovereignty and superiority of divine grace, which does not depend on some creaturely factor to actualize or complete it. He therefore posits the soteriological and ontological priority of Christ over Adam, gospel over law.

In the soteriological position that I have already outlined, I have attempted to overcome this apparent opposition by stressing both the *priority* of grace and the *existential context* of salvation. The two positions are not necessarily opposed but merely examine the same christological reality from two different vantage points. Jüngel comes to the same conclusion in his response to the dispute between Barth and Bultmann over Romans 5. While Barth's soteriological perspective correctly understands that the eschatological grace of God is dependent on nothing and no one, nevertheless "the connection to humanity opened up by Christ remains dependent on Adam, because the new history determined by the future needs a corresponding history terminated by it in order to come to expression in a theologically

---

102. Ibid., 154.

103. It is important to emphasize that Bultmann does *not* think we have epistemological access to Adamic existence (i.e., the law) prior to faith in Christ. Bultmann differentiates between the phenomenological and the theological: phenomenologically it is the case that there must be a sinner prior to the gift of faith; theologically, however, he argues that we only know our prior sinful existence from the position of faith because our sinfulness is a matter of revelation that can only be disclosed to us by God. For Bultmann, therefore, gospel precedes law at the level of theological truth, but law precedes gospel at the level of human experience. For more on this, see Congdon, *Mission*, 1.2.2.3.

appropriate way. The old is therefore soteriologically dependent on the new, but the new is theologically dependent on the old."[104]

This debate in itself is not the issue here. What interests me about the Barth-Bultmann dispute is the way it shapes their respective christologies. Each approaches the question of Christ's humanity in light of a distinctive soteriological logic, which I have identified with the reformational particles *sola gratia* and *sola fide*. In *Church Dogmatics* 4.2, Barth explains his *sola gratia* logic, which leads him to take up the patristic anhypostatic-enhypostatic christology, with its concept of the assumption of flesh (*assumptio carnis*), in a robust fashion. He says there that the "divine act" of reconciliation has a specific "*object*," namely, the creaturely reality that "is assumed into unity with the Son of God and his own being. This is the *human being* [*menschliche Sein*] on which he had mercy and which he therefore adopted from all eternity and then in time."[105] He goes on to say he could also describe this object as a "human '*nature*,' like the older dogmatics."[106] While what resulted in the incarnation was *a* human being, Jesus of Nazareth, what was actually assumed was the totality of humanity as such:

> What God the Son assumed into unity with himself and his divine being was and is—in a specific individual form elected and prepared by him—not merely "a human being" but the *humanum* [*Menschliche*], the being and essence, the kind and nature, which is that of all human beings, which characterizes them all as human beings, and differentiates them from other creatures. . . . [I]n this form it is the human in all human beings: the concrete *possibility* of the existence of a human being which will be *like* the *concrete* possibility of the existence of *all* human beings, in the actualization of which he will be our brother like ourselves. . . . [Christ's] existence as a human existence, as this one human being, directly concerns *all* other human beings, and in all the singularity in which it is an event in Jesus Christ his incarnation signifies the promise of the basic alteration and determination of what we *all* are as human beings. In Jesus Christ it is not merely one human being, but in fact the *humanum* of *all* human beings, which is posited and exalted as such to unity with God. . . . At this point we have reached what the older dogmatics—using the language of later Greek philosophy—described with the

104. Jüngel, "Das Gesetz," 168.
105. *CD* 4.2:47; *KD* 4.2:50, rev.
106. *CD* 4.2:47; *KD* 4.2:50, rev.

concept of *anhypostasis*, the *impersonalitas* of the human nature of Jesus Christ.[107]

Barth is able to speak in this passage of a universal human nature (or being or essence) that belongs to all individual human beings. He identifies the *Menschliche* or *humanum* as the general essence of all human beings, the genus within which each actual person is a species. In doing so he borrows Aristotle's distinction between primary and secondary substance.[108] Moreover, Barth describes this secondary substance as the general *potentiality* of human existence that is actualized in particular human beings, thus adopting Aristotle's distinction between potentiality (δύναμις) and actuality (ενέργεια/ἐντελέχεια).[109] This makes sense, given that the category of substance provides the continuity between actuality and potentiality. God the Son thus assumes in the incarnation the secondary substance of humanity ("the *humanum* of *all* human beings"), which is the potentiality for each and every human person to exist in his or her concrete actuality. By assuming this essence, and so reconciling all humanity in potentiality, Christ transforms each actualization of this potentiality. All human individuals are thus reconciled in truth at the level of secondary substance, while each person, each primary substance, must come to acknowledge their reconciled state in faith.[110]

---

107. *CD* 4.2:48–49; *KD* 4.2:51–52, rev.

108. *Categories* 2a11–19; see Aristotle, *Complete Works*. See van Driel, *Incarnation Anyway*, 107. Robert Jenson argues that Barth "retain[s] the general structure of classical theology but put[s] the historical event of Jesus' existence in the place formerly occupied by changeless 'Being'" (*Alpha*, 140). This leads to a dangerous separation in Barth between "God's eternal history and temporal history including the history of Jesus of Nazareth" (ibid., 162). Colin Gunton adds that "Barth appears to be not quite interested enough in the human story. I mean he is interested in it but I think he tries to say that he is mainly interested in divine terms more than he is in human terms. Unless you spell out the humanity a bit more strongly then I think you are in danger of treating Christ as a sort of timeless Platonic principle in—time. This is excusable, I mean much better this than all of this proving Jesus by messing around in history. . . . The way you do it, as I am always saying, is by a strong doctrine of the Spirit" (*Barth Lectures*, 199–200). A strong doctrine of the Spirit is precisely the answer proposed here.

109. *Metaphysics*, 9.

110. Because the general *humanum* exists in God's eternal being by way of election in distinction from the human beings who exist in history, I also refer to these two human substances as "primary humanity" (the universal human essence in eternity) and "secondary humanity" (individual human existence), drawing on Barth's distinction between God's primary and secondary objectivity (Congdon, *Mission*, 205–6). But this can be confusing, since the use of "primary" and "secondary" here is the opposite of Aristotle. Regarding primary and secondary objectivity, see *CD* 2.1:16: "As He certainly knows Himself first of all, God is first and foremost objective to Himself. We shall return to this point in the second part of the present section. In His triune life as such,

The key to Barth's position, as he says, is the concept of *anhypostasis*, the notion that the human nature of Christ is "impersonal" on its own and only becomes personal (i.e., *enhypostasis*) in its assumption into unity with the Logos. The anhypostatic-enhypostatic christology historically served to oppose views that the church deemed to be erroneous, such as adoptionism. "The second person of the trinity did not assume an already existing individual person, but rather assumed human nature," a nature that has no independent status but exists entirely in dependence on the Son of God. The humanity of Christ is "only an abstract, universal concept of humankind, . . . only the idea of humanity, not a human person."[111] But this means these terms are rooted in certain metaphysical presuppositions, the very ones we interrogated above in the analysis of Chalcedon.

Barth claims to have "actualized" that schema and translated it into a historical conceptuality.[112] While it is true he does use new language—as a modern European theologian must by necessity—he retains the same basic logic. The central feature of this logic, the piece that holds Barth's entire position together, is the notion that there is some secondary substance, called "human nature," in which each person ontologically participates as a primary substance, so that what God does with respect to this secondary substance has actual implications for each person's relation to God. This substance ontology is implied in Barth's doctrine of election in the sense that God elects the general human nature of Christ, in whom all particular human beings are elect by virtue of their participation in Christ's nature. It is this participation of the primary in the secondary that Barth takes for granted. He assumes it is meaningful to speak about God acting on us by acting upon a general abstraction, as if the idea of a universal *humanum* bears some kind of intrinsically significant relation to the individual person within history. But just because one can speak notionally about all humanity does not mean that "humanity as such" is somehow a real object in itself that can be acted upon. The fact that each human being shares the same basic genetic code does not then mean there is some supratemporal form of this code existing "out there," which then makes possible the actualization of this code in particular persons. Any attempt to abstract in this way from the

---

objectivity, and with it knowledge, is divine reality before creaturely objectivity and knowledge exist. We call this the primary objectivity of God, and distinguish from it the secondary, i.e., the objectivity which He has for us too in His revelation, in which He gives Himself to be known by us as He knows Himself. It is distinguished from the primary objectivity, not by a lesser degree of truth, but by its particular form suitable for us, the creature."

111. Ebeling, *Dogmatik*, 3:70.

112. *CD* 4.2:105. See Sumner, *Karl Barth*, 128–40.

concrete situation of human existence leads to a thoroughly metaphysical position, as we have defined it, in the sense that the object of such discourse is general and ahistorical, not connected to the actual historicity of each person. For this reason, a hermeneutical reconstruction of our participation in Christ will have to historicize the doctrine of *anhypostasis* in a radical way.

Bultmann offers the initial resources for this hermeneutical reconstruction. As we have seen already, Bultmann's critical-historical analysis of early Christian christology leads him to the conclusion that, in the kerygma, the proclaimer has become the proclaimed, that is, the prophet of God's eschatological reign has himself become the eschatological event. What this means is that the believer is no longer permitted to search behind the kerygma for a purportedly prekerygmatic Jesus of history. Even if one could do so, there would be no neutral way to guarantee that this man is identical with the Christ who encounters us in the kerygma; one can identify the two only retrospectively from the position of faith. Bultmann explains this by saying that faith is only concerned with the *Dass* or the "that" of Jesus, not the *Was* or the "what." The distinction appears as early as 1925, where he says, with regard to the Gospel of John, that "the author is interested only in the *that* of the revelation, not in the *what*."[113] And in his 1930 lecture on NT christology, he says: "Not the what but rather the that of [Jesus'] proclamation is the decisive thing."[114] This distinction between the "what" and the "that" is a historical version of Bonhoeffer's distinction between the "what" and the "who." The "what" for Bonhoeffer refers to the dogmatic categories that attempt to explain Christ's person, whereas the "what" for Bultmann refers to the historical details that are the object of scientific inquiry (i.e., the quests for Jesus). In both cases, the "who" and the "that" refer to Christ in his saving significance as the one who is crucified and raised. Faith is concerned with Jesus as savior and lord, as the agent of the eschatological event.

Gerhard Ebeling sees in this distinction between the *Was* and the *Dass* a postmetaphysical appropriation of the *anhypostasis* doctrine. By denying that God assumes a specific human being, the concept of *anhypostasis* prevents the isolation of Jesus's human attributes and actions from his divine or saving identity (i.e., from his *person*). And this is precisely what Bultmann is doing with his emphasis on the "that" of Jesus. According to Ebeling, therefore, Bultmann's "concentration on the pure That corresponds structurally . . . to the orthodox doctrine of anhypostasis, except of course that it has its place in a different field of interpretation, in historical (*geschichtlich*) rather

---

113. Bultmann, *Exegetica*, 103.
114. *GuV*, 1:265. Cf. Bultmann, *Das Verhältnis*, 9.

than metaphysical thought."[115] The orthodox doctrine is metaphysical because it ascribes the *anhypostasis* to the properties of the human nature or
substance, whereas Bultmann ascribes the doctrine to the historical event
itself. In both cases the *anhypostasis* means the humanity of Christ is inseparable from his divinity; it does not have a "personality" of its own. In more
Bultmannian terms, Jesus's historicity is inseparable from his work as the
revealer. Classical orthodoxy achieves this "by setting the divine person in
the place which would otherwise be occupied . . . by a purely human person.
Bultmann does it by setting God's action in the place which would otherwise be occupied, historically speaking, by the appearance of human action
in its What and How."[116] Both christologies see Jesus entirely in terms of his
character as the revelation of God, but the nature of this revelation is dramatically different in each case. Since the *anhypostasis* belongs to the human
nature in orthodoxy, the act of the *unio* that makes this nature enhypostatic
in the Logos gives the human properties a share in the divine attributes;
Jesus becomes, among other things, omniscient and omnipotent. For Bultmann, by contrast, "the *unio* does not occur on the level of the natures, but
on the level of the historical (*im Geschichtlichen*)." As a result, the revelation
that comes into history through him does not appear in his *what* or *how*
but in the pure *that*, in the event of his "witness to the saving event which
completely eludes examination. . . . For only through the Word can God be
related to history. The act of God can only appear in history as kerygma."[117]

We can start to see in Ebeling's interpretation of Bultmann the contours of a potentially postmetaphysical response to Barth. Ebeling's examination of the *anhypostasis* in Bultmann focuses on the divine aspect of the
Christ-event, but we are interested here in the *human* aspect, in the relation
between this Christ and the rest of humankind. If, however, the act of God
"can only appear in history as kerygma," then it follows that this act of God
cannot relate to all human beings apart from the historical site in which the
kerygma addresses particular persons in their concrete historicity.

We thus return, by way of a circuitous route through twentieth-century theology, to our thesis that the saving event is an existential apocalypse. The apocalypse of salvation is the existential dislocation that places
us outside ourselves and into the hands of God. To be saved is to live an
eccentric existence on behalf of others, in utter dependence upon God,
and in this way to share in Christ's death. Salvation, as the apostle Paul
would say, is our being-in-Christ, and our being-in-Christ takes place in

115. Ebeling, *Theology*, 118.
116. Ibid., 119–20.
117. Ibid., 120.

our being-outside-ourselves. If we are then going to understand Christ as universally inclusive of humankind, it cannot be through a metaphysical abstraction from the eschatological encounter between a person and the kerygma. Christ's universality will have to be understood *in* and *through* the apocalyptic event. And this means our hermeneutical reconstruction of christology will have to be, at the same time, the reconstruction of pneumatology. As Ebeling states in his *Dogmatik*, "being in Christ is a being in the Spirit."[118]

The Repetition of the Cross: *Fides Directa*

The Spirit of God is, according to the New Testament, the Spirit of *Christ*. This is the consistent witness of the NT from its earliest to its latest documents. Paul, for instance, speaks of "the Spirit of life in Christ Jesus" (Rom 8:2; cf. Phil 1:19) and says that "anyone who does not have the Spirit of Christ does not belong to him" (Rom 8:9). In the letter to the Galatians, he says that "God has sent the Spirit of his Son into our hearts" (Gal 4:6). To share in the Spirit, in other words, is to participate in Christ. It even seems that the risen Christ and the Spirit are essentially identical within the context of the early Christian community. While the earliest Christians confessed that "Jesus is Lord" (1 Cor 12:3; Rom 10:9), Paul could also declare that "the Lord is the Spirit" (2 Cor 3:17). The Gospels reinforce the unity of Jesus and the Spirit. Each account narrates the Spirit's descent at Jesus's baptism (Mark 1:10; Matt 3:16; Luke 3:22; John 1:32–33), followed in the Synoptics by the Spirit propelling him into the wilderness (Mark 1:12; Matt 4:1; Luke 4:1). Whereas Mark is satisfied with Jesus receiving the Spirit in his baptism, Matthew and Luke add a mythical prologue regarding his birth from the Spirit as a way of proclaiming the truth that Jesus is Spirit-empowered from the beginning.[119]

The paradoxical unity, even identity, between the Spirit and Christ is most clearly pronounced in the Johannine texts. In his encounter with

---

118. Ebeling, *Dogmatik*, 3:63.

119. The Gospel of Luke narrates a pneumatological promiscuity unlike anything else in the NT. The Spirit comes upon Mary, fills Elizabeth, fills Zechariah, rests on and guides Simeon, before finally descending upon Jesus. Whereas the other Synoptics say that Jesus was led by the Spirit into the wilderness, Luke reinforces it to the point of redundancy: "Jesus, full of the Holy Spirit, returned from the Jordan and was led by the Spirit in the wilderness" (Luke 4:1). And shortly afterwards we read: "Then Jesus, filled with the power of the Spirit, returned to Galilee" (Luke 4:14). Such phrases are evidence of later composition, driven by the community's growing need to emphasize the uniqueness of the person of Jesus in the face of competing religious claims and the failed expectation of the parousia.

Nicodemus, Jesus declares cryptically that "what is born of the flesh is flesh, and what is born of the Spirit is Spirit" (John 3:6, my translation).[120] Based on the Synoptics we would have to say that Jesus is the one who is uniquely born of the Spirit. The Gospel of John has its own way of connecting Jesus and the Spirit. When Nicodemus asks, "How can these things be?" (John 3:9), Jesus answers by telling him about the "Son of Man" who has "descended from heaven" and who must be "lifted up" (John 3:13–14). John adds later that the one "whom God has sent . . . gives the Spirit without measure" (John 3:34), so to believe in Jesus *is* to be born of the Spirit.[121] In fact, we learn that "as yet there was no Spirit [οὔπω γὰρ ἦν πνεῦμα], because Jesus was not yet glorified" (John 7:39), a statement that more ideologically conservative translations modify to say that "as yet the Spirit had not been given." But we must not soften the close Johannine association of the Spirit with the glorified Christ. As Bultmann provocatively but accurately states, *"the Paraclete therefore is a parallel figure to Jesus himself."* He further supports this claim with reference to the Evangelist's description of the Spirit as "another Advocate [ἄλλον παράκλητον]" in John 14:16, which shows that the same term applies to both Jesus and the Spirit.[122] Later in the text Jesus tells the disciples that he will send the "Advocate," the Holy Spirit, who "will testify on my behalf" (John 15:26; cf. John 14:26), and this Advocate will not come unless Jesus goes away (John 16:7).[123] The Spirit "will not speak on his own, but will speak whatever he hears" (John 16:13). Jesus even "breathes" the Spirit upon his disciples, which is John's remarkable way of describing how the Spirit is an extension of Jesus's presence and power in the midst of his bodily absence (John 20:22). This Spirit, according to Jesus, "abides with you" and "will be in you" (John 14:17)—indeed, the Spirit will "be with you forever" (John 14:16, lit. "in the age" or "in eternity"), a statement reminiscent of Jesus's words at the end of Matthew, "I am with you always" (Matt 28:20).

120. Standard English translations translate one or both instances of πνεῦμα here as "spirit," rather than "Spirit," even though there is nothing in the Greek text to indicate a difference. The decision to use "spirit" seems largely driven by a concern to protect the metaphysical otherness of the divine Spirit. I follow Bultmann here in understanding πνεῦμα as "the divine power . . . as it impinges on human existence" (Bultmann, *Gospel of John*, 139n1).

121. When Jesus says, "Whoever believes in me, as Scripture has said, rivers of living water will flow from within them," the narrator glosses this by saying, "By this he meant the Spirit" (John 7:38–39 NIV).

122. Bultmann, *Gospel of John*, 567.

123. The latter statement seems transparently to be a retrospective defense of Jesus on the part of the church in light of his death and the fact that Christ did not come in glory as expected.

We need to resist the pressure to conform the NT witness to later trinitarian dogma. While we need not deny that it is possible to read the biblical text in the direction of the Niceno-Constantinopolitan Creed, we must refute the claim that reading the text in accord with the creed is the *only* responsible or permissible interpretation. The NT is a far more complex and messy witness than we would often like. Other theological options present themselves once we remove the lens that sees either orthodoxy or heresy. With respect to the topic at hand, there is no straightforward understanding of the Spirit's identity. Certain texts suggest that the Spirit has a distinct agency all her own, while other texts suggest that the Spirit is a proxy for Jesus.[124] The dominant theme on the whole is that the Spirit is the Spirit *of* Christ; she does not speak on her own but speaks whatever she hears him say. The Spirit, we might say, *is* the risen Christ, insofar as the resurrection means that Jesus is not locked in the past but is able to be with us forever. But like Christ himself, the Spirit has to be understood as an event affecting each person. Within our soteriocentric approach, the Pauline-Johannine witness to the Spirit's work leads to the following thesis: *the Holy Spirit is the saving action of God in Christ "as it impinges on human existence" in the*

---

124. The use of the female pronoun with reference to the Spirit should not be taken to mean that I view the Holy Spirit as the "female" member of the trinity. I would be just as happy to use the female pronoun for God as such or for God the Creator/Father. My practice here is to use no gender for God (the Creator), the masculine for Jesus, and the feminine for the Spirit—not because a balance of imagery is more faithful to *God* but because it more effectively disrupts *our* culturally-captive assumptions about the divine. Gendered language is for our benefit; it reminds us that God relates to the world personally rather than as an impersonal, objectifiable "It." Since God absolutely transcends the creature, neither male nor female language gives direct access to the divine. Indeed, Father and Spirit are, as Kathryn Tanner and Janet Soskice argue, "more than" any one set of gender imagery can adequately communicate: "The gendered imagery in classical trinitarianism is always considered in tandem . . . with other forms of biblical imagery of a quite impersonal sort—light and water imagery, for example. . . . The Son comes out of the Father, for example, like a ray from a source of light, so as to share its nature. No one set of biblical images, furthermore, is privileged; each has its particular theological strengths and weaknesses. . . . Multiple images are therefore commonly employed together so that they might mutually modify one another's theological shortcomings. . . . One might grant too that in classical trinitarian thinking this is a Father who acts like a mother: he births or begets the Son. . . . The closeness of the relationship is at issue: the absence of any temporal or spatial distinction between originator and originated. Birth as the primary metaphor for developing whatever the Father is doing in relation to the Son is therefore often quite strong in classical trinitarianism. One might even say, following Psalm 120:3, as Hilary of Poitiers does, that the Son is begotten of the Father's womb. . . . Gendered imagery is 'exceeded' in a 'baffling of gender literalism,' as Janet Soskice puts it. 'Roles are reversed, fused, inverted: no one is simply who they seem to be. More accurately, everyone is *more than* they seem to be . . . the Father and the Spirit are more than one gender can convey'" (Tanner, *Christ the Key*, 213–15; Soskice, "Trinity," 146).

present moment, and thus pneumatology within a soteriocentric dogmatics accomplishes the work traditionally ascribed to the christological doctrine of the assumption of flesh.[125] The Spirit is the continuation of Christ's presence, the ongoing efficacy of his saving work, the mode of his interruption of our existence.

We argued above, following Jüngel, that "the presence of Jesus Christ and the absence of Jesus Christ should be conceived in the unity of the same being."[126] Christ is himself the unity of God's presence and absence—a presence that encounters us precisely *as* absence. In his theses on the Holy Spirit, Jüngel develops this theme pneumatologically. He observes, as we have, that "the presence of the Holy Spirit presupposes the absence of the earthly Jesus (John 7.39)." In the absence of Jesus, "the Holy Spirit reveals who Jesus was, and so fulfills Jesus's work of revelation."[127] In other words, "the Spirit, like Jesus himself, is Revealer."[128] But if "the material climax of revelation" is located in the "death of the Revealer," then the Spirit fulfills this work by making the absence of the crucified Jesus present to us *as absence*. That is to say, "in the Holy Spirit, Jesus Christ is present as the absent one."[129] Christ is the presence-in-absence of God, while the Spirit is the ongoing presence-in-absence of Christ. If the saving action of God is the apocalyptic event of Jesus's death in God-abandonment, then the Spirit—if the Spirit is defined and determined by Christ—is the event of our participation in this death. The Spirit is what makes crucifixion into *co*crucifixion. Barth posits a universal human nature in which we all share in Christ's death irrespective of our concrete existence, so that our present situation is referred *backwards* to the past event of Christ. A pneumatological approach to this problem, by contrast, understands the Spirit as the one who instead relates the past event of the cross *forwards* to our present situation. Whereas Christ within the classical model *represents* all human individuals in his action, the Spirit within the model proposed here *repeats* the action of Christ in the specific encounter with each individual. In place of Christ as the event of representation, we have the Spirit as the event of repetition. The Spirit fulfills the saving revelation of Christ by *repeating* it, so that God's absence in Christ becomes identical with our own experience of divine abandonment.

Speaking about the "repetition" of the crucifixion hearkens back to one of the main Protestant criticisms of the Roman Mass, namely, that it

---

125. Bultmann, *Gospel of John*, 139n1.

126. Jüngel, "Thesen," 277.

127. Jüngel, "Zur Lehre," 108.

128. Bultmann, *Gospel of John*, 570.

129. Jüngel, "Zur Lehre," 108.

is a "bloodless repetition" of Christ's sacrifice. According to Luther and the other reformers, the Roman doctrine of the Lord's Supper, in which transubstantiation establishes a metaphysical identity between the elements and the crucified Christ, repeats a sacrifice that is unrepeatable and "once for all." Roman Catholic theologians, for their part, respond by denying the charge. They argue that the Mass was always understood by them as a *representation* (a re-*presentation*) of Christ's sacrifice, and they can point to pre-Reformation sources to prove it. For instance, Thomas Aquinas's defense of the Mass as a sacrifice affirms that the "celebration of this sacrament is an image representing the passion of Christ, which is the true sacrifice."[130] And Gabriel Biel, in his *Sacri canonis Missae expositio* (1499), says that "our offering is not a repetition [*reiteratio*] of his offering but its representation [*rep[rae]sentatio*]."[131] The details of the debate aside, what is interesting is the way both sides—Protestant and Catholic—agree in rejecting repetition as a valid category for understanding the eucharist. The death of Christ is apparently something that can be recollected and remembered but never repeated.

Modern theology and philosophy, however, have opened up new ways of understanding repetition. The basis for the recent discussion comes from the work of Søren Kierkegaard. In Kierkegaard's early pseudonymous work on *Repetition*, Constantine Constantius confounds the easy distinction between recollection and repetition: "Repetition and recollection are the same movement, just in opposite directions, because what is recollected has already been and is thus repeated backwards, whereas genuine repetition is recollected forwards."[132] By placing repetition in contradistinction to Platonic recollection (as well as Hegelian mediation), Constantius recognizes that the contrast between them is not a contrast between the remembrance of a past event (recollection) and the addition of new events (repetition), but rather both are fundamentally temporal vectors: recollection moves backwards into the past while repetition moves forwards into the future. Repetition is not the supplementation of new occurrences but the movement of the singular occurrence out of the past into new historical moments. The French poststructuralist tradition—notably, Jacques Derrida and Gilles Deleuze—developed Kierkegaard's concept of repetition in generative directions. Derrida's 1967 work *Speech and Phenomena* critically examined the role of repetition and representation in Husserl. The follow-

---

130. *ST* 3.83.1 resp. As he elsewhere states, "this sacrament works in human beings the effect that the passion of Christ worked in the world" (*ST* 3.79.1 resp.).

131. Biel, *Sacri canonis Missae*, Lect. 53U, 361.

132. Kierkegaard, *Repetition*, 3.

ing year Deleuze published the most important philosophical work on the
topic in the twentieth century, *Difference and Repetition*. Like others before
him, he distinguished between two kinds of repetition. The first, also called
representation, is a static, negative "repetition of the Same." True repetition, by contrast, he calls "complex repetition," which is a dynamic, positive
repetition that includes difference within itself by way of excess.[133] Deleuze
illustrated this with reference to "the apparent paradox of festivals: they repeat an 'unrepeatable.' They do not add a second and a third time to the first,
but carry the first time to the 'nth' power."[134]

The concepts of identical and nonidentical repetition have also caught
on among theologians engaged in conversation with continental philosophy, including David Ford and the Radical Orthodox theologians John Milbank and Catherine Pickstock.[135] Pickstock takes a metaphysical approach
and develops a doctrine of the immanent trinity as the unity of identical
and nonidentical repetition, a unity that is held together in the Holy Spirit.[136]
Free of the old Protestant concerns, Ford takes a more nonmetaphysical approach and sees in the eucharist the paradigmatic instance of nonidentical
repetition. Paradoxically, each celebration is a new iteration of the same
Christ-event: "In gratitude the past is repeated in such a way that it is fruitful in a new way for the present and future. It is somewhat paradoxical:
what has been completed continues. The more decisively and gloriously
completed it is the more richly it can continue in repetition. In this way the
good of the past can overflow into continuing life."[137] In the eucharist we do
not sacrifice Christ again and again but rather encounter in new ways what
has already been completed.

By drawing on Kierkegaard, Deleuze, and Ford—along with Pickstock's talk of the Holy Spirit, though shorn of Radical Orthodoxy's Platonic
metaphysics—we can define the Spirit's role in the saving work of God as
the agent of the nonidentical repetition of Christ's death in God-abandonment.

133. Deleuze, *Difference and Repetition*, xx, 24. See also ibid., 287.

134. Ibid., 1.

135. See Ford, *Self*; Milbank, *Theology* and *Word*; Pickstock, *After Writing* and
Repetition.

136. "God can consequently be regarded as the coincidence of the opposites of
identical and non-identical repetition. And the Holy Spirit's further expression of this
generative repetition is the expression of their unity in, and despite, their difference. In
the Holy Spirit, God returns to and consummates himself. . . . The Son expresses nothing other than the identical self-repetition of the Father, which already pertains, though
it only pertains through the Father's non-identical repetition as Son. . . . The Holy Spirit
expresses nothing other than the equality or identity of identical and non-identical
repetition" (Pickstock, *Repetition*, 196).

137. Ford, *Self*, 154.

The Spirit unites the abandoned Jesus with the person who is placed outside herself. The Spirit does not actualize an identical repetition, since that would ignore or nullify one's particular historical situation; she instead actualizes a creative, complex repetition that makes the christological event present in surprising and unanticipatable ways. The Spirit is the parousia (i.e., presence) of Jesus that, according to Giorgio Agamben, "does not signal a complement that is added on to something in order to complete it, nor a supplement, added on afterward." Instead, this pneumatological parousia is a moment of *kairos* that "stretches" the historical arrival of the Messiah by "seiz[ing] hold" of an instant of time and "bring[ing] it forth to fulfillment."[138] The kairotic, parousial Spirit does not add anything to the original event but stretches the event to include new historical contingencies. She thereby interrupts each moment with the presence-in-absence of God. By carrying the cross to the "nth power," the Spirit makes the "once" into the "once for all." Apart from the Spirit's repetition of Christ, the death on the cross would be a mere fact of history, the crucifixion of one more Roman criminal. Only the Spirit saves Jesus from historical oblivion.

The repetition of the cross, moreover, actualizes a specifically *existential* apocalypse. Repetition for Kierkegaard is "actuality and the earnestness of existence."[139] He illustrates this existential significance with reference to the story of Job. After enduring the loss of everything in his life while remaining faithful to God, "Job is again blessed: 'and the Lord gave Job *twice* as much as he had before.' This is what I call a *repetition*."[140] Here we see a particularly vivid example of nonidentical repetition; the new reality is a *gain* over Job's previous life. The event of repetition is not a *return* to an earlier existence, which would be a form of recollection, but a *resurrection* into eschatological existence. Kierkegaard describes this as a reparative occurrence, in which the act of repetition heals the wounds in one's self: "This 'self' . . . is mine again. The schism in my being has been removed. I am whole again. . . . Is repetition not possible? Have I not received everything back, only doubled? Have I not myself again, and in such a way that I have a double appreciation of what this means?"[141] The eschatological moment of repetition is the experience of an existential blessing in which one's identity is received anew, whole and restored.

If this existential gift of repetition occurs in our cocrucifixion with Christ, then we gain ourselves by being placed outside ourselves. Following

138. Agamben, *Time*, 70–71.

139. Kierkegaard, *Repetition*, 4.

140. Ibid., 69.

141. Ibid., 74.

Bonhoeffer we can identify this pneumatic gift of a new self as the event of "direct faith" (*fides directa*).[142] The classical Christian tradition understands faith as a gift of the Holy Spirit, the "Lord and giver of life," according to the creed. Thomas Aquinas, for instance, says that faith—along with the other theological virtues of hope and love—requires "the prompting or motion of the Holy Spirit," that is, "the gift of the Holy Spirit."[143] John Calvin states that "faith is the principal work of the Holy Spirit."[144] There is direct biblical support for this idea. In his list of the various manifestations of the Spirit, Paul says that "to another [is given] faith [πίστις] by the same Spirit" (1 Cor 12:9). And his description of the "fruit of the Spirit" includes πίστις (Gal 5:22). There is also more indirect support, such as the claim that we are no longer "captive" to the law but are "slaves in the new way of the Spirit" (Rom 7:6, my translation), or that "the law of the Spirit of life in Christ Jesus has set you free from the law of sin and death" (Rom 8:2)—given that Paul elsewhere contrasts the law with the apocalyptic reality of faith (Gal 2:16; 3:23–24). But where and to whom does the Spirit give this gift of faith? Traditionally, πίστις is understood as the reflective faith of the adult, and the work of the Spirit is thus circumscribed within the confessing ecclesial community. If, however, saving faith occurs where one participates in the Christ-event, and if this participation is fundamentally the experience of receiving a new identity—what we have defined as the unconscious, direct faith of the child—then the action of the Spirit is by no means circumscribed by the community of those with a conscious, reflective faith. The existential event of faith is universal in scope: in the instant of our being-outside-of-ourselves each person becomes the site of the Spirit's eschatological work of repeating the death of Christ.

In this way, the category of repetition achieves the same end as Barth's universalistic doctrine of Christ's election and incarnation, but it does so without trading on the abstract presuppositions that led to the incoherence of Chalcedon. God's interruption of the world in the apocalyptic death of Jesus interrupts each person in the apocalyptic repetition of the Spirit. The person of the Spirit is therefore the event in which the saving act of God invades a person's existence and empowers a new self-understanding in solidarity with the neighbor.

---

142. Bonhoeffer, *Act and Being*, 158.

143. *ST* 1–2.68.2 resp.

144. Calvin, *Institutes*, 3.1.4.

The Spirit of Adoption: Election as Interruption

The foregoing account of the Spirit as the eschatological agent of faith raises pressing questions regarding the nature of election. As we mentioned above, Barth constructed a christocentric doctrine of election in his *Church Dogmatics*, in which Jesus Christ, as both divine and human, is simultaneously the subject and object of election; all other human persons are derivatively elect in him by virtue of the *assumptio carnis*. Barth's doctrine depended on a strongly representative and substitutionary account of Christ's humanity as universal human nature. While Barth succeeded in overcoming metaphysics with respect to God by letting the history of Jesus determine the meaning of all God-talk, he did not succeed in overcoming metaphysics with respect to humankind, since he let an abstract concept of humanity stand in the place of the actual historicity of human persons. The account we have sketched here addresses this problem by replacing the purportedly universal humanity of Christ with the existential event of the Spirit's repetition of Christ. We must therefore replace Barth's christocentric election with a christo(pneumato)centric election.[145] The Holy Spirit is the subject of election, not *alongside* Christ but *as* the agent by which the elected Christ interrupts the human person. While a departure from Barth's own position, the seeds for this reconstruction of election are already present in his work.

Barth's doctrine of election is a sustained gloss on the confession that the God of the gospel is the *living* God. Barth begins his treatment of the doctrine in *CD* 2.2 by reiterating his thesis from *CD* 2.1 that God "is the living God as the One who loves in freedom."[146] It is precisely this axiom that grounds his opposition to the "absolute decree" (*decretum absolutum*) or "general decree" (*decretum generale*) of Protestant orthodoxy. For Barth, there is no such thing as a general divine decree. God makes decisions regarding particular concrete realities, not abstractions. For this reason Barth rejects the scholastic line of thought that views God as an abstract metaphysical being who relates to the world in a general manner: "According to this conception God is everything in the way of aseity, simplicity, immutability, infinite, etc., but [God] is not the living God, that is to say, [God] is not the God who lives in concrete decision."[147] God exists in no other way

145. By placing the "pneumato" in parentheses in the middle of the word, this neologism indicates that the Spirit is not a second agent alongside Christ who accomplishes a second work in addition to the work of Christ. Instead, the Spirit simply *is* Christ in his present efficacy and existential actuality. The Spirit is an extension and repetition of Christ and to speak of one is necessarily to speak of the other.

146. *CD* 2.2:3.

147. *CD* 2.2:79.

than "in this concrete liveliness [*Lebendigkeit*]."[148] And for Barth, this concreteness is the history of Jesus Christ, in which God determines Godself to be the one who exists for and with humanity. In Christ we encounter the being and will of God *in toto*. Barth thus criticizes the "traditional teaching" that "saw in predestination an isolated and given enactment."[149] According to this view, "God *willed once* in the pre-temporal eternity when the decree was conceived and established," and therefore "the *living quality* of this action is *perfectum*, eternal *past*."[150] God elected at one time, but this electing decision "now *no longer* takes place."[151] What God does in the present is merely an "echo" (*Nachklang*) of the past decree of God. As a result, such a God is not living but dead. Barth compares this view of predestination with deism: God acted once in the past, and everything since is simply the logical and necessary outworking of what God has already done.[152]

Against the deistic model of election that he finds in Protestant orthodoxy, Barth claims that "God's decree is not lifeless, but rather infinitely more alive than any human decree."[153] Barth criticizes the Reformed tradition for isolating the act of election from the being of the God who elects— and specifically from the being of Jesus Christ in his historical reality. For Barth, election is the personal self-determination of God to become incarnate. Election is consequently as much a matter of the present and future as is Jesus Christ himself. Barth corrects the tradition by focusing not on the decree itself but on the divine *subject* of the decree. To speak about election is to speak about the one who elects. In contrast to the *decretum absolutum*, "God is never a mere echo; God is and remains and always will be an independent tone and sound."[154] By identifying Jesus Christ as the subject (and object) of election, Barth is able to say that the event of election is a "concrete decree," and for this reason it "never ceases to be *event*."[155] The event of election occurs as "history, encounter, and decision"; it is an act determined by a concrete occurrence within time and space.

---

148. *CD* 2.2:79, rev.

149. *CD* 2.2:181, rev.

150. *CD* 2.2:181; cf. *KD* 2.2:199. Original italics restored. All future italics are restored from the original German.

151. *CD* 2.2:181, rev.

152. *CD* 2.2:182.

153. *CD* 2.2:183, rev.

154. *CD* 2.2:183, rev.

155. *CD* 2.2:184.

Somewhat surprisingly, this leads Barth to describe election as an "act of divine life in the Spirit" (*Akt göttlichen Geisteslebens*).[156] This peculiar phrase is unique to this section of the *Church Dogmatics*.[157] Throughout the rest of the work, Barth almost exclusively uses *Geistesleben* to speak of *human* life-in-the-Spirit or "spiritual life," and often pejoratively because of the Schleiermacherian connotations.[158] In its antideistic context, Barth's use of the phrase "act of divine life in the Spirit" indicates that election is concretely and actively related to the particularities of historical existence. It is not an abstract decision in eternity over against time; rather, it is a living decision in the Spirit of Jesus Christ. Support for this can be found indirectly in §35, where Barth examines the election of the individual. There he argues that election "comes to fulfillment in one's calling." The election of the individual is "an election to participation in the service of the community."[159] The elect individual "is as such a *messenger* of God. . . . He [or she] is sent. He [or she] is an *apostle*: on the basis of the fact that Jesus Christ was elected to be the apostle of grace and in connection with the apostolate of grace that is the meaning and order of the life of [Christ's] whole community."[160] Election, in other words, is a divine commission to become a missionary witness to God's reconciliation of all things in Christ. What Barth is describing here is what he later explains as the *awakening* of a person to faith, an awakening

---

156. *CD* 2.2:184; cf. *KD* 2.2:202. The phrase occurs three times: "Only as concrete decree, only as an act of divine life in the Spirit, is it the law which precedes all creaturely life" (*CD* 2.2:184). "Since it is itself history, encounter and decision, since it is an act of divine life in the Spirit, since it is the unbroken and lasting determining and decreeing of the one who as Lord of all things has both the authority and the power for such activity, it is the presupposition of all movement of creaturely life" (*CD* 2.2:184, rev.). "But it is an act of divine life in the Spirit, an act which affects us, an act which occurs in the very midst of time no less than in that far distant pretemporal eternity" (*CD* 2.2:185, rev.). The translators of this volume rendered the latter two instances as "divine life in the spirit," rather than "in the Spirit," for no apparent reason.

157. Eberhard Jüngel, in his interpretation of Barth's doctrine of election, makes this phrase ("act of divine life in the Spirit") central to Barth's theology in a way that is creative and interesting, though perhaps a stretch considering how marginal it is to the *Church Dogmatics*. Nevertheless, as an interpreter of Barth who seeks to bring him into a positive relation with Bultmann, Jüngel is right to emphasize this concept. It also shows his keen eye for easily overlooked, but deeply insightful, elements in Barth's theology. See Jüngel, *God's Being*, 91–92.

158. A typical example is this passage from the first volume: "God reveals Godself as the Spirit, not as any spirit, not as the basis of humanity's spiritual life [*des menschlichen Geisteslebens*], which we can discover and awaken, but as the Spirit of the Father and the Son" (*CD* 1.1:332, rev.).

159. *CD* 2.2:410, rev.

160. *CD* 2.2:415, rev. For a fuller discussion of this material, see Congdon, "*Apokatastasis*," 475–80.

that occurs by the power of the Spirit: "In the justification of the sinner that has taken place in Jesus Christ [the divine No and Yes] have both become an event that comprehends all people. And it is the awakening power of the Holy Spirit that this impossibility [of faith] as such and this necessity [of faith] as such thus confront and illuminate a person."[161] The "ontological impossibility" of unbelief and the "ontological necessity" of faith is an objective reality "for *all*, for *every* person," and this involves both the justifying work of Christ and the awakening power of the Spirit.[162] But there is a strict order here between the *primary* work of Christ and the *secondary* work of the Spirit. The "divine decision" of election, Barth writes, does not take place "in the person, in one's spirit," but rather it is "only reproduced [*nachvollzogen*]."[163] He even says that God's eternal decision "has the full weight of the eternal 'perfect,'" is "completed and isolated," "precedes all creaturely life," and finally "stands harder than steel and granite before and above all things and all events."[164] Just as Barth comes to the edge of developing a pneumatological account of election, he pulls back.

Despite his opposition to the deistic, dead god of Protestant orthodoxy and his valiant effort to reconceive election in a way that is postmetaphysical and historically grounded, Barth's project nevertheless remains incomplete. More precisely, it remains *pneumatologically* incomplete.[165] Barth's account

161. *CD* 4.1:747–48, rev. Cf. *KD* 4.1:835.

162. *CD* 4.1:747, rev.

163. *CD* 4.1:748, rev. The English translators use "repeated."

164. *CD* 2.2:183, rev.

165. This is not to suggest agreement with Robert Jenson and Eugene Rogers, who charge Barth with being pneumatologically deficient. Their claim is that, precisely where an appeal to the Spirit would seem most natural or appropriate, Barth either expunges the Spirit's unique agency by reducing the Spirit to a property or power of Christ (a problem often traced back to Augustine's definition of the Spirit as the *vinculum caritatis* or "bond of love"), or he simply replaces the Spirit with Christ altogether. For this reason, Jenson charges Barth with an "apparent binitarianism," and Rogers claims that, in Barth, "Christological statements render pneumatological ones superfluous." See Jenson, "You Wonder," 296–304, here 298; Rogers, "Eclipse," 173–90, here 175. Jenson and Rogers take issue with Barth's doctrine of the trinity as one subject in three modes of being. Rogers criticizes the lack of a "Trinitarian *interval* between the Son and the Spirit" that grants the Spirit her own "autonomy" ("Eclipse," 179). Jenson goes further and says that "the Spirit is condemned by the *vinculum*-doctrine to remain a *modus* only," and thus "the Spirit does not appear as an historical party" ("You Wonder," 302). Ultimately, Jenson's real critique concerns Barth's ecclesiology. Jenson claims that Barth's "Spirit-avoidance . . . is avoidance of the *church*" (ibid.) and represents his Protestant resistance to Catholic conceptions of the church as "the active *mediatrix* of faith" (ibid., 303). In short, both Rogers and Jenson have larger theological agendas driving their criticism of Barth's pneumatology. The approach taken here is a far more immanent critique, insofar as the pneumatological deficiency I have diagnosed is *internal* to

is only plausible if we accept his claim that, in the incarnation, God assumed into unity with Godself "the *humanum*, the being and essence, the kind and nature, which is that of all human beings."[166] If Jesus Christ ontologically includes every human being in his own person, then it follows that the Holy Spirit is not involved in the saving and electing action of God. The Spirit's role is merely noetic; she enables the *recognition* of what has already occurred in Christ. Personal knowledge of our redemption through the Spirit is a secondary moment subsequent to the ontological actualization of redemption in Christ. In addition to the problem of incarnational metaphysics, there is the issue of the divine being. Barth's doctrine of the trinity understands God to be a single subject in three modes of being. He strongly adheres to the Augustinian axiom that "the external works of the trinity are indivisible" (*opera trinitatis ad extra sunt indivisa*). If that is the case, however, then the Spirit ought to be as much the subject of election as the Son, and in a sense Barth would agree. The Spirit is certainly involved in the history of Christ, just as Christ is present and active in the awakening power of the Spirit. But Barth refuses to allow election to be fully and equally an act of the Spirit alongside Christ, since that would entail identifying the justifying work of Christ with the awakening work of the Spirit.

For Barth, the existential apocalypse of faith can only look *backward* in acknowledgment and remembrance to the historical apocalypse of Jesus, and therefore he regards any attempt to make the two events paradoxically identical as a betrayal of the Reformation:

> There have been many attempts to make the history of Jesus Christ coincide with that of the believer, and *vice versa*. The theology of the younger Luther (up to 1519) was nothing but a powerful move in that direction. But we can approve and make common cause with it neither in its earlier forms nor in that authoritatively represented today by R. Bultmann. . . . Christian faith takes note of [the history of Jesus Christ], and clings to it and responds to it, without itself being the thing which accomplishes it, without any identity between the saving act of God and faith as the free act of the human person. . . . What takes place in the recognition [*Erkenntnis*] of the *pro me* of Christian faith is not the saving act of God itself, *not* the death and *not*

Barth's doctrine of the trinity. Put another way, my argument is not that Barth collapses Christ and Spirit but that he fails to collapse them *enough*. Barth isolates Christ from the Spirit and gives him independence from the Spirit. The solution is not to give the Spirit a reciprocal independence but rather to reject any independence on either side. Christ and Spirit are instead a single agent.

166. *CD* 4.2:48, rev.

the resurrection of Jesus Christ, not the presentation and not the reproduction [*Nachvollzug*] of his obedience and sacrifice and victory. What is Bultmann's conception but an existentialist translation of the sacramentalist doctrine of the Roman Church, according to which, at the climax of the mass, with the transubstantiation of the elements—in metaphysical identity with what took place then and there—there is a "bloodless repetition" of the sacrifice of Christ on Golgotha? Those who regard this teaching of the mass as basically untenable will find it impossible to make what took place ἐφ᾽ ἅπαξ in Jesus Christ coincide with what takes place in *faith*.[167]

Like the younger Luther, Barth's own early theology posited the unity of past and present in the moment of revelation. His early doctrine of election, as seen especially in the Göttingen dogmatics of 1924–25, understood the decision of God to occur in the present event of faith.[168] Barth's later theology, however, opposes the unity of past and present in virtually every form—whether it is the presence of Christ's self-offering in the eucharist or the presence of God's electing decision in the awakening of faith—on the grounds that salvation would become a human work. With respect to election, Barth says "there can be no question of a limiting and conditioning of the freedom of God . . . by the mystery of the existentiality of a complementary human decision." The God-human relationship would then have "two sources," and given the variable and capricious character of the creature, the human partner would determine the nature of the relationship.[169] Barth understandably seeks to avoid such a conclusion. He states "there is no synergism of any kind in the history of Jesus Christ's election" and thus "no cooperation or reciprocal action of any kind."[170] Barth thus rejects including the Spirit in election in an effort to secure the universal graciousness of God toward humankind. The question is (a) whether we can affirm Barth's conclusion that God says a clear and unequivocal Yes to every human person without relying on a metaphysical "logic of assumption"[171] whereby Christ's humanity is the general *humanitas* of all human beings, and (b) whether we can affirm that election includes the particular histories of each person

167. *CD* 4.1:767, rev. Cf. *KD* 4.1:858.

168. See McDonald, "Barth's 'Other' Doctrine," esp. 135–38.

169. *CD* 2.2:193.

170. *CD* 2.2:194.

171. Cf. van Driel, "Logic of Assumption," 265–90. See also van Driel, *Incarnation Anyway*, 138–42. While I accept some of van Driel's critiques of Barth on this point, I do not accept his christological proposal as the appropriate alternative.

without making the God-human relationship conditional upon one's conscious decision of faith.

We can achieve this, I suggest, by taking Barth's idea of election as an
"act of divine life in the Spirit" further than he was willing to go, and the
place to start is Paul's declaration in Romans: "For those who are led by the
Spirit of God are children of God. For you did not receive a spirit of slavery
to fall back into fear, but you have received the Spirit of adoption. When
we cry, 'Abba! Father!' [αββα ὁ πατήρ] it is that very Spirit bearing witness
with our spirit that we are children of God" (Rom 8:14–16, my translation).[172]
Paul is here discussing what it means to be "in Christ." He explains this
through a series of eschatologically-charged binaries: the "law of the Spirit"
versus the "law of sin and death" (Rom 8:2), walking "according to the flesh"
versus walking "according to the Spirit" (Rom 8:4), setting "the mind on the
flesh" versus setting "the mind on the Spirit" (Rom 8:6). The one is "death,"
while the other is "life and peace" (Rom 8:6). Within this apocalyptic scenario, the presence of the Spirit confirms that one belongs to the new aeon
of Christ rather than to the enslaving power of the flesh that belongs to the
old aeon: "Anyone who does not have the Spirit of Christ does not belong
to him" (Rom 8:9). To be led by the Spirit is therefore to be a "child of God"
(Rom 8:16), one of "God's elect" (Rom 8:33). The Spirit confirms our eschatological identity as children of God, according to Paul, in the cry of "Abba!"
In this cry the Spirit does not compete with or control a person's action.
She does not operate like a divine puppet master. She does not force faith
upon people against their will.[173] Paul says the Spirit "bears witness with
our spirit." The verb συμμαρτυρέω means "to witness [*martus*] with [*sum*]"
or "cowitness." The Spirit acts *as* the human person acts; she cries *as* we cry.

172. I mostly follow the NRSV here, with the exception that I have replaced "a spirit
of adoption" with "the Spirit of adoption." The decision to interpret πνεῦμα as a human spirit in 8:15 makes little sense, given that 8:16 refers to that same Spirit (αὐτὸ τὸ
πνεῦμα) as the one who bears witness that we are children of God. The NIV and ESV
translate the Greek correctly here.

173. Paul speaks in a more competitive and unilateral way in Galatians, when he
writes: "Because you are children, God has sent the Spirit of his Son into our hearts,
crying, 'Abba! Father!'" (Gal 4:6). This can be explained largely in terms of context.
Galatians 4 describes an apocalyptic situation of bondage and liberation: "we were
enslaved to the elemental spirits [στοιχεῖα] of the world" until the "fullness of time," in
which "God sent his Son . . . so that we might receive adoption as children" (Gal 4:3–5).
Paul here describes the same scenario as in Romans, but in a way that highlights our
utter inability to liberate ourselves. Our existential egocentrism and estrangement from
others—what Luther called being curved in upon oneself—requires a radical act of
interruption from outside ourselves. In that soteriological sense, it is indeed the Spirit
who compels our cry of *Abba*.

The Spirit's act of witnessing coincides with the person's witness, so that the two occur paradoxically as a *single action*.

The cowitnessing act of the Spirit coincides not only with the cry of the human person but also with the cry of the suffering Jesus. Besides Romans 8 and Galatians 4, the cry αββα ὁ πατήρ appears in one other text. In the Garden of Gethsemane, Jesus prays, "Abba, Father, for you all things are possible; remove this cup from me; yet, not what I want, but what you want" (Mark 14:36).[174] If one accepts the widely (though not uncontroversially) held position that Paul's theology influenced Mark's Gospel—for which Mark 14:36 provides significant support—then one could argue Mark means to suggest that the Spirit is here bearing witness to the truth that Jesus is the original child of God, the first of God's elect.[175] This would be appropriate, given that Paul in Galatians connects this cry of "Abba" to God's sending of the Son "to redeem those who were under the law, so that we might receive adoption as children" (Gal 4:5). Even apart from this question of historical influence, the text itself warrants the theological interpretation that to be adopted as God's child is to be adopted into Jesus's experience of divine silence and God-abandonment. Election is always election-to-cocrucifixion; it is an election into the existential abandonment of God's presence-in-absence. As the agent of this election, the Spirit joins Jesus to the believer and the believer to Jesus—a joining represented in the common cry: Abba![176] This cry need not be a literal vocalization, in the same way that cocrucifixion does not mean we must actually crucify ourselves. We share in the Abba-cry of Jesus—and so live according to the Spirit as a child of God—by participating unconsciously in Christ's total eccentricity, his being-outside-of-himself.

As mentioned above, I thus propose a christo(pneumato)centric doctrine of election in which the divine life-in-the-Spirit that constitutes the living actuality of election takes place *within* the event of Jesus Christ; conversely, we might say the cruciform history of Christ occurs *within* the agency of the Spirit. Christ and Spirit do not act in a sequence or order but as a single agent and event: the Christ-Spirit. In contrast to the logic of

---

174. The Greek in this text is the same: αββα ὁ πατήρ. Perhaps it would be more accurate to translate Jesus's prayer more emphatically as "Abba! Father!"

175. Regarding the debate over Pauline influence on Mark, see Becker, Engberg-Pedersen, and Mueller, *Mark and Paul*.

176. According to Kevin Vanhoozer, "The 'spirit' that Jesus expired on the cross and then breathed out on his disciples (Jn. 20:22) in turn speaks on behalf of the believers that he unites to Christ, indwells, and enlivens. It is this same Spirit who now prompts believers to cry out to God with the same term that characterized Jesus's own prayers: 'Abba' (cf. Gal. 4:6)" (*Remythologizing Theology*, 56–57).

assumption, this account includes every person through the logic of repetition: each person *becomes* elect in a particular historical encounter that places a person outside of herself and so constitutes the repetition of Christ's death. In contrast to a conditional election that limits the freedom of God, this proposal understands the work of the Spirit not as a conscious awakening but as an unconscious interrupting.[177] The direct faith of the child is a wholly divine act that does not depend upon the autonomous cooperation of the individual. God elects *as* the individual acts, but not *because* the individual acts. The Abba-cry of Jesus is paradoxically and pneumatologically identical with the Abba-cry of each person. Election and faith occur simultaneously as part of a single divine-human, christo-pneumatic event.

Election, in short, is *interruption*. To be elect is to be interrupted, to be placed outside oneself. In this sense, Jesus is indeed the elected human as the one who experienced the ultimate interruption of divine abandonment on the cross. But as a human person, he is not himself in any straightforward sense the one who elects. Instead, as the agent of interruption, the *Spirit* is the agent of Christ's election.[178] The Spirit interrupts and elects Jesus from his baptism to his journey to Golgotha. And as the one who elects Jesus, the Spirit elects and interrupts others, thereby constituting Jesus's deity at the same time she constitutes his universality. She simultaneously includes other individuals in this event of election by nonidentically repeating the cross in every moment of existential interruption, however hidden or manifest. Each person is elected in and for interruption—that is to say, elected in and for participation in the suffering of Christ. The interrupting work of the Spirit points neither toward a finished reality in the past nor a

177. By emphasizing *unconscious* rather than conscious faith, we are addressing Barth's criticism of *apokatastasis* as a "metaphysics of history," which claims that every person will be a *conscious* witness to Christ. See CD 2.2:417–18. Cf. Congdon, "*Apokatastasis*," 476–79.

178. Traditionally election is appropriated to God the Creator as the one who chose Israel (Ezek 20:5) and later chose us in Christ (Eph 1:4). Karl Barth famously argued that Jesus Christ is the subject (and object) of election, an argument developed from his own christocentric account of revelation. His christocentric election does not contradict the biblical tradition but rather clarifies it, since the triune God is a single subject. The NT itself legitimates the shift of election from the first to the second trinitarian mode of being in the way that it concretizes election "in Christ," but also in the way that the NT already displays a similar shift regarding creation by acknowledging, in contrast to the OT, that all things were created through Christ and in him all things hold together. Barth's christocentric understanding of revelation picks up on these threads and develops them further. Similarly, my soteriocentric understanding of revelation picks up on the textual witnesses to the agency of the Spirit, such as Romans 8 and Galatians 4, and develops out of these elements a pneumatological account of election that clarifies the biblical tradition in light of the apocalypse of salvation.

final consummation in the future; it is rather constitutive of the event itself in its present contingency and historicity. The saving event is always a decision-in-becoming that remains "new every morning," and thus the saving agent—the Christ-Spirit—is always a being-in-becoming whose identity is determined ever anew in the apocalypse of salvation.

DEUS PRAESENS:
APOCALYPTIC PNEUMA-CHRISTOLOGY

We began this chapter by looking at the problem with classical Chalcedonian christology and its definition of deity and humanity prior to any consideration of the saving action of God in history. The result was an incoherent account of the saving event. In its place we developed a soteriocentric christology that takes the apocalyptic interruption of the human person as its starting point. But this interruption only encounters each particular human person through the agency of the Spirit, since the metaphysical reliance on the assumption of a universal human nature is theologically and hermeneutically impossible. For this reason, the reconstruction of christology is simultaneously the reconstruction of pneumatology. Indeed, following the New Testament, we must speak of Christ and Spirit as a single divine agent in different historical modalities. Christ and Spirit are two modes of God's saving action: Christ is the event itself in its historical actuality, while the Spirit is the nonidentical repetition of the event as it existentially impinges upon a person.[179]

We can therefore reconstruct Chalcedon historically. Jesus of Nazareth, as the one who experiences the abyss of God's presence-in-absence, is simply a human being. It is precisely the scandal of the incarnation that God's Word becomes manifest in flesh—not alongside or behind the flesh

179. In all of this I am offering a correction to Barth's bifurcation and hierarchical ordering of christology and pneumatology, which allows him to say that Bultmann's theology is "an attempt at a 'theology of the third article' and therefore of the Holy Spirit" (Barth and Bultmann, *Briefwechsel*, 197; *Letters*, 108). Barth posited a sharp distinction between objectivity and subjectivity, between the theological and the existential, between Christ and the Spirit. In his *Table Talk* he was thus able to say: "A good theology can be based on any of the three articles of the Creed. You could base it on the Doctrine of the Holy Spirit. . . . A good critique of Bultmann and existential theology would lie along this same line. . . . I personally think that a theology of the Spirit might be all right after A.D. 2000, but now we are still too close to the eighteenth and nineteenth centuries. It is still too difficult to distinguish between God's Spirit and man's spirit!" (*Karl Barth's Table Talk*, 27–28). The mistake Barth makes is to think that we can isolate Christ or the Spirit as an independent starting point for theology. We either have Christ and the Spirit together as a single event or not at all.

but *as* flesh. This flesh is not a generic, universal substance (i.e., *humanum*), but rather the very particular Jewish flesh of a single person, whose "humanity" cannot be generalized. There is nothing about him as a human being to set him apart from others. In his words and deeds he is a witness to the reign of God; he points away from himself to the coming eschatological event. How then can we translate Chalcedon's claim that Christ is "of one substance with the Father as regards his deity, and at the same time of one substance with us as regards his humanity"? If we only know deity in terms of God's saving action, then we will translate the former ("of one substance with the Father") in our translation of the latter ("of one substance with us"). And with respect to the latter, we have argued that the New Testament describes Christ's ongoing presence and agency in terms of the Holy Spirit. Christ relates to other human persons not through a universal substance but through the Spirit's repetition of Christ as the saving event. The Spirit repeats the historical particularity of Jesus, thereby establishing his relation to every other people. And insofar as being "of one substance with the Father" means that Jesus's history is not a mere datum of the past but is in some sense eternal, then we can say that the Spirit constitutes Jesus's "deity" at the same time that she constitutes his "humanity." We can therefore formulate our thesis as follows:

1. Jesus is the one who dies in God-abandonment;

2. Jesus is the saving event (i.e., the Christ) insofar as other human beings participate in his death in God-abandonment;

3. other persons participate in his death insofar as their existence non-identically repeats the existence of Jesus;

4. other persons repeat the existence of Jesus when they unconsciously share in his eccentricity, his being-outside-of-himself;

5. to be outside of oneself is to be interrupted;

6. the Spirit of Christ is the agent of interruption;

7. every person is, at some moment, interrupted by the Spirit.

The only christology is a *pneuma-christology*, a christology determined by the agency of the Spirit. Jesus is divine as the one who is no longer lost to history but is present with us as the event of salvation. Jesus is divine, therefore, in his unity with others—that is to say, in the pneumatic repetition of his existence within the manifold array of human history. Because the Spirit is not a secondary moment in addition to the event but is the event itself in its existential efficacy, it follows that our concrete experience of abandonment is constitutive of Christ's being as the Abandoned One. His divine being-in-abandonment includes the interruption, alienation, and abandonment of each person. The Christ-Spirit is thus "ontologically located" in the saving apocalypse.[180] Instead of speaking of one Christ in two natures, we should speak of one saving event in two modes: the historical actuality of the event in the crucified Jesus and the existential repetition of the event in the agency of the Spirit. The *anhypostasis* is historicized as the event of interruption, while the *enhypostasis* is pneumaticized as the act of repetition.

If we are going to understand God soteriocentrically—and so christo(pneumato)centrically—then we must conclude that the divine being as such is constituted in relation to the multiplicity and diversity that characterizes historical existence. It is insufficient to speak merely of *Christus praesens* or *Spiritus praesens*; we must speak instead of *Deus praesens*. The only object of Christian theological discourse is the God present in the eschatological event of faith. The *Deus praesens* is the ongoing and infinite repetition of the apocalypse of Jesus Christ through his Spirit. In the Christ-Spirit, God creatively and nonidentically repeats the saving event, thereby repeating God's own being. We can thus say that God's being "is singularly unique by virtue of the fact that it can *repeat itself*."[181] And if God's being is a being-in-repetition, then transcendence and immanence coincide in each moment of historical existence: God is transcendent as the event of existential interruption, while God is immanent in that this event happens ever anew in the context of a person's particular existence. Divine immanence takes the form of repetition so as to ensure its simultaneous transcendence. God's inclusion of human historicity in the Christ-Spirit is not a process of development that grows and evolves. Repetition seeks to preserve the eventfulness of the Christ-event, its singularity and irruptive agency. It is a *happening* that does not give rise to any measurable development or institutional stabilization. The *Deus praesens* thus establishes the ecclesial apostolate.

180. Jüngel, *Gottes Sein*, vi; cf. Jüngel, *God's Being*, xxv: "God's being is ontologically located." The phrase is perhaps better translated as "God's being is ontologically localized [*lokalisiert*]," meaning that God's being is ontologically determined by its concrete location in history.

181. Jüngel, *Gottes Sein*, 117.

5

The Site of Salvation
Apostolate

In the last days it will be, God declares,

that I will pour out my Spirit upon all flesh,

and your sons and your daughters shall prophesy,

and your young men shall see visions,

and your old men shall dream dreams.

ACTS 2:17

In that renewal there is no longer Greek and Jew, circumcised and uncir-
cumcised, barbarian, Scythian, slave and free; but Christ is all and in all!

COLOSSIANS 3:11

EXTRA ECCLESIAM NULLA SALUS?

When it comes to developing a soteriocentric ecclesiology, one has to
be mindful of the fact that, for most of Christian history, it was as-

sumed the church mediated salvation—indeed that it was the *exclusive* mediator of salvation. As Cyprian's famous axiom states, *extra ecclesiam nulla salus* (outside of the church there is no salvation). Christian theologians since at least the early catholicism of the second century located this mediatorial work of the church in the sacraments, particularly in baptism.[1] This sacramental ecclesiology is rooted in a sacramental soteriology, which "understands Christ to have objectively wrought the material of salvation which must be subjectively applied to us before it can be considered effective."[2] By positing this gulf between the objective and the subjective, traditional theology makes the church necessary as the bridge between "then" and "now."

Given how invested the church has been throughout its history in retaining its spiritual and political hegemony, any change to this doctrinal framework would be seen as a direct threat to the church's sociocultural power. The Reformation was precisely such a threat. The reformers rejected the mediatorial nature of the church's liturgy and practices. They did not abolish the gap between objective and subjective—that would come later with Barth—but they shifted the site of application from the sacraments to individual faith. This effectively abolished the power of clerics to determine a person's eternal fate. Now each person could find eternal security through her own faith in the promises of the gospel. This did not, in the minds of the reformers, mean the church was no longer necessary, but now the necessity was of a different character. A person needed the church not to guarantee salvation but to learn about where to find salvation and to find encouragement and nourishment in the life of faith.

The reformers could thus still appeal to Cyprian's axiom. For example, in a 1522 Christmas sermon, Luther preaches: "Therefore the one who would find Christ must first find the church. How should we know where Christ and his faith are, if we do not know where his believers are? . . . For outside of the Christian church there is no truth, no Christ, no salvation."[3] According to John Calvin, while "it is by faith in the gospel that Christ becomes ours," nevertheless "we need outward helps to beget and increase faith within us." And for this reason Calvin follows Cyprian in the view that

1. A sacrament is "a rite performed by the church, involving tangible media, which is understood as a divine act that either imparts to the individual the salvation achieved in Christ or else sustains and deepens it" (McMaken, *Sign*, 60–61). McMaken argues that Thomas Aquinas ascribes to the sacraments the power of imparting salvation, while reformational theology ascribes to them the power only to sustain and deepen the salvation acquired by faith.

2. McMaken, *Sign*, 59–60.

3. *WA* 10:140.8–11, 16–17.

"those to whom [God] is Father the church may also be Mother."[4] Indeed, Calvin goes on to say that "away from her bosom one cannot hope for any forgiveness of sins or any salvation," since "the Lord has promised his mercy solely in the communion of saints."[5]

These statements by Luther and Calvin suggest that one has to first find the church before one can find salvation. While the church itself does not save, the church is where one finds salvation. But where do we find the church, the visible communion of saints? To answer that question, the reformers appealed to two marks of the church (*notae ecclesiae*): the preaching of the gospel and the administration of the sacraments. Of course, the marks in themselves were not unique; what distinguished reformational theology was their distinctive understanding of the gospel (justification by grace alone) and their distinctive understanding of the sacraments (two nonsalvific sacraments effective only for faith). The reformers did not rethink the marks themselves.[6] While the reformers overturned the Catholic doctrine of the church as the mediator of salvation, they did not interrogate the *identity* of the church itself. They reassessed *how* the church functions but not *what* the church actually is. Talk about the church was taken for granted as part of their Christendom context: "The Reformers presupposed the existence of Christendom. This is one of the reasons, no doubt, why they did not develop a full doctrine of the church. Their purpose was, not to create new communities, but to reform those already in existence."[7] There was no need to rethink the nature of the church since everyone already knew what the church was. Both Luther and Calvin, along with virtually everyone else at that time, assumed that the church—defined by various liturgies, practices, structures, and teachings—was a self-evident given. The church itself was not the problem, only what it taught.

The problem with this is the same one we examined in the previous chapter. The reformers—like most theologians before or since—saw the church as being significant for salvation, but they did not rethink the church *itself* in light of the saving event of God. Theirs was still a metaphysical ecclesiology because their church-talk was not determined and normed by salvation-talk. The result was the ecclesiological parallel to the

4. Calvin, *Institutes*, 4.1.1.

5. Ibid., 4.1.4, 4.1.20.

6. The reformers certainly did argue with Roman Catholics over the details of the marks. Second- and third-generation Protestants disputed with Cardinal Bellarmine, for instance, over his list of fifteen marks of the church. See Gerhard, *Loci theologici*, 5:604. The reformers put forth a minimalist account of the marks, but the *object* described by these marks remained essentially the same.

7. Hoekendijk, *Church*, 14.

metaphysics that has plagued christology: just as the being of Christ was defined independently of the saving event, so too the church was defined independently of the saving event. A prior understanding of the church has predetermined the nature and location of the church in the world. But whereas the metaphysical aporia within christology has been the subject of heated debate for decades and even centuries, there has been relatively little attention given to the problem of ecclesiology. In a sense the doctrine of the church is even more inviolable than the doctrine of Christ's two natures, since to question the structure of the church would seem to call into question the dogmatic decisions rendered by this church throughout history, thus ostensibly undermining the Christian faith. Theologians can dispute every aspect of church doctrine so long as no one disputes the nature of the church itself. The consequence has been an *ecclesiological foundationalism and fundamentalism* that has blinded theologians to the fundamental underlying question: what exactly *is* the church?

A soteriocentric ecclesiology aims to overcome this problematic theological legacy by critically examining this question anew. Doing so in today's theological context, however, is much more difficult than overcoming the legacy of metaphysical christology. While christology was widely interrogated and demetaphysicized in the twentieth century, ecclesiology became progressively *more* metaphysical, and this trend has continued into the twenty-first century. Over a half-century ago Stephen Neill observed that "all our ecclesiologies are inadequate and out of date. Nearly all of them have been constructed in the light of a static concept of the Church as something given, something which already exists."[8] The years since have only compounded the theological crisis. Theologians have lulled themselves into a dogmatic metaphysical slumber where the church is concerned. Before we can develop a positive soteriocentric understanding of the church, we will first have to rouse ourselves from this theological torpor by coming to terms with the ecclesiocentrism that pervades contemporary theology.

THE PROBLEM OF ECCLESIOCENTRISM

In his magisterial history of *The Christian Tradition*, the late Jaroslav Pelikan observes that the twentieth century marked a new stage in the history of doctrine. In the first several centuries, the point of division was christology and trinity; in the medieval era, it was the sacraments; in the Reformation, soteriology; in Protestant orthodoxy, election and the inspiration of

---

8. Neill, *Creative Tension*, 111. Cf. Flett, *Apostolicity*, 32–35.

scripture.[9] But the late nineteenth century saw a shift, which then flowered in subsequent decades. "As previous periods of church history had found their distinctive theological vocation in the doctrine of the Trinity or in the doctrine of justification," Pelikan comments, "so now it was to be the doctrine of the church that would become the leitmotiv of this age."[10] According to Everett Ferguson, "ecclesiology may be regarded as the organizing theme for twentieth-century theology."[11] The principal reason for this "turn to the church," as we might call it, was the rise of the ecumenical movement:

> As the twentieth century began, each of the major churches of a divided Christendom was obliged, for reasons of its own, to address anew the doctrine of the church. . . . Ecumenicity was the great new fact in the history of the church, and hence also in the history of Christian doctrine; and the doctrine of the church became, as it had never quite been before, the bearer of the whole of the Christian message for the twentieth century, as well as the recapitulation of the entire doctrinal tradition from preceding centuries.[12]

The driving force behind the ecumenical movement was the growing pluralism within western society and the corresponding dissolution of Christendom. As Christians realized their estrangement from the bonds of nation and culture, they began to establish new bonds with fellow believers from other confessions and communions. "The theological rediscovery of the doctrine of the church was thus closely tied to the existential rediscovery of the reality of the church itself," according to Pelikan.[13]

The rise of ecumenism and the turn to ecclesiology led to major changes in both mission and theology. Prior to the twentieth century mission largely took the form of a "civilizing" colonization: since the gospel was communicated in terms of the culture of the missionaries, mission was simply the spread of western civilization, with religion constituting one factor alongside sociopolitical and economic factors. But as Christendom fell apart, and Christianity was disentangled from nation, mission had to change. Unfortunately, it changed by replacing one sociohistorical bond for another. Mission-as-civilization instead became mission-as-*churchification*.[14] Mission became conversion not to a national culture but to a transnational

9. Pelikan, *Christian Tradition*, 5:281.

10. Ibid., 5:289.

11. Ferguson, *Church*, xiv.

12. Pelikan, *Christian Tradition*, 5:282.

13. Ibid., 5:287.

14. Hoekendijk, *Church*, 23.

ecclesial culture that purported to unify the disparate members of the global church.[15] Johannes Hoekendijk, the main voice speaking out against this in the mid-twentieth century, calls this "church-centric missionary thinking," according to which "the church is the starting point and the goal of the mission."[16] The result was not merely the churchification of mission but also the *churchification of theology*. This church-centrism or ecclesiocentrism became the dominant presupposition in theology and mission in the twentieth century to such an extent that very few bothered to point out that the NT presented a powerful witness against this ecclesiasticization.

The Eschatological Body of Christ

The German Lutheran New Testament scholar Ernst Käsemann was keenly aware of this turn to the church. As one who initially participated in the German Christian movement and then later joined the Confessing Church, the turn to the church had deep existential significance. And it was significant for his fellow Christians in Germany, as he notes at the beginning of his essay on "The Theological Problem Presented by the Motif of the Body of Christ" in his 1969 volume on Pauline theology:

> In all probability, the nature and task of the church has seldom been the subject of more intensive consideration in the Protestant churches than during the last forty years. In Germany the reaction against liberal individualism, the struggle against national socialism, and the ecumenical movement, have all played their contributing parts here. In this way the theme of the body of Christ has also taken on a significance for my generation which would have been unthinkable earlier; and it has frequently been of determining importance.[17]

In light of this context, Käsemann turns to investigate the Pauline notion of the "body of Christ" that had become such an important theme in twentieth-century investigations of ecclesiology. Käsemann writes as a historical-critical scholar, and he insists on a "historical interpretation" that locates the Pauline concept within "its historical situation." Because the concept has a long reception history within Christian dogmatics, there is "the danger of treating the text as evidence of a dogma and of interpreting the dogma . . .

15. See Flett, *Apostolicity*, 103–37.

16. Hoekendijk, *Church*, 38.

17. Käsemann, *Perspectives*, 102.

but not the apostle's intention."[18] And indeed, he argues, that is precisely what has happened.

The apostle Paul, according to Käsemann, was not centrally concerned with the church but with *Christ*, and his argument about the "body of Christ" was "a Christological one."[19] Paul uses the concept in an "exclusively Christological" way to indicate the "universal sovereignty" of Christ.[20] The concept serves to flesh out Paul's other idea of being "in Christ," which indicates our participation in the apocalyptic advent of new creation.[21] Paul understands both Christ and the church eschatologically: "the centre of ecclesiology is now the contrast of the aeons of Adam and Christ, of fallen and redeemed creation."[22] Ecclesiology, for Paul, is simply a function of his christology and pneumatology. The church is that place where Christ through his Spirit exercises God's eschatological rule over the cosmos. What this means is that "the apostle is not interested in the church *per se* and as a religious group. He is only interested in it in so far as it is the means whereby Christ reveals himself on earth and becomes incarnate in the world through his Spirit." The church community is "the sphere in which and through which Christ proves himself *Kyrios* on earth after his exaltation."[23] The role of the Christian, and thus the church more generally, is to "be a 'place holder' for Christ until death."[24] The problem is that "what Paul preached in Christological terms has now been turned into the function of ecclesiology," and we see this already in the deutero-Pauline work of Ephesians.[25]

Despite a number of similarities with Paul's writings, the letter to the Ephesians, likely written by a disciple of Paul, inverts the Pauline order of Christ and the church, elevating "the idea of the people of God" in a way that "overshadows the decisive and permanent primacy of Christology over ecclesiology. . . . Christology and ecclesiology merge into one another: the church becomes the prolongation and representative of her Lord."[26] As the *incarnatus prolongatus*, "the church has become the central eschatological

18. Ibid., 105.
19. Ibid., 103.
20. Ibid., 109.
21. Ibid., 106.
22. Ibid., 108.
23. Ibid., 117.
24. Ibid., 119.
25. Ibid., 121.

26. Ibid., 112. There is a conservative trend in recent NT scholarship that argues for the authenticity of the Pauline authorship of Ephesians and Colossians. I see this as further confirmation of the ecclesiocentrism that plagues theology, especially within Anglo-American evangelical scholarship.

event," so that what Paul proclaims as an eschatological reality in *Christ* has become instead a reality in the church.[27] Käsemann summarizes the problem in Ephesians as follows:

> The theme of the church moves into the centre and takes on independent life ... even as against Christology, although the motif of the body of Christ still remains dominant. ... The thematic treatment of the concept of the church cannot be called Pauline. *Wherever ecclesiology moves into the foreground, however justifiable the reasons may be, Christology will lose its decisive importance, even if it does so by becoming integrated, in some form or other, in the doctrine of the church.* ... What Paul preached in Christological terms has now been turned into the function of ecclesiology. ... The function of Christology in the letter to the Ephesians consists in caring for the orderly growth of the church.[28]

Long before Constantine, it was the abandonment of the eschatological consciousness of the apostles and the corresponding conflation of Christ with the church that constituted the true fall of Christianity. Whereas Paul exalted Christ alone and understood the church to be constituted by his Spirit, the Christian community after him began to see itself as the historical extension of Christ incarnate and understood the Spirit as serving merely to "sustain, foster and nourish" its existence.[29] Whereas Paul focused on the crucified body of *Christ* in whom we participate, the later church focused on the communal *body* of Christ that subsists in the church's teachings and practices. Christianity became concerned with, as Käsemann says, "caring for the orderly growth of the church," as opposed to the ecstatic missionary proclamation of Christ's apocalypse.

The Alternative Society

The rise of early catholicism was historically inevitable. As Rudolf Bultmann observes, "no human society can have permanence in history without regulations. ... As the congregations grew and Christianity spread, these regulations were formed, unified, and solidified until the organization of the

---

27. Ibid., 121. Is it an accident that the transition toward ecclesiology in the early church coincided with a transition toward viewing salvation as a process of *growth* (cf. Eph 4:15; Col 1:10; 1 Pet 2:2; 2 Pet 3:18)?

28. Ibid., 120–21. Emphasis mine.

29. Ibid., 112.

ancient catholic Church stood created, or, rather, had grown into being."[30] But as the organization developed and grew, the primitive church inevitably left behind the original expectation of the imminent end of the world. The moment of eschatological fulfillment was pushed out to the indefinite future: "one day is like a thousand years" (2 Pet 3:8).[31] The result of this development was a transformation in the church's self-understanding. Instead of a community oriented toward a transcendent, inbreaking future, the church began to see its eschatological character *"in its present possession of institutions* which are already mediating transcendent powers in the present: a sacramental cultus and finally a priestly office."[32] The community "changed from a fellowship of salvation to an institution of salvation."[33] The defining mark of the church shifted from the *imminent* expectation of Christ's coming to the *sacramental* expectation of the priest's consecrating action. As the church became the mediator of salvation, the sacrament, rather than the kerygma of Christ's eschatological lordship through the power of the Spirit, "comes to be regarded . . . as the factor which is constitutive for the Church."[34] The transcendent, eschatological community knew its provisionality and was defined entirely in terms of its mission in the last days; the immanent, sacramental church, by contrast, had to secure its permanence and continuity. The replacement of eschatological consciousness with sacramentalism thus led to the formation of ecclesiastical offices, with the bishop becoming the priest of the sacramental cultus and the rest of the congregation becoming the laity.[35]

With the loss of the community's self-understanding as "an eschatological community ruled by the Spirit,"[36] the church began to take on the character of an alternative culture, a separate social entity in competition with the surrounding cultural milieu. In order to articulate this new self-understanding, early Christian leaders turned to the one paradigm of an

30. Bultmann, *Theology*, 2:95.

31. Ibid., 2:114.

32. Ibid., 2:112.

33. Ibid., 2:114.

34. Ibid., 2:109.

35. "Then eschatological consciousness is over-shadowed or supplanted by sacramentalism, and *the bishop* who leads worship and administers the sacrament *becomes the priest,* whose office gives him a quality which separates him from the rest of the congregation, making them laymen. . . . The order which regulates the cultus is now regarded as that which guarantees its efficacy. Thereby the persons who carry out the cultus achieve priestly character, and the distinction between priests and laymen, unknown to the New Testament and, indeed, contradictory to it, develops" (ibid., 2:110).

36. Ibid., 2:97.

alternative culture they all knew best: the people of Israel. The church soon appropriated the identity of Israel for itself.[37] As the first letter of Peter articulates it, the church is "a royal priesthood" (1 Pet 2:9).[38] Here already we can see the seeds of later anti-Jewish supersessionism, according to which the Christian church is the *only* true Israel. For good reason, the early church's relation to Judaism has been a topic of much discussion. What has been ignored, however, is the way this co-opting of Jewish identity was unfaithful not only to the Jewish people but also to *Christianity*.

We have to tread carefully here. The topic of the church's appropriation of Israel's mission rests on the edge of a knife. On the one side we risk conflating Israel and the church and failing to acknowledge the distinctiveness of each community. On the other side we risk dividing Israel and the church and failing to acknowledge the proper continuity between the two testaments. If Peter—with his talk of the church as a "royal priesthood"—represents the former, then Marcion—with his sharp division between Jesus and the God of Israel—represents the latter. The trend in recent decades, given the desperate need of the Christian community to address the horror of the Shoah, has been to side with Peter.[39] But this has come at a deep theological cost—namely, at the cost of the earliest community's eschatological consciousness. The apocalyptic gospel, which was lost in the transition to an ordered institution, has become systematically excluded from Christian theology. Today it is in vogue even among Protestants to say the "eucharist makes the church."[40] Even those who do not go this far often still think of the church as an alternative culture, treat doctrine as providing universal rules for faith and action, and view the institutional order of the church as normative and inviolable. Any attempt to reclaim the pneumatological, apocalyptic spirit of early Christianity is associated with dispensational cults

37. According to Bultmann, "in the course of time the more development there is toward the formation of Christian regulations for living, the more the territory of divine law will expand outward from its center in the cultic ordinance. This tendency takes on concrete form by the fact that the Old Testament is taken over by the Church" (ibid., 2:111).

38. Ibid., 2:101.

39. We see this especially in Anglo-American postliberalism. Lindbeck, for example, argues for an "Israel-like view of the church." See Lindbeck, "Confession"; cf. Ochs, *Another Reformation*.

40. The phrase comes from Henri de Lubac, who writes: "Literally speaking, therefore, the Eucharist makes the Church" (*Corpus Mysticum*, 88). It has been taken up and popularized in Anglo-Catholic circles through Radical Orthodoxy. According to John Milbank and Catherine Pickstock, "the giving of Body and Blood in the Eucharist gives also the Body of the Church. The Eucharist both occurs within the Church and gives rise to the Church in a circular fashion" (*Truth*, 94).

that believe Jesus might rapture them away tomorrow. But we must make the attempt if we are to reclaim the soteriocentric identity of the Christian community.

The transformation of the church from an eschatological event into a new Israel required abandoning precisely what made the new age of Christ *new*. Israel was called by God to be a people set apart from the nations. Their mission was to remain faithful to their distinct culture, a culture defined by the law, by Torah. They were called to be "a light to the nations" (Isa 42:6, 49:6). Mount Zion, according to Isaiah, "shall be established as the highest of the mountains," so that "all the nations shall stream to it" (Isa 2:2). The vision of Micah declares that the nations will "go up to the mountain of the Lord, to the house of the God of Jacob; that he may teach us his ways and that we may walk in his paths" (Mic 4:2). In other words, the Jewish eschatological vision is that all the nations will participate in the life of Israel; the nations will adopt the law of God and conform to the culture of the Hebrew people.[41] In missiological terms, Israel has a *centripetal* mission: the gentile periphery moves *in* toward the center—the mountain of Zion. If, according to the Babel myth, God judged the tower (i.e., the false mountain) of the world by scattering the people to the periphery, then Israel's mission is to restore the lost unity by bringing all people together again at the true mountain.

For those who confess that Jesus is the Christ, however, a very different mission follows. The birth of the church at Pentecost, according to the Acts of the Apostles, is the key turning point. When the Spirit fills the apostles, they "began to speak in other languages" (Acts 2:4). Jews in Jerusalem "from every nation under heaven" heard the apostles "speaking in the native language of each" (Acts 2:5-6). Whereas the tower of Babel involved the loss of a unified language and so the loss of communication, Pentecost involves the restoration of communication precisely *through the plurality of human languages*. Pentecost is the *blessing* of Babel's curse; it sanctifies the very diversity that is the cause of our cultural fragmentation and miscommunication. Through the apostles God speaks a single kerygma in and through the multiplicity of tongues, cultures, and contexts. In contrast to a single culture into which all nations are eschatologically assimilated, Peter

---

41. Theodore of Mopsuestia, in his commentary on Micah 4, thus writes: "Large numbers from all quarters, even from foreign peoples, would hasten to assemble to reach this mountain of God, on which God is believed to dwell, and learn how they should regulate their lives and live as they ought. The result would be that the law that is in force there would be a law also for those from foreign parts, and all would seem to hear a divine voice by which they would be obliged to live in keeping with the laws of Jerusalem" (*Commentary*, 220).

declares that, "in the last days," God "will pour out [God's] Spirit upon *all* flesh" (Acts 2:17; emphasis mine). The nations are sanctified *as the nations*, rather than receiving God's blessing only insofar as they are incorporated into the people of Israel.

The logic of this apocalyptic outpouring of the Spirit leads inexorably to the decision of the Jerusalem Council in Acts 15 to accept the gentiles *as gentiles*.[42] The early community recognized that God "[gave] them the Holy Spirit, just as he did to us" (Acts 15:8), and for this reason they decided "we should not make it difficult for the Gentiles who are turning to God" (Acts 15:19 NIV). Remarkably, the instructions given to the gentiles by the Jerusalem church did not require circumcision, thereby including within the family of God those people previously deemed unclean sinners. One did not have to become a Jew in order to follow the God of Israel. A person could follow Jesus within the framework of her native cultural context. It follows that the Christian community has a *centrifugal* mission: the apostolic church moves *out* to the gentile periphery. Acts thus concludes with the declaration that "this salvation of God has been sent to the Gentiles [or nations]" (Acts 28:28) echoing the conclusion of Luke, which says that "repentance and forgiveness of sins is to be proclaimed in his name to all nations [or Gentiles]" (Luke 24:47). Followers of Christ are *sent* (ἀποστέλλω) out to *proclaim* (κηρύσσω) the gospel; theirs is an apostolic and kerygmatic mission. The church has no defining cultural form, but rather "all cultural forms that distinguish and define human life and experience are in principle worthy of bearing the truth of Christianity." Christianity is "without a revealed language or a founding original culture." Following the inclusion of the gentiles, Christians "pursued mission through multiple cultural idioms, convinced that no language was exempt from God's salvific work."[43] The genuine church is no alternative society or culture but rather a kerygmatic presence within every society and every culture.

By describing the church as a "royal priesthood," the author of the first epistle of Peter applied language belonging to Israel's centripetal mission to a community pneumatically defined by a centrifugal mission. The result was the silencing of the Holy Spirit. The Christian community was born in a pentecostal event that shattered the old bond between covenant and culture, liberating the transformative power of God from attachment to any single

42. The word "gentiles" translates the Greek τὰ ἔθνη (*ta ethnē*), which means the nations or peoples. When we read Jesus's commission to "go therefore and make disciples of all nations [τὰ ἔθνη]" (Matt 28:19), this could also be translated, "go therefore and make disciples of all gentiles." It is also worth pointing out that the LXX uses ἔθνη to translate *goyim*.

43. Sanneh, *Translating*, 74.

historical moment. The eschatological Spirit of this liberation empowers acts of faith and witness that cannot be circumscribed by tradition, culture, state, polity, or doctrine. The redefinition of the church as the "new Israel," however, shackled the Spirit to a sacramental institution:

> The Spirit is no longer the power that now and again breaks out in the "gifts"—the words and deeds and conduct of the believers—but is a power immanent in the institutions, particularly in the sacramental cult; it is the office-bearers' equipment for office. The officers have taken on the quality of priests, while it is only through their mediation that the Spirit is indirectly at work in the laymen.[44]

The church's replacement of eschatological consciousness with cultic-priestly consciousness was a betrayal of Pentecost. The church exchanged its migratory, crosscultural, diasporic mission for historical permanence and cultural security. This development—even if, in certain respects, historically inevitable—set in motion a trajectory that includes everything from monastic communities to medieval Christendom, from the missionary movement to American evangelical subcultures. It is a trajectory, in other words, that we live with today.

By appropriating the identity of Israel for itself, the church lost sight of its distinct calling in the world—a calling neither to extend nor to supplant Israel but to exist alongside of it. "Christian mission is a *shared* mission," according to Clark Williamson, "one in which both the church and synagogue are called to be witnesses of the God of Israel before the world and each other."[45] The move to appropriate Israel's identity for itself and thus to identify the church with the eschatological kingdom of God "indicate[s] nothing more than theological chaos and institutional self-justification."[46] It is imperative to recover the eschatological consciousness of the early Christian community, not only to restore the pentecostal identity of the church within a pluralistic society but to heal relations with the Jewish people in a post-Shoah age.

Cultural Ecclesiocentrism

The ecclesiocentric turn from Christ to church has taken a number of different forms, but in each case it has involved setting up the church as an

---

44. Bultmann, *Theology*, 2:114.
45. Williamson, *Guest*, 251.
46. Ibid., 252.

alternative society (the divine *polis* or *civitas*)—an exclusive community set apart from others in some clearly demarcated way. Doctrinally, it led to the view of the church as the exclusive mediator of salvation (*extra ecclesiam nulla salus*); socially, it led to Christendom and the joining of spiritual and imperial power; liturgically, it led to the sacramentalization of Christianity and the elevation of the priestly office as the center and foundation of the Christian life. The Reformation initially unsettled many of these shifts, but in the last half-century we have seen the entrenchment of this old Christendom mentality within Protestant ecumenical theology in response to the rise of pluralism in modernity and the corresponding dissolution of Christendom in the West. The new version of ecclesiocentrism, which has roots going back to the nineteenth century, conceives the church as an alternative culture.[47]

There are a host of factors that contribute to this, some of them causally connected, others largely coincidental. Probably the most important is the Second Vatican Council in the mid-1960s, and especially the promulgation of *Lumen Gentium* in 1964, which placed ecclesiology at the center of the global theological agenda for over a generation. Other factors include: the disillusionment with and abandonment of existential and hermeneutical theology in the late 1960s and the corresponding rise of postliberalism in Anglo-American theology through Hans Frei's work in the mid-1970s (*Eclipse of Biblical Narrative*, 1974) and George Lindbeck's work in the mid-1980s (*The Nature of Doctrine*, 1984); the turn to patristic theology and precritical exegesis in the 1980s, along with the subsequent development of what is known as theological interpretation of scripture; the turn to classical virtue ethics with the publication in 1981 of Alasdair MacIntyre's *After Virtue*; and finally, as part of the second generation of postliberalism, the ecclesiological hegemony that took hold in the 1990s and beyond, initiated by the work of Stanley Hauerwas (*Resident Aliens*, 1989) and John Milbank (*Theology and Social Theory*, 1991).

Lindbeckian postliberalism is especially important insofar as it makes the cultural institution of the church the norm for the meaningfulness of God-talk, thereby establishing ecclesiology as the foundation for all theology in a way that was unprecedented for Protestants. Lindbeck achieved this by arguing, ostensibly on the basis of Ludwig Wittgenstein and Clifford Geertz, that the truth of doctrine is relative to a particular community of faith. Doctrine makes sense within a specific "cultural-linguistic"

---

47. Here I am thinking, especially, of Friedrich Schleiermacher's development of the *Volkskirche*, Adolf von Harnack's "brotherhood of man," and the Anglo-American missionary movement.

context and is "incommensurable" with other contexts.[48] Postliberal theology thus interprets scripture by engaging in "intratextual social or ecclesial embodiment."[49] Scripture is understood only as it is socially embodied within the church. For this reason, Lindbeck says, "the Bible exists for the sake of the church."[50] Ronald Thiemann, a second-generation postliberal who studied under Frei at Yale University, summarizes the essence of postliberalism when he states that "theology seeks its criteria of judgment within the first-order language of church practice."[51] But postliberalism does not limit itself to the view that church practice is only a hermeneutical criterion. If, as he says, interpretation involves "social or ecclesial embodiment," and if "to interpret the Bible is to use it to interpret other things,"[52] and if "the text . . . absorbs the world, rather than the world the text,"[53] then interpretation involves absorbing the things of the world into the social orbit of the church. The goal of biblical interpretation becomes the construction of an ecclesial society, or the universal expansion of the church—i.e., Christendom.[54] In other words, the church has the responsibility to reinterpret and absorb all other cultural frameworks and thought-forms so that they become subservient to the church: "the Bible as interpreted within the Christian mainstream purports to provide a totally comprehensive framework, a universal perspective, within which everything can be properly construed and outside of which nothing can be equally well understood."[55] It is only natural that Lindbeck, like early catholic theologians, advocates an "Israel-like view of the church," and claims that "Christians can now apply Israel's

---

48. Lindbeck, *Nature of Doctrine*, 18–27, 34–35.

49. Lindbeck, "Atonement," 145.

50. Ibid., 152.

51. Thiemann, *Revelation*, 75.

52. Lindbeck, "Atonement," 151.

53. Lindbeck, *Nature of Doctrine*, 104.

54. Lindbeck's postliberal version of Christendom does not conflict with his earlier statement that Christians in our post-Christian world "must become, sociologically speaking, sectarian" ("Sectarian Future," 230). For Lindbeck, it is precisely the church's distinctiveness over against the modern secular world which enables it to practice its intratextual intussusception of all things. In its separation from secularism, the church can do its work of practicing the scriptural interpretation of reality, and through this the world will benefit. The Christian community is in possession of the true meaning of all things in the world, and it is responsible for enacting or embodying this meaning in the social body of the church. Paul DeHart thus describes Lindbeck's position in the following way: "liberal social values must be harnessed to an ecclesial vision which is sociologically sectarian but also catholic and orthodox" (*Trial*, 60).

55. Lindbeck, "Gospel's Uniqueness," 429.

story to themselves without supersessionism or triumphalism."[56] But this is precisely what Christians must *not* do if they are to avoid triumphalism and supersessionism, which postliberalism does not. Indeed, Christianity within Lindbeck's theological framework is an untranslatable worldview that seeks to circumscribe everything within the bounds of the church. The end of this path lies in the return to Christendom and the establishment of the church as the arbiter of social and political power.

The work of Robert Jenson, a postliberal contemporary of Lindbeck, is another key factor in the churchification of theology in the late twentieth-century. Jenson, particularly in his later work, develops the most robust version of the church-as-culture position. In a 2003 lecture he begins by defining culture, without interacting with cultural theorists or anthropologists, as "the mutual behavior of a group in so far as this behavior is sustained by teaching and not only by genetics and physical ecology," or "in so far as this can be abstracted from those doing the behaving, as in itself a coherent system of mutually determining signs."[57] Let us assume for the sake of argument that this is an adequate definition. Jenson asserts that, based on either definition, "the church obviously has—or rather is—a specific identifiable culture." He goes on to say that "if the church is, or has, a culture of her own, then the church's claim somehow to *be* Israel must also be a claim somehow to continue the culture of Israel."[58] The "argument" here goes something like this: if (a) the church is Israel, and (b) Israel is a culture, then (c) the church is a culture—specifically the culture of Israel. Jenson can thus claim that "a relation between, say, Christ and Chinese culture is in itself a relation between Jewish culture and Chinese culture."[59] By claiming that the church is Israel, Jenson begs the very question under dispute and makes the loss of eschatological consciousness normative for Christianity.[60]

Jenson draws three decisive implications from this that bear directly on our argument. The first is that "like any community, [the church] is

56. Lindbeck, "Confession," 495.

57. Jenson, "Christ as Culture 1," 323–24.

58. Ibid., 324.

59. Ibid., 323.

60. It is important, of course, to oppose anti-Judaism and antisemitism wherever they occur, and certainly Jenson and Lindbeck believe that their identification of the church with Israel is a philosemitic move. On both historical and theological grounds, I find this logic questionable. Furthermore, if the price of opposing anti-Judaism is the loss of the distinctive essence of Christian self-understanding as the eschatological community of Jesus Christ, then it is a price too high to pay. Thankfully, it is not the only option available to us. My argument here is that a more carefully defined *distinction* between the church and Israel not only does justice to the NT kerygma but also addresses the problem of supersessionism.

responsible to cultivate her culture, and can lose her identity if she does not." The cultivation of the church's culture—including polity, liturgy, doctrine, art, and the like—that Käsemann and Bultmann identify as the fall of the church is, for Jenson, the church's divinely authorized mission! The second implication naturally follows: "since the church is a culture, there are limits on 'inculturation'. With any culture, there are some elements of other cultures that it can assimilate and others that it cannot without self-destruction."[61] If the church already has its own given culture, then the mission of the church can only take one of two forms: colonialism or separatism. Jenson takes the path of colonialism: the church can, at best, "assimilate" other cultures into its culture.[62] Here we see the wholesale adoption of Israel's centripetal mission, the result of which is a rejection of crosscultural translation and contextualization. In his *Systematic Theology* Jenson says that the church's culture comprises signs "that are not items of a language"—for example, images, processions, ritual practices, music, and architecture—and thus are not "disposable by translation."[63] Robert Wilken extends this line of thinking. "Culture lives by language," he argues, and "if there is a distinctly Christian language, we must be wary of translation." The only acceptable form of translation is assimilation: "There must be translation *into* the Lord's style of language, bringing alien language into the orbit of Christian belief and practice and giving it a different meaning."[64] Jenson's third implication brings everything to a head: "if the church is the body of Christ, . . . and if this body of Christ, the church, is a culture, it follows that Christ is a culture."[65] Whereas Käsemann argues that the turn to the church involved a turn away from Christ, Jenson makes the more radical leap and simply identifies Christ with the church—more specifically, with the church's culture. One can now comfortably concern oneself with cultivating the church's institutional culture in the safe knowledge that one is advancing the cause of Christ.

The fact that this position has no basis in the New Testament is of little concern to Wilken and Jenson. Wilken in fact traces the history in which "Christ becomes culture." Referring to the well-known *Epistle to Diognetus*, he observes that in the second century Christians "did not bear the marks usually associated with a distinctive community." Christian art at the time involved selecting a conventional symbol or image and "invest[ing] [it] with

61. Jenson, "Christ as Culture 1," 324.

62. John Flett develops this argument at length in *Apostolicity*, esp. 103–85.

63. Jenson, *Systematic Theology*, 2:60.

64. Wilken, "Church's Way," 30.

65. Jenson, "Christ as Culture 1," 325.

a Christian meaning. . . . What the symbols represented lay in the eyes of the beholder, not in the object. As far as Roman society was concerned Christianity was invisible."[66] Wilken clearly views this stage of Christianity as deficient. Like Jenson, he claims that the church is an alternative *polis*, and this *polis* is the historical prolongation of Christ himself: "Christ entered history as a community, a society, not simply as a message, and the form taken by the community's life *is* Christ within society."[67] Wilken and Jenson both make Christendom definitive for Christian theology—indeed, definitive for God's self-revelation in the person of Christ. Christianity's development into a distinctive culture, which occurred historically along with the co-opting of Israel's identity, becomes for them the hermeneutical criterion of the gospel. Any possibility of God disrupting and invading the institution of cultural Christianity has been prohibited in principle.

If the postliberalism of Jenson and Wilken represents the colonialist mission of cultural Christianity, then the contemporary evangelical focus on the "church in exile" represents the separatist mission. Talk of the exilic nature of the church has exploded in the early twenty-first century.[68] One reason for this is no doubt a reaction to the bellicose, belligerent nature of the colonialist mission of the Religious Right. Instead of fighting the culture, these younger conservatives seek to escape it. This approach, however commendable as an alternative to the so-called "culture wars," remains trapped within the same logic of Christendom. It still assumes the church is a culture; the only difference is that this culture is supposed to remain pure and undefiled by the world, abstaining from the pursuit of worldly power. In short, conservative (ecclesiocentric) evangelicalism, like postliberalism, assumes a noneschatological Christianity that has made self-care its primary mission and task in the world. These are not the only instances of Christendom logic, but they exemplify the problem in the present situation. Whatever form it takes, ecclesiocentrism reduces the eschatological event to a worldly reality concerned with spatiotemporal continuity.

To summarize, the twentieth-century turn to the church has thus replicated in the history of doctrine the original turn to the church that occurred within the primitive Christian community between Paul's missionary proclamation and the rise of early catholicism. And in both cases the consciousness of God's apocalyptic action in Christ was lost, while the ecclesial institution became the de facto center of Christian existence. Ecclesiocentrism thus appears whenever Christianity loses sight of the

66. Wilken, "Church's Way," 32–33.

67. Ibid., 32.

68. For example, see Frost, *Exiles*; Thompson, *Church*; Beach, *Church*.

eschatological horizon of the gospel, that is, whenever it fails to remain conscious of Christ's interruptive incursion into our unconscious existence. Ecclesiocentrism is a betrayal of the apocalypse of God. With the loss of a constant expectation of a new encounter with Christ, faith settles down in the world and takes up permanent residence within the structures of society. The problem with ecclesiocentrism—both ancient and modern—is that, in the end, soteriological christology loses its normative character and becomes subservient to the preservation of a particular cultural institution. Both doctrine and liturgy become auxiliaries in the church's quest for sociocultural stability and dominance. Those who espouse an ecclesiocentric vision may not themselves be pining after Christendom (though some are), but their steadfast concentration on protecting and promoting the visible work of the *church*—with its virtues, practices, liturgies, and doctrines— ensures they will lose sight of the invisible work of *God*. *Ecclesiocentrism is incompatible with the bifocal vision of faith.* And once we lose our capacity to see and follow the inbreaking of Christ, our work becomes subsumed within the brick-laying machine of the empire.

THE CHURCH AS THE APOCALYPTIC APOSTOLATE

The hermeneutical reconstruction of ecclesiology has to begin by clearing away our natural assumptions about what the church is. We are so accustomed to hearing that "the church" does this and "the church" thinks that, that we do not stop to ask whether we know what we mean when we speak about the church. Just as Bultmann asked in 1925, "what does it mean to speak of God?" so we must ask today, "what does it mean to speak of the church?" And like Bultmann, we need to begin our reconstruction by looking at the eschatological origins of Christianity.

The Church as Eschatological Community

The earliest church community understood itself as an eschatological community standing at the turning point of the ages. Within the Synoptic traditions, the community of believers are sent out to proclaim the news that "the kingdom of God [or heaven] has come near" (Luke 10:8–11; Matt 10:7). Followers of Jesus are ambassadors, according to Paul, of God's apocalyptic act of reconciliation, which marks the end of history and the coming of God's reign (2 Cor 5:19–20). The Matthean tradition thus tells the story of

Jesus giving his followers the "keys of the kingdom" (Matt 16:18–19). In light of the prophetic witness, the community saw themselves as the elect remnant of Israel heralding the coming of the Messiah. They are "an exemplary anticipation and advance representation of the righteous eschatological fellowship for which humanity is destined in the kingdom of God."[69] The small band of disciples represents "the vestibule, so to say, of God's Reign that is shortly to appear."[70]

Central to this consciousness of being the eschatological community is the gift of the Holy Spirit as the "first installment" (2 Cor 1:22) or "first fruits" (Rom 8:23) of God's eschatological promises. The Christian community "knew that it had been given *the Spirit*, that gift of the end of days . . . whose impartation was promised for the end of days."[71] For the eschatological community of faith, the gift of the Holy Spirit supplanted God's gift of the law. Whereas the law was tied to a particular sociocultural form and specified in advance what a person should do, the Spirit is open to every cultural form (cf. Acts 2) and does not determine what faithful existence looks like in advance but guides the believer in each new moment according to the command to love one's neighbor (Rom 13:8–10).[72] Paul thus says "we are discharged from the law, dead to that which held us captive, so that we are slaves not under the old written code but in the new life of the Spirit" (Rom 7:6; cf. Rom 8:2), and "where the Spirit of the Lord is, there is freedom" (2 Cor 3:17)—freedom not only from the powers of sin and death but also from the principalities that enslave people to a code, written or

69. Pannenberg, *Systematic Theology*, 3:463.

70. Bultmann, *Theology*, 1:37.

71. Ibid., 1:41.

72. Tom Greggs, commenting on Acts 2, rightly sees the "event of the Holy Spirit" as the ground of the church in contrast to postliberal-ecclesiocentric accounts of the church: "The church begins at Pentecost with the coming of the Holy Spirit. The primary condition of the church is not ecclesial form, patterns of worship or structures of ministry. The primary condition of the church is the event of the coming of the Holy Spirit, who is present within the variety and plurality of the community in all its diversity, and acts upon the community to make it the church. The church is made holy (is sanctified) from without by an event of the *Holy* Spirit. . . . The vast majority of engagements in contemporary ecclesiology fall prey to precisely the problem of locating the identity of the church in the institutional organization of the church. . . . There has been a propensity in many ecclesial settings to think about the church in resolutely non-theological categories; and this runs deep. Much discussion of the church has focused on aping the church of Acts 1, and not attending to the condition of the existence of the church in Acts 2—the event of the outpouring of the Holy Spirit of God. Much ecclesiological discussion has become obsessed with questions of *how* to be church, sometimes at the expense of thinking about the question of what the church actually is" ("Church and Sacraments," 160–61).

unwritten, dictating what defines genuine life. "If you are led by the Spirit," Paul writes, "you are not subject to the law" (Gal 5:18).

This freedom in the Spirit translates into a different understanding of the community's missionary task. Mission determined by a cultural law is always centripetal. Israel is thus missionary by bringing the rest of the world into its own culture; the world must become Israel.[73] Mission determined by the Spirit is always centrifugal. The Christian community is thus missionary through diasporic self-translation into the multiplicity of cultural contexts; the world becomes Christian *as world*, not by conforming to an ecclesial culture. The Spirit of Pentecost blesses the languages—and, by extension, the sociocultural frameworks—of "every nation under heaven" (Acts 2:5) and grants the community an eschatological vision of new creation in which "a great multitude . . . from every nation, from all tribes and peoples and languages" are gathered together, unified precisely in their diversity (Rev 7:9). The Spirit empowers the community with this eschatological vision to carry on the healing ministry of Jesus and propels them to go out into the ends of the earth with the message of the Messiah's coming. Their self-understanding as the eschatological community is therefore the impetus and ground for their missionary activity, which is reflected especially in the Synoptic accounts of Matthew and Luke-Acts.[74]

Not only do they bear the message of the eschatological advent, but they order their lives to correspond to this expectation of God's coming. The practices of baptism and Lord's Supper are of chief importance. Through baptism the church concretizes the turning of the ages with respect to each person; the baptizand dies to the old age and rises again as a member of Christ's eschatological body (cf. Rom 6:5–11). Likewise, the church's table fellowship at the Lord's Supper is a "provisional representation of the fellowship of God's kingdom," a celebration of the Lord's impending inbreaking.[75]

---

73. There is a formal similarity between the mission of Israel and the ecclesiocentric mission of Christendom, in the sense that both are world-encompassing and culturally defined. But there are important differences: the mission of Israel is explicitly eschatological and theocentric, constituted wholly by God's sovereign action at the end of history and not through the mechanisms of colonial and imperial power; biblically speaking, the mission of Israel—at least in the prophetic tradition as opposed to the royal, Davidic tradition—is the liberative mission of an oppressed and marginalized minority, not the mission of an empire seeking to convert the heathen; the mission of Israel is a mission of estrangement rather than assimilation and appropriation, in the sense that it calls people out of their contexts to adopt an entirely foreign way of life, whereas ecclesiocentrism subsumes particular cultural artifacts into its hegemonic vision.

74. See Bultmann, *Theology*, 1:42.

75. Pannenberg, *Systematic Theology*, 3:464.

As Paul informs the Corinthian church, "as often as you eat this bread and drink the cup, you proclaim the Lord's death until he comes" (1 Cor 11:26). Properly understood, the eucharistic celebration has the imminent advent of Christ always in view. Paul censures the Corinthians because they still have divisions and factions in their communal gatherings (1 Cor 11:18–19), which means they have forgotten the eschatological essence of their ecclesial existence. Earlier in the same letter he exhorts them, "in view of the impending crisis [ἀνάγκη]"[76] that comes with the end of history, to "let each of you remain in the condition in which you were called" (1 Cor 7:26, 20). Those who are single should not seek a spouse (1 Cor 7:27), and those who are slaves should "not be concerned about it" (1 Cor 7:21). This passage has wreaked ethical havoc because it has been read as a timeless, transhistorical prescription, rather than as a situational ethic in the face of the fact that "the present form of this world is passing away" (1 Cor 7:31). The community lives in the "appointed time," the καιρός, that has "grown short" or "contracted itself" (συνεσταλμένος) (1 Cor 7:29). As Giorgio Agamben observes, the verb συστέλλω "signifies the act of brailing up sails as well as the way in which an animal gathers himself before lunging."[77] The eschatological καιρός is time pulled taut, the moment of tense expectation for the embarkment of history upon its final voyage.

The origins of the Christian community reveal that the church was, from the start, *constituted* by its eschatological consciousness. The church had no *raison d'être* apart from its anticipation of the Messiah's appearance. The Christian community has no proper existence outside of the eschatological moment, what Walter Benjamin calls the time of the messianic "now"

---

76. At a 2014 session at the annual meeting of the Society of Biblical Literature, John Barclay argued for a correction of the English translation of τὴν ἐνεστῶσαν ἀνάγκην, translated in the NRSV as "the impending crisis," which suggests that the ethic Paul provides in 1 Cor 7 is an "interim ethic" for the time that remains until Christ's imminent return. Barclay argues that the word ἀνάγκην should be translated as "necessity" or "constraint," referring to the nature of the world as such. Paul's phrase, "the present constraint," thus has nothing to do with an imminent parousia. According to Barclay, Paul is articulating an ethic that is generally applicable to all Christians. Even if we concede that this phrase should not be interpreted to refer to an imminent eschatological crisis, it does not follow that Paul is providing us with a general ethic for all times, for the simple reason that Paul's *entire theology* is conditioned by imminent expectation. Isolating this one pericope does not change the fact that Paul expects the end of the present evil age in the near future, and this expectation shapes his entire theological and ethical thought. I agree with Barclay that we cannot and should not isolate this one passage as problematic and explain it away. But that is because Paul's theology as a whole has to be translated from his antiquated world-picture to our contemporary context.

77. Agamben, *Time*, 68.

(*Jetztzeit*).[78] Whether it was because the Messiah did not appear within the lifetimes of the apostles as they had expected or simply because the growth of the church demanded greater attention to institutional structure, the community lost this eschatological consciousness and became a religious society among others, vying for attention and struggling for adherents like any other cultural institution. The eschaton was deferred indefinitely and so rendered practically irrelevant. The apocalyptic Christ became the sacramental Christ. Perhaps this was inevitable, given the cultural assumptions of the day, but it is not the only available option. As I have been arguing throughout, the alternative is to rethink the apocalypse as an existential interruption, which means rethinking Christ as the agent of an existential event and so rethinking the church as the historical community that lives in constant remembrance and expectation of this event, which occurs anew in the repetition of Christ's cruciform reality. To understand the church in this light is to understand it as the eschatological *apostolate*.

The Church as Apostolate

The apocalyptic words of Jesus in the Olivet discourse provide us with a starting point for conceiving the church as the community of the apocalypse. In a private conversation about the coming end of history, Jesus tells his disciples: "And this gospel of the kingdom [εὐαγγέλιον τῆς βασιλείας] will be proclaimed [κηρυχθήσεται, "kerygmatized"] throughout the whole world [οἰκουμένη]" (Matt 24:14, my translation; cf. Mark 13:10).[79] We find in this passage, which Johannes Hoekendijk calls his "favorite missionary text,"[80] an essential correlation between kingdom, proclamation, and world. At the end of history the reign of God is not limited to a particular community, culture, or society, but rather it has cosmic significance: "The ends of the earth and the end of time belong together."[81] The kerygmatic message of God's eschatological reign concerns the entire unclean, heathen, nonelect "οἰκουμένη," rather than just the Jewish people.[82]

---

78. Benjamin, "On the Concept," 397.

79. Cf. Hoekendijk, *Church*, 31.

80. Ibid., 38.

81. Ibid., 30.

82. The word οἰκουμένη only occurs fifteen times in the NT. It is particularly distinctive of Luke-Acts, which is appropriate given the Lukan focus on the mission to the gentiles, that is, "to the ends of the earth [γῆ]" (Acts 1:8). The more common NT term, especially in the Johannine literature, is κόσμος.

Within this apocalyptic spatiotemporal matrix, the action that unites kingdom and world is the "kerygmatizing" of the gospel, the proclamation of God's reign. The kerygma is the eschatological event that ushers in the end of the old age and the birth of the new. This kerygmatizing act, and the people commissioned as its creaturely auxiliaries, is what Hoekendijk calls the apostolate.[83] The apostolate is the site where kingdom and world intersect. The apostolate is not the church referred to in common parlance.[84] Instead, this apocalyptic community "is an absolute novum in history with which the world knows not what to do. It cannot be classified sociologically or forced into line politically."[85] If the church were properly understood as the intersection within history of kingdom, apostolate (or kerygma), and world, then talk of the church would be nothing other than talk of the

83. The kerygma is to theology what the apostolate is to the church. The kerygma and apostolate are the divine events to which theology and the church are the creaturely correlates.

84. Nor is the apostolate (i.e., the genuine church) the kingdom, in contrast to the claims of Scot McKnight, and before him the theologians of the nineteenth century, both liberal and conservative. Albrecht Ritschl famously maintained that talk of the kingdom in the NT was a way of speaking about the church as the ideal moral community within history. The rediscovery of apocalyptic by Johannes Weiss and others was a shock to the liberal establishment, since it undercut the connection they had drawn between Jesus's preaching about the kingdom and their modern Protestant churches. Conservative Protestant theologians in modernity were not all that different from the liberals, a point often (and conveniently) forgotten. A. B. Bruce, for instance, says that the kingdom of God "concerned men here and now; all men eventually, Israelites in the first place. . . . It was to become a society on earth, ever widening in extent, for a kingdom is a social thing; it could not fail to become such . . . for the spirit of the kingdom is love, and impels to fellowship. It was the highest good of life. . . . It was accessible to all. . . . It was spiritual. . . . It was associated with, may almost be said to have consisted in, a certain doctrine of God, and a kindred doctrine of man" (*Kingdom*, 59–60). At this point he quotes a passage from the mediating theologian, Karl Theodor Keim, regarding the kingdom concerning the "Fatherliness of God" and the "sonship of men." To take another example, Charles Hodge begins his treatment of the kingdom with a section entitled "The Church God's Kingdom," where he says that "the kingdom of God . . . as consisting of those who acknowledge, worship, love, and obey Jehovah as the only living and true God, has existed in our world ever since the fall of Adam" (*Systematic Theology*, 2:597). He goes on to say that since "religion is essentially spiritual, an inward state, the kingdom of Christ . . . is not a visible body, except so far as goodness renders itself visible by its outward manifestations. Nevertheless as Christ has enjoined upon his people duties which render it necessary that they should organize themselves in an external society, it follows that there is and must be a visible kingdom of Christ in the world. . . . They therefore form themselves into churches, and collectively constitute the visible kingdom of Christ on earth, consisting of all who profess the true religion, together with their children" (ibid., 2:604). The point is that, in the nineteenth century, liberals and conservatives both dismissed New Testament eschatology and identified the kingdom of God with the church.

85. Hoekendijk, *Kirche*, 214.

apocalyptic event of the kerygma, the existential encounter with God's word of revelation. Unfortunately, talk of church too often remains talk of a certain sociological phenomenon, a cultural institution with its own history and identity that has to be maintained in the face of competition for attention. Theologically speaking, it is another element of the οἰκουμένη awaiting salvation. For this reason, eschatology necessarily displaces every ecclesiocentric ecclesiology.

> It is true that the context Kingdom–apostolate–oikoumene does not leave much room for the church. Ecclesiology does not fit here. When one desires to speak about God's dealings with the world, the church can be mentioned only in passing and without strong emphasis. Ecclesiology cannot be more than a single paragraph from Christology (the *Messianic* dealings with the world) and a few sentences from eschatology (the Messianic dealings with the *World*). The church is only the church to the extent that she lets herself be used as a part of God's dealings with the oikoumene. For this reason she can only be "ecumenical," i.e., oriented toward the oikoumene—the whole world.[86]

The notion that Hoekendijk dispenses with the church as a body is unfounded and presupposes the very ecclesiocentrism that he subjects to theological critique.[87] What Hoekendijk rejects is a conception of the church that does not arise out of the apocalyptic event of kingdom–apostolate–world. The "church" has its own independent existence; it has its *raison d'être* in itself. The apostolate, by contrast, has no independent existence; its *raison d'être* resides wholly outside of itself in the inbreaking event of the kerygma.

Hoekendijk illuminates the distinction between church and apostolate by drawing a contrast between centripetal "Jewish proselytism" and centrifugal "Christian mission," a contrast we thematized above in our discussion of ecclesiocentrism:

> Jewish ... *proselytism* is the opposite of Christian *mission*. ... In the centripetal movement of proselytism, people are invited to come to the center where salvation is localized. In order to become a participant of salvation, they will have to join the group that mediates the redemption, i.e., emigrate completely from all other life relationships: in short, become a Jew. ... Mission is centrifugal. It leaves Jerusalem and the Jewish group and is on its way to the ends of the earth and the end of time. To

---

86. Hoekendijk, *Church*, 38.

87. Some of the main critics include Hendrikus Berkhof, Hans Margull, Konrad Raiser, and Georg Vicedom. See Flett, *Apostolicity*, 222–34.

join means here: to join the journey away from the center. The symbol is the light for the Gentiles, which goes forth toward the people, seeking them out and taking them by surprise in their darkness.[88]

Ecclesiocentrism rears its ugly head again, however, precisely at this point. While theologians and pastors are often quick to affirm the centrifugal emphasis in Christian mission, they tend to add immediately that this outward mission has to be stabilized by an inward, centripetal movement back to the church. Hence one hears about the need to keep mission and worship in balance. Some even say that this inward worship is both the origin and the goal of mission. Mission without proselytism, according to this account, is only a half-truth that undermines God's purposes for the world.

What these ecclesiocentric thinkers have failed to grasp is that the genuine church of Jesus Christ only exists where the world confronts the invasive reign of God. According to the apocalyptic perspective of the New Testament, there is no church prior or subsequent to this confrontation, no inward substance that persists independently of the event itself. This is what differentiates Israel and the New Testament church: Israel has a salvation *history* and persists as a culture within the world; the church only has a salvation *eschatology* and exists exclusively as an encounter with the coming age. "Strictly speaking, the church has no history," writes Barth.[89] Recognizing this requires the "radical abandonment of all that is reminiscent of proselytism in our practices," and that means abandoning the notion that mission serves to bring people into the church.[90] *Mission is not churchification.* On the contrary, mission serves to confront people with the reign of God, and this confrontation is constitutive of the church properly understood. The church does not *have* an apostolic function, as if "apostle" were an office supporting the larger institution. Instead, the church *is* its apostolicity.[91] If, as Karl Barth says, the church's "act is its being, its dynamic

---

88. Ibid., 43–44.

89. *KD* 2.2:377. Cf. *CD* 2.2:342.

90. Hoekendijk, *Church*, 44.

91. Eberhard Jüngel, in his 1999 lecture on mission, argues that "if the church had *a heart*, a heart that was still beating, then mission and evangelization would in great measure determine the rhythm of the church's heart. . . . Whoever is interested in a healthy circulatory system for the church's life must therefore be interested in mission and evangelization" ("Mission," 115). As helpful as this metaphor is, it is insufficient to view mission as merely the heart of the church—much less as the church's pacemaker setting the heart's rhythm. This assumes there is a dimension of the church that is not engaged in mission, as if mission expands the size of the church rather than constituting its very existence.

its status, its existence its essence," then the church is nothing other than the missionary action of the apostolate.[92] The church "is a function of the apostolate, that is, an instrument of God's redemptive action in this world. . . . The church is (nothing more, but also nothing less!) a means in God's hands to establish shalom in this world."[93] The church-as-apostolate is the bearer of the kerygma, the messenger of God's interruptive word, the proclaimer of the day of the Lord. More accurately, the church-as-apostolate *happens* where the kerygma takes worldly form. Dietrich Bonhoeffer writes that "the church is not a religious community of those who revere Christ, but Christ who has taken form among human beings. . . . The church is nothing but that piece of humanity where Christ really has taken form."[94] If Christ, as we argued in the previous chapter, is the kerygmatic event of interruption, then the church is simply that "piece of humanity" where this interruption occurs. Christ is the apostle of God as the one who embodies this interrupting event within history, and thus the church is the apostolate of God as the site where this event is repeated anew.

The implication of this conception of church as apostolate is that the Christian community has no permanent place of residence or cultural form. Within Christendom, by contrast, the church is understood as a culture or *polis*, and this takes the institutional form of the parish. The parish model of the church belongs to a hierarchically ordered cosmos that manifests itself in medieval European society, in which the church building resides at the center of town with everything else structured around it. These parishes, and the political body associated with them, are then structured around the cathedral, and the cathedrals around Rome. This geopolitical order is mirrored macrocosmically in the Ptolemaic universe and microcosmically in the moral psychology of the virtuous Christian. In the words of Thomas Aquinas, "man is called 'a little world,' because all creatures of the world are in a way to be found in him."[95] Ultimately, the microcosm of the human person, the sociocosm of the political order, and the macrocosm of the universe are reflective not only of each other but of the ontological order of the Great Chain of Being.[96] The parish resides at the center of town because

92. *KD* 4.1:727. Cf. *CD* 4.1:650.

93. Hoekendijk, *Church*, 22.

94. Bonhoeffer, *Ethics*, 96–97.

95. *ST* 1.91.1 resp.

96. The mirroring goes even deeper, beyond structural and ontological analogies into temporal analogies between past, present, and future: "Terrestrial events could be accounted for by changes in the celestial spheres, while physiological changes in the human being relate to changes in the material world. . . . Even knowledge of the future could be gleaned from the study of resemblances, for 'structural' analogies were

God resides at the center of all being. It is certainly true, as David Bentley Hart says, that "this cosmos was at once a scientific and a metaphysical conjecture, but also an object of great imaginative beauty, full of heights and depths and intricacies, splendor and sublimity and delicacy."[97] But this imaginative metaphysical picture produced, or perhaps existed to serve, the Christendom fiction that the church is a cultural institution whose mission is coextensive with the destiny of its culture and society—indeed, an imperialist European culture and society. The beautiful medieval world-picture is thus inseparable from the abandonment of the apostolate's apocalyptic consciousness. The church-as-parish is only possible where the church has lost its eschatological expectancy.

In contrast to the elegantly ordered cosmos of Christendom, the apocalyptic community of Christ resides within a precarious cosmos on the brink of a new epoch—on the edge between the end of history and the arrival of the messianic age. Even though we can no longer reside within the apocalyptic cosmos taken in a straightforward sense as empirically true, the precariousness of this cosmic picture remains valid in an existential, historicized register. The apocalyptic world exists today in the eccentricity of the eschatological moment. The community of faith—the apostolate—lives within this moment, in all its exigency and contingency. "Only in the last days . . . can we speak of the apostolate in the strict sense of the word."[98] Given that this moment is always newly determined by the demands of the present situation—every day confronts us as the "last day"—the church-as-apostolate is permanently on the move, constantly occurring in new forms and bearing the kerygma in new ways. Each moment is a "mission situation," and as such the community is daily faced with the reality that the apostolate may require a fundamentally different structure than it did yesterday. The community can be the missionary event of the apocalypse "only if she consistently structures herself as a missionary congregation. That means that she divests herself of all that cannot be used for mission, no matter how venerable, 'classic,' or orthodox it may be."[99] Long-held cultural forms and practices, no matter how historically significant they may

---

accompanied by temporal analogies. As the firmament above resembles the earth below, as the world within resembles the world without, so the future resembles the past" (Harrison, *Bible*, 53). What we have in this ontological order is an implicit doctrine of providence, since every occurrence, however small or large, can be accounted for by movements in another sphere, which continue higher and higher until one reaches the empyrean itself, the realm of God.

97. Hart, *Experience*, 52.

98. Hoekendijk, *Kirche*, 236.

99. Hoekendijk, *Church*, 95.

be, can never be more than provisional and contextual expressions of the apostolate. What defines the apostolate is not any culture or tradition, but rather the eschatological consciousness that occupies a particular moment in history and mobilizes bodies to become the form of the kerygma.

To live at the end of history is to live in the midst of sociocultural upheaval. The apocalypse existentially crucifies us with Christ, but in doing so it crucifies our historical contexts, subjecting them to permanent, revolutionary critique. The kerygmatizing act that constitutes the apostolate centrifugally places us outside ourselves through an interruptive encounter with the stranger—namely, with the strange God who meets us in the strange neighbor. This confrontation with the divine shatters the security of our cultural imaginary and thrusts each person into the insecurity of the eschatological moment, where cultural hybridity is not only possible but necessary and inexorable. At the turning point of the ages, "Christ is all and in all" (Col 3:11). No creaturely form is more suited for the apostolate than another; none has a privileged position before God.[100] The light of the apocalypse dissolves all worldly distinctions and cosmic orders, both religious ("circumcised and uncircumcised") and political ("slave and free"). This cosmic dissolution of all things in Christ opens up a space of anarchic freedom—not ἀναρχία in the political sense of being "without a ruler" but in the theological sense of being "without a first principle," meaning without a stable, rational, and divinely ordained cosmic order. The death of Christ is the death of every such order.[101]

Christ is the divine anarchist. In his abolition of the principles of nature he reveals himself to be "all and in all." Anything and everything may become the occasion for the kerygmatic intersection of kingdom and world

100. Paul Tillich famously remarked that "what makes Protestantism Protestant is the fact that it transcends its own religious and confessional character, that it cannot be identified wholly with any of its particular historical forms. . . . Protestantism has a principle that stands beyond all its realizations. It is the critical and dynamic source of all Protestant realizations, but it is not identical with any of them. It cannot be confined by a definition. . . . The Protestant principle is the judge of every religious and cultural reality, including the religion and culture which calls itself 'Protestant'" (*Protestant Era*, 162–63). The present work is self-consciously Protestant in precisely the terms described by Tillich, and yet I also contend that this "principle" is, in some sense, the inevitable consequence of interpreting the New Testament within a modern historical context. Perhaps, as Gerhard Ebeling suggested, modernity is essentially Protestant.

101. David Bentley Hart captures this well: "The new world we see being brought into being in the Gospels is one in which the whole grand cosmic architecture of prerogative, power, and eminence has been shaken and even superseded by a new, positively 'anarchic' order: an order, that is, in which we see the glory of God revealed in a crucified slave, and in which (consequently) we are enjoined to see the forsaken of the earth as the very children of heaven" (*Atheist Delusions*, 174).

that constitutes the apostolate. All forms, concepts, practices, and experiences are necessarily included at this apocalyptic juncture. Wherever this divine interruption takes place, therefore, the kerygma is *translated* into a worldly body. If translation occurs wherever the divine takes worldly form, then the kerygma, as the existential interruption that crucifies one with Christ, is itself the event of translation, and the apostolate, as the place where kingdom and world intersect, is the bodily site in which this event takes place. The church-as-apostolate does not engage in translation as a secondary, practical application for certain situations. The apostolate exists solely as an act of translation—indeed, as an ongoing *translating* into ever new forms of historical existence. "It is impossible to bathe in the same river twice," according to Käsemann, "even if one enters it at the same point. There is no such thing as an unchangeable ecclesiology."[102] The apostolate thus occurs in as many modes and appearances as the kerygma itself. Each new form is not a deviation from a normative configuration, because the proliferation of new forms precisely *is* the apostolate. Insofar as eccentricity and repetition define the kerygma, the apostolate is necessarily a complex multiplicity. Each moment of interruption is an intercultural encounter that recontextualizes the apocalypse. Each repetition of the saving event is a translation of God into new cultural forms. The ecclesiocentric rejection of translation should therefore be seen not merely as impossible but as genuinely unfaithful to the work of the Christ-Spirit.[103]

---

102. Käsemann, *Perspectives*, 120.

103. Translation, like the community's consciousness of the apocalypse, lies at the origins of Christianity. Lamin Sanneh identifies translation as central to the gentile mission of Paul. If gentiles can become Christian *as gentiles*, this implies that the gospel is not tied to a single culture as universally normative, in contrast to the assumption of postliberal ecclesiocentrism. Christianity is thus translatable from one context to another; it does not assimilate other contexts into an all-encompassing worldview, but rather it hybridizes itself through intercultural dialogue. The early church community recognized that it had to "relativize [Christianity's] Judaic roots" and to carry out the "destigmatization of Gentile culture" (Sanneh, *Translating*, 1). Early Christianity had to decenter itself; it could no longer assume the superiority of any context or language, including even the cultural framework of Israel. Paul's gentile mission thus forced him to search for a "fresh criterion . . . by which the truth of the gospel is unscrambled from one cultural yoke in order to take firm hold in another culture" (ibid., 29). According to Andrew Walls, "Christian faith rests on a divine act of translation: 'the Word became flesh, and dwelt among us'" (*Missionary Movement*, 26). If so, then the criterion for translation is the gospel itself. Cultural plurality is part of the internal logic of Christian faith. Translation of some kind is thus essential to Christianity on any account of the kerygma. Faithfulness to the God revealed in Christ requires a community engaged in missionary translation—including from Jew to gentile, from ancient to modern, from north to south.

The apostolate exhibits what Theo Sundermeier calls "a pluralism intended by God, who deals creatively with differences . . . and joins them into a creative coexistence."[104] The pluralism of the apostolate not only involves ethnic backgrounds and linguistic diversity, but it also embraces social, political, and religious practices. If the apostolate occurs as an event of translation that embraces the full scope of human experience, then it may frequently come into existence where Christ is unrecognized—even where God is actively denied. This should come as no surprise. As we noted in previous chapters, the saving encounter with the Christ-Spirit occurs unexpectedly at the level of our prereflective, unconscious existence. It is only natural, then, that the apostolate should exist primarily as an unconscious community. Indeed, the translation proper to the eschatological event of the kerygma may require the complete divestment of every traditional vestige of "church."

The Church as Unconscious and Conscious

If the apocalypse is the event of salvation, then *the apocalypse makes the church*. This is the starting point for a soteriocentric ecclesiology. There is a seed of truth in Cyprian's axiom *extra ecclesiam nulla salus*, but only if we invert it: instead of "outside the church there is no salvation" we should instead say "outside of salvation there is no church" (*extra salutem nulla ecclesia*). Salvation is not defined by the church; the church is defined by salvation. The church is not constituted by its institutional history, its liturgical rites, its confessions and creeds, its public gatherings and proclamations. The community of Jesus Christ is instead brought into existence ever anew by the eschatological act of God. If the apocalypse is not a publicly visible occurrence on the surface of history, but rather occurs in the unconscious existence of each person in her or his historicity, then the church is essentially an *unconscious community* that is always *becoming conscious* in particular historical situations.

Traditional Christian dogmatics differentiates between the visible and invisible church. This distinction is fraught with danger. The category of the invisible is often loaded with metaphysical baggage—such as when Christians speak of the hidden community of those elected by God in eternity or the community of the saints in heaven. As the church triumphant (*ecclesia triumphans*), the invisible church is supposedly the whole community of Christians who are truly elect or who have died and are now with Christ in some eternal society outside of history. There is a Platonic ecclesiology

104. Sundermeier, *Mission*, 112.

at work in such claims that posits an otherworldly, idealized church. With Barth we can describe this as an "ecclesiological Docetism" that "tries to overlook the visibility of the Church, explaining away its earthly and historical form as something indifferent, or angrily negating it, or treating it only as a necessary evil, in order to magnify an invisible fellowship of the Spirit and of spirits."[105] If not fully docetic, an ecclesiology grounded in a metaphysically invisible church is at least instrumentalist in the sense of Apollinarian christology, where the Logos acts in the world through the passive medium of Jesus's flesh—a flesh that it can all too easily cast off as a temporary accommodation. An instrumentalist ecclesiology similarly views the essential church as a uniquely divine and inviolable communion that colonizes worldly cultures for its earthly sojourn, only to slough them off at the end of history. The same instrumentalist thinking governs those approaches to revelation that see the Bible as God's infallible word directly communicated through the passive medium of the prophets and apostles. A metaphysics of invisibility ultimately serves to bypass the hermeneutical problem by denying the significance of our historicity in our relationship with the divine.

But the category of visibility is no less dangerous. It is fashionable in many circles to define the church in terms of its visible practices (hence the common slogan: "the eucharist makes the church") or to reduce the church to its sociocultural characteristics. In contrast to docetism, this position runs to the opposite extreme of ebionite (or adoptionist) christology, in which Jesus is adopted or possessed by the Spirit of God at his baptism. This view makes his divine identity directly visible in his flesh. The ecclesiological parallel here would be a flatly visible communion, that is, a reduction of ecclesiology to sociology. Barth refers to this as a "two-dimensional" church that lacks "the third dimension of its existence."[106] Some theologians have tried to charge Barth himself with neglecting the concrete visibility of the church. Reinhard Hütter claims that Barth loses the "church's concreteness" and advocates a "disembodied pneumatology" because he does not understand the church as "*a way of life*, i.e., a distinct set of practices interwoven with normative beliefs, concretely and distinctly embodied."[107] Hütter argues the Holy Spirit is the "real subject" of these practices, such that these "core practices . . . subsist enhypostatically in the Spirit."[108] By using the

105. *CD* 4.1:653.

106. *CD* 4.1:655.

107. Hütter, "Dialectical Catholicity," 148–49. Others have addressed in detail the problems with both Hütter's reading of Barth and his conception of the church. See Bender, *Confessing*, 40–64; Flett, "Communion"; McCormack, "Witness."

108. Hütter, *Suffering*, 132–33.

language of post-Chalcedonian christology to describe the relation between church and Spirit, Hütter directly identifies the traditions and practices of the church with the third person of the trinity. In this way he gives a specific visible form of the church—namely, a western European form rooted in the contingent history of Christendom—divine authorization and permanent validity. That is to say, he makes a particular sociology normative for the church universal. A metaphysics of visibility ultimately ends up in the same position as a metaphysics of invisibility: it too circumvents the hermeneutical problem by lifting a particular set of norms and practices out of their historical context, making them ahistorical and thus unimpeachable.

Whether in the mode of invisibility or visibility, ecclesial metaphysics manifests itself wherever there is a "sacred inflation" of the church, which entails "that the Church will be sharply distinguished from the world."[109] The metaphysically invisible church differentiates itself from the world by positing a perfect community outside of history. The metaphysically visible church differentiates itself from the world by making a specific historical community—marked by cultural assumptions, moral norms, practices, aesthetic forms, confessions, doctrines, and the like—identical with the divine will, in contrast to every other cultural context. If we are going to recover the element of truth in the doctrine of the visible and invisible church, it will not come through the mere assertion that the church is both visible and invisible, as if the only problem is letting one aspect predominate. The problem with the visible-invisible schema is that, at best, it is a misleading metaphor. If we set aside its metaphysical interpretation, the concept of invisibility simply means there are genuine Christians outside the walls of the confessing church community (and likewise that not everyone within those walls is a genuine Christian). But this makes a nontheological datum—namely, the walls that visibly demarcate a social gathering—the benchmark for the church's existence. In other words, the visible-invisible schema takes for granted a public church tradition and structure, and the only question is whether the communion of saints is completely identical with this structure or not. The schema thus presupposes the church; it is inextricably bound up with the ecclesiological fundamentalism that has to be subjected to thoroughgoing scrutiny.[110]

109. Pickard, *Seeking*, 65.

110. The visibility schema provides a convenient way of avoiding the tension between the sociological and the theological. The visible church corresponds to the sociological entity, while the invisible church corresponds to some theological or metaphysical reality. What are we to make of the fact that "what appears sociologically to be an odd sort of club is often spoken of theologically as the 'body of Christ'" (van Buren, *Secular Meaning*, 184)? The problem with the history of ecclesiology is that the

The norm of the apocalypse renders the visible-invisible distinction irrelevant, since the apocalypse is simultaneously both: "it is not visible, demonstrable, or provable in the categories and with the means of perception native to 'everyday' existence," and yet those who have encountered the invasive event of salvation are able to see "both the evil age and the new creation simultaneously."[111] The eschatological action of God is intrinsically beyond observation, and yet this action takes place within the historical situation of the present age and not in some metaphysical realm beyond history. But as we have seen already in chapter 3, the invisibility and visibility of the apocalypse is not at the empirical but rather at the *existential* level. The saving event is not generally invisible because there are divine spirits operating within the world in some hidden dimension, nor does it become literally visible for those with faith. The apocalypse does not take a stable and readily identifiable bodily form, such as the institution of the church. Instead, the apocalypse remains invisible for faith because it occurs as an event of the *unconscious*. It is hidden even for those whom it encounters. And yet it is not truly invisible, since it genuinely occurs in concrete moments of worldly existence. For this reason, any attempt to elaborate an ecclesiology by examining the conscious and visible community of faith is already at least two steps removed from the actual apostolate. Attempting to understand the community of the apostolate by examining the institution of the Christian church is like trying to understand love by examining the vows exchanged at a wedding chapel in Vegas.

Instead of the invisible and visible church we should speak of the unconscious and conscious apostolate. Both forms of the apostolate are empirical realities in the world with real bodies, but neither form is directly or necessarily visible as a distinctly religious social organization. The apocalypse of salvation, as we have seen, occurs when a person is existentially interrupted and placed outside herself. This existential dislocation is a prereflective act of faith (*fides directa*). If we understand this apocalypse as identical with the divine act of justification, then we can state, in agreement with John Calvin, that "forgiveness of sins . . . is for us the first entry into the church and Kingdom of God. Without it, there is for us no covenant or bond with God."[112] Unlike Calvin, however, we acknowledge that this forgiveness belongs to each person insofar as he or she exists as the child who shares in

---

sociological entity is taken for granted as the starting point, and then we ask to what extent the Pauline phrase "body of Christ" is an apt description of this "odd sort of club." But this has it precisely backwards. We must first discern what constitutes the "body of Christ" and only then speak of public manifestations of this body.

111. Martyn, *Galatians*, 104.

112. Calvin, *Institutes*, 4.1.20.

God's reign without being conscious of it. The divine act of faith constitutes the apostolate as an unconscious community of those who participate in Christ's death in God-abandonment. It follows that "we need not ... see the church with the eyes or touch it with the hands. Rather, the fact that it belongs to the realm of faith should warn us to regard it no less since it passes our understanding than if it were clearly visible. And our faith is no worse because it recognizes a church beyond our ken."[113]

The apocalypse constitutes the apostolate by simultaneously dissolving the distinction between the apostolate and the world. Karl Barth grasped this truth better than almost anyone who preceded him. In the early pages of his *Church Dogmatics* he remarks:

> If the Church is visible, this need not imply that we actually see it in its full compass, that the dimensions of its sphere might not be very different from what we think we know them to be. God may suddenly be pleased to have Abraham blessed by Melchizedek, or Israel blessed by Balaam or helped by Cyrus. . . . [God] can establish the Church anew and directly when and where and how it pleases Him. . . . God may speak to us through a pagan or an atheist, and thus give us to understand that the boundary between the Church and the secular world can still take at any time a different course from that which we think we discern.[114]

Barth makes a similar claim in his Göttingen dogmatics lectures, where he affirms that God's word may come to us from the most unexpected quarters:

> I will open my ears wide to be convinced that God's Word might even come through voices that belong to no church, that are perhaps directed against every church, that have nothing to do with what we call religion, and yet that I have to listen to if I am not to be disobedient to the heavenly voice [cf. Acts 26:19]. I hope I am ready at any time to be open to God's Word as in fact it may be spoken to me also in nature, history, art, and, who knows, even my own heart and conscience.[115]

Barth arrived at this insight on the basis of his doctrine of revelation. But what for him was a *possibility* grounded in divine freedom is for us an *actuality* grounded in God's saving act in Christ. God not only can speak through pagans and atheists, but pagans and atheists belong to the apostolate—even if only unconsciously. Not only can God establish the church

---

113. Ibid., 4.1.3.

114. *CD* 1.1:54–55.

115. Barth, *Göttingen Dogmatics*, 34.

anew in ways that redefine the boundary between church and world, but God in fact constantly does so, since the apocalypse occurs anew in each moment in social and existential configurations that demolish the boundaries between religious and secular, boundaries that belong to the passing age that was crucified with Christ. Now we say instead: "Christ is all and in all" (Col 3:11). The unconscious apostolate thus appears wherever persons are corporately placed outside themselves, that is, wherever people share in God's self-abandonment. If the proclamations of the Jewish prophets and Jesus himself are any indication, we will find this apostolate among the socially, politically, and economically marginalized and among those struggling for their emancipation.[116] Today we see the apostolate especially in the many black lives suffering under mass incarceration and systemic violence, as well as in those protesting this injustice and fighting for black liberation.[117]

The movement from the unconscious to the conscious apostolate is not necessarily or even predominantly a movement to the institution of Christianity. According to Paul van Buren, salvation is an act of liberation in which a person is "set free" in order "to be concerned and compassionate, to become involved for the sake of our neighbor in the world about us."[118] Freedom in this sense corresponds closely to what we have called the being-outside-oneself of cocrucifixion. Van Buren then says that "the 'church' was the people who shared in this freedom *and were aware of its source.*"[119] He combines in his definition of the "church" two aspects that we

116. A recent example, not without complications, is the Euromaidan Revolution that took place in Ukraine in February 2014, in which people from all backgrounds gathered in solidarity to protest the government's actions and ultimately to oust the Ukrainian president, Viktor Yanukovych. Near the end of the documentary, *Winter on Fire: Ukraine's Fight for Freedom*, a woman says: "Maidan was a singular experience, when everyone felt real unity, real patriotism, and felt the presence of God." We cannot directly identify the apostolate with any social movement, but we can discern a paradoxical identity that corresponds to the kerygma.

117. James Cone has discerned this truth with prophetic power: "It is on the basis of the soteriological meaning of the particularity of [Jesus'] Jewishness that theology must affirm the christological significance of Jesus' present blackness. He *is* black because he *was* a Jew. . . . The blackness of Jesus brings out the soteriological meaning of his Jewishness for our contemporary situation when Jesus' person is understood in the context of the cross and resurrection. . . . The resurrection means that God's identity with the poor in Jesus is not limited to the particularity of his Jewishness but is applicable to all who fight on behalf of the liberation of humanity in this world. And the Risen Lord's identification with the suffering poor today is just as real as was his presence with the outcasts in first-century Palestine. His presence with the poor today is not docetic; but like yesterday, today also he takes the pain of the poor upon himself and bears it for them" (*God*, 134–35).

118. Van Buren, *Secular Meaning*, 182.

119. Ibid., 184. Emphasis mine.

need to distinguish. The *unconscious* apostolate is the community of people who share in this freedom. They are the people who existentially participate in the apocalypse of God and so experience inner freedom from themselves and their context; they have learned "to rely not on [them]selves" (1 Cor 1:9). The unconscious apostolate is thus the site of the Christ-Spirit's repetition. The *conscious* apostolate, by contrast, is the community of people *who are aware of the source of this freedom but do not necessarily participate in it.* While the Christian churches would indeed count as part of the conscious apostolate, they can by no means claim this category exclusively for themselves. The category of the conscious apostolate admits a wide and varied range of communities, depending on how minimal or maximal is one's awareness of the source. A minimal awareness could simply identify the source of our existential liberation as being "outside of ourselves." Extrinsicality of some kind is thus the bare minimum for the conscious apostolate. This can include everything from a monotheistic deity to the uncountable event of Alain Badiou, which is "the advent of what subtracts itself from all experience."[120] A maximal awareness would acknowledge with van Buren that "it was the free man Jesus of Nazareth who on Easter began to set them free."[121] But a greater awareness of the source does not correspond in any way to a greater participation in the saving event—in keeping with the truth that justification is by faith alone and not by the works of the law. Indeed, consciousness as such is a departure from the source, since a defining feature of this source is that it is an eschatological event that cannot be objectified in the form of doctrines or practices; it is intrinsically and infinitely repeatable in a multiplicity of historical modalities. Insofar as conscious, reflective awareness of this event is by definition to grasp it in a *single* particular modality—that is, within a particular language, culture, and world-picture—one has only grasped an *occurrence* of the event and not the event itself. The best that the conscious apostolate can do is provide a space for becoming consciously unconscious. This is the highest and most crucial task of religion.

TOWARD A NEW LETTER TO DIOGNETUS

The anonymous second-century *Epistle to Diognetus* defended the fledgling Christian community to the Roman authorities, and among its many well-known arguments is the following observation: "For Christians are not distinguishable from other people either by country, language, or customs.

120. Badiou, *Logics*, 387.
121. Van Buren, *Secular Meaning*, 134.

For nowhere do they live in their own cities, speak some unusual dialect, or practice an uncommon lifestyle."[122] According to Robert Wilken, "as far as Roman society was concerned Christianity was invisible."[123] He illustrates this using the example of art. A Christian living in 200 CE who wanted an object to express Christian belief "would go to a craftsman and select a lamp stamped with a conventional symbol that could yield a Christian interpretation: a dove, a fish, a ship, an anchor, or a shepherd carrying a lamb." The same object meant two different things depending on whether it was in a Roman or a Christian home: "what the symbols represented lay in the eyes of the beholder, not in the object."[124] Wilken makes these observations as evidence of how culturally underdeveloped Christianity was at the time and how marvelous was the transition to imperial Christendom. For Wilken, Christians should have their own culture, dialect, art, and lifestyle. They should be clearly and visibly set apart as their own society and *polis*. To ecclesiocentrists like Wilken, the *Epistle to Diognetus* represents a form of Christianity the church has thankfully left behind.

A soteriocentric ecclesiology, however, affirms a Christianity that is "indistinguishable from other people"—not through the idealization of a primitive stage of development, as we find in communities that attempt to repristinate the "Acts 2" church, but through an apocalyptic theology that dissolves the boundary between church and world. Insofar as "church" names a distinct social and cultural body, the apocalypse of Jesus Christ annuls such an entity as part of the passing age. The apostolate that it establishes instead is nothing more or less than the site where the kerygma interrupts the world. This interruptive event does not generate an outward, visible separation between church and world but rather elicits an invisible, existential crisis between world and world. It ruptures our common, mundane existence—not by establishing an "uncommon lifestyle" but by denying our attempts to secure, deify, and universalize our existence. The apocalypse is a permanent critique of our habits and practices. It is the constant impetus toward freedom, both a freedom *from* the past and a freedom *for* the future.

> What is this freedom? It is freedom by and for grace, and this means, at the same time, for the freedom of God. That is, it is release from all worldly conditions and radical openness for encounters with God in all that comes. Further, it is the renunciation of every security that a man might acquire by assent to

122. *Ep. Diognetus* 5.1–2; Jefford, *Epistle*, 145.

123. Wilken, "Church as Culture," 33.

124. Ibid., 32–33.

"right doctrine" or by appropriate practical conduct; it is the renunciation of every "standpoint" by which he could make the free grace of God his possession. In other words, it is the renunciation of every "legalism"; for every such security is a legalistic security. The genuine freedom of faith is man's radical surrender to God's grace as the sole means whereby he is saved from his factual insecurity, his total lostness. But this grace "must necessarily appear to the man who lives in legalism in the form of an offending, perplexing, and frightening annihilation" (Gross, p. 710). Thus freedom is the readiness to sink into the "abyss of nothingness" (p. 708), or, to express the matter with Luther, it is the readiness to go out into utter darkness.[125]

If the apostolate is going to live within this freedom, it must ever again surrender the temptation to become a separate society with its own language, customs, and lifestyle. The cocrucifixion of the apostolate is a constant dying to oneself that frees the community from attempting to secure its existence. The witness of the church-as-apostolate will not be found in drawing people to itself but in sharing more fully in the sufferings of the world, in expending itself on behalf of its neighbors. The mission of the apostolate is thus, again and again, to become unconscious and invisible, to journey with Christ on the way of the cross into utter darkness.

A half-century ago the German missionary and theologian Paul Gerhard Aring issued a treatise on the church as an event (*Kirche als Ereignis*) that still resounds today with the force of a manifesto. He concludes with a vision of the church as the site where people dare to live freely without the security of tradition and in revolt against the unjust powers of the status quo. The church-as-apostolate is not a stable *thing* in the world—a culture, institution, or doctrinal system—but an *event*, an uprising, an occurrence of genuine freedom.

> The event of the church takes place where people grasp that Jesus Christ is God's protest against the status quo of a world that is peaceless, desolate, unreconciled, and so misunderstands itself. It takes place where people feel the invitation, the compulsion, the energy, and the ability to rebel against the lovelessness and misuse of human power, against inhumanity and injustice, and in this rebellion to dare to live. . . . The event of the church takes place where, precisely because of their own powerlessness and questionableness in the revolt against the inhumanities of human structures of order and coercive systems, people discover and become aware of the fact that God has made them

125. Bultmann, "On Behalf," 95.

free to relinquish their questionableness and surrender in obedience to the service of *God*. ... The church takes place where people accept the future of the world as already begun in Jesus Christ and thus as clear and defined, and for that very reason stand in the present—without preconceived programs, without binding doctrines, without selfish restrictions, without egotistical anxiety. The church takes place where people abandon their securities, their positions, their traditions, their missions and so dare to ground their credibility entirely on the credibility of the gospel manifest in the humility, the self-emptying, and the passion of ... Jesus Christ.[126]

The apostolate is the site of the apocalypse by existing purely as event. In correspondence to Christ it pursues fidelity, not permanency; credibility, not authority; vitality, not stability; justice, not legality; translatability, not universality. The apostolate may be here today and gone tomorrow, but in each today it arrives as the emancipatory sign of God's eschatological grace.

126. Aring, *Kirche*, 154–55.

6

The Space of Salvation
Unnature

*May I never boast of anything except the cross of our Lord Jesus Christ,
by which the world has been crucified to me, and I to the world. For
neither circumcision nor uncircumcision is anything; but a new creation is
everything!*

GALATIANS 6:14–15

*So if anyone is in Christ, there is a new creation: everything old has passed
away; see, everything has become new!*

2 CORINTHIANS 5:17

THE DESTROYER OF EDEN

In his recent study of the Shoah as a warning for the world today, Timothy Snyder highlights Hitler's *Weltanschauung* or worldview, according to which the Jews were a disease corrupting the natural order:

When paradise falls and humans are separated from nature, a character who is neither human nor natural, such as the serpent of Genesis, takes the blame. If humans were in fact nothing more than an element of nature, and nature was known by science to be a bloody struggle, something beyond nature must have corrupted the species. For Hitler the bringer of the knowledge of good and evil on the earth, the destroyer of Eden, was the Jew. It was the Jew who told humans that they were above other animals, and had the capacity to decide their future for themselves. It was the Jew who introduced the false distinction between politics and nature, between humanity and struggle. Hitler's destiny, as he saw it, was to redeem the original sin of Jewish spirituality and restore the paradise of blood. . . . Hitler saw the species as divided into races, but denied that the Jews were one. Jews were not a lower or a higher race, but a nonrace, or a counterrace. Races followed nature and fought for land and food, whereas Jews followed the alien logic of "un-nature." They resisted nature's basic imperative.[1]

Hitler viewed the natural order as the scene of racial struggle, as each race battles for supremacy and survival. The highest goal of human beings, according to Hitler, "was not 'the preservation of any given state or government, but the preservation of their kind.'"[2] The Jewish people violated this law of nature by promoting universal concepts and norms that encompass all humanity. As Snyder puts it, summarizing Hitler's position, the Jews "invented general ideas that draw the races away from the natural struggle. . . . Ideas of political reciprocity, practices in which humans recognize other humans as such, came from Jews."[3] The Jews worship a transcendent God who is sovereign over the entire earth and whose covenant with Israel concerns all the nations of the world. By undermining the pursuit of national self-preservation, the universal scope of Judaism is "a violation of the logic of being."[4]

If the Jews within Hitler's worldview represent the destructive force of "unnature," then Christianity augments and intensifies the same tradition. The Synoptic Gospels present Jesus as an apocalyptic prophet proclaiming love for enemies and a cosmic messianic reign. Over against the "present evil age," Paul announces the arrival of "new creation" in Christ (Gal 1:4; 6:15), which annuls the usual divisions and conflicts between persons and

1. Snyder, *Black Earth*, 4–5.
2. Ibid., 5.
3. Ibid.
4. Ibid., 6.

declares that "all of you are one in Christ Jesus" (Gal 3:28). John proclaims God's love for the world and describes Christ not only as the savior of the world but as the truth "which enlightens everyone" (John 1:9). Throughout the New Testament, Christ is the invasion of an alien logic that violates the laws of nature—both literally, in the miracle stories, and figuratively, in the violation of religious and political laws that defined the natural social order at the time. Insofar as the religious system sought to establish Eden on earth—since Eden and the Jewish temple intentionally mirror each other[5]—Jesus indeed appeared as the destroyer of Eden. The apocalyptic Olivet discourse in each of the Synoptic Gospels begins with Jesus prophesying the temple's destruction. And in Matthew and Mark, Jesus's accusers claim: "We heard him say, 'I will destroy this temple that is made with hands, and in three days I will build another, not made with hands'" (Mark 14:58; cf. Matt 26:61).[6] These false accusers unwittingly bear witness to the truth of Jesus's apocalyptic inbreaking. To a social system that has grown comfortable with the dynamics of religious and imperial power, Jesus comes as the great destroyer, the disruptor of nature, the alien invader who corrupts the species with the truth of a kingdom not of this world.

Counterintuitive as it may seem, this is the appropriate starting point for reconsidering the doctrine of creation—as a doctrine not of nature, but of the apocalyptic event of *unnature*.

REVERSING THE LOCI: TWO WAYS

Traditional systematic theologies have, for centuries, followed a standard order arranged according to the trinitarian framework of the creed and determined by the ancient doctrine of appropriations. The first, second, and third articles of the creed correspond to Father, Son, and Holy Spirit, while each member of the trinity corresponds to the divine work traditionally appropriated to that trinitarian mode of being. And to the Father, in particular, the church has appropriated the work of creation, due to the fact

---

5. According to Gordon Wenham, "The garden of Eden is not viewed by the author of Genesis simply as a piece of Mesopotamian farmland, but as an archetypal sanctuary, that is a place where God dwells and where man should worship him. Many of the features of the garden may also be found in later sanctuaries particularly the tabernacle or Jerusalem temple. These parallels suggest that the garden itself is understood as a sort of sanctuary" ("Sanctuary Symbolism," 19).

6. In both Mark and Matthew, the same claim is thrown in Jesus's face while on the cross (Mark 15:29–30; Matt 27:40). Only in the Gospel of John do we have a story that explains why people would accuse Jesus of this (John 2:19–21), since nowhere else in the Synoptics does Jesus claim to rebuild the temple in three days.

that, narratively prior to the revelation of Son and Spirit, God is already presented as the creator of the world. That, combined with the ancient doctrine of the monarchy of the Father, has led to a long habit of treating creation prior to reconciliation and redemption.

There is a certain self-evidentness about this, insofar as it seems natural to say that there has to *be* something first before it can be *saved*. But the New Testament is largely about upending what appears self-evident and natural: "You have heard that it was said . . . but I say to you . . ." (Matt 5); "God has made him both Lord and Messiah, this Jesus whom you crucified" (Acts 2:36); "the wisdom of this world is foolishness with God" (1 Cor 3:19). But of all the counterintuitive claims in the NT, one of the most extraordinary is the claim that Jesus is himself the one through whom all things were created. The Gospel of John declares that "all things came into being through him, and without him not one thing came into being" (John 1:3). The author of Colossians states that "in him all things in heaven and on earth were created, things visible and invisible, whether thrones or dominions or rulers or powers—all things have been created through him and for him" (Col 1:16). And the author of Hebrews says that God has spoken to us by a Son "through whom he also created the worlds" and "who sustains all things by his powerful word" (Heb 1:2, 3).

We would misunderstand these claims if we took them to mean simply that, before his earthly history, Jesus existed as a divine being who exercised power in the cosmos. That is the *mythical framework* in which these statements made sense to their original audience, but it is not their essential or kerygmatic *meaning*. The NT writers are instead bearing witness to what Richard Bauckham calls "the inclusion of Jesus in the unique divine identity."[7] Jesus is identified with the creator, but more than that, the creator is identified *with Jesus*. The Christ in history has become the criterion for identifying the eternal creator—the "exegesis" of the one whom "no one has ever seen" (John 1:18)—and by implication, for understanding the work of the creator. The upshot of this is that we cannot treat the first article on creation in isolation from the second article on christology and soteriology. If the agent of salvation is the agent of creation—and if salvation is the norm and starting point for thinking about God—then we must reverse the traditional order of the loci, as I have done here.

In reversing the loci, we preclude the possibility of natural theology. The long tradition of natural theology is rooted in the notion of natural (or general) revelation, the belief that God is first and foremost revealed to all people through nature. This tradition is only possible on the assumption

---

7. Bauckham, *Jesus*, 19.

that creation has a certain autonomy and self-evidentness about it—and a given relation to God that preexists salvation—which allows creation to be thematized independently of soteriology. If, however, soteriology precedes creation both epistemologically and ontologically, then what we mean when we talk about creation is no longer what theologians have generally meant. To let salvation be the criterion for what counts as creation—to make the first article into the third article—means that the object in view is the *new* creation (Gal 6:15; 2 Cor 5:17), not the *old* creation, what Paul calls the "present evil age" (Gal 1:4) or the "present form of this world [that] is passing away" (1 Cor 7:31). The new creation is the *eschatological truth* of the old creation.[8] The old and new creation are radically distinct but do not stand alongside each other as competitive entities, just as the one who participates in the crucifixion of Christ is no longer the same person as the one who existed prior to cocrucifixion. And yet the event of cocrucifixion constitutes the truth of the person in a way that annuls any prior identity: "I no longer live, but Christ lives in me" (Gal 2:20 NIV) and "you have died, and your life is hidden with Christ in God" (Col 3:3). Creation viewed soteriocentrically is equally crucified and nullified in the Christ-Spirit. The creation revealed in the apocalypse is not what generally passes for nature; it is rather the advent of the wholly unnatural within the natural, the unnaturing of nature.

But on what basis do we arrive at a soteriocentric doctrine of creation? There are two main approaches we could take, which I will call the *mythical* way and the *existential* way. The mythical version of soteriocentric creation tries to probe the eternal mind and will of God. It posits a divine being consciously willing the creaturely order with the history of salvation in mind. This position is exemplified best by Reformed scholasticism and the dispute over infralapsarianism and supralapsarianism. According to the logic of lapsarian theology, and especially the supralapsarian version, the historical events of creation, fall, and redemption have their ground in the pretemporal, predestinating decrees of God—decrees regarding creation, the permission of the fall, the election of individuals, and the provision of a mediator. The Reformed scholastics split between the infralapsarians and

---

8. Jesus, as the one who actualizes the eschatologically new creation, is the concrete self-definition of God and the concrete definition of humanity: "The eschatologically new being, by reference to which theology decides what ought properly to be called human being, is that man in whose historical existence God defined himself and, in the act of his self-definition, also defined us: the man Jesus. It is fundamental to a Christian understanding of God and humanity that we neither advance a view of humanity on the basis of a preconceived understanding of God, nor advance a view of God on the basis of a preconceived understanding of humanity—even if it be humanity's indefinability. Rather, judgments about God and humanity can only be made on the basis of one and the same event" (Jüngel, "Humanity," 132).

the supralapsarians regarding whether God elected fallen (infralapsarian) or unfallen (supralapsarian) human beings. Either way, creation unfolds according to God's eternal decrees regarding the election of human creatures and the provision of a redeemer to fulfill that election. I call this account mythical, because it takes the biblical description of divine creation and predestination literally. It presents God as a supersized sovereign, the infinite projection of a human monarch. Just as an earthly king makes decrees regarding his realm, so too this mythical deity makes decrees regarding the cosmic realm. This kind of metaphysical theism "appears guilty of a particular sort of idolatry, namely, that of attempting to speak of God by speaking of human persons in a loud voice."[9] It is insufficient to retain this description of God as metaphorical rather than literal, since the description itself misrepresents the nature of God's being-in-act.

The alternative is what I designate the existential approach. This view shares with the mythical approach the belief that creation is determined by soteriology. Whereas the mythical account understands this soteriology in terms of a salvation-historical narrative beginning with election and ending with consummation, the existential account—which is premised on the need to demythologize this narrative in light of the hermeneutical problem of historicity that we explored in the prolegomena on soteriocentrism—understands salvation as an apocalyptic encounter with the crucified God in the concrete historical moment. The doctrine of creation is a derivative claim that relates *this* particular encounter to the wider cosmos. An existentially soteriocentric account of creation does not speculate about divine actions not revealed in the saving act of the Christ-event. On the contrary, it sees in this saving act the disclosure of the truth about the creaturely order—a truth that calls this order into question by calling it outside itself. To confess that God is the creator is thus to acknowledge the absolute dependence of our existence *upon* God and the eschatological character of our existence *before* God. A soteriocentric doctrine of creation is thus primarily an *existential theanthropology* and secondarily an *existential theocosmology*.

EXISTENTIAL THEANTHROPOLOGY:
A THEOLOGY OF THE CREATURE

Soteriocentric theology is concerned specifically with the God-human relationship. It is thus unashamedly anthropocentric. Calling something anthropocentric has become a theological slur, however, so it is important to clarify which kind of anthropocentrism we mean.

9. Hector, *Theology*, 13.

Karl Barth placed theology on the right track when he said in 1949 that "Christian proclamation . . . is the proclamation of *God's humanism*."[10] By 1957 this idea had crystallized into the concept of "theanthropology" (humanity included in God), which he later contrasted with "anthropotheology" (God included in humanity).[11] For Barth there is a certain kind of humanism and anthropology that is essential to Christian theology because it belongs to the very being of God. Given his christological lens, there is no theology for Barth that is not also anthropology. Christocentrism is not only theocentrism but also anthropocentrism—that is to say, theanthropocentrism.[12] Barth was thus able to turn Ludwig Feuerbach on his head. Feuerbach famously makes the charge in his *Essence of Christianity* that "religion is the *reflection*, the *mirroring*, of human essence in itself. . . . *God is the mirror of the human person*." Consequently, he argues that "the *mystery of theology* is nothing other than *anthropology!*"[13] Barth agrees with Feuerbach's criticism of religion, but Barth understands the God revealed in Jesus Christ to be qualitatively other than the god of religion. Even though both gods are human, the God revealed in Christ is human as the result of an eternal divine act to be united with the man Jesus, whereas the god of religion is the projection of human wishes and ideals upon the divine. Instead of a god who mirrors the human person, Barth argues that the human person mirrors the human God.

Barth sets his theanthropology over against the deity of classical theism, which is "everything in the way of aseity, simplicity, immutability, infinity, etc., but is not the living God."[14] He even sets it against his own earlier theology of the "wholly other" God in the *Epistle to the Romans*, which showed "greater similarity to the deity of the God of the philosophers than to the deity of the God of Abraham, Isaac, and Jacob." This deity

10. Barth, "Christian Proclamation," 3.

11. See Barth, "Evangelical Theology," 11; Barth, *Evangelical Theology*, 12. The earliest use of the term appears to be in *Church Dogmatics* §43 (*KD* 3.2:12; *CD* 3.2:13), published in 1948, where he says that Christian faith sees the cosmos "*theanthropozentrisch*" (theanthropocentrically).

12. In his *Evangelical Theology*, Barth writes: "The knowing subject can be interested either primarily in God or primarily in man. Its wish can be to comprehend, possess, enjoy, and, in this sense, to know either God above all or man above all. In the theology of antiquity and of the Middle Ages, scientific Eros expressed itself more in the first and theocentric direction. Conversely, in the more recent theology determined by Descartes, it tended more in the second and anthropocentric direction. To the extent that this object in fact has to do with both God and man, both emphases were not without foundation in the true object of theology" (*Evangelical Theology*, 198).

13. Feuerbach, *Wesen*, 93, 309. Cf. Feuerbach, *Essence*, 62, 206.

14. *KD* 2.2:85; *CD* 2.2:79.

did not appear to be "the *deity* of the *living* God," who lives in a "sovereign *togetherness*" with humanity. The problem with his earlier theology is that it viewed God "in isolation, abstracted and absolutized, and set it over against man."[15] Despite his attempt to overcome the one-sidedness of his earlier work, Barth's later theology merely replicated the same problem at the human level. He viewed Christ's human nature, so to speak, in isolation, abstracted and absolutized, and set it over against the concrete historicity of human existence. Barth was able to define theology as theanthropology only by identifying a universal human essence (belonging to Christ in eternity by way of election) in distinction from individual persons in history (those who share in Christ's election).[16] In doing so Barth bore witness to God's universally inclusive Yes to the world, but he did so only by objectifying humankind. He presented the divine-human relationship as a metaphysical *what* instead of an apocalyptic *that*.[17]

Ultimately, the problem with Barth's theanthropology is that he sets it over against anthropotheology and views them as mutually exclusive options. Anthropotheology moves from the human person to God, whereas theanthropology moves from God to the human person. Only the latter order, for Barth, is theologically appropriate: "If theology wished to reverse this relationship, and instead of relating man to *God*, related God to *man*, then it would surrender itself to a new Babylonian captivity."[18] Barth is at least half-right. Viewed in isolation, anthropotheology leads to a natural theology that forms God in the image of the creature; the result is an idolatrous objectification of the divine. But if Barth wishes to avoid classical theism, which assumes a deity metaphysically opposed to humanity, then he has to embrace some kind of anthropotheology, or else the humanity that belongs to God has no genuine relation to the humanity actualized in history. Barth inverts Feuerbach when he should rather *sublate* him—that

15. Barth, *Humanity*, 45.

16. See chapter 4 above.

17. By drawing on an Aristotelian substance ontology, Barth's position—like that of classical orthodoxy—is pre-Darwinian, in the sense that "the logic of Darwinism" disposes of the view "that an organism has an essence that determines its necessary place in a unique nested hierarchy of kinds." Organisms do not have essences that clearly bind them together. No single taxonomy or order is capable of pinning a creature down as self-evidently of a certain kind, since every creature is constantly in flux and can be identified by multiple categories. John Dupré thus argues for what he calls "promiscuous realism" (Dupré, *Humans*, 4). This applies as much to human beings as to any other creature. The language of "humanity" or "humankind" has no ontological basis; it is a convenient placeholder, a communicative shortcut, more like synecdoche than literal description.

18. Barth, *Evangelical Theology*, 8.

is to say, he should assimilate Feuerbach's position into its opposite, thereby simultaneously negating and affirming it. The solution, in other words, is not to pit theanthropology against anthropotheology, but to develop a theanthropology that constructively incorporates anthropotheology. We must think at the same time from God to world *and* from world to God. This is what I call an *existential theanthropology*: a theology of the creator-creature relationship that begins with the apocalyptic encounter between God and world, an encounter that is constantly being repeated anew in each moment. In agreement with Barth, we can speak of the humanity or humanism of God; in contrast to Barth, however, we must understand this humanity in its historical multiplicity and diversity. There is no human *nature*. The apocalypse of God constantly places nature outside of itself. The creature of the apocalypse is thus something permanently new and unnatural.

In explicating this existential theanthropology we will first defend our focus on the God-human relationship against theological and ethical objections. We will then develop a soteriocentric theology of the creature as eccentric, unconscious, and unnatural—corresponding to our key dogmatic themes of crucifixion, Spirit, and apocalypse.

Soteriocentric Anthropocentrism

Before we explore this further, it is necessary to defend our theanthropocentric theology against the compelling ethical objection that anthropocentrism of any kind elevates the human creature above all other creaturely life, thus lending support to those who use the claim of human superiority to justify the abuse of the earth and nonhuman animals. David Clough, in his work *On Animals*, mounts the most extensive and persuasive case against anthropocentrism, which is any perspective that views "the world with human beings as central."[19] Clough begins by differentiating between five different interpretations of the term that have confused the conversation: (1) teleological, meaning the world was created for human beings; (2) epistemological, meaning we only know God in relation to human beings; (3) perspectival, meaning we inevitably view the world from a human position; (4) metaethical, meaning that human beings are the sole source of value; and (5) ethical, meaning that human interests alone matter. Clough dismisses the perspectival sense of the term as "platitudinous" and rejects the metaethical as "atheistic."[20] The ethical is dependent on the teleological, and so his primary concern is with teleological anthropocentrism. As

19. Clough, *On Animals*, xvi.
20. Ibid., xviii.

Clough points out, some "distinguish an *inclusive* teleological anthropocentrism that allows that other creatures have a peripheral place in God's
purposes from an *exclusive* teleological anthropocentrism (labelled 'anthro-
pomonism' by these authors) that denies that non-human creation is of any
interest at all."[21] Clough argues against every teleological anthropocentrism,
inclusive or exclusive, as an overly narrow understanding of God's purposes
in creation. His response—driven by the ethical question, "what should we
do in our relationships with other creatures?"—is that "Christianity should
be distinguished by its theocentrism, rather than anthropocentrism."[22] He
clarifies what he means by theocentrism by arguing that God's purpose in
creation is neither simply to glorify Godself nor simply to display God's
goodness toward creatures, but instead it is both at once.[23]

Clough's *On Animals* is a sustained attack on human hubris. He carries
out this attack using the standard creedal structure of creation, reconciliation, and redemption. In the discussion of creation, he argues against the
claim that human beings are the goal of God's creative work. The goal is
instead "to include creatures into the trinitarian fellowship," which includes
humans alongside other creatures.[24] He explores the debate over what differentiates human beings from nonhuman animals and rejects any obvious
and essentialist line of demarcation that could warrant elevating humans
above other creatures, as represented, for example, by the Great Chain of
Being and substantialist interpretations of the *imago Dei*.[25] In his treatment
of christology and atonement Clough argues that, in becoming "flesh" (John
1:14), Christ became a creature in unity with all living animals. The incarnation, he argues, is a "cosmic event" that reveals the destiny of all creaturely

---

21. Ibid., xix.

22. Ibid., xiv, xx.

23. Ibid., 22–23.

24. Ibid., 24.

25. Clough clarifies his position as follows: "My argument here is not that there are
no differences between human beings and other animals: clearly, it only makes sense to
speak of human beings at all because such differences identify us uniquely among other
creatures. Nor am I trying to minimize our sense of the differences between humans
and other animals: it seems to me that these differences are significant and worth[y]
of careful comparative investigation. My objection is to the routine and thoughtless,
theological or philosophical, drawing up of a list of attributes supposedly possessed by
all human beings, and excluding all non-human beings. . . . If our aim is to characterize
the difference between humans and other animals in order to understand what it is to
be human, it seems that the more accurate and detailed our list becomes, the less likely
it is that we can claim it to be universally true of human beings, and the harder it is to
attribute significance to the differences we find" (ibid., 72–73).

life.[26] The atoning work of Christ addresses the sin that affects all creaturely life and so reconciles all creatures to God. In conversation with John Wesley and John Hildrop, Clough concludes by claiming that the scope of redemption encompasses all of creation on the grounds that "what God had reason to create, God has reason to redeem." At stake here is "the coherence of Christian theology as such."[27] Any attempt to limit sin or redemption to human beings alone is thus sheer superciliousness.

Clough takes for granted the creedal tradition and modifies each doctrinal locus to embrace the entire creaturely world. It is noteworthy that Clough focuses on the problem of "teleological anthropocentrism"— which he replaces with a cosmic theocentrism—but largely bypasses the subjective aspects of anthropocentrism, namely, the perspectival and the epistemological. The former he rejects as "unhelpful," while the latter he says "may cause us to be appropriately cautious before presuming too much knowledge of God's relationship to other creatures, but should not prevent us from seeking the knowledge concerning our place before God in relation to other creatures that we need to guide our actions towards them."[28] Clough is particularly critical of Barth's christocentric anthropocentrism, which combines agnosticism about nonhuman animals with the fact that God specifically became a human being:

> In respect of all other creatures, we can and must look confidently to the same ontological basis [in Jesus Christ]. But in the case of non-human creatures we do not know what it means that they have this basis. We state their (for us) impenetrable secret when, looking in the same direction as we may and must look in regard to ourselves, we say of them too that they are with God. We know only that they are this. We do not know how. For when we say of them, too, that they are with Jesus and therefore with God, the decisive and distinguishing thing is that the God who is also their God did not become like them. He was not made an animal, a plant, a stone, a star or an element of the invisible heavenly world. But He did become man.[29]

In addition to the christological argument, Barth differentiates between humans and other animals on the basis that humans are able to respond to God's address in a unique way. For example, human beings alone can thank God, be responsible before God, and be baptized as a Spirit-filled partner

26. Ibid., 84–86.
27. Ibid., 144.
28. Ibid., xviii.
29. *CD* 3.2:137.

in the covenant.[30] Barth thus claims that human beings are "more noble" than other creatures and that "creation finds its conclusion" in humans.[31] Clough agrees with Barth's attempt to take a christocentric approach to the covenant, but he finds no reason to limit the scope of the incarnation to humankind, nor does he think our epistemological limitations permit us to make definite claims about God's relationship with nonhuman creation. He appeals to recent scientific evidence that indicates other creatures have "capacities for thinking."[32]

Clough's argument has much to commend itself within the context of classical Christian orthodoxy, but it is precisely this context that we must scrutinize, even if we seek to arrive at a similar conclusion. If Clough is justified in denying that "a Christocentric interpretation of creation is thereby an anthropocentric one,"[33] a soteriocentric interpretation of creation complicates matters by requiring that we take the subjective dimensions of anthropocentrism more seriously. Our starting point is no longer Jesus taken in isolation, but only Jesus as he interrupts us in the Spirit. The epistemological limitation thus becomes an ontological determination: God's being is exclusively located in God's saving action towards us in the apocalypse. The restriction of our knowledge is God's self-restriction, so to speak. God is the existential and eschatological event of the Christ-Spirit that places us outside ourselves. To put it another way, God is not a discrete personal agent who then enters into relationship with creatures; rather, God *is* the relationship—a specifically saving relationship—with creatures. This theanthropic relationship only exists in the correlation between objectivity and subjectivity, that is, between the crucified Jesus and the cocrucifixion of the individual believer. Mere modifications of the classical creedal tradition are no longer possible. A soteriocentric theology refracts every doctrine through the declaration: "I no longer live, but Christ lives in me" (Gal 2:20 NIV).

All of this suggests that a certain anthropocentrism necessarily follows, insofar as soteriocentric theology speaks about and from a concrete divine-human encounter—indeed, God's encounter with *me*. And yet, as we have argued, this encounter is primarily and normatively an *unconscious* event. To share in Christ's death in God-abandonment only requires that the creature is placed outside of itself and has its being defined by the future. The creature does not need to respond in thankful obedience to God in

30. *CD* 3.2:169, 176, 359.
31. *CD* 3.1:177.
32. Clough, *On Animals*, 92.
33. Ibid., 89.

order to participate in the saving event. The epistemological and ontological restriction of theology to the existential event of the Christ-Spirit thus paradoxically results in a cosmic soteriology. In contrast to Barth, there are no phenomenological marks of distinction between human and non-human animals where the scope and significance of God's saving action is concerned. In contrast to Clough, it makes no difference whether creatures have the capacity to think, since conscious reflection is not the condition for relationship with God; nor does it matter whether the flesh of Christ is understood to be creaturely flesh in general, as opposed to specifically human flesh, since that debate presupposes a substantialist metaphysics that no longer obtains within soteriocentric theology. We can thus arrive at a similar destination but without the mythical framework that Clough takes for granted. The problem with teleological anthropocentrism is not the anthropocentrism but the teleology. We need to replace *teleological* anthropocentrism with *archaeological* anthropocentrism. Humans are not the goal of divine activity but the paradigmatic origin, out of which we can discern the universal scope of the apocalypse. We discover this normative starting point in our cocrucifixion with Christ.

Creature as Eccentric: Cruciform Creaturehood

If salvation is cocrucifixion, then the creature—seen in the new light of the apocalypse—is fundamentally a being-outside-itself. To be a creature is to be eccentric. David Kelsey, in his magisterial *Eccentric Existence*, argues that human beings are "eccentric, grounded outside themselves in the concrete ways in which the triune God relates to all that is not God."[34] That is to say, "the ground of meaning in human life is eccentric to that life. What makes their lives meaningful wholes is not that they have been unified by the lifelong project of actualizing their true 'selves,' but simply the fact that the triune God has been creatively relating" to them in the various projects and practices they concretely enact in community with others. As such the meaning of their lives "cannot be undercut by the inevitability of death."[35]

Kelsey explores three ways in which God relates to what is not God: creation, consummation, and reconciliation. In creation the creature lives on "borrowed breath" (*what* are we?), in consummation the creature lives on "borrowed time" (*how* ought we to be?), and in reconciliation the creature lives "by another's death" (*who* are we?). Corresponding to these

34. Kelsey, *Eccentric Existence*, 1008.
35. Ibid., 327–28.

three questions are the concrete "existential hows" of faith, hope, and love.[36] Kelsey treats these questions as separate but interrelated; each has its own narrative framework that cannot be conflated with the others. For this reason Kelsey strongly resists taking a christological or soteriological view of the human person in favor of letting the canonical texts of scripture frame the question of anthropology. The emphasis clearly falls on creation and consummation. Jesus appears at the end as the one who images God as the paradigmatic and exemplary human creature.[37] Kelsey especially and novelly refuses to conflate eschatological consummation and reconciliation, despite acknowledging the centrality of the incarnation to both narratives. Those that insert the "Incarnation-focused story of God relating to bless eschatologically" into the "Incarnation-focused story of God relating to reconcile estranged creatures" take the way of infralapsarianism, while those who order the stories inversely (inserting reconciliation into consummation) take the way of supralapsarianism.[38] Kelsey insists that each has an irreducibly distinct "narrative logic"; neither story implies or requires the other.[39] Kelsey takes the postliberal route of making the canonical narratives themselves the norm for theology. He embraces the mythical stories in their plurality but does not press beyond them. There is no kerygma that functions as a hermeneutical criterion for critically testing the narratives. While there is much to gain from his work, particularly with respect to the existential "hows," Kelsey's approach stands in stark contrast to the method of the present work, which focuses on the existential encounter with God, rather than the canonical narrative *about* the encounter, as the norm for Christian doctrine. The "Christian particularism" that Kelsey advocates is ultimately not particularist enough.[40]

The eccentricity of the human creature, according to our soteriocentric perspective, is rooted not in the general ways in which God relates to what is not God, but in the concretely *saving* action of God. The creature is not naturally eccentric by virtue of being grounded in something outside itself. Instead, the creature continuously *becomes* eccentric in the constantly new event in which what is outside a person—namely, the alien action of God that meets us in the strange neighbor or worldly occurrence—interrupts and invades creaturely existence. We have identified this event as the repetition of the cross. The creature is not an ontological *what* but an existential

---

36. Ibid., 340–42.

37. Ibid., 1009–11.

38. Ibid., 609–10.

39. Ibid., 611.

40. Ibid., 6–7.

how: a cruciform mode of existence defined first by passive receptivity. Eccentricity is thus not a given property of the creature but an act that has to be received, experienced, and suffered again and again. Indeed, if the cross is the norm of creaturely life, then suffering—which comes from the Latin meaning "to carry," as in, to carry one's cross—becomes a hermeneutical key for a theology of creation.

In his reflections "After Ten Years," written at the end of 1942 a few months before his imprisonment, Dietrich Bonhoeffer remarks on the need to empathize with other human beings and enter into communion with them. To do so means that "we must learn to regard human beings less in terms of what they do and neglect to do and more in terms of what they suffer."[41] Genuine creaturehood is defined by what happens to us, rather than by what we do or accomplish. "As a person I am, before all my own activities, primarily one who receives, that is, a self who not only receives something but above all receives myself."[42] One first receives life, love, and language before sharing these with others. For Jüngel we *become* truly human when we are able to receive our being "continually anew as a gift. Truly human persons are those who are gifted—not with any special advantages, but—with themselves."[43] But we are inveterate doers habitually accustomed to the demands of self-realization and addicted to the accolades of personal achievement. For this reason the reception of our being as a gift does not come as a peaceful, natural process of life. The possibility of becoming truly human is more violent purgation than pleasant donation; it manifests itself as existential crisis rather than evolutionary progress. The human achiever "must be *elementally interrupted* in his or her being-active. And, like the *individual*, the human *society* oriented to achievement must also undergo an elemental interruption, by which we are transposed out of our *activities* into a very lively, very intensive, indeed highly *creative passivity*."[44] By "creative passivity" Jüngel means that, in the interruptive event of faith, human beings *receive themselves* by becoming "recipients of the salvific activity of God that was enacted in history in the sacrificial death of Christ."[45] In other words, each person receives, in the moment of existential eccentricity, the creative divine act that establishes their existence anew. Faith discerns the

---

41. Bonhoeffer, *Letters and Papers*, 45.
42. Jüngel, "On Becoming Truly Human," 237.
43. Ibid., 237–38.
44. Ibid., 238.
45. Nelson, *Interruptive Word*, 74.

truth of creaturely life in the death of Christ as the act that places the crea-ture in the position of creative receptivity.[46]

A creature that is creatively receptive is an inherently social and em-bodied creature. The event of the cross thus has significant ethical and so-ciopolitical implications. If the being or identity of the creature lies outside itself, then a society corresponds to the truth when it privileges those who suffer, when it demonstrates a "preferential option" for those who are poor and marginalized, those who exist at the mercy of the principalities and pow-ers. Those who see creation soteriocentrically "will allow their eyes to follow the inexorable downward gaze of the God who justifies us."[47] For Jüngel this has special implications for the people trapped in the criminal justice sys-tem, who are reduced to what they have done (or what the state claims they have done), and for those who are not able to do what "our achievement-oriented society" values as productive, such as children, the elderly, and the disabled.[48] An apocalyptic ethic will seek to make human justice *consistent* with Christ's death in God-abandonment "without being misconstrued as an *extension* of it."[49] Creaturely existence is able to *correspond* to and even *coincide* with divine existence in its absolute and irreducible *otherness*. If God is paradoxically present in absence and the apocalypse is paradoxically present in history, then divine justice is paradoxically present in those mo-ments of worldly justice—perhaps even in those moments the world takes to be injustice—that treat the creature in view of its eschatological identity as a genuine participant in the crucifixion: "from now on we understand no one according to the flesh" (2 Cor 5:16, my translation). Secular justice actualizes the justice of God—the δικαιοσύνη θεου—when and where society considers a person not as a self-realizing monad determined by the past (what *has* happened) but as a systemically connected political agent open to the future (what *may* happen). The social order in this sense becomes the space for the repetition of the cross. Indeed, a cruciform account of creation sees creation *as* repetition, insofar as creation is the apocalyptic space for "the birth of something *other* than God. . . . Creation is the breach of divine immanence, . . . the instant in which God relates to an other that

46. "The Christian doctrine of justification sees human beings fundamentally as those who can do nothing towards their salvation. . . . It is the question of the *truth* of human life. The Christian faith is distinguished from all other systems of meaning by its deep interest in the truth of human existence" (Jüngel, *Justification*, 264).

47. Ibid., 271.

48. Ibid., 270–71.

49. Ibid., 274.

cannot be taken back into identity."[50] The cosmos corresponds to God in its centrifugality.

Creature as Unconscious: Pneumatic Creaturehood

The saving event of the apocalypse reveals the creature to be not only eccentric and social but also primarily *unconscious*. If the absent God is pneumatically present to us principally in our unconscious existence, a soteriocentric theology of the creature will prioritize unconsciousness over consciousness as the defining locus of personal identity.

We find a similar priority in the latest research in cognitive science. As summarized by George Lakoff and Mark Johnson, this research has discovered "that most of our thought is unconscious, not in the Freudian sense of being repressed, but in the sense that it operates beneath the level of cognitive awareness, inaccessible to consciousness and operating too quickly to be focused on."[51] These unconscious activities include: accessing memories, making sense of sentence structure, picking out words, interpreting body language, constructing mental images, and planning what to say next in a conversation.[52] The "cognitive unconscious," as it is called, "consists of all the mental operations that structure and make possible conscious experience."[53] These operations include intentionality, representation, inference, propositions, semantic meaning, imagination, and causality.[54] In other words, the building blocks of basic social interaction occur, in a sense, "automatically and without noticeable effort."[55] Our capacity to comprehend and conceptualize our experience is fundamentally prereflective and preattentive. According to Lakoff and Johnson, the cognitive unconscious constitutes "95 percent of all thought—and that may be a serious underestimate." Without our unconscious thought laying the necessary groundwork, "there could be no conscious thought."[56] One implication of this is that we are unable to be directly aware of the vast majority of our cognitive activity. Most of what we do and who we are is thus "wholly other" even to ourselves.[57]

50. Kangas, *Kierkegaard's Instant*, 101.

51. Lakoff and Johnson, *Philosophy*, 10.

52. Ibid., 10–11.

53. Gibbs, *Embodiment*, 40.

54. Lakoff and Johnson, *Philosophy*, 116–17.

55. Ibid., 11.

56. Ibid., 13.

57. The cognitive unconscious is thus not a direct object of research but a hypothesis posited to explain the empirical evidence from our experience and behavior (ibid.,

As Raymond Gibbs points out, the cognitive unconscious is inseparable from the body, "because all of our cognitive mechanisms and structures
are grounded in patterns of bodily experience and activity."[58] For this reason
neuroscientists and cognitive scientists speak of "embodied cognition" or
"situated cognition," according to which "human cognition is fundamentally
shaped by embodied experience."[59] This is still an emerging field of research
with competing theories about the precise relation between brains, bodies,
and environments. What everyone rejects is the classic western separation
between (and hierarchical ordering of) mind and body, a tradition that
stretches from Plato to Descartes and is exemplified by Alan Turing's notion
that the mind is a computer.[60] The body and brain together form human
cognition. The cognitive unconscious, for instance, is constantly operating
in response to social and physical stimuli. Those who work in the area of
situated cognition further share "a *rejection* of the ideas that cognition is
individualistic (accomplished by each human individually), general (true of
all individual humans and applicable in all situations), abstract, symbolic,
explicit, language based and located in the brain as mediator between sen-
sory input and action output."[61] The nature of the situatedness varies and
is highly complex. Some of the situations include: environment, social location, political location, historical context, and individual embodiments.
Cognitive activities are typically determined by more than one situation.[62]
And since "bodily experience is shaped by cultural practices," there is a
growing recognition by cognitive scientists that embodied cognition is a
culturally situated cognition.[63]

Human identity is thus located in an embodied mind, in which it is
impossible to isolate the mind from the body. To be a self is to be situated
concretely within history. Rudolf Bultmann, in his analysis of the Pauline
concept of σῶμα (*soma*, body), remarks that "the *soma* is not a something
that outwardly clings to a person's real *self* (to his soul, for instance), but
belongs to its very essence, so that we can say one does not *have* a *soma*,
but rather *is soma*."[64] Bultmann uses the example of Romans 6 where Paul
says "do not let sin exercise dominion in your mortal bodies [*soma*]" (Rom

---

103).

58. Gibbs, *Embodiment*, 40.

59. Ibid., 3.

60. Ibid., 5.

61. Solomon, "Situated Cognition," 413.

62. Ibid., 423.

63. Gibbs, *Embodiment*, 39.

64. Bultmann, *Theology*, 1:194, rev. Cf. Bultmann, *Theologie*, 190–91.

6:12), but rather "present *yourselves* to God as those who have been brought from death to life" (Rom 6:13; emphasis added). The *soma* is the self, the whole person, the human being as a living historical subject. A person is a *soma* "*insofar as one is able to make oneself the object of one's action or to experience oneself as the subject of some occurrence or suffering*," that is to say, "*insofar as one has a relation to oneself,* and can in a certain sense distance oneself from oneself."[65] Bultmann conceives the self-as-*soma* as the subject of creative passivity, as a creature capable of becoming eccentric and existing outside itself. The self-as-*soma* experiences itself as the object of suffering. Somatic existence is thus *pneumatic* existence, inasmuch as the Spirit is constantly repeating in our bodies the apocalyptic event of the cross. Bultmann's conception of the self as *soma* in the theology of Paul thus anticipates not only our soteriocentric understanding of the creature but also the recent scientific understanding of the self as an embodied mind, in which one's self-relation is constituted within the historical relation to others. There is no disembodied soul or psychological faculty in which the true self resides. Moreover, as this research has demonstrated, most of the cognitive activity that forms our self-relation occurs unconsciously—which corresponds to Bultmann's own theological observation that our relation to God, which is always simultaneously the relation to ourselves, is fundamentally prereflective and unconscious.[66]

We are in a position now to understand what it might mean for the creature to exist in the "image of God" (*imago Dei*, εἰκὼν τοῦ θεοῦ). As the NT testifies, Jesus Christ is himself "the image of God" (2 Cor 4:4). He is "the image of the invisible God, the firstborn of all creation" (Col 1:15), even "the exact imprint of God's very being [ὑπόστασις]" (Heb 1:3). The word for

---

65. Bultmann, *Theologie*, 192.

66. Bultmann, "On the Problem," 112, 116–17. Cf. Congdon, *Rudolf Bultmann*, 79–84. The claim here is not that divine action operates exclusively in the processes of the cognitive unconscious. That would be the cognitive equivalent of the claim by some that divine action operates in the indeterminism of quantum physics. Both are forms of natural theology that establish a direct identity between physical processes and divine action. Following this path would lead us back to an objectifying metaphysics that makes God an object of our rational inquiry. The argument here is not that cognitive science reveals where God acts, but rather that it provides an analogy or "secular parable," to use Barth's famous term (*CD* 4.3:115–17). Put another way, we have already learned from the kerygma that God acts in us unconsciously. From this starting point we should expect to find creaturely analogies and witnesses to this truth about human existence, and this is precisely what we find in the latest research in cognitive science. It is not that this research constrains where God acts. The God of the gospel simply cannot be objectified as a natural, causal force among others. We know the character of divine action independently of science, but science can offer its own corroborating witness to this theological truth.

"exact imprint" (χαρακτήρ) generally refers to the way a coin or seal bears the royal trademark. The primary use of image language in the NT is in reference to Christ. I thus agree with Kelsey when he says that "the principal anthropological significance of the notion of the *imago Dei* emerges, not from its role in Genesis 1:26–27, but from its role in christological contexts in the New Testament."[67] We can only speak about other creatures bearing the image of God in the sense of sharing in and conforming to the image of Christ. Other creatures image God, in other words, by "imaging the image of God."[68] The concept of the *imago Dei* is therefore a soteriological and eschatological doctrine. We see this especially in the Pauline letters. Paul uses his Adam-Christ typology to contrast two different images. Historically "we have borne the image of the earthly man," he writes, but eschatologically "we shall bear the image of the heavenly man" (1 Cor 15:49, my translation). In his second letter to the Corinthian community, Paul says that those who share in the freedom of the Spirit "reflect [κατοπτρίζω, lit. to mirror] the glory of the Lord" and are "being transfigured [μεταμορφόω] into the same image" (2 Cor 3:18, my translation).[69] Paul says in Romans that "those whom he foreknew he also predestined to be conformed to the image of his Son" (Rom 8:29), and since Christ is the image of God (2 Cor 4:4), we can say that "imaging the image" is the heart of his soteriology. The author of Colossians furthers this line of thought by saying that those who live in Christ have "clothed [themselves] with the new self, which is being renewed in knowledge according to the image of its creator" (Col 3:10).

The point is that to speak of any creature as existing in the image of God is to speak about how that creature exists *in relation to Christ*. And as we have argued in previous chapters, the relation to Christ is an unconscious existential event of the Spirit, what we have described above as an elemental interruption that places us in a position of creative passivity. The *imago Dei* is therefore not some essence or faculty—in agreement not only with our hermeneutical inquiry into human historicity but also with the results of cognitive science research—but what we might call an *act-relation*: a relation between the image-giving act of God and the image-receiving act

---

67. Kelsey, *Eccentric Existence*, 938.

68. Ibid., 1011.

69. The word μεταμορφόω (*metamorphoō*) is the verb translated as "transfigure" in the transfiguration episodes recorded in Mark 9:2 and Matt 17:2. It is also typically translated as "transform" in Rom 12:2. But in the context of 2 Cor 3, where Paul is speaking about the glory (δόξα) of God that was reflected in the face of Moses and is now reflected by all believers through the Spirit, "transfigure" is the most appropriate translation. Jesus's transfiguration was a proleptic anticipation of the eschatological transfiguration of all people through the liberating work of the Spirit.

of the human person. Dietrich Bonhoeffer calls this an analogy of relation (*analogia relationis*) in contrast to the analogy of being (*analogia entis*):

> The likeness, the analogia, of humankind to God is not analogia entis but *analogia relationis*. What this means, however, is, firstly, that the relatio too is not a human potential or possibility or a structure of human existence; instead it is a given relation, a relation in which human beings are set, a justitia passiva! And it is in this relation in which they are set that freedom is given. ... Analogia relationis is therefore the relation which God has established, and it is analogia only in this relation which God has established.[70]

Bonhoeffer here achieves two things. First, he identifies the image or likeness of God with an active relationship, one whose efficacy depends upon the continuation of that relationship by God and does not consist in a static property or structure of the creature itself. Second, he identifies this relationship with the saving relation of divine justification that places a person in the position of passive receptivity.[71] The definition of justification as *iustitia passiva* (passive righteousness) hearkens back to Luther's Galatians commentary, in which he differentiates the righteousness of faith from all other forms of righteousness (e.g., political, ceremonial, legal) on the grounds that "it is a merely passive righteousness, while all the others, listed above, are active. For here we work nothing, render nothing to God; we only receive and permit someone else to work in us, namely, God."[72]

Following Bonhoeffer, then, bearing the image of God is identical with sharing in the righteousness of God. The *imago Dei* is not an essence but an event. If we share in this event in the existential moment when we are placed outside ourselves, then we bear the *imago Dei* in the unconsciousness of faith. We correspond to God not in *what* we are but in *how* we are—namely, in how we exist eccentrically as creatures who constantly find themselves outside themselves, not only in our sociohistorical community with others but also and simultaneously in God.[73]

---

70. Bonhoeffer, *Creation and Fall*, 65.

71. "In its formal aspect, 'justification' means that it is through the event of divine justice that human beings first become themselves: the *righteousness of God* which occurs in the being of Jesus Christ constitutes our humanity" (Jüngel, "Humanity," 133).

72. *LW* 26:4–5.

73. By understanding the *imago Dei* in terms of a "how" rather than a "what," we are able to redress the historical use of this doctrine to perpetuate "Christianity's longstanding misuse and abuse of the body," an abuse manifested especially in the oppression of women and ethnic minorities (Teel, *Racism*, 39). Racism and white supremacy within Christian churches exemplifies a distorted theological anthropology. Karen Teel

Creature as Unnatural: Apocalyptic Creaturehood

The creature is eccentric and unconscious because ultimately—that is, apocalyptically—the creature is *unnatural*. To many this will sound odd at best, scandalous at worst. Is not the doctrine of creation a theological way of speaking about "nature"? Wolfhart Pannenberg argues this position most forcefully. In his 1970 essay, "Contingency and Natural Law," he claims that the theologian who speaks of creation refers to the same reality as the scientist who speaks of nature:

> Theology must not become prey to the all too comfortable escape to the idea of creation on a special or exclusively theological level which is inaccessible to any critique by the natural sciences, for example, as an interpretation of the first two chapters of the Bible. This protection from critique by the natural sciences signifies at the same time the irrelevancy of theological statements, not only for the work of the natural scientist but also for the worldview of today's humanity which is rightfully informed by the results of the natural sciences. *Exactly that nature which is researched by natural science would have to be claimed by theology as the creation of God.*[74]

If theology is going to be relevant to a world that thinks in scientific terms about the world, then it must be willing, Pannenberg argues, to take on modern scientific language about nature when speaking about what Christians have traditionally called creation. Since "the one God of the Christian faith is also the Lord of nature," a theology of creation "is better characterized as a 'theology of nature.'"[75]

----

thus argues that "the body is the image of God" (ibid., 42), since "the traditional view of the image of God as soul or mind has failed to challenge racism and related ills that plague our society and churches" (ibid., 163). While certainly an improvement over the position she critiques, Teel's argument remains trapped within the logic of the classical tradition, which identifies the image with some faculty or property of the person. She continues to speak of "bodies as well as spirits," as if the problem is merely the order of the two rather than the dualism as such (ibid.). As important as it is that our theology advance the cause of justice, it is systematically insufficient to make theological judgments on pragmatic and functional grounds (i.e., this doctrine is correct because it will produce such and such an effect in the world). Teel simultaneously goes too far and not far enough. If we reconstruct anthropology on a soteriocentric basis, we will achieve a coherent anthropology that also and correlatively addresses the problems associated with the metaphysical separation of body and spirit.

74. Pannenberg, *Toward a Theology*, 74. Emphasis added.

75. Ibid., 72. Pannenberg goes on to say that "a God who would not be the origin and perfecter of this nature could not be the power that determines all reality of being, and therefore not truly God" (ibid., 75).

Alister McGrath criticizes Pannenberg for being hermeneutically naïve in his talk of nature. Pannenberg uses the term as if it is universal and objective—a self-evident fact about the world that all people can observe and affirm. He is far too sanguine about the capacity of modern natural science to establish a common foundation across all disciplines and traditions. The problem, according to McGrath, is that "nature cannot be thought of as a neutral or uninterpreted entity, in that it is *seen as* something."[76] What we call "nature" is always the world viewed from a particular historical perspective. There is no knowledge that is free from presuppositions. We do not have direct access to the world as such but only to the world as we encounter and experience it. It follows that there is no "nature" as such but only nature as we experience it.

> "Nature" is thus not a neutral entity, having the status of an "observation statement"; it involves seeing the world in a particular way—and the way in which it is seen shapes the resulting concept of "nature." Far from being a "given," the idea of "nature" is shaped by the prior assumptions of the observer. One does not "observe" nature; one constructs it. And once the importance of socially mediated ideas, theories and values is conceded, it is impossible to avoid the conclusion that the concept of nature is, at least in part, a social construction. If the concept of nature is socially mediated—to whatever extent—it cannot serve as an allegedly neutral, objective or uninterpreted foundation of a theory or theology. *Nature is already an interpreted category.*[77]

Recognizing there is no uninterpreted nature means, for McGrath, that the theologian can understand her or his theology of creation *as* a theology of nature, without having first to demonstrate that the category conforms to what scientists call "nature." "Christians see *nature* as *creation*," according to McGrath. "'Creation' is a specific way of viewing 'nature.'"[78]

McGrath's position on nature can be seen as an extension of the postliberal argument regarding God-talk in general: each cultural-linguistic community has its own socially-mediated grammar for identifying certain statements about God (or nature) as true. Pannenberg, by contrast, is a more classically modern theologian in his insistence on a universal grammar of nature and history that enables theologians, philosophers, historians, and scientists to engage in shared discourse. The present work is post-postliberal in the sense that I acknowledge, with McGrath, the cultural and

76. McGrath, *Scientific Theology*, 1:137.

77. Ibid., 1:113.

78. Ibid., 1:137–38.

hermeneutical character of all God-talk while simultaneously affirming the possibility of intercultural translation and communication, since the criterion of meaningful God-talk—the kerygma—is a transcultural event that is irreducible to social construction. The nature of this criterion means that the (soteriocentric) theologian is not concerned with developing a worldview that embraces the same domain as the philosopher or the scientist. This is where I differ from McGrath, who aims for the same universality as Pannenberg: "we wish to affirm that a Christian 'theology of nature' is contained and subsumed in the insight that the natural order, including humanity, is God's creation."[79] Whereas McGrath reverses Pannenberg, the present argument is that a doctrine of the creation is strictly concerned with the *creature* seen and defined in terms of the existential event of the apocalypse, and then only with the so-called "natural order" as the space within which the creature exists.

Nature, as McGrath correctly recognizes, is always hermeneutical: it is "*seen as* something."[80] If this calls into question the scientific universality posited by Pannenberg, it also calls into question the *moral* universality posited especially by neo-Thomists and American evangelicals, along with anyone else who appeals to "natural law" or the "order of creation" as the basis for universal ethical norms. The details of natural law ethics are beyond the scope of our inquiry. What the various parties take for granted is that natural law provides "the grammar of a common moral discourse . . . by which the public square not only *can* but *must* be preserved."[81] This public discourse presupposes a shared concept of nature as its condition of possibility. According to Jesse Covington, this common grammar "reflects the inescapable structures of the created order."[82] We can have a universal morality because we share a universal nature. In other words, "public morality must rest upon public principles—principles that are rooted in the fabric of creation" and "are accessible to all people by virtue of God-given reason."[83] We can apply McGrath's critique of Pannenberg to the natural law theorists. Once again the concept of "nature" is being used in a way that is hermeneutically naïve. These ethicists speak of "created order" and "structures of creation" as if these structures and orders are objectively public, as if the mere exercise of reason is sufficient to show there is an inherent configuration in nature that ought to determine our moral reasoning. The truth is that

79. Ibid., 1:137.
80. Ibid.
81. Charles, "Burying," 20.
82. Covington, "Grammar," 179.
83. Charles, "Burying," 21.

these ethicists are *interpreting* nature to serve this role. Just as Pannenberg interprets nature to provide the basis for a public scientific reasoning, so too these ethicists interpret nature to provide the basis for a public moral reasoning. Either way the purported neutrality and universality of "nature" in these accounts is an illusion. In every case the argument from nature is an instance of special pleading.

The appeal to nature (φύσις) as the basis for universal norms suppos-edly gains its legitimacy from the apostle Paul himself. For scholastic theo-logians the natural law "is nothing other than the law to which Paul refers in Romans 2:14, which is written on the hearts of the men and women of the nations."[84] Paul claims in this passage that certain gentiles "do by nature [φύσει] the things of the law" (Rom 2:14, my translation),[85] which seems to follow from his earlier claim that the invisible properties of God "have been seen and understood through what has been made" (Rom 1:20, my translation).[86] Paul makes a handful of other references to φύσις, which sug-gest he sees the concept of nature in moral and cultural terms. For instance, Paul speaks about women and men exchanging "natural" (φυσικός) for "un-natural" (παρὰ φύσιν) sexual relations (Rom 1:26–27). In his first letter to the Corinthians he asks rhetorically, "Does not nature [φύσις] itself teach you that if a man wears long hair, it is degrading to him, but if a woman has long hair, it is her glory?" (1 Cor 11:14–15).[87] Paul identifies "nature"

---

84. Porter, *Nature*, 327.

85. Peter Leithart follows N. T. Wright and others in translating φύσει as a modifier of "Gentiles," in which case the verse would read: "When Gentiles, who do not have the law by nature, do the things of the law . . . ." A key point in favor of this reading is that Paul speaks elsewhere of being "Jews by nature [φύσει Ἰουδαῖοι]" (Gal 2:15), referring to those who are born into the Jewish faith. This reading only further confirms the cultural conception of φύσις in Paul's thought. See Leithart, *Delivered*, 27.

86. Douglas Campbell has argued that Romans 1:18—3:20 does not actually repre-sent the views of Paul at all but is rather the position he aims to attack (see Campbell, "Natural Theology"; Campbell, *Deliverance*). Even if we do not go this far, Paul's state-ment in Romans 1 clearly stands in tension with his claims that the mind set on the flesh "is hostile to God" (Rom 8:7) and that "in the wisdom of God, the world did not know God" (1 Cor 1:21). Ernst Käsemann uses these countertexts to minimize the apparent *theologia naturalis* in Romans 1. Paul is not simply taking Hellenistic Judaism on board. Doing so would involve "advocating a natural theology which could scarcely be reconciled with his eschatology and christology" (*Commentary*, 41). Whatever else Paul means it is clear that "God remains 'invisible' here to the extent that we cannot get power over him or calculate him metaphysically; rather, he 'has' us" (ibid., 42).

87. Alan Padgett argues that 1 Cor 11:14–15, typically translated as a question, should in fact be translated as a statement: "But nature herself has not taught you that if a man has long hair it is a shame while if a woman has long hair it is her glory; for hair is given to her instead of a covering" (*As Christ Submits*, 108). He cites the Vulgate in support of this reading. For Padgett, then, Paul is using nature to *oppose* the cultural

here with a cultural custom. Elsewhere he speaks of himself and Peter as "Jews by nature" (φύσει Ἰουδαῖοι), while referring to gentiles as those who are "uncircumcised by nature" (ἡ ἐκ φύσεως ἀκροβυστία), in which φύσις apparently refers not to a biological quality but to one's participation in a certain sociocultural context (e.g., Torah). Certain people are "naturally" circumcised Jews, while others are "naturally" gentiles—and all people, according to the author of Ephesians, are "naturally" children of wrath who live according to the flesh" (Eph 2:3).

Not unlike the modern theologians cited above, Paul speaks of nature as something generally accessible and self-evident, even though it clearly comes laden with culturally specific norms. Counterintuitively, Peter Leithart sees this as Paul's central insight. He observes that "for Paul constructed orders also have the force of 'nature.' . . . For Paul, *physis* and *nomos*, physics and law, nature and culture, are not finally separable." Paul has thus "socialized" the concept of nature. Leithart draws from this an anthropological axiom: "Human beings are defined by the social and cultural setting in which they live, move and have their being."[88] Paul, according to Leithart, provides us with a social ontology. The human person, the creature, is ontologically defined by the sociocultural context that determines its existence. Leithart insightfully connects talk of "nature" with the even more enigmatic phrase "elements of the world" (τὰ στοιχεῖα τοῦ κόσμου).[89] The concept of στοιχεῖα is used in ancient Greek philosophy to refer to the elements and entities that constitute the cosmos, but as with φύσις Paul uses this term "to describe a change in the basic constituents of the social and cultural cosmos."[90] In Galatians Paul says that, before the coming of faith (namely, Christ), we were imprisoned "under sin," "under the law," and "under a guardian" (Gal 3:22, 23, 25). He reiterates this when he says several verses later that we were children "under stewards and managers," that is to say, enslaved "under the elements of the world" (Gal 4:2–3, my translation). Sin, law, guardian, and cosmic elements are thus ways of speaking about the

---

custom of head coverings. In support of this he refers to verses 11–12, where Paul presents a more egalitarian position: "Nevertheless, in the Lord woman is not independent of man or man independent of woman. For just as woman came from man, so man comes through woman; but all things come from God" (1 Cor 11:11–12). Padgett here uses a retranslation to restore harmony within the Pauline corpus, though the appeal to nature remains. On Padgett's reading, Paul uses nature to support an egalitarian position rather than a patriarchal one. This does not solve the problem posed by the use of φύσις, but it does make the concept more flexible by recognizing that one can use φύσις to criticize rather than confirm culture.

88. Leithart, *Delivered*, 28–29.

89. On τὰ στοιχεῖα τοῦ κόσμου, see Martyn, *Galatians*, 393–406.

90. Leithart, *Delivered*, 38.

same social reality from which Christ sets us free. In other places Paul uses "flesh" (σάρξ) to convey the same idea. This conflation of the cultural and the cosmic means that Paul can describe the end of the law in apocalyptic terms as the end of the old cosmos, indeed as the death of the self (e.g., Gal 2:19–20). The author of Colossians says that those who have "died with Christ" have died "to the elements of the world" (Col 2:20), which the author also describes as "putting off the body of flesh" (Col 2:11).[91] The crucifixion of oneself with Christ is the death of τὰ στοιχεῖα, the annulment of φύσις, the end of the age.[92] "For Jews like Philo, for Egyptians, Babylonians, Greeks and Romans too," writes Leithart, "liberation from *stoicheia* simply means liberation from order itself, for there appears to be no conceivable order besides stoicheic order. For many, the gospel Paul announces is no good news, it seems, but a threatening wave of chaos."[93] Indeed, we must go further than Leithart here and say that it is a liberation from order and security *for the followers of Christ*.

For all his insight into the apocalypse of Christ as the cosmic destruction of the old sociocultural order, Leithart ends up returning to the comfort of the cultural fleshpots of Egypt instead of bravely entering the promised land of new creation. He marshals the resources of apocalyptic only to advance a thoroughly ecclesiocentric vision of cultural Christendom. On the one hand, "stoicheic *order* has been completely dismantled by the advent of the Son and Spirit," and yet on the other hand, "the order of *ta stoicheia* comes to fulfillment, maturity, in the practices and life of the church."[94] The *telos* of Christ's work of reconciliation is that humankind will "acquire a common *physis*, operate by the same *stoicheia* and come to occupy the same *kosmos*."[95] The culture of the church establishes a new cosmic, stoicheic order. Leithart thus aligns himself with the postliberal conception of the church as an alternative society and *polis* when he says that the church is "the socioreligious entity that operates by matured forms of purity and holiness." This account

91. Ibid., 78n5.

92. This is, in effect, a demythologizing of Paul's eschatology. Leithart agrees with N. T. Wright and others in interpreting the apocalyptic imagery in the NT as figurative language for "the collapse of a political universe" (ibid., 134). The imminent catastrophe was not the end of the actual world but only of a certain social order. There were no dashed expectations, because this apocalyptic expectation was actually fulfilled. I side here with Bultmann and others in viewing the apocalyptic language of the NT as genuinely about the physical cosmos, though Paul and John do provide the basis for a demythologizing of this eschatological expectation in their interpretation of the Christ-event as the fulfillment of the apocalypse, albeit for faith alone.

93. Ibid., 42.

94. Ibid., 224, 226.

95. Ibid., 207.

of the church has direct implications for the conception of mission. If the church's very being is located in its sociocultural practices, then as Leithart states, "the church's first mission is to be the church."[96] Once the primary mission becomes the centripetal cultivation of a particular social order, the church becomes a culture and any centrifugal mission is inevitably a form of cultural imperialism. Indeed, Leithart embraces this implication. He purports to show "how tribal peoples continue to live *hypo ta stoicheia tou kosmou*," drawing on examples from the Toda people of south India, the Hua people of New Guinea, and traditional Hawaiian religion.[97] He concludes: "The church would necessarily confront and subvert these stoicheic patterns. It is not politically correct to say so, but traditional cultures cannot be preserved intact if they enter the Christian era, the new creation."[98] Christian mission in this sense is indistinguishable from colonialism. As we have argued in the previous chapter, such an ecclesiology and missiology is diametrically opposed to the eschatological and emancipatory event of the apostolate. To put it plainly, it is a betrayal of the gospel.

When it comes to the new creation in Leithart, talk of dismantling the old order gives way to far less invasive metaphors: "the patterns of stoicheic life are not lost but transposed into a new key."[99] He ends up turning the new creation into a mirror image of the old, and he makes this argument by referring to Paul's description of the Christian life as "slavery" (Gal 5:13), as obedience to the "law of Christ" (Gal 6:2).[100] The cultural patterns of the old age have been retained, he claims, though transformed with new content. He calls this the "spiritual alchemy of Easter and Pentecost," which translates the old cosmic elements into a new configuration.[101] In one sense this is certainly true: the new Christian community clearly understands itself as the authentic continuation of the old covenant community. But what is the actual nature of this continuity? For Leithart, the new creation remains a culture, a "socioreligious entity" that competes with the cultures of the world. The form remains largely the same, though the content is different; the church is the new cosmos, the new temple.[102] The problem, exegetically

96. Ibid., 230.

97. Ibid., 240.

98. Ibid., 246.

99. Ibid., 227.

100. Ibid., 226.

101. Ibid., 227.

102. Leithart even says that "Christ is himself the new cosmos of the believer," but this is only because "he is the principle of coherence and unity in the cosmos as a whole" (ibid., 42n39). We can understand Christ as the cosmos only if we redefine cosmos in a cruciform, apocalyptic way—not by fitting Christ into a prior concept of the

speaking, is that the NT—especially Paul—does not use the terms κόσμος, στοιχεῖα, or φύσις to describe the new reality in Christ. These terms are almost exclusively used to name the "present evil age" (Gal 1:4).[103] The κόσμος is the realm of sin (Rom 5:12–13), false wisdom (1 Cor 1:20–21), and the elements that enslave (Gal 4:3). The new age is not κόσμος or φύσις but rather καινὴ κτίσις—new creation (Gal 6:15; 2 Cor 5:17)—and this reality is "a genuine *novum*, a first-order reversal of all previous arrangements—an altogether new creation *ex nihilo*, out of nothing."[104] If Leithart thus advocates a version of *gratia non tollit sed supponit et perficit naturam* (grace does not destroy but supports and perfects nature), we must ask what it means for nature—and thus for law and the cosmos—if grace does not destroy but *crucifies* nature: *gratia non tollit sed crucifixit naturam*.[105] The human situation is such that "nothing short of the crucifixion of the old *kosmos* (Gal 6:14) will suffice."[106] For all his exegesis of Galatians, Leithart does not once mention Galatians 6:14, where Paul writes: "May I never boast of anything except the cross of our Lord Jesus Christ, *by which the world has been crucified to me, and I to the world*" (emphasis mine). Given the connection of κόσμος with σάρξ, στοιχεῖα, and φύσις, our eschatological crucifixion with Christ is the crucifixion not only of the world but of nature itself. Christ comes as the great destroyer of Eden. The apocalyptic event of cocrucifixion puts an end to nature along with the principalities and powers. To participate

---

cosmos as creation. We should, in fact, jettison the language of cosmos altogether and speak of Christ as the "new creation" of the believer, as the eschatological reign of God.

103. In the Johannine texts, the soteriological dualism between God and the world, between light and darkness, is "not a contrast between two ages," as in Paul, but a contrast between two modes of existence, two ways of being in the world—the way of truth and faith and the way of falsehood and unbelief (Bultmann, *Theology*, 2:15). As Barth puts it, "the epitome of κόσμος is of course unredeemed humanity" (*Erklärung*, 220).

104. Rutledge, *Crucifixion*, 355. Barth, commenting on John 1:13, says that "the truth of their own existence . . . is a miracle, a creation, a new birth . . . in relation to the existence of the cosmos that is covered by darkness, to their own existence insofar as it belongs to this cosmos" (Barth, *Witness*, 82–83).

105. Al Wolters provides a typology of four positions on nature and grace (see Wolters, "Nature"): (1) *gratia contra naturam* (associated with Anabaptism), (2) *gratia supra naturam* (associated with Roman Catholicism), (3) *gratia iuxta naturam* (associated with Lutheranism), and (4) *gratia intra naturam* (associated with Calvinism). The position of *gratia crucifixit naturam* does not fit within any of these categories but draws on elements of each—especially *contra* and *intra*, which are held in a paradoxical tension.

106. Rutledge, *Crucifixion*, 356. Cf. Martyn, *Galatians*, 406: "The cosmos that was crucified on the cross is the cosmos that was founded on the distinction between Jew and Gentile, between sacred and profane, between the Law and the Not-Law. When we contemplate the identity of this crucified cosmos, it is not difficult to see how its departure could lead a Pharisee to speak of his own death (Gal 6:14)."

in the crucified Christ is continually to put nature to death and to live the *unnatural* existence of faith.

To speak of faith as unnatural is not to commend an ahistorical or disembodied existence. It is rather to observe that a faith constituted by the apocalypse is *acosmic*—that is to say, it no longer operates according to the norms and structures of the κόσμος, the passing age. The cosmos crucified in Christ is constituted by certain essential elements; it has its own natural physics, its own stable φύσις. The cosmos is turned-in-upon-itself, since "*physis* is that mode of being whereby an entity relies on itself for its existence and operations."[107] With reference to *this* nature we can indeed speak about a natural law. But the new creation has no such nature since it is always being created anew in its constant cocrucifying participation in Christ. It has its being outside of itself; its being is thus unnatural, set in antithesis to nature. For Paul, "neither circumcision nor uncircumcision is anything—but rather new creation" (Gal 6:15, my translation). Both circumcision and uncircumcision are "natural" in the sense of being static, permanent, and objectifiable structures of existence.[108] They belong to the logic of φύσις and the norms of κόσμος. By contrast, the new creation is not a creation so much as a *creating*—a *creatio continua*—that happens in each new existential moment. Creaturehood is thus constituted by the ever-new event of our being outside ourselves, *extra se*. There can be no generic, universal norm for what counts as "natural" or "creational." All talk of nature is simultaneously talk of culture, given that "the very idea of nature itself is not natural; *nature is cultural*" and also that "nature has cultures: *culture is natural*."[109] The attempt to establish such a norm not only bypasses our historicity and ignores the hermeneutical problem, but it also imperialistically sets up a single sociocultural framework as authoritative over against global cultural multiformity. The imperial-ecclesiastical campaign to autho-

107. Przywara, *Analogia Entis*, 119.

108. This is not to proscribe *all* talk of nature, since sometimes it is necessary to use the language of natural and unnatural in nonoppressive ways. According to Nicole Seymour, "while it may not be possible to escape altogether the construction of some things as natural and some as unnatural, it might at least be possible to combat the kinds of naturalizations and denaturalizations that enable exploitation and discrimination, or that deny the complexities of humans and non-humans" (Seymour, *Strange Natures*, 5).

109. Bell, "Queernaturecultures," 143. David Bell is here developing the idea of "naturecultures" proposed by Donna Jeanne Haraway, who speaks of "situated histories, situated naturecultures, in which all the actors become who they are *in the dance of relating*" (Haraway, *When Species Meet*, 25). The field of queer ecology seeks to explore the paradoxical construction of "alternative cultures of nature" (Mortimer-Sandilands and Erickson, *Queer Ecologies*, 35).

rize permanent "laws of nature" and "structures of creation" is to participate in κόσμος rather than Christ, to engage in oppressive propaganda rather than emancipatory proclamation, and "any acts seen to upset this agenda are constituted as not just unnatural, but *toxic* to nature."[110]

The unnatural creature is therefore always free for new configurations of authentic existence: "For freedom Christ has set us free" (Gal 5:1).[111] The creaturely freedom of the apocalypse is a freedom from metaphysical substances that purport to define creaturely identity in advance. Judith Butler refers to a "metaphysics of gender substances" that posits a static gender identity prior to its actual practice and performance; it is a being that subsists prior to becoming.[112] Her actualistic alternative understands the gendered body to be *performative*, meaning "that it has no ontological status apart from the various acts which constitute its reality."[113] Creaturely identity is "a term in process, a becoming, a constructing that cannot rightfully be said to originate or to end."[114] Butler's account of gender identity is a secular parable (to borrow Karl Barth's term) of the cruciform-pneumatic creature defined by the saving apocalypse. Barth himself argues that "human beings do not first have some kind of nature, only then to be addressed by God in this nature. They do not have something different, earlier, and more basic, no deeper stratum, no original substance of being, in which they are without or prior to the word of God."[115] The only "nature" of the

110. Gosine, "Non-white Reproduction," 151. To return to Hitler's worldview, the linchpin of the German Christian position was the identification of *creation* (as a normative, divinely authorized order) with the *Volk* (referring to the people as a nation of "blood and soil"). Friedrich Gogarten, a supporter of the German Christians, wrote in his 1932 work on political ethics that "faith recognizes . . . God's eternal will of creation in this *lex civilis*," which he defines as the "political orders of human life" (*Politische Ethik*, 113). Despite the collapse of the German Christian movement, Gogarten continued to propound these ideas. In 1937 Bultmann wrote to Gogarten to criticize him for his "identification of the law of the people [*Volksnomos*] with the law of God [*Gesetz Gottes*]" (Bultmann and Gogarten, *Briefwechsel*, 212).

111. The word ἐλευθερόω (to set free) is elsewhere used by Paul in Romans, where he writes: "For the law of the Spirit of life in Christ Jesus has set you free [ἠλευθέρωσέν, the same form of the verb used in Gal 5:1] from the law of sin and of death" (Rom 8:2). And later in the same chapter Paul says that "creation itself will be set free [ἐλευθερωθήσεται] from its bondage to decay and will obtain the freedom of the glory of the children of God" (Rom 8:21). For the other uses of the verb by Paul, see Rom 6:18, 22. The only other occurrences in the NT are found in the famous lines of the Fourth Gospel: "you will know the truth, and the truth will make you free [ἐλευθερώσει]," and "if the Son makes you free [ἐλευθερώσῃ], you will be free indeed" (John 8:32, 36).

112. Butler, *Gender Trouble*, 30.

113. Ibid., 185.

114. Ibid., 45.

115. *KD* 3.2:179.

creature is its existence in the divine word, and if we recognize this word as the repeating and pluralizing eschatological event, then the creature exists as an *unnatural* disruption of cosmic order, an open process of (re)construction within history that neither begins nor ends. Apocalyptic creaturehood is *queer* creaturehood: a plastic, praxical, performative being-in-becoming. The apocalypse does not free the creature for just any becoming, however, but for modes of becoming that place the creature outside of itself and so place it in solidarity with others. The apocalypse queers the creature by *interrupting* the creature.[116]

Armed with the queer kerygma of Christ, we can return to Paul's statements about nature with fresh hermeneutical eyes. Jean Porter, referring to Romans 1–2, claims: "The existence of the natural law is thus confirmed by revelation."[117] Here in this sentence we confront the fundamental challenge posed by this book, namely, whether we will acknowledge and address the hermeneutical problem within theology. It is the identification of the Pauline texts—indeed, of *any* text—with divine revelation that leads to the evasion of hermeneutics. If we do not presuppose the direct divine authorization of the biblical texts, and thus do not force them into a false harmony, we are free to recognize their historically and culturally situated character. We are free, in particular, to recognize Paul's assumption of a heteropatriarchal culture that took certain expressions of gender and sexual identity for granted as natural and normative. These presuppositions about φύσις were part of his cultural κόσμος.[118] So much of the exegetical literature attempts

---

116. Laurie Zoloth, in her ethics of interruption, describes the disruptive nature of interruption according to the religious texts of Judaism, Christianity, and Islam. In these narratives, "the given, stable hierarchies of power, the truth claim, the natural order of the empirical world, the dark and steady pull of cultural customs, even the sequence of narrative, is interrupted by God" ("Interrupting," 8).

117. Porter, *Nature*, 327.

118. This is the central aporia in Leithart's analysis of Paul. He affirms (a) that Paul's talk of nature is actually about culture and (b) that Christ dismantles the old order and cosmos in order to establish a new order. And yet, when it comes to Romans 1, Leithart decides that, "in this passage, *physis* names a *permanent* structure of creation. From the beginning, God made them male and female, and the gospel does not dissolve the created structures of human sexuality. Human desires should be conformed to the Creator's design, which Paul calls 'nature'" (*Delivered*, 27). Nature here is not a passing cultural perspective but a permanent fact of creation. Without any justification from the text itself Leithart treats Romans 1 as a grand exception to the usual talk of φύσις in the New Testament, as he analyzes it in his book. As the above quote indicates, he reads into this passage an entire theology of creation—in particular, one that assumes God designs normative *structures* of creation. According to Leithart, a certain moral imagination and logic—that is to say, a certain *culture*—is built into the fabric of nature itself. So perhaps it would be more accurate to say that he reads "nature" in Romans 1 as referring not to the passing cultural framework constituted by the cosmic elements

to explain passages like 1 Corinthians 11:2–16 in light of Paul's other statements, generally through some version of the principle that "scripture interprets itself" (*scriptura sui interpres*), in order to show that Paul points in a
consistently liberative or repressive direction.[119] The way forward, however,
is not through a salvage operation based on the premise that scripture itself,
even if only a textual "canon within the canon," is the norm for responsible
God-talk. Such an approach views the Bible as a "mythical archetype" that
"can be either accepted or rejected, but not critically evaluated. A mythical
archetype takes historically limited experiences and texts and posits them
as universals, which then become authoritative and normative for all times
and cultures."[120] In contrast to a mythical approach, soteriocentric theology
discerns the kerygma *through* the text but not *in* the text.[121] The kerygma as
hermeneutical norm exists beyond the text—both historically behind and
contextually in front of the text—at the existential and praxical intersection
of God and the world. Soteriocentrism presupposes "that, as kerygma, the

---

but to the new cultural order established by Christ, which he then secures for all time by
calling it a "permanent structure of creation." In other words, one gets the impression
that Leithart's interpretation of Romans 1 is largely driven by a reactionary culture war
agenda.

119. On this principle see Mostert, *Glaube*, 9–41; Forde, *More Radical Gospel*, 68–
74. As noted above, Alan Padgett harmonizes Paul's writings in an egalitarian direction
by interpreting 1 Cor 11:14–15 as a statement rather than a question (Padgett, *As Christ
Submits*, 108). Elisabeth Schüssler Fiorenza, despite being critical of the "canon within
the canon" approach, reads the same passage as a question but interprets it in harmony with a feminist understanding of Paul based especially on Gal 3:28. According
to Schüssler Fiorenza, Paul argues "for the custom of bound-up hair, as the symbol of
women's prophetic-charismatic power" (Schüssler Fiorenza, *In Memory*, 230). Lone Fatum, by contrast, harmonizes Paul by arguing that he is consistently androcentric, not
only in 1 Corinthians 11, but also in Gal 3:28, the verse used most frequently to support
a feminist interpretation of his letters. The phrase "no longer male and female" is not
a critique of gender norms but a rejection of human sexuality as such: "it is a negation
in so far as sexuality and sexual activity to Paul are negative concepts in themselves"
(Fatum, "Image," 63). Likewise, in 1 Corinthians 11, "Paul pleads for male control in
the shape of practical suppression of women." The attempt to read this passage in a
feminist direction is "apologetically misleading to Paul's moral purpose" and "distorts
Paul's argumentative point, that the image of God is an expression of superiority and
hierarchic order." The image of God represents "a definite and absolute order of creation
reflecting the qualitative difference between man and woman" (ibid., 71).

120. Schüssler Fiorenza, *Bread Not Stone*, 10.

121. Tom Greggs comments on Bonhoeffer and religionless Christianity by stating:
"It is the very God pointed to in the text who cannot be confused with our religious
speech about God. Scripture relativizes the confidence with which the theologian can
speak of God because Scripture is not the LORD but points to the LORD who is within,
but also beyond the text itself. Put otherwise, the Bible will not allow fundamentalism
as the Bible relativizes the Bible before God. . . . There must be no idolatry, not even
biblio-idolatry" ("Religionless Christianity," 305).

New Testament texts are language captured by revelation, but they have not remained free from the opposite movement as human speech of their time."[122] The historical location of the texts demands a content criticism (*Sachkritik*) that tests the biblical texts against the eschatological event of the kerygma. As with the Bible's androcentric language, the talk of nature must then be reconstructed critically in light of the queer kerygma of the apocalypse. The event that crucifies the κόσμος and liberates us from the στοιχεῖα puts to death the patriarchal structures of φύσις that Paul takes for granted. A soteriocentric theology of the creature is thus a theology of *unnature*.

Adapting Paul we can say: *From now on we regard nothing according to nature (κατὰ φύσιν); if anything is in Christ—new creation!* We no longer regard human persons κατὰ φύσιν, as if gender, racial, and sexual identities are fixed substances and natural facts of creation, as if our stories are defined at birth rather than through the complexities of lived existence. We no longer regard economic systems κατὰ φύσιν, as if modern market capitalism is the natural mode of financial transaction. We no longer regard cultures κατὰ φύσιν, as if the assumptions and prejudices with which we are raised are natural and static, incapable of hybridization and transculturation. We no longer regard societies κατὰ φύσιν, as if economic inequality, systemic racism, and libertarian individualism are natural features of human community with which we must come to peace. We no longer regard religions κατὰ φύσιν, as if certain religious traditions are inherently violent or peaceful, as if religions are not complex, open systems capable of historical development. We no longer regard God κατὰ φύσιν, as if divinity is a substance that we can define and analyze in the abstract and not a concrete historical event in the Christ-Spirit. *So if anything is in Christ—new creation.*

EXISTENTIAL THEOCOSMOLOGY: A THEOLOGY OF CREATION

The move from the creature to the cosmos is not, as it was in the ancient church, a move from microcosm to macrocosm within a stable ontological hierarchy, nor is it a move from the elected individual to the theater of election, as in the covenant theologies of Protestant orthodoxy, with their carefully managed accounts of creation and providence. The transition within a soteriocentric theology is far more modest. As indicated by our shift from a mythical to an existential theology, a doctrine of creation cannot claim to be about the cosmos as such but only about the cosmos as it relates to the

122. Jüngel, *Gottes Sein*, 24n34. Jüngel is here describing Bultmann's program of demythologizing. See Congdon, *Mission*, 626–37.

saving event, as seen from the vantage point of God's incursion into the world in the Christ-Spirit. It is thus a *theocosmology* rather than simply a cosmology in theological perspective. The word "creation" is not the "natural world" by another name. A soteriocentric theocosmology speaks of the cosmos as the presupposition and context of the new creation. It is not a theology of κόσμος but of the cosmic scope of God's saving act.

A theocosmology is not interested in the cosmos for its own sake. The creation accounts in Genesis 1–2 are minimalist in their description of the world itself. What appears in the foreground is not the world but *God*, and only then humankind as the creature chosen to exist in a unique relation to God. The account in Genesis is not a cosmology in the classical sense; there is no interest in nature as an object of rational inquiry. Rudolf Bultmann highlights the contrast between the Jewish understanding of creation and the Greek understanding of the world:

> The problem of the relation between form and matter, which so much exercised the Greek mind, is conspicuously absent from the Old Testament. There is no conception of the "cosmos" (κόσμος = harmonious structure), of "nature" (φύσις), of the law of nature (νόμος φύσεως). The world is never objectified as a natural order whose eternal laws are open to intellectual apprehension. There is no natural science or physics. The Greek saw the divine power in the cosmic law whose existence he had apprehended by reason. . . . The Bible on the other hand regards God as transcending the world.[123]

What interests the Hebrew scriptures is not the world as nature but the world as *history*. History is the space in which God acts. The creation story is not a primitive cosmogony but "the first chapter in history," a history that is not a mere record of facts and laws but a mythic chronicle that speaks of God as the sovereign judge of the earth and the nations.[124] History is where God encounters and confronts human beings, and the world is only of interest insofar as it is the space where this encounter takes place: "The human person is not understood in terms of the world, but rather the world is understood in terms of the human person."[125]

If we therefore understand the human creature as eccentric, unconscious, and unnatural—as the existential site where the eschatological event occurs—then the world, as the given space for this encounter, is understood as the scene of the apocalypse, that is to say, as *unnature*. The world, of

123. Bultmann, *Primitive Christianity*, 17.
124. Ibid., 21.
125. Bultmann, *Urchristentum*, 17. Cf. Bultmann, *Primitive Christianity*, 20.

course, is not the scene of an objective Armageddon, as in the mythical stories of ancient apocalyptic literature; the world is rather the spatiotemporal
locus of the conflict between the cruciform power of the Christ-Spirit and
the cosmic powers of the present age. The bifocal vision of the apocalypse
compels us to interpret the world in terms of the future that is constantly
inbreaking in the moment. In continuity with the Hebrew prophets, "there
is no idea of order and purpose in the universe. Instead there is a future to
be inaugurated by God."[126] The world is the creation of God insofar as it is
the place where God interrupts us, where the future comes to meet us. "God
is always a God who comes," and thus we "wait for God's coming in every
future moment."[127] As we come to understand ourselves in light of God's
advent, we understand the world as the unnature, the creation, of God.

The word "creation," like the word "nature," is thus a hermeneutical
category. "Nature" interprets the worldly space in which we exist in terms
of a universalizing discourse. To speak about nature or essence is to speak
about what something is in itself in a way that can be generally known and
observed. But talk of something "in itself" (an sich) is always already an
interpretation of that thing, since there is no genuine in-itself apart from the
knowing subject. In this case, talk of the world-as-nature is an exercise in
scientific discourse that reduces the object to what is empirically given and
universalizable. Such talk is antithetical to faith, which sees the world bifocally, not in terms of what it is but in terms of how it may be—that is to say,
in terms of its future rather than its past. Faith sees the world according to
what is outside of itself, namely, the transcendent, eschatological act of God.
Faith in the world-as-creation "is thus not a cosmological theory about the
origin of the world but the obedient and confident acceptance of the world
in which I live as God's creation, . . . insofar as I understand my here and
now as qualified by the proclamation."[128] Whereas "nature" interprets the
world in terms of a directly given and universalizing discourse, "creation"—
which is always new creation and therefore unnature—interprets the world
in terms of a nongiven and paradoxical proclamation. Nature refers to the
world's objectifiable substance, while unnature refers to the world's eschatological goal; nature is its past, while unnature is its future.[129] To confess that
God is the creator and the world is God's creation is not a native possibility,
a basic structure of our existence; it can only be perceived against appear-

126. Bultmann, *Primitive Christianity*, 34.

127. Ibid.

128. Bultmann, "Truth," 187.

129. The relation of nature to unnature/creation is analogous to John Walton's distinction between "material ontology" and "functional ontology" (Walton, *Lost World*,
22).

ances as a *novum*, an act of grace. To see the world-as-creation is thus to see the resurrection of the dead.

This apocalyptic vision of the world-as-creation does not mean we invest the world with divine meaning and activity, as if the world itself participates in God. The distinctive feature of the Old Testament creation accounts in comparison to the ancient Near East is the absolute transcendence of God: God speaks and it is so, and "when you take away their breath, they die and return to their dust" (Ps 104:29). We understand the world as unnature when we recognize it is "constantly encompassed and threatened by nothingness" and that "in and of itself it is nothing."[130] The doctrine of creation thus serves primarily to emphasize the radical *distinction* between creator and creature, incomparably expressed by Deutero-Isaiah:

> Who has measured the waters in the hollow of his hand
> and marked off the heavens with a span,
> enclosed the dust of the earth in a measure,
> and weighed the mountains in scales
> and the hills in a balance?
>
> Who has directed the spirit of the Lord,
> or as his counselor has instructed him?
> Whom did he consult for his enlightenment,
> and who taught him the path of justice?
> Who taught him knowledge,
> and showed him the way of understanding?
> Even the nations are like a drop from a bucket,
> and are accounted as dust on the scales;
> see, he takes up the isles like fine dust.
> Lebanon would not provide fuel enough,
> nor are its animals enough for a burnt offering.
> All the nations are as nothing before him;
> they are accounted by him as less than nothing and emptiness.
> To whom then will you liken God,
> or what likeness compare with him? (Isa 40:12–18)

The God who saves has no given likeness, no creaturely analogy, no natural point of connection (Exod 20:4). This God is utterly hidden from sight, present to us only in absence. Faith in God the creator is "the knowledge of our complete abandonment."[131] The revelation of God, according to Barth, is a revelation "in *hiddenness*, which therefore means the radical dedivinizing

---

130. Bultmann, "Faith," 175.
131. Ibid., 177.

of the world and nature and history, the complete divine *incognito*."[132] God's apocalyptic otherness frees the world to be the *world*, which is the space of the apocalypse precisely in its secularity. But it also frees God to be *God*, that is, to be the one who dies within the world, so that in participating in this death we die to the world and ourselves. Commenting on Dietrich Bonhoeffer's famous statement that "God consents to be pushed out of the world and onto the cross," Eberhard Jüngel observes that "to let oneself be pushed out, to depart, to go away, are all something other than a total lack of relationship. This can actually signify the most intensive relationship."[133]

The cross is the existential "twilight of the gods," the *Götterdämmerung* that emancipates the world from its bondage to the old order—its gods, religions, social norms, economic systems—so that the world is free to be the unnatural creation and human beings are free to be unnatural creatures. The dedivinizing of the world is not the opposite but the very actualization of God's saving presence. Only a thoroughly secular world, liberated from its enslaving idols and elemental powers, can thus exist in truth as God's creation.

EXISTENTIAL *EPEKTASIS*: THE END OF CREATION

Creation-as-unnature has, in a paradoxical way, already arrived at its eschatological end. The third article thus comes before the first article. We know God as the redeemer, as the agent of the apocalyptic undoing of nature, before we know God as creator. This necessitates a fundamentally different approach to the so-called "last things."

In his work of speculative theology on the last things or *novissima*—that is, those things that cannot be followed by anything new, by a *novum*—Paul Griffiths identifies "three possible last things ... for any creature or creaturely kind."[134] These are annihilation, simple stasis, and repetitive stasis. In each case there is no longer any novelty. The conditions are permanent and unchanging. Griffiths identifies a fourth option, however, that he calls epektasy, which is the denial of a *novissimum* or last thing. The word comes from the Greek επεκτείνω, meaning "to stretch out toward" or "to extend toward." In the NT it appears only once in the middle form of ἐπεκτείνομαι in Paul's statement about himself as "forgetting what lies behind and straining forward [ἐπεκτεινόμενος] to what lies ahead" (Phil 3:13). While it "has

---

132. Barth, *Göttingen Dogmatics*, 144, rev. Cf. Barth, *Unterricht*, 177.

133. Jüngel, *God as the Mystery*, 61. Cf. Bonhoeffer, *Letters and Papers*, 479.

134. Griffiths, *Decreation*, 13.

no immediate reference to the last things in Philippians," the word "has been applied to the heavenly condition of human beings, and when it is, this amounts to a denial that there is . . . a heavenly *novissimum* for humans."[135] Specifically, epektasy for Griffiths means "the future of such a creature is always, at least in principle, narratable, because there is always something new yet to happen to it."[136]

Griffiths does not mention anyone by name but he evidently has in mind ancient Greek mystical and ascetic theology, above all the work of Gregory of Nyssa. The great fourth-century theologian is famous especially for his doctrine of *epektasis* or eternal progress, developed most extensively in his *Life of Moses*. For Gregory of Nyssa, the soul is created with a desire for God that is eternally inexhaustible, given the ineffable transcendence of the divine essence. The true vision of God is "never to be satisfied in the desire to see him."[137] Once released from the body that holds it down, the soul thus "becomes light and swift" and "rises ever higher and will always make its flight yet higher—by its desire of the heavenly things *straining ahead* [συνεπεκτεινομένη] *for what is still to come,* as the Apostle says."[138] Participation in the divine is thus a "never-ending ascension into God."[139] It never ends because "it is not in the nature of what is unenclosed to be grasped."[140] The ungraspable God draws the soul ever higher and ever deeper for all eternity, and the soul "attracted to that ascent constantly expands [συνεπεκτείνεται] as one progresses in pressing on to the Good."[141] For Gregory, eternal life is an infinite extension of the pilgrimage begun in one's earthly life. Eternity is a never-ending sojourn toward God, an ascent without arrival.

If the apocalypse is constitutive of both God and world, this means that God is a denaturalizing event and the world is the unnatural space of this event—and thus to participate in God is to exist not in stasis but in dynamic, historical movement. True creaturely existence consists in constantly going outside oneself. There is no end to novelty; the creature has no divinely ordained *novissimum*. For this reason we must side with the epektasy of Gregory of Nyssa against annihilation or permanent stasis, whether simple or repetitive. But Gregory's appropriation of a Platonic metaphysics has to be demythologized—and so historicized and existentialized. In place

135. Ibid., 26.
136. Ibid., 25.
137. Gregory of Nyssa, *Life*, 116.
138. Ibid., 113. Cf. Gregorii Nysseni, *De Vita Moysis*, 112.13–20.
139. McGinn, *Foundations*, 129.
140. Gregory of Nyssa, *Life*, 116.
141. Ibid. Cf. Gregorii Nysseni, *De Vita Moysis*, 116.17.

of a body-soul dualism that allows the eternal soul to embark on a bodiless journey toward God, we must reinterpret *epektasis* within creaturely existence as the ever-new encounter with the divine apocalypse within history. The soul, according to a nonreductive physicalism, is not a substance separate from the body but rather the total orientation of the human person in relation to God, the world, and oneself. The truth or "soul" of the creature consists in what Jüngel calls the *adaequatio totus homo ad rem*, the correspondence of the whole person to the object (i.e., God), which occurs when the interruptive encounter with the divine "moves [the person] to a new existential location."[142] This existential relocation occurs anew in each concrete historical moment, and we never arrive at our destination. There is always a new denaturalizing interruption that takes us outside ourselves and destroys the elements of the cosmos to which we cling. The Christ-Spirit leads us ever onward—not vertically into the empyrean heights but *horizontally* into the existential depths of human community; not vertically toward the ungraspable divine nature but horizontally toward the ungraspable human neighbor, where alone we will genuinely encounter God and so discover ourselves.

Having said all that, the *epektasis* does eventually come to an end, namely, at death—whether our own death, the death of the planet, or perhaps of the cosmos. This is not a true *novissimum*, however, because we cannot speculate as to whether the creature has an existence beyond this limit.[143] The theologian can only speak of God and the creature within history, where the apocalypse of salvation occurs, but this history has an inexorable and impenetrable cosmic horizon beyond which we cannot gaze. Faith is the act of facing this horizon in correspondence to the Christ who "set his face to go to Jerusalem" (Luke 9:51). We will understand the end of creation when we understand the end of Christ.

On July 1, 1934, Rudolf Bultmann gave a sermon at Marburg University on faith in God the creator, in which he connected the first article of the creed on creation with the second article on christology.[144] While cosmic nothingness hems us in on all sides, Christ freely entered into the darkness

---

142. Jüngel, "Die Wahrheit," 49.

143. On the question of life after death, see the concluding "Epilogue" below.

144. The text for the sermon was 1 Cor 8:4–6: "Hence, as to the eating of food offered to idols, we know that 'no idol in the world really exists,' and that 'there is no God but one.' Indeed, even though there may be so-called gods in heaven or on earth—as in fact there are many gods and many lords—yet for us there is one God, the Father, from whom are all things and for whom we exist, and one Lord, Jesus Christ, through whom are all things and through whom we exist."

of death and, as the "pioneer and perfecter of our faith" (Heb 12:2), he now leads us into the nothingness of the future with confidence.

> If we know [Christ], we know God; and if we do not know him, we do not know God. . . . He has died on the cross—for us; and he now lives in eternity—for us! And only when we understand this do we understand that God is the Creator; and so it is through him that the world becomes God's creation—for us! . . . To have faith in the crucified one means to permit oneself to be crucified with him, to permit this judgment also to be passed against oneself. To have faith in the cross of Christ means to be prepared to let God work as the Creator. God creates out of nothing, and whoever becomes nothing before [God] is made alive. Whenever the cross really leads me to the knowledge of my own nothingness and to the confession of my sin, I am open for God's rule as the Creator who forgives me my sin and takes from me nothingness, death. Thus Christ as the one who leads us to God, the Creator of life, is our Lord, through whom we exist.[145]

To see the world as creation is to see ourselves as crucified with Christ. The apocalyptic event of his death destroys the power that death has over us and so opens us eccentrically to the future. To be a creature is therefore to exist in the eschatological space of unnature—to know ourselves as dead in our φύσις, and yet alive in Christ. This is the scandalous paradox of faith: "For the word of the cross is foolishness to those who are perishing, but to us who are being saved it is the power of God" (1 Cor 1:18, my translation). The existential *epektasis* of creation is thus a journey toward the crucified God who calls both creature and cosmos to become unnature by "enter[ing] the darkness of the future hopefully and confidently."[146]

Creation reaches its end, its *telos*, in the cross, in the undoing of the cosmos, in the stripping of the altar of nature. The end of creation bears witness, however, to the endlessness of the apocalypse, the incompletable—*unvollendbar*—scope of the saving kerygma that knows no predetermined perimeter. The saving event ripples outwards from the cross deep into the invisible, unconscious underside of history, interrupting all creatures, human and nonhuman alike, in its eschatological wake until the sun, in the ultimate eccentricity, expands beyond itself and consumes the earth in the conflagration of its cosmic communion with the crucified one, offering

---

145. Bultmann, "Faith," 179–81. Cf. Bultmann, *Das verkündigte Wort*, 270–72.
146. Bultmann, "Humanism," 83.

itself as a final perishable testament to imperishable grace. "The grass withers, the flower fades; but the word of our God will stand forever" (Isa 40:8).

7

The God of Salvation
Trinity

Our God is a God who saves.

PSALM 68:20

*My word and my kerygma were not with plausible words of wisdom, but
with a demonstration of the Spirit and of power.*

1 CORINTHIANS 2:4

*Then comes the end, when he hands over the kingdom to God the Father,
after he has destroyed every ruler and every authority and power.*

1 CORINTHIANS 15:24

TRINITY AS *SCHLUSS*

Christian theology must begin with the doctrine of God, and specifically the doctrine of the trinity—or at least so it is widely claimed today. Anything else is regarded as tantamount to denying Christian faith altogether. Within this context Friedrich Schleiermacher is often lifted up as the paradigm of liberal theology's dismissal of the doctrine of the trinity as irrelevant to the Christian life. The chief evidence for this is allegedly the way this doctrine "is placed right at the end of the work [*The Christian Faith*], as an appendix."[1] Despite being "the most popular charge" cast against Schleiermacher's theology, "it is a perfectly absurd charge."[2] While the doctrine of the trinity does appear at the end of *The Christian Faith*, it appears not as an appendix (*Anhang*) but as the conclusion (*Schluss*), the summation and capstone of all that came before. Despite the many spurious claims about Schleiermacher, this is precisely where the doctrine belongs. The trinity properly appears at the *end* of Christian dogmatics.

While Karl Barth is often held up as the anti-Schleiermacher on the grounds that he begins his *Church Dogmatics* with the trinity, in truth he proves the validity of Schleiermacher's approach. In the final, unfinished fourth volume on the doctrine of reconciliation Barth effectively has to reconstruct his doctrine of the trinity on a christocentric basis, though he does not carry out the job consistently or completely.[3] The formal doctrine in the first volume, derived from an abstract concept of revelation, is unable to do justice to Barth's later emphasis on the history of Jesus. Without announcing it as such, Barth expounds the trinity *in the light of christology*, as opposed to the other way around. The Son is the one who goes into the far country in obedience to the command of the Father, while the Holy Spirit actualizes this "vertical" relationship in a "horizontal" direction by gathering and empowering the community of Christ's body.[4] By developing the trinity in light of christology Barth merely repeats the logic displayed in the history of doctrine: beginning with the worship of Jesus as the Son of God, the early Christian communities began to develop various christologies (and eventually also pneumatologies) to understand the relation between Jesus of Nazareth and YHWH.[5] In other words, the ancient church did

---

1. McGrath, *Christian Theology*, 258. For more charges against Schleiermacher on this score, see Kim, *Deus Providebit*, 129.

2. Powell, *Trinity*, 90.

3. See McCormack, "Doctrine."

4. See esp. *CD* 4.1, §§59, 62.

5. For an accessible account of five early christologies from the second century, see Papandrea, *Earliest Christologies*.

not presuppose the trinity; rather, the doctrine of the trinity presupposed an existential and soteriological faith in Jesus. Once the councils made the trinity into dogma, however, the church turned what was a conclusion into a presupposition.

We cannot speak meaningfully of God unless we know *which* God we are talking about, that is to say, unless we know *who* this God is. And we only know who this God is based on *what* this God has done. We can therefore only talk about the trinity *after* we have spoken of revelation, namely, the apocalypse. *Soteriology, not trinity, is the ground of Christian dogmatics.* If our only access to the being of God is through revelation in history, then the trinity, if valid, can only be something we learn from the saving event. Eberhard Jüngel thus proposes a trinitarian axiom: "The trinity is a mystery of *salvation*." This can serve as our dogmatic starting point "because [the trinity] is revealed in the event of σωτηρία [salvation]."[6] The epistemological point is grounded in an ontological one: we come to know God in the saving event because God *is* the saving event. God is ontologically located in this event. The word "God" names the agent and actuality of the existential apocalypse of faith. When we speak of the triune God, we are not speaking of some being that exists behind or apart from the event, but rather the paradoxically transcendent and immanent reality of the event itself. A dogmatic sketch of the triune God who saves will thus interpret the three *tropoi* of Christ, Spirit, and Creator as, respectively, the historical inbreaking, existential power, and eschatological ground of the apocalypse.[7]

---

6. Jüngel, "Verhältnis," 269.

7. I use the Greek language of "tropos" in place of the language of "person" or "mode." Historically the church has used a variety of terms to identify the three divine realities traditionally named Father, Son, and Holy Spirit: ὑπόστασις, πρόσωπον, *persona*, τρόπος. The Greek and Latin traditions of ancient Christianity disputed the appropriate language for the Godhead; the Greek term ὑπόστασις was taken to be equivalent to the Latin term *substantia*, which the West used for the shared divine essence, while the Latin term *persona* was taken to be equivalent to πρόσωπον, which in the East meant the mask worn by an actor. The West thus accused the East of tritheism, while the East accused the West of modalism or Sabellianism. By modalism we mean the view that the "persons" or "modes" of the trinity are merely historical manifestations of the single divine nature and do not have eternal existence in the being of God. Eventually these three terms were understood to be synonymous, so long as πρόσωπον was understood in the sense of the Latin *persona*, while *substantia* was understood as equivalent to οὐσία. The language of τρόπος, which means "mode," was also used in Greek Christianity to refer to the individual ὑπόστασις or *persona*, in distinction from the common divine λόγος or essence. Of course, τρόπος is not meant in a modalistic sense. Maximus the Confessor thus speaks of God as one λόγος (*logos*, principle) of essence in three τρόποι (*tropoi*, modes) of existence: "God is truly Unity and Trinity: Unity according to the principle of essence and Trinity according to the mode of existence [τρόπος τῆς ὑπάρξεως]" (*Maximus Confessor*, 111). Karl Barth also speaks of God as one subject in

GOD THE CHRIST:
THE INBREAKING OF THE APOCALYPSE

Christian dogmatics begins with the claim, "God was in Christ . . ." (2 Cor 5:19 KJV). Metaphysical theology assumes we already know what it means to speak of God, and the only question is how this God is *in* Christ. Soteriocentric theology reverses the method of theology: what we know, inasmuch as we know anything, is what it means to speak of Christ, and the only question is *who* is the God that is in him. For this reason, the genuine "first article" of Christian theology is not about God the Creator[8] but about God the Christ. Dogmatic theology has for centuries followed the pattern of the creed by moving from creation (Creator) to reconciliation (Christ) to redemption (Spirit), thereby associating the first *tropos* of God's being with the Creator. This makes sense if, following the example of Jesus and the apostles, we associate the Creator with the YHWH of the Old Testament. The problem arises when we move from the faith of Jesus who proclaims the reign of *YHWH* to the faith of the early Christian community that proclaims the reign of *Jesus*, the Christ of YHWH. Taking the latter seriously means letting the advent of Christ become the hermeneutical norm for responsible God-talk. Following this starting point leads us to affirm "that the Triune God is YHWH, and that YHWH is the Triune God."[9] No single *tropos* of God can be identified with the God of the old covenant. This then frees us to reconsider trinitarian *taxis*. The order of the divine *tropoi* no longer needs to be Creator, Christ, and Spirit on the assumption that priority has to be given to God the Creator in order to give precedence to YHWH, the God of Israel.

three modes of being (*Seinswesen*): "The God who reveals Himself according to Scripture is One in three distinctive modes of being subsisting in their mutual relations: Father, Son, and Holy Spirit" (*CD* 1.1:348). Barth uses *Seinsweise* to translate τρόπος ὑπάρξεως (*CD* 1.1:359). With Barth I prefer the language of "mode of existence" over that of "person," given the connotation of an individual mind and will that the latter has in modernity. But since the word "mode" in English tends to connote a kind of modalism, I have opted for *tropoi*.

8. I have chosen to refer to the traditional *tropos* of God the Father as God the Creator to avoid the masculine and patriarchal connotations associated with father-language. The use of "father" for God is also a problematic projection upon God of imagery derived from the human family, which encourages one to view God as a supersized human rather than as the utterly transcendent saving event. The fact that the NT uses the language of "father" is no reason to insist on its use by the community of faith today, any more than the NT's use of myth obliges us to speak in mythical terms today about God, the world, or ourselves. In the same way that God is not really "above us," so too God is not really our "father." Father-language belongs to an ancient cultural world-picture that we no longer share today. We are free to explore different or even new language for bringing the object of our faith to expression.

9. Soulen, "YHWH," 32.

Since Christian faith confesses Jesus the Christ to be the constitutive revelation, norm, and ground of the triune being of God, the doctrine of the trinity must begin with God the Christ as the subject of the saving apocalypse.

1. God the Christ is the *inbreaking* of the apocalypse. Christ is where the saving power of God intersects worldly existence. The language of inbreaking and intersection metaphorically expresses the truth that he inaugurated a definitive turning point between two ages. Christ was a shattering disruption of the cosmos as understood and experienced by those who received his message of the coming reign of God. His proclamation of repentance involved a radically new self-understanding, "a turning away from the whole of the world as it existed at the time."[10] Following the message of Jesus did not merely entail a change in one's inherited piety and practice but "a turning away from the structure of the world which [this piety] presupposed and guarded."[11] The advent of Christ was thus "the total transformation of all things," the actualization of "a completely new mode of human existence."[12] As J. Louis Martyn interprets Paul's theology, the Christ-event breaks fundamentally with the Deuteronomic logic of the "Two Ways"—life or death, faith or works, obedience or disobedience, circumcision or uncircumcision.[13] What counts as real and true now is only *new creation* (Gal 6:15), and according to the faith of the early community, the new creation became historical actuality in Jesus the Christ.

2. God the Christ is the apocalyptic *past*: the event that *was*. Christ is the moment when the apocalypse becomes historical in a definitive, spatio-temporal way. This does not mean that talk of God the Christ depends upon determining the historicity of the Jesus-tradition apart from faith. This was and is the abiding error of all quests for the historical Jesus, as Bultmann saw clearly. Bultmann acknowledges that the Synoptic Gospels are "a combination of historical report and kerygmatic christology," but this combination does not serve "to legitimize the Christ-kerygma through history [*Historie*], but just the opposite, to legitimize the history [*Geschichte*] of Jesus, so to speak, as messianic history, by placing it in the light of the kerygmatic christology."[14] The statement that Christ is the historical actuality of the apocalypse is a *kerygmatic* claim, meaning it is a confession of faith. There is no possibility of reaching behind the kerygma through historical research.

10. Gogarten, *Christ*, 141.

11. Ibid., 142.

12. Ibid., 142, 143.

13. See Martyn, "Apocalyptic Gospel."

14. Bultmann, *Das Verhältnis*, 13. He adds: "The attempt to prove the legitimacy of the kerygma through scientific research serves a modern interest, for it poses a question to the kerygma with which it is wholly unconcerned" (ibid.).

We can only discern its historicity *through* the kerygma, not apart from it. Nevertheless, with kerygmatic eyes we can see and acknowledge that in Jesus the apocalypse *has happened.* In the Christ-event faith and history are paradoxically identical.

3. God the Christ is the vector of *faith.* The paradoxical identity of faith and history in the apocalypse means that the exclusive starting point for thinking and speaking about this event is faith. The possibility of faith, however, is itself a gift of the apocalypse and not a native human capacity (Gal 3:23–25). Christ is the vector of faith in that the actuality of his advent makes possible the very mode of existence required to participate in this event. The act of faith sees the past event of Christ's death *as* the present event of his resurrection life. Faith sees in Christ, in other words, the living vitality of the Spirit.

GOD THE SPIRIT:
THE POWER OF THE APOCALYPSE

The doctrine of God the Christ brings to expression the historical norm of the apocalypse, but this norm is only an actuality *for us* insofar as it is not merely located in the past but becomes a living event for us today. The tradition names the eventfulness of the apocalypse the Holy Spirit.

1. God the Spirit is the *power* of the apocalypse. The NT identifies Jesus as a man of δύναμις or power. Throughout the Synoptic Gospels he is recorded as actualizing δύναμις: "What deeds of power [δυνάμεις] are being done by his hands!" (Mark 6:2; cf. Matt 13:54).[15] The narrative of Luke-Acts, which joins the life of Jesus with the life of the Christian community by way of Pentecost, connects the δύναμις of Jesus with the Spirit. The Gospel of Luke signals this already in the birth narrative, when the angel tells Mary that "the Holy Spirit will come upon you, and the power of the Most High will overshadow you" (Luke 1:35). Following his Spirit-impelled journey into the wilderness, "Jesus, in the power of the Spirit [ἐν τῇ δυνάμει τοῦ

---

15. The NRSV translates δυνάμεις as "deeds of power" in the Gospels but as "miracles" elsewhere in the NT. Interestingly, the NRSV is one of the few modern translations that retains the language of "power." The NIV uses "miracles" throughout. The ESV uses a variety of phrases, but it primarily uses "mighty works" in the Gospels and "miracles" in the rest of the NT. Whether there is any valid basis for describing the works that Jesus performs differently is a question worth considering. In any case, the word should literally be translated as "powers," though "deeds of power" is a suitable translation as well. But the inconsistency in translation can disguise the fact that the very same word is used in quite distinct contexts. So Paul can ask, "Do all work powers?" (1 Cor 12:29, my translation), but he can also list "powers" as one of the things that cannot separate us from the love of God (Rom 8:38–39).

πνεύματος], returned to Galilee" (Luke 4:14, my translation). Luke-Acts tells the story to Jesus to reinforce the fledgling church community. For this reason it describes the followers of Jesus as sharing in his δύναμις, both before (Luke 9:1; 10:19) and after Pentecost (Acts 3:12; 4:33; 6:8; 8:13; 19:11). At the heart of the narrative is the sending of the Holy Spirit, who is presented as the agent of δύναμις, the presence of the divine power that launches the mission of the church: "You will receive power when the Holy Spirit has come upon you; and you will be my witnesses in Jerusalem, in all Judea and Samaria, and to the ends of the earth" (Acts 1:8; cf. Luke 24:49). Luke-Acts describes in a mythological way the theological truth that, wherever and whenever the apostolate comes into existence, the dynamic energy animating the apostolate comes from outside itself. The presence of this divine δύναμις in the world, according to the Gospels, is a sign of the coming messianic age. In the apocalypse "the powers in the heavens will be shaken" and his disciples will "see 'the Son of Man coming in clouds' with great power and glory" (Mark 13:25–26; cf. Matt 24:29–30; Luke 21:26–27).[16] For this reason the present participation in the Spirit's δύναμις by Jesus and the apostolate indicates that both belong to the eschatological reign of God; they are ambassadors of God's coming future.

Whereas the Gospels ascribe to Jesus and his Spirit the δύναμις of God, the earlier writings of the apostle Paul ascribe this same δύναμις to the gospel itself (1 Thess 1:5: "our message of the gospel came to you . . . in power"; Rom 1:16: "[the gospel] is the power of God for salvation") and to the word of cross (1 Cor 1:18: "For the message [λόγος] about the cross is . . . the power of God"). Paul even says that his "word [λόγος] and kerygma [κήρυγμά]" are a demonstration "of the Spirit and of power" (1 Cor 2:4, my translation). God's power is manifest in the world not through miraculous deeds but through the word of the gospel, the kerygma of the crucified one. While Paul does speak of the "power of the Holy Spirit" at the end of Romans (Rom 15:13, 19), he primarily speaks of the δύναμις of God—a δύναμις that apocalyptically confronts the anti-God "power of sin" (1 Cor 15:56). Christ's work is finished, according to Paul, when he has "destroyed every ruler and every authority and power" (1 Cor 15:24).[17] Given the apocalyptic

16. The language of "powers in the heavens" refers to the stars, which in the ancient world were thought to be spiritual beings with their own agency.

17. The word for "ruler" here is ἀρχή, which means origin or first principle—a ruler in the sense of something that determines the course of what follows. Aristotle uses it as the word for God in the sense of first cause or ultimate principle (*Metaphysics* 1.983a). There is a connection between this word and the concepts of φύσις and στοιχεῖα explored in the previous chapter. To say that Christ destroys every principle, along with every authority (ἐξουσία) and power (δύναμις), can be taken to mean that Christ destroys not only the sociopolitical structures of oppression (authority and power), but also the

conflict in Paul between God and the powers of sin and death that mark the present evil age, Martyn interprets Paul's expression "to be under" (ὑπὸ τίνα εἶναι) as "to be under *the power of*," so that, according to Martyn's translation of Galatians, "the scripture imprisoned everything *under the power of Sin*" (Gal 3:22), "we were confined *under the Law's power*" (Gal 3:23), and "we were held in a state of slavery *under the power of the elements of the cosmos*" (Gal 4:3). This reading reinforces the understanding of the Spirit as the power of the apocalypse, since, according to Paul, "If you Galatians are led by the Spirit, then in fact you are not *under the power of the Law*" (Gal 5:18).[18] To be led by the Spirit is to be under the emancipatory δύναμις of God.

While Paul and the Evangelists employ mythical language to describe the apocalypse, Paul's claim that the kerygma manifests the Spirit and power of God (1 Cor 2:4)—not to mention the Johannine replacement of power language altogether with talk of faith and obedience—provides the basis for a hermeneutical reconstruction of the Spirit's apocalyptic agency. We can understand the Spirit as the power of the apocalypse only if we do not conceive the Spirit "as a mysteriously magical power at work behind our doing, so that our doing is no longer *ours*, and our faith is no longer *ours*."[19] The scholastic notion that "the powers of faith and love worked by God exist beyond consciousness as mysterious qualities" is "to speculate like an Augustinian and to live like a Pelagian."[20] The δύναμις of the Spirit is only at work *as* we are at work; she operates *in* our existence and not alongside it. The Spirit is not some tangible, objective, or causal force in the world, which has evident effects that can be isolated from the apostolate as the site of the apocalypse. Following Paul, the Spirit of God interrupts us *in the kerygma* with the apocalyptic dynamism of God's reign as the new mode of our eschatological existence within history.[21]

2. God the Spirit is the apocalyptic *present*: the event that *is*. If God the Christ is the past-tense occurrence of the apocalypse, then God the Spirit is its present-tense realization. Jesus the Christ is a first-century Palestinian man. Isolated from the Spirit, he is merely a historical figure and so only the possibility of the apocalypse and not its actuality. The Spirit makes present the historical inbreaking of the apocalypse in Christ, and she does so,

---

entire cultural-metaphysical framework for understanding the world (principle). Paul in this passage reinforces our thesis that the apocalypse is the inbreaking of unnature.

18. Martyn, *Galatians*, 370–71.

19. Bultmann, *What Is Theology?* 142.

20. Herrmann, "Die Busse," 41–42. Cf. Bultmann, *What Is Theology?* 82.

21. "The Spirit denotes a how of our historical existence" (Bultmann, *What Is Theology?* 142).

as we discussed in previous chapters, by way of repetition. The Spirit will "remind you of all that I have said to you" (John 14:26) and "will testify on my behalf" (John 15:26). This repetition occurs when and where persons are placed outside themselves in an existential participation in the experience of God's cruciform presence-in-absence. The act of the Spirit is not a simple repetition of the same but a *nonidentical repetition of interruption* that is new in each moment because of the particularities of the one being interrupted. The pneumatic act of repetition is thus an act of novelty-in-continuity: a multiplicity of persons contingently crucified with Christ.[22]

3. God the Spirit is the vector of *love*. The material norm for the Spirit's act of repetition is Christ's total being-outside-himself, actualized in his death in God-abandonment, and thus God the Spirit does not repeat the apocalypse in every moment but only in those moments that correspond to, and so participate in, the mode of Christ's crucifixion. The NT calls this norm ἀγάπη or love. The experience of genuine love is an existential repetition of the apocalypse. Paul makes this connection in the pivotal moment of his letter to the Galatians. The new existence of faith—that is, the "faith of Christ" (Gal 2:16)—means that I "have been crucified with Christ" so that Christ himself now lives "in me" as the new ego, the new subject of my existence (Gal 2:19–20). Paul then goes on to clarify the nature of this new subjectivity: "And the life I now live in the flesh I live by faith in the Son of God, *who loved me and gave himself for me*" (Gal 2:20; emphasis mine).[23] Paul thus defines the new existence enacted in Christ as an act of self-donating love, in which Christ is "handed over" (παραδίδωμι) on our behalf.[24] This act of love, which is the new life of faith, is what now lives

---

22. Alain Badiou rejects repetition in his early work on the grounds that it lacks novelty and thus justice: "It is quite a step into the dialectic to understand, in a nontrivial sense, that every rightness and every justice are, in principle, novelties; and that everything that repeats itself is invariably unjust and inexact" (*Theory*, 39).

23. As Richard Hays and others have pointed out, the phrase ἐν πίστει ζῶ τῇ τοῦ υἱοῦ τοῦ θεοῦ is perhaps better translated as "I live by the faith of the Son of God," reading the genitive as a subjective rather than objective genitive (see Hays, *Faith*). Since my point is valid either way, I have chosen to leave it in the form used by most modern translations. I do so in part, however, to protest against the attempt by many to make Jesus's own faithfulness—much less a speculative reconstruction of his personal experience of faith—salvific in itself, independent of one's participation in Christ. I worry, too, about the futile and naïve attempt to pry into Jesus's consciousness, as if the historical record grants such access.

24. Paul uses both the active and passive forms of παραδίδωμι with reference to Christ being given over to death. Here in Galatians Paul says that Christ "gave himself for me" (παραδόντος ἑαυτὸν ὑπὲρ ἐμοῦ), but in Romans he says that Christ "was handed over [παρεδόθη]" (Rom 4:25) and that God "gave [Christ] up for all of us [ὑπὲρ ἡμῶν πάντων παρέδωκεν αὐτόν]" (Rom 8:32).

in me by virtue of the fact that I no longer live because I have been crucified with Christ. In other words, to live in self-giving love *is* to be crucified
with Christ, to have Christ in me as my new subjectivity. Paul reinforces
this very point when he tells the Corinthians that "while we live, we are
always being given up [παραδίδωμι] to death for Jesus's sake, so that the life
of Jesus may be made visible in our mortal flesh" (2 Cor 4:11). As in Galatians Paul speaks here of a correspondence between our present existence
("while we live") and the existence of Christ ("the life of Jesus") that consists
in the handing-ourselves-over-for-others that characterizes Christ's death.
We participate in the crucified Christ insofar as we hand ourselves over on
behalf of another. Or to use the characteristically straightforward language
of the Johannine epistles: "if we love one another, God lives in us" (1 John
4:12). The missing link in this is the Spirit. For Paul, especially, the new
life of faith—meaning the act of self-donating love, which is the event of
our cocrucifixion, the sublation of our subjectivity—happens when we "live
by the Spirit," when we are "guided by the Spirit" (Gal 5:25). To bring this
full circle, the Spirit repeats the apocalypse in those moments in which we
hand-ourselves-over in love and so exist truly outside ourselves. God the
Spirit, as the agent of apocalyptic repetition, is thus the vector of love.

GOD THE CREATOR:
THE GROUND OF THE APOCALYPSE

The doctrine of God the Creator is usually articulated in a nonsoteriological
way to refer to the prime mover or first cause for the material cosmos. God,
according to Thomas Aquinas, is the "first exemplar cause of all things"
(*prima causa exemplaris omnium rerum*).[25] God-talk on this way of thinking is a way of explaining world-talk. In other words, one begins with the
observable fact that we exist, that there is a universe of matter around us,
and then one posits "God" as the necessary explanation for this observation: "God is necessary in order to understand the world as world."[26] For
example, C. S. Peirce begins *A Neglected Argument for the Reality of God*
by asserting that "God" identifies the necessary explanation for human experience: "The word 'God' . . . is *the* definable proper name, signifying *Ens
necessarium* [necessary being]; in my belief Really [*sic*] creator of all three
Universes of Experience."[27] When God the Creator becomes an *ens necessarium*, one speaks *about* "God" as a metaphysical projection, a mere idea

25. *ST* 1.44.3 resp.
26. Jüngel, *God as the Mystery*, 30.
27. Peirce, *Essential Peirce*, 434.

that has no existential significance. In order to speak *of God* as the living God who saves one must understand even the Creator in terms of the saving event of the apocalypse.

1. God the Creator is the *ground* of the apocalypse. The element of truth in the claim that God is the "ground of being" is found in the more concrete claim that God—specifically, God the Creator—is the ground of the apocalypse.[28] The Creator is the transcendent possibility or ontological presupposition, so to speak, of the apocalyptic event of interruption. But the ontological ground of this event does not lie behind but in front of it; the ontological ground is the *eschatological goal*. God grounds the apocalypse by ensuring its perpetual provisionality in light of the future. Rather than guaranteeing some measure of stability, God the Creator ensures the instability and incompleteness of salvation. The apocalyptic God of unnature undermines every pursuit of an *ens necessarium*. Paul Tillich clarifies his claim that God is the ground of being or being-itself by defining God more specifically as "the power of being in everything and above everything, the infinite power of being."[29] If we concretize this soteriologically, we can say that God is the power of the apocalypse, the infinite power of the saving event. Whereas God the Spirit is the power of this event in the repetition of the present moment, God the Creator is the power of this event in the orientation toward *future expectation*. God the Creator is the eschatological horizon of salvation and in that sense we can say that the Creator creates or grounds the apocalypse from the future.

The NT describes God the Creator in this way by locating the Creator's place within the salvation myth in the eschatological future. The Markan and Pauline texts, which share the same genetic profile, are focused strictly on Jesus the suffering and crucified one, so for them the "Father" has a very limited presence; the Creator largely remains on the distant horizon. The key text in Paul's letters appears at the end of 1 Corinthians, where he writes: "Then comes the end, when he hands over the kingdom to God the

---

28. Tillich, *Systematic Theology*, 1:235.

29. Ibid., 1:236. Tillich later defines the divine first principle as "the power of being infinitely resisting nonbeing, giving the power of being to everything that is" (ibid., 1:250–51). In discussing the omnipotence of God, Tillich says that "God is the power of being, resisting and conquering nonbeing. . . . It is more adequate to define divine omnipotence as the power of being which resists nonbeing in all its expressions and which is manifest in the creative process in all its forms" (ibid., 1:272–73). This is a more apocalyptic conception of God, but whereas Tillich makes this action universal and general, I have located it more concretely in the local, particular action of the Spirit. God conquers nonbeing in the existence of the person who is placed outside herself in participation in Christ, who conquers nonbeing through his or her self-abandonment to nonbeing.

Father, after he has destroyed every ruler and every authority and power"
(1 Cor 15:24). God the Creator is the eschatological goal of the saving work
of the Christ-Spirit. The Creator is not an active participant in this work
but rather the *teleological ground*. In Mark, the Creator is the object of Jesus's prayer in Gethsemane—"Abba, Father, for you all things are possible"
(Mark 14:36)—but otherwise remains the absent, silent deity, whose glory
will only appear when the "Son of Man" comes "with the holy angels" (Mark
8:38; cf. Mark 13:32). The other Gospels, which represent a later development of the tradition, contain numerous references to the "Father," but still
the eschatological orientation remains. Jesus refers to the "Father in heaven"
who "will reward you" if you practice piety with the right intentions (Matt
6:1–18). God the Creator appears at the *end* of the salvation myth, which is
the end of history, as the one who will consummate the story and settle accounts. In the meantime, within history, "all things have been handed over"
to Jesus (Matt 11:27; Luke 10:22). At the end of his life Jesus commends his
spirit to the Father (Luke 23:46), a proleptic anticipation of his eschatological self-offering. The Fourth Gospel contains numerous references to the
Creator, but they serve primarily as a way for Jesus to assert his identity with
YHWH or at least the divine authorization of his mission (see esp. John
5:17–23, 26, 36–37; 6:45–46; 8:16–19). But even here the Creator serves an
eschatological purpose: "Whoever serves me, the Father will honor" (John
12:26). Believers go *to the Creator* but *through Jesus* (John 14:6). If we dispense with the mythology of a Son in pretemporal eternity who then takes
on human flesh in the incarnation, we can interpret Jesus's statements about
coming from the Creator as also eschatological in character: Jesus comes
from the Creator in the sense that his existence is divinely authorized and
so eschatologically paves the way *to* the Creator.[30] In light of the NT texts
we can therefore understand God the Creator as the eschatological *telos* of
the apocalypse.[31]

30. Even this, however, cannot be attributed to the Jesus of history. These are
kerygmatic claims of the church *about* Jesus and not direct indications of Jesus's self-
consciousness, to which we have no access.

31. Identifying the Creator with the *telos* or goal of the apocalypse inverts Eberhard
Jüngel's interpretation of the trinity. Jüngel develops his trinitarian dogma around the
insight that "God's being is in coming" (*Gottes Sein ist im Kommen*), which subdivides
in the following way: God comes *from* God (Father), God comes *to* God (Son), and
God comes *as* God (Spirit). God's triune being is thus "the event of God's coming-to-
Godself" (*Gott als Geheimnis*, 521; cf. *God as the Mystery*, 380). Within this interpretation "God the Father" means that "God is the origin of Godself" (*Gott als Geheimnis*,
522). But because this primal originality of God is "earlier than being and nonbeing,"
God is "not the Father of what exists," unless God wills to be, which is to say, unless
one believes God to be (ibid., 522–23). In this way Jüngel ensures that the doctrine of
God the Creator is *not* an explanation of the world but rather strictly an explanation of

2. God the Creator is the apocalyptic *future*: the event that *will be*. Given what we have concluded in light of the NT witness, we can identify the Creator as the future of the apocalypse. God the Creator is the future mode of God's being. This is superficially reminiscent of Wolfhart Pannenberg's claim that "it is necessary to say that, in a restricted but important sense, God does not yet exist."[32] By this, however, Pannenberg means that God's being has to be conceived in terms of God's rule over the world, and thus God's being is only fully manifest at the end of world history, when the rule or kingdom of God becomes objectively present. For Pannenberg, then, God is "the power of the future"[33] in an immanent, chronological sense: God's being is bound up with the future of the empirical world, a future that connects "prehistoric saurians" with the kingdom proclaimed by Jesus, as if dinosaurs and divine justice belong on a single historical continuum.[34]

A critical, soteriocentric hermeneutic interprets the future of the apocalypse not as the chronological future of world history—as is the case with the mythological eschatology of the NT, which presupposes a literal arrival of the Messiah in either the imminent or the distant future—but as the existential future of God's inbreaking in the kerygma. God the Creator is the apocalyptic future in the sense that God *transcends* the moment. The Creator is the divine being-out-ahead-of the present situation. God the Creator is thus the *futurity* of the apocalypse, the constant beyondness of the eschatological event, which enjoins faith to sustain a posture of expectancy with respect to the elemental interruption of our existence. The futurity of God the Creator is at the same time God's *invisibility*, which is "God's being removed in principle from the domain of objectifying thinking."[35] The invisibility is not a contingent limitation of our creaturely faculties but a corollary of the Creator being eschatologically withdrawn from us and thus inaccessible apart from faith. "God is invisible," writes Martin Luther, "and

---

God—more concretely, of God's saving action in Jesus Christ. The positioned I develop in this work shares much in common with Jüngel. The shift of the Creator from the *from* (*von Gott*) to the *to* (*zu Gott*) addresses two issues: (a) it adheres more closely to the NT witness, in terms of the Creator's determinative position at the *end* of history; and (b) it more closely remains an interpretation of the historicized saving event in the Christ-Spirit, and thus avoids giving the impression of referring to an abstract generation of the "Son" by the "Father" in eternity. It also completely avoids the problem of making God (the Creator) into the metaphysical explanation of the world, thus more completely fulfilling Jüngel's intention.

32. Pannenberg, *Theology*, 56.

33. Ibid., 56–57.

34. Ibid., 61.

35. Bultmann, "Science," 144.

you will not make God visible."[36] God the Creator is invisible in the sense that God "cannot be apprehended in any now as one who remains [*der Bleibende*]," but instead "God ever stands before me as one who is coming [*der Kommende*]."[37] God is eschatologically invisible, and thus we encounter God—we can *see* God—in the existential event of the apocalypse. God is apocalyptically revealed precisely as the hidden God.[38] The *Deus revelatus*—the *Deus apocalypticus*—is the *Deus absconditus*; but conversely and simultaneously, the *Deus absconditus* is the *Deus apocalypticus*.

3. God the Creator is the vector of *hope*. The futurity of the apocalypse—the futurity of *God*—validates faith taking the posture of hope. The hope promised in the gospel of the one crucified in God-abandonment is not a message of future escape from worldly tribulations, whether at the end of history or the end of one's life. Such a hope is ultimately either vain wish-fulfillment or speculative metaphysics—and probably both. Genuine hope is a mode of faith's *confidence* in the promise of God to save. Faith takes the form of hope because it is "the conviction of things not seen" (Heb 11:1). While salvation is actualized in our being-outside-ourselves, in the encounter with the Christ-Spirit, this saving action cannot be made visible and objectifiable; God the Creator is by nature invisible and transcendent. To be faithfully expectant for the apocalypse is to live in hope. The apocalypse is therefore an event of imminent expectation, a looking ahead to the new moment that awaits us.[39] The hope of the gospel is the confident expectation that *this* moment will become an encounter with the future, an eternal moment—the "acceptable time" and the "day of salvation" (2 Cor 6:2).

THE APOCALYPTIC TRINITY

The God who saves is the apocalyptic trinity whose being is ontologically located in the event of salvation, in the existential interruption of the apocalypse. We cannot speak of a divine subject, much less a *triune* divine subject, behind or apart from the saving event. God's being, as Eberhard Jüngel argues, is indeed in becoming (*Gottes Sein ist im Werden*). But this act of

36. WA 43:459.14. Cf. *LW* 26:44.

37. Bultmann, "Science," 144; *GuV*, 3:121.

38. Ebeling, "Existenz," 285: "*Deus revelatus* does not remain *Deus revelatus* if God is not known as *Deus absconditus*."

39. I have thus existentialized the definition of apocalypse formulated by Ernst Käsemann in 1962: "I speak of primitive Christian apocalyptic to denote the expectation of an imminent parousia [*die Naherwartung der Parusie*]. . . . The beginnings both of church and theology were conditioned by 'imminent' expectation" (Käsemann, *New Testament Questions*, 109n1).

becoming occurs in the historical site of salvation, which takes place simultaneously in the past, present, and future modalities of faith, love, and hope.
We can thus say that *Gottes Sein ist im Heilen*—God's being is in saving; or
perhaps *Gottes Sein ist im Unterbrechen*—God's being is in interrupting. In
other words, *God's being is in apocalypse*. God is apocalyptically triune.

Apocalypse is thus logically prior to triunity, even if the two are ontologically equiprimordial.[40] Triunity is a corollary of the saving event: the
former is an implication of the latter. We cannot speak of a triune God that
is not the God who saves. Any attempt to do so, no matter how rooted in
Christian texts and traditions, is to speak of a human construct, an idolatrous projection. The event of salvation is the event of triune differentiation.
God differentiates God's own being in a trinitarian way *in* the existential
dislocation of the person who is placed outside herself in her cocrucifying participation in Christ's death in God-abandonment. *God is always
becoming-triune in each new kerygmatic event.* Each new encounter with the
christo(pneumato)centric apocalypse of salvation simultaneously differentiates and unites Christ, Spirit, and Creator. We must therefore collapse the
classical distinction between the processions and the missions. The divine
processions distinguish between the *tropoi* in eternity, while the missions
distinguish between the *tropoi* in history. In those theologies that bifurcate
between the immanent and economic trinity, the processions and missions
form two separate acts in the life of God—the former necessary and the
latter contingent. Other theologies posit "a single eternal act in which both
the processions and the missions take place," according to which the processions in eternity are ordered *toward* the missions in time, resulting in an
ordered relation between the two aspects of the one act.[41] If, however, the

40. To say this is to weigh in on one side in the ongoing dispute within contemporary Barth scholarship over whether Barth's mature doctrine of election, with its claim
that Jesus Christ in his divine-human unity is the eternal subject of election, requires
a shift in the logical priority of triunity and election. Bruce McCormack argues that it
does, though he acknowledges that Barth remains inconsistent. Many of the key writings in the debate are available in Dempsey, *Trinity.* See also McCormack, *Orthodox.*
With respect to Barth I am in agreement with McCormack's interpretation, but constructively I demur from Barth's emphasis on an eternal decision of God to become
incarnate, which retains too much of the mythological-metaphysical conception of deity as a supreme, personal being willing certain courses of action to take place in world
history. For this reason I replace (eternal) election with (existential) apocalypse, thus
further historicizing the event that determines God's self-differentiation.

41. McCormack, "Processions," 115. In this essay Bruce McCormack argues that
both Thomas Aquinas and Karl Barth have a single-act divine drama in which the
processions and missions are coposited in eternity, with the difference that Thomas
works more "from above" in his analysis of the divine essence, while Barth works "from
below" in reflection on the history of Jesus Christ as the event of election: "To say that

apocalypse is the ground and event of God's triunity, then the immanent processions are paradoxically identical with the economic missions. The triune *tropoi* process *as* the *tropoi* actualize the saving event. The immanent trinity, we can say, is the *eternality* of the economic trinity. God's eternal immanence brings to expression the truth that the apocalypse of God transcends the particular historical moment, and thus the event of the trinity is not only present but also future. God's being is trinity is in fact permanently future as a being-in-apocalypse.

The apocalypse is a paradox without reservations: revelation is hiddenness, presence is absence, transcendence is immanence, repetition is novelty, death in God-abandonment is life everlasting, economic mission is immanent procession. The being of God *is* a permanent revolution.[42] The apocalypse comes to expression in the epistemological abyss of this dogmatic "is." Neither side of the *est* can be reduced to the other. The paradox of a God whose being exists in the existential event of faith, love, and hope that is new every morning cannot be resolved without denying the God we encounter in the kerygma. The eccentricity of faith abides in the paradox of the gospel, because it participates in the God who is eternally eccentric. God constantly abandons Godself in the eschatological moment of interruption and, paradoxically, thereby constantly realizes God's being in an ever new way. God determines Godself in the act of delivering Godself over to the obscurity of the future—which is the hiddenness of God. Faith therefore follows the way of the triune God in its recognition that "they alone find security who let all security go, who . . . are ready to enter into inner darkness."[43]

Jesus Christ is the subject of election and to mean it as Barth means it requires, at a minimum, that the event of God's self-constitution as triune (i.e., the processions) and the event of his turning toward the human race in the covenant of grace (i.e., the missions) be one and the same event—albeit *one event with two terms*" (ibid., 114–15). McCormack originally developed this reading of Barth a decade earlier in his "Grace and Being" essay, using the distinction between God *ad intra* and God *ad extra*: "The *decision* for the covenant of grace is the ground of God's triunity and therefore of the eternal generation of the Son and the eternal procession of the Holy Spirit from Father and Son. In other words, the works of God *ad intra* (the trinitarian processions) find their ground in the *first* of the works of God *ad extra* (viz., election)" (McCormack, *Orthodox*, 194).

42. Paul Lehmann argues that Barth is a "theologian of permanent revolution," in the sense that his theology leaves us "with a perspective and a power to discern the reality of revolution, to accept its permanence as the condition and direction of our involvement in what God is doing in the world for the objective desacralization of power and for the making of room, in space and time, for freedom" (Lehmann, "Karl Barth," 79–80).

43. Bultmann, "On the Problem," 122.

THE EX-CENTERING GOD

The apocalyptic abyss at the heart of God's being is not a modern discovery, nor does it trace its origins to the Reformation. We must go back much earlier to the heart of the medieval period, to the twelfth-century pseudo-Hermetic text, *Liber viginti quattuor philosophorum* (*Book of the Twenty-Four Philosophers*). In this text, which was influential for later theologians like Meister Eckhart, Thomas Bradwardine, and Nicholas of Cusa, we find twenty-four theses answering the question: *quid est Deus?*—who or what is God? Of particular interest to us are theses 2 and 18:

> 2. *Deus est sphaera infinita cuius centrum est ubique, circumferentia nusquam.* (God is an infinite sphere whose center is everywhere and whose circumference is nowhere.)

> 18. *Deus est sphaera cuius tot sunt circumferentiae quot puncta.* (God is a sphere that has as many circumferences as [center] points.)[44]

The other theses make similarly paradoxical claims, such as "God is the principle without principle" (*Deus est principium sine principio*), "God is love which the more one holds the more it hides" (*Deus est amor qui plus habitus magis latet*), and "God is the unmoved that always moves" (*Deus est semper movens immobilis*). As Peter Sloterdijk observes, this theosophical text "leads directly into the highlands of Neoplatonic philosophy, ten thousand feet beyond the priesthood and the catechism."[45] Its metaphysical trappings notwithstanding, the *Book of Twenty-Four Philosophers*, with assistance from Sloterdijk, leads us also into the apocalyptic depths of the kerygma.

The second thesis, made famous by its use by later medieval theologians, proposes the thoroughly disorienting notion that God is an *infinite* sphere whose center is everywhere and whose circumference is nowhere. In addition to paving the way for modern astronomy—thanks to Nicholas of Cusa's transference of the metaphor from God to the world—such an idea explodes the distinction in God between transcendence and immanence, between above and below.[46] One has "to think the eternal *generatio* of the Son from the Father along with the *incarnatio* of the Son," such that "the

44. For the text see Baeumker, "Das pseudo-hermetische Buch," 194–214.

45. Sloterdijk, *Globes*, 512.

46. On Nicholas's application of this metaphor to the world, see *De docta ignorantia* 2.12 in Nicholas of Cusa, *Selected Spiritual Writings*, 161, where he writes: "The world machine will have, one might say, its center everywhere and its circumference nowhere, for its circumference and center is God, who is everywhere and nowhere." Cf. Grant, *Much Ado*, 138–41.

immanent and economic trinity are not strictly separate but rather inter-
twined with one another."[47] God, as Luther says, is "both the highest and the
lowest," both the *Deus summus* and the *Deus infirmus* (cf. Ps 139:8).[48] But
the implications extend beyond the doctrine of God into the very depths of
human existence. If taken seriously this thesis undermines every attempt
to establish either a fixed center or fixed boundaries. Every point is equally
near and equally far from God. God is simultaneously wholly present and
wholly absent. Consequently, "there is no longer an inside," but instead
"everything is outside." Long before the Reformation, then, this "infinitist
turn" means "there is nothing to support the sacerdotal notion that certain
persons and institutions are 'closer to God.'"[49] Such a God cannot be used
to prop up any human cultural norm or political regime. The infinite sphere
offers no security for those with religious or social power. The infinitizing
of God "fundamentally put an end to the use of God for regional and imperial spatial enchantments. . . . The god [*sic*] with the circumference nowhere
would never again be of use as the accomplice of a finite worldview or world-
presumption."[50] One cannot appeal to a God with no stable center or boundary to authorize one's particular ideology, justify one's actions, grant special
treatment, or provide safety from the strange and unknown—for nothing
is more strange or more Other than this boundless God. Sloterdijk thus
calls the God of this "eccentric thesis" an "ex-centering force of the greatest
virulence; the thought of him eliminates the minor residential right of the
souls that rely on their salvation in private chapels, landscapes, prerogatives
and grandiosities. . . . Whoever meditates this god finds themselves moving
further out into the boundless, the unstable and the extra-human."[51] The
infinite God is the queer God who unsettles all norms and traditions. An
eccentric, decentering God establishes an eccentric, decentering existence:
"Existence *in* so ex-centered a god amounts to a stay in the bottomless and
borderless outside."[52]

The bottomless and borderless outside—here we have the apocalyptic
gospel *in nuce*. To be crucified with Christ, to participate in this ultimate
eccentricity, is to be utterly displaced, to find oneself in a new creation
without borders or boundaries, without orders or natures, where the divine

47. Beuttler, *Gott*, 135.

48. Jüngel, "Nemo contra deum," 247. Cf. *WA* 43:580.3–14.

49. Sloterdijk, *Globes*, 524.

50. Ibid., 531. Cf. ibid., 525: "The infinitized theosphere no longer offered protec-
tion; it released."

51. Ibid., 523, 526.

52. Ibid., 528.

center is at home in the most marginalized extremities. The eccentricity that seems to Sloterdijk so terrifying and disturbing is, for precisely that reason, the basis for an emancipatory freedom from the principalities and powers that attempt to restrict the divine to authorized channels of mediation, to normative cultural forms, to the orders of φύσις and κόσμος. The triune God of the apocalypse is the ground, not of our stability and security, but of our existential undoing: "God signifies the radical negation and sublation of humanity; theology, whose object is God, can therefore only have the λόγος τοῦ σταυροῦ [word of the cross] as its content."[53] The God who saves is the eccentric and ex-centering God of the cross. Theology follows this God by journeying to its death—in the confident expectation that in this death there is life anew and for all. "For those who want to save their life will lose it, and those who lose their life for my sake will find it" (Matt 16:25).

---

53. *GuV*, 1:2. Cf. Bultmann, "Liberal Theology," 29. Bonhoeffer's "outline for a book," sketched in prison, asks: "Who is God? . . . Encounter with Jesus Christ. Experience that here there is a reversal of all human existence, in the very fact that Jesus only 'is there for others.' Jesus's 'being-for-others' is the experience of transcendence! Only through this liberation from self, through this 'being-for-others' unto death, do omnipotence, omniscience, and omnipresence come into being" (Bonhoeffer, *Letters and Papers*, 501).

Epilogue
Faith, Love, Hope

This dogmatic sketch began by looking at the conditions for a universalism free from metaphysical presuppositions. We identified three conditions:

1. Salvation is freely actualized by God in history.

2. Salvation relates to each person in concrete historicity; it is situated but not synergistic.

3. Salvation is not a once-for-all ontological transformation of nature but an ongoing ontic transformation of existence.

Our soteriocentric theology meets these conditions by arguing: (a) that God acts savingly and definitively in the historical event of Christ's crucifixion; (b) that the Spirit of God repeats this event in each new elemental interruption of existence; and (c) that each person participates in this event through an unconscious act of cocrucifixion that places us outside ourselves in solidarity with others in the apostolate. Salvation is thus a reality rather than a possibility, eschatological rather than protological, existential rather than mythical. The result is a version of Christian universalism that has been hermeneutically reconstructed in a dialectical and postmetaphysical way so as to avoid general categories that render salvation abstract and ahistorical. It is a universal salvation that does not rely on a general concept of humanity, nor does it depend on any pretemporal or posttemporal activity such as divine predestination or postmortem faith; instead it locates salvation *in* the act of human faith without making it contingent upon a conscious decision of faith—a universalism without universals.

Despite the systematic nature of this work, many questions remain unanswered. Indeed, when it comes to matters of eschatology, many questions *must* remain unanswered. Some matters lie beyond the scope of human inquiry. That being said, three matters warrant additional comment in this epilogue: (a) the implications of soteriocentrism for understanding other religions, (b) the question of justice for victims of horrific evils, and (c) the validity of traditional belief in conscious life after death. The last of these, being the most historically and theologically complex, will receive an extended treatment.

FAITH: UNIVERSALISM AND RELIGIONS

Soteriocentric theology confesses the actuality of God's saving act in the Christ-Spirit. As an exercise in Christian theology, it interprets the norm of salvation on the basis of the scriptural witness to the apocalypse of Christ, which is intrinsically open to a plurality of cultural contexts and religious expressions. It is thus a distinctively *Christian* interpretation of the God-world relationship. But it makes claims about people who are explicitly *not* Christian, who openly reject any form of Christian self-understanding and practice. It does so by proposing the notion of unconscious Christianity, in which faith is primarily and normatively an unconscious act of existence. This raises a question about those who *consciously* confess a faith that is not Christian—or those who confess no faith at all. What would a soteriocentric theology of religions look like?

For starters, soteriocentric theology stands in clear contrast to pluralistic theologies that suggest there are multiple paths of salvation. The error of soteriological pluralism is the notion that *religion* saves. A Christian pluralist assumes that Christianity saves and then seeks to understand how other religions can save as well. But this is to start with a faulty presupposition about the saving significance of religion as such. Christianity does not save any more than Islam or Buddhism. For this reason, soteriocentric theology also stands in contrast to Jesucentric theologies that make explicit acknowledgment of Jesus a condition for participating in the authentic life that characterizes redemption. Conscious faith is not in itself saving; it is a contextual interpretation of unconscious faith.

If the condition for salvation is the event of being placed outside oneself—particularly in sociopolitical praxis—then any situation where this occurs becomes a genuine encounter with God. Religion is a primary site for this encounter, insofar as it is simply a way of organizing human life for the sake of regularly and predictably facilitating this experience of being-outside-oneself. But this experience is by no means limited to religion. It may often occur outside of any religious or cultic context. The experience of elemental interruption can occur almost anywhere at any time. Our soteriocentric analysis thus serves to identify the existential ground of religion, the transcendent unity of human existence.[1] Each religion is but a contingent, contextual manifestation of this transcendent ground, but no religion can claim exclusive access to this ground.

Does this mean that, in fact, "all religions agree"? Lenn Goodman criticizes the separation of religious essence from accident as the bowdlerizing of religion: "Here pluralism turns monistic: Trappings may differ, but ultimately, we are assured, the great teachings speak with one voice. Splitting hairs only overlooks the inner truth that all religions share."[2] Whereas bowdlerization claims a unifying essence *internal* to the religions themselves, the position developed here is an absolutely *transcendent* unity that lies only in God—and is thus recognizable only by faith. The religions themselves are irreducible to some ideal essence. Nothing unifies the *religions* as such. Instead, the saving event of God *sublates* the religions—nullifying them as religions but affirming them as potential sites of existential encounter. This also addresses the common charge that universalism makes each religion an equally valid "path to God." In fact, no religion is *in itself* a path to God. Rather, God acts savingly wherever one is elementally interrupted and placed outside oneself. But this simultaneously means that every religion is a path to God, insofar as every moment of existence—religious or nonreligious—is potentially the site where God's saving apocalypse invades one's existence.

LOVE: UNIVERSALISM AND JUSTICE

Universalism is either praised or blamed for its response to suffering and horrendous evils. Many praise it for promising "ultimate divine comfort

---

1. This last phrase is an intentional variation on Frithjof Schuon's famous book, *The Transcendent Unity of Religions*, which is one of the key texts in the Traditionalist (or Perennialist) School. Schuon, along with other Traditionalists, argues that all religions derive from a common point of origin, a shared metaphysical essence. The religions are unified esoterically (inner essence) but differ exoterically (external form). What makes Schuon distinctive is his mystical, even apophatic, variation on this distinction, which places the esoteric or transcendent unity beyond reason and experience; it is a mystical unity that surpasses the subject-object distinction (see Schuon, *Transcendent Unity*, xii–xv). The position I develop here does not share the belief in a *philosophia perennis* or the notion that there is a common essence *of the religions themselves*. But I do share with Schuon the idea of a transcendent unity, one that lies beyond the creaturely distinctions between religions. I speak of a unity of *human existence* because it is existence as such that is unified in the saving event; the religions do not have special access to this unity, nor are they genetically connected to each other or to the transcendent origin.

2. Goodman, *Religious Pluralism*, 20.

for all the victims of this world." For those who experience suffering and abuse in this life, universalism provides one with confidence that God will rectify all things in the life to come.[3] Others, however, reject universalism for the very same reason—namely, on the grounds that it does not require the punishment of those who have abused others. This objection only applies to those versions of universalism that do not have a purgatory or hell at all. Gregory MacDonald's evangelical universalism is not liable to this critique, since his position makes salvation contingent on a conscious decision of faith, whether that occurs in this life or in the life to come. This book, however, takes a broadly post-Barthian approach in that, if there is a hell—and I do not think there is—it is an empty set; the reconciling work of the Christ-Spirit is already final for each person.

Does this make soteriocentric theology morally suspect? That depends on whether one thinks the point of eschatology is to ensure that abusers are punished and victims are avenged. Christian thinkers that construct heaven and hell to satisfy this human thirst for justice have to ask whether their pictures of the "afterlife" are genuinely grounded in revelation—that is, in the saving event of the Christ-Spirit—or only in a sociobiological desire for recompense. I have more to say about the afterlife below. Here I want to inquire into our *moral imaginations*. The gospel challenges us to see each person no longer "according to the flesh," but instead according to the new creation—a new creation that includes every person through the existential power of the Spirit (2 Cor 5:16–17). This certainly scandalizes our natural moral instincts, which are shaped especially in our modern world by notions of one's "just deserts." It may seem morally scandalous to suggest that God is *pro omnibus*, for all—that God redeems Judas and Hitler as well as me and you—but this is precisely what the gospel speaks of when it calls the cross an "offense" (Gal 5:11) and "foolishness" (1 Cor 1:23). What could be more offensive than a God who crucifies each person in solidarity with Christ?

HOPE: UNIVERSALISM AND THE AFTERLIFE

The debate over universalism has focused so exclusively on the question of *where* we go after death that very few have bothered to ask if we *go* anywhere at all. The assumption on all sides is that there is an "afterlife" of some sort. But why is this assumed? And is this assumption actually essential to the Christian faith?

3. MacDonald, *Evangelical Universalist*, 157.

A brief review of the research in the history of religion will be helpful
here. Scholars of comparative religion point out that hunter-gatherer groups
and tribal peoples throughout the world believe not in an afterlife (in the
sense of final destinations that reward or punish) but in rebirth.[4] Their view
of human existence is closely connected to the natural world with its annual
cycles of death and new life, and in some cases this involves a blurring of the
distinction between human and nonhuman animals.[5] Insofar as there is an
otherworld, "entry into that otherworld is a privilege available to all." These
societies occasionally have reward and retribution built into the cycles of
rebirth: those who led destructive lives are often "punished by being denied
a human reincarnation."[6] Karmic eschatology emerges, according to Gananath Obeyesekere, "when ethicization is systematically introduced into
any rebirth eschatology," which transforms and bifurcates the otherworld
into a place of reward ("heaven") and retribution ("hell") and makes reward
contingent upon morally good action.[7] A full theory of karma appears when
the rebirth cycle extends this bifurcation and contingency, so that the human world into which one is reborn furthers the process of reward and
retribution.

4. See Bellah, *Religion*, 102; Obeyesekere, *Imagining Karma*, 19–71. The work of
Gananath Obeyesekere especially has demonstrated how widespread rebirth eschatologies are among tribal peoples on every continent, especially the Americas, Africa, and
Asia. Obeyesekere argues that these rebirth eschatologies "show considerable similarity
across regions," in which "a person after dying returns to the world he or she has left
behind, sometimes sojourning in an intermediate world located in the space between
death and rebirth" (Obeyesekere, *Imagining Karma*, 15–16). On Amerindian rebirth
cycles, see Mills and Slobodin, *Amerindian Rebirth*.

5. Amerindian myth, in particular, "often postulates a homology of a physical
and spiritual nature between humans and animals, and this is manifest in the constant
transformations, the boundary crossings, and the blurring of categorical distinctions
between the two." This results in different kinds of rebirth and reincarnation cycles:
human-to-human, human-to-animal, and human-to-animal-to-human (Obeyesekere,
Imagining Karma, 44). The work of Philippe Descola has demonstrated in great detail,
especially on the basis of South American indigenous societies, that the separation between nature and culture, between the nonhuman and the human, is a modern western
invention. He identifies three other ontologies—animism, totemism, and analogism—
that blur the distinction or dissolve it altogether. For many of these societies and tribes,
all creatures, both human and nonhuman, are made up of "a multiplicity of mobile
components whose combinations, all different, produce particular identities" (Descola,
Beyond Nature, 222). The mobility of these components is what makes possible "the
transmigration of souls, reincarnation, metempsychosis, and, above all, possession"
(ibid., 213).

6. Obeyesekere, *Imagining Karma*, 74.

7. Ibid., 78–79.

Throughout much of the ancient world, with the famous exception of Egypt, the dead were believed to enter a dismal otherworld rather than experience rebirth. We find this especially in the texts of the ancient Near East, such as the Epic of Gilgamesh, Ugaritic myths, and the Hebrew scriptures.[8] Societies with a strong generational and/or national consciousness—such as ancient Israel and ancient Greece—viewed divine reward and punishment in terms of personal fame, the blessing of children, and/or the future prosperity of the nation.[9] As in rebirth and karmic eschatologies, these generational and national eschatologies emphasize the connection to one's ancestors, kin, and descendants. Sin and righteousness were familial acts that reaped long-term familial punishments or benefits: "For I the Lord your God am a jealous God, punishing children for the iniquity of parents, to the third and the fourth generation of those who reject me, but showing steadfast love to the thousandth generation of those who love me and keep my commandments" (Exod 20:5–6).

The Pythagorean and Orphic philosophers of the sixth century BCE inaugurated a "revolution" in the idea of the afterlife with their notion of the immortality of the soul and its ascent to heaven after death.[10] In contrast to the idea of immortality as fame in classical Greek tradition, Plato conceived of immortality as something that could be achieved through the cultivation of wisdom and the intellectual life.[11] It was during this period of Israelite exile and Second Temple Judaism that the Jewish people came into contact with Persian and Greek thought, which introduced them to the notion of a life after death—though "the right social and historical situation had to arise before a beatific afterlife was expressed in Jewish thought."[12] The Hellenization of Judaism laid the foundation for the rise of Christianity by conceiv-

---

8. See Johnston, *Religions*, 470–92.

9. Alan Segal notes that "fame is better than immortality" in the *Odyssey* (Segal, *Life*, 211), and Jon Mikalson observes that "for most Greeks, it seems, the only immortality envisioned was through one's children, through the memory of one's deeds in this life" (Mikalson, *Ancient Greek Religion*, 208). The famous "valley of dry bones" passage in Ezekiel 37 is not a prophecy of resurrection, but rather it "uses the metaphor of resurrection to promise national regeneration. There is no suggestion that resurrection is supposed to happen to anyone personally or individually" (Segal, *Life*, 256). Regarding Isa 26:19 and Ezek 37:1–14, Karl Barth says that in these passages "we obviously have pictures of the promised renewal of Israel in history. The fact that these images are selected is not insignificant, but they cannot be regarded as evidence of Israel's concrete hopes for the solution of the problem of death" (*CD* 3.2:619).

10. Johnston, *Religions*, 470. See Segal, *Life*, 220–21.

11. Segal, *Life*, 230.

12. Ibid., 249. On the development of the afterlife in ancient Judaism, see Bernstein, *Formation*, 133–202.

ing a fulfillment of God's promises beyond history and by distinguishing between national identity and personal identity.

We can thus identify the following as the key factors in the development of heaven and hell as destinations in the afterlife within the Christian tradition:

1. *A strong sense of salvation history as a narrative.* Every narrative has a beginning, middle, and an end. Narratives that lack any part of this basic structure feel incomplete and unfinished. A deep narratival consciousness, especially one cultivated over centuries of oral tradition and written chronicles, has a lasting impact on one's world-picture. Evolutionary anthropologists Terrence Deacon and Tyrone Cashman argue that "the tendency to believe in an afterlife might be a natural by-product of the narrative tendency." The development of a mind that thinks in terms of narrative has "the ability to discover that everyone's history both begins and ends." A religious narrative that includes an afterlife is able to make sense of one's personal narrative by embedding it "in a larger story that links it with before and after events, and, thus, does not ever come to an unequivocal end."[13] But Robert Bellah is surely right to observe that this is not sufficient in itself to account for belief in an afterlife, given that many narratival cultures do not have any such belief.[14] But it is nonetheless a constitutive component. "Human beings are narrative creatures," notes Bellah, and narrative addresses the basic anxiety of human existence by "tak[ing] the fundamental anxiety into itself and . . . transform[ing] the anxiety into some kind of resolution."[15] Insofar as religion can be understood as an existential narrative that responds to human anxiety, it has a built-in need to reach some kind of resolution. If such resolution is unattainable within this life, it is only natural that people look for resolution in the afterlife.

2. *Oppression and exile.* Failure to achieve this-worldly resolution was at the heart of the Jewish turn to the afterlife. The exile at the hands of the Assyrian and Babylonian empires and postexilic persecution under Greek rule shattered faith in the Deuteronomic tradition, which promised that God would bless the righteous and punish the wicked. The prolonged suffering of God's covenant people was a crisis of faith: "If God was letting his faithful suffer, the very promises of the Bible

13. Deacon and Cashman, "Role," 501.

14. Bellah, *Religion,* 102.

15. Ibid., 34, 36.

are brought into doubt."[16] The writings from the Persian and Hellenistic periods of Judaism attempted to grapple with this new situation. Whereas Job and Ecclesiastes sought to assuage Jewish anxieties by helping people to come to peace with their situation—Job by showing that God is gracious enough to hear Job's complaint,[17] and Ecclesiastes by teaching people to make the most of their time on earth in whatever situation they find themselves—the apocalyptic writings of Second Temple Judaism under Seleucid domination raised a protest against imperial oppression by envisioning a radical alternative.[18] Systemic and sustained oppression rendered implausible the expectation of this-worldly rewards and punishments and stripped the Jewish people of hope in anything except the invasive act of God. The Book of Daniel thus responds to Antiochus IV Epiphanes by speaking for the first time of resurrection. The dead "shall awake, some to everlasting life, and some to shame and everlasting contempt" (Dan 12:2).[19] Apocalyptic was therefore a narratival way of regaining control over their future destiny; it was a prophetic resistance to imperial power.[20] These texts

16. Segal, *Life*, 265.

17. I follow C. L. Seow in locating Job "between the very late sixth and the first half of the fifth century" (Seow, *Job 1–21*, 45).

18. See Portier-Young, *Apocalypse*, esp. 78–222. According to Portier-Young, "the writers of the apocalypses countered hegemonic cosmologies, imperial spectacle, and false claims to power by articulating and promulgating an alternative vision of the world" (ibid., 217).

19. Candida Moss comments regarding Daniel 12: "Prior to this, the prophets had promised people that if they kept God's commandments they would be rewarded in the here and now with prosperity, family, and success. . . . Notions of the afterlife in this period were still amorphous and imprecise, because justice could be found in the present and God could be trusted to make good on his promises. . . . Scholars hypothesize that this idea of delayed judgment and eschatological reward developed because these promises of immediate reward were constantly unfulfilled. As a result and in order to avoid the conclusion that God was either notoriously unreliable or fundamentally incompetent, the idea of future eschatological reward and punishment emerged. Injustices that were not righted in one's lifetime would be settled at the end of time" (Moss, *Myth*, 47). According to Alan Bernstein, "Belief in future punishment is a manifestation of the sublimated desire for vengeance. Belief in punishment after death becomes necessary when no sign of restoration is visible in life" (Bernstein, *Formation*, 202).

20. Jacob Taubes thus discerns a connection between apocalyptic and revolution: "Apocalypticism is at first not concerned with changing the structure of society, but directs its gaze away from this world. If revolution were to mean only replacing an existing society with a better one, then the connection between apocalypticism and revolution is not evident. But if revolution means opposing the totality of this world with a new totality that comprehensively founds anew in the way that it negates, namely, in terms of the basic foundations, then apocalypticism is by nature revolutionary. Apocalypticism negates this world in its fullness. It brackets the entire world negatively" (Taubes,

claimed access to divine mysteries promising their vindication by God and the destruction of their oppressors. The early Christian community shared this apocalyptic consciousness, which is only natural given the persecution they experienced. The promise of eternal bliss after death can be a powerful source of courage in the face of imminent death, as it was for early Christian martyrs.

3. *The rise of the individual.* Another significant factor is Christianity's development of the idea of individual worth and responsibility. Scholars have noted the way in which Christianity granted each individual equal dignity before God, including women, children, and slaves.[21] Moreover, the emphasis on personal faith, coupled with a uniquely strong belief in an afterlife and future resurrection, gave the actions of an individual person an eternal religious significance. Each person was accountable before God for her actions. Combined with a strong sense of narratival continuity and apocalyptic redemption, it was only natural that this led to robust conceptions of individual reward and punishment in the afterlife.

There is certainly much more that could be said regarding the sociohistorical development of Christian views about the afterlife. The point of this all-too-brief review of religious history is that belief in a conscious afterlife, complete with rewards for the faithful and retribution for the unfaithful, is a historically situated notion that developed over time in response to cultural, philosophical, and political pressures and influences. We should be careful to avoid the genetic fallacy: the history of an idea does not indicate whether it is true or false. But the history should lead us to question how essential the idea is to the Christian kerygma. The history of the West has been so thoroughly "Christianized" that we rarely stop to ask whether the kerygma could be translated into a cultural form that did not presuppose belief in a conscious afterlife.

The historical development of the afterlife aside, there are reasons to question the validity of a conscious life after death on the grounds of the gospel itself. Here we can follow the insights of Karl Barth and Eberhard Jüngel. In his discussion of human temporality in the *Church Dogmatics* (§47), Barth reflects on what scripture has to say about death. His overall thesis is that "our consolation, assurance and hope in death are restricted to the existence of God."[22] He develops this claim by looking at key Old and

---

Occidental Eschatology, 9).

21. See "A Revolution of the Person: The Invention of Human Dignity," in Aquilina and Papandrea, *Seven Revolutions*, 33–54.

22. *CD* 3.2:616.

New Testament texts. He finds the central OT insight to be "the superiority and decisiveness in which Yahweh confronts death and the underworld."[23] God is the source of consolation and deliverance. The Psalmist especially cries out for salvation from "the world of death and the realm of the dead depicted as a sea or wilderness," and this salvation involves being taken to the land of the living.[24] But there is no life beyond this life: "The Old Testament says *nothing* of a renewal of human beings in a time after their death, of a continuation of their lives, of resurrection in this sense, and therefore of an eternal life granted to them."[25] With respect to Daniel 12:2, Barth comments: "here on the fringe of the Old Testament canon we have the exception which proves the rule." And the rule in question is "to be content with a strict *opposition* between the temporally completed being of humanity in death on the one side and the temporally unlimited being of God on the other as the Lord not only of life but also of death and the underworld."[26] To the extent that God is still living and active, the covenant relationship that God has with both the living and the dead still remains. In that sense they are still God's covenant partners. Their lives are eternally "enclosed in God."[27]

The NT, Barth says, remains fundamentally consistent with the OT—the former is "indirectly identical" with the latter.[28] The difference is that the enclosure within God that constitutes the hope of the covenant people is now concretely located in Jesus Christ: "For you have died, and your life is hidden with Christ in God. When Christ who is your life is revealed, then you also will be revealed with him in glory" (Col 3:3–4).[29] The NT defines the eschatological hope of the Christian as having our life *in* and *with* Christ. The death of Jesus is "the event in which . . . time is fulfilled" and his resurrection is the "preliminary indication" of this event, and thus our own death and resurrection—that is, our participation in the eschatological end of history—is strictly and exclusively dependent on Christ.[30] This "concrete grounding of the Old Testament hope" in the NT results in a "radical *change of perspective*," manifested in the Christian's joy and confidence in the face of

23. *CD* 3.2:616, rev. See *KD* 3.2:750.

24. *CD* 3.2:617.

25. *CD* 3.2:618, rev.

26. *CD* 3.2:619, rev. Cf. *KD* 3.2:753.

27. *CD* 3.2:620.

28. *CD* 3.2:623.

29. See *CD* 3.2:624: "Does not [Jesus's] resurrection usher in the last day, when even the believer in Jesus can only live a life hidden with God in Christ?"

30. *CD* 3.2:623.

death.[31] But it is not a hope for a conscious existence beyond death. Christian hope is materially identical to Jewish hope: it is a hope solely in the contrast between God's eternal existence and humanity's temporal existence, with the change that divine existence is actualized in the particularity of Jesus. Every NT statement about our creaturely future is a statement about Christ.

The last day is not the start of a new history in some heavenly realm. Just as "the event of creation took place in a present without a past, so *this* event is that of a *present without a future*, in which ... there does not follow any further communication or the promise of further occurrences but only the sounding of the 'last trump' (1 Cor 15:52)."[32] In this eschatological event, according to Paul, what is *perishable* and *mortal* "puts on" imperishability and immortality (1 Cor 15:53). The mortal is not supplemented by or replaced with immortality, but rather the mortal *as mortal* is what puts on immortality. This putting-on-of-immortality is the event of the last day.

> But *nothing* further will follow this happening, for then "there shall be time no longer" (Rev 10:6). There is no question of continuing into an unending future and in this future having a somehow altered life; what New Testament hope expects beyond human death is rather the "eternalizing [*Verewigung*]" of our *ending* life. This corruptible and mortal life *as such* will be stripped of its character as "flesh and blood," ... will put on incorruption and immortality. ... Our *past* life, which we lived in our limited time, which did not begin before its time and does not continue beyond it, our *real* but also our *only* life, will then fully, definitively, and manifestly participate in that καινότης ζωῆς [newness of life] (Rom 6:4); it will then be eternal life in God and in fellowship with God. Indeed, the *past life* of every person in its limited time has a place in this fellowship with God, who was and is and will be the Eternal One. It can only be a matter, therefore, of this *past life* in its limited time undergoing a *transition* and *transformation* (1 Cor 15:51) and participating in eternal life in fellowship with God. This transition and transformation is ... the *resurrection of the dead*, which according to the indication following the resurrection of Jesus is our participation in his future revelation and therefore in the time that we still have, which is our *hope*.[33]

The NT does not abandon the "sober realism" of the OT. What it does instead is view the finite existence of human beings in the light of the revelation of

31. *CD* 3.2:620, rev.

32. *CD* 3.2:624, rev.

33. *CD* 3.2:624, rev. Cf. *KD* 3.2:759–60.

Christ. It is *this* particular history that is raised up to participate in the life of God. The life we have is the gift of God; to pine after a different life in the future is to be ungrateful for the gift we have already been given. Those who want the NT to guarantee us something more should see "whether they are pursuing pagan dreams of all kinds of good times after death and not letting the New Testament say the radically good thing that it has to say in the realism which it has in common with the Old Testament."[34]

Turning now to Jüngel's 1971 book, entitled in German simply *Tod* (*Death*), we find a position substantially identical to Barth's. For Jüngel, the Old Testament views death strictly in relation to life as the highest good. To be alive is to live in relationship—to be related to God and thus also to ourselves.[35] Death is an evil in the sense that it is the "event of relationlessness."[36] But this event is given in the gift of life. "Life is the condition of possibility also of death," and thus death is part of the goodness and mercy of God.[37] The faith of Israel thus affirms finitude as integral to the distinctive value of each human life.[38] This means that death is constrained by the power of God; it does not have any autonomous significance. In contrast to the societies and cultures around them, Israel avoided "any independent religious interest in death."[39] Their relationship with death was "decidedly aloof."[40] Jüngel thus says that "inherent in the faith of Israel is a tendency to demythologize death, which then works itself out in the New Testament in an extremely radical way."[41] Despite this basic continuity, there is a decisive contrast between the Old and New Testaments based on the fact that with the death of Jesus Christ death itself has changed.[42] The New Testament sees death in terms of "the certainty of a divine victory over death," grounded in faith in the resurrection of Jesus Christ from the dead.[43] Whereas in the Old Testament a person looks ahead to death as the conclusion to a well-lived

---

34. *CD* 3.2:625, rev.

35. "'Life' in the Old Testament means: *to have a relation*. Above all it means: to have a relation to God" (Jüngel, *Tod*, 99; Jüngel, *Death*, 77). All translations from Jüngel are my own.

36. Jüngel, *Tod*, 145; Jüngel, *Death*, 115.

37. Jüngel, *Tod*, 91; Jüngel, *Death*, 72.

38. "The *affirmation of the finitude* of human beings leads the faith of Israel to place a high value, even the highest value, on life as the *rejection* of death" (Jüngel, *Tod*, 98; Jüngel, *Death*, 77).

39. Jüngel, *Tod*, 93; Jüngel, *Death*, 73.

40. Jüngel, *Tod*, 92; Jüngel, *Death*, 72.

41. Jüngel, *Tod*, 93; Jüngel, *Death*, 73.

42. Jüngel, *Tod*, 76; Jüngel, *Death*, 60.

43. Jüngel, *Tod*, 103; Jüngel, *Death*, 81.

life, in the New Testament a person "already looks back on one's death," and because death is already in the past one recognizes that life is not one's own.[44] Death as the event of relationlessness, which breaks one's relationship with God, is the death that one has already died in Christ. In contrast to this sense of death as a curse, the new creation consists in "a new relation of God to human beings, through which the *human being* is created anew." And since these eschatologically new relations are actualized by God, they "cannot be broken off" by the creature. It follows that "the end of a life is not [their] termination. God's creative relation with human beings precludes the termination of these relations."[45]

We are now in a position to understand Jüngel's interpretation of Christian hope in the face of death. The human person, according to Jüngel, is a "*temporal* being." Human beings are defined by the fact that they "have time"—more specifically, they "have a *history*."[46] The history of each person has to be understood theologically "as a moment of God's history with all human beings. Each person participates in this history."[47] Each person is thus irreplaceable and of unique importance to God, and yet it is important precisely in its finitude. The infinite importance of each life does not mean each life must itself be infinite. While each life is lived within the temporal boundaries of past and future, it is lived "in communication with the history of God," and this gives each life "an *eternal* past and an *eternal* future. Life is created by God and life enters into the resurrection of the dead."[48] Hope in the resurrection, however, does not mean "the expectation of the abolition of the temporal boundaries of human life." Given that these temporal boundaries are precisely what constitute the distinctiveness of human existence, the abolition of these boundaries would imply "the abolition of the individuality of the life of a person."[49] Jüngel gives the example of someone who lived before her birth. Such a person would obviously be someone else, since the identity of the person would not be defined by the history that this person actually lived. The same would be true for someone who lived beyond her death. That person is again someone else; she would have a new history and therefore a new individual identity. For this reason

---

44. Jüngel, *Tod*, 107; Jüngel, *Death*, 84.

45. Jüngel, *Tod*, 114–15; Jüngel, *Death*, 90.

46. Jüngel, *Tod*, 148; Jüngel, *Death*, 117–18. He adds: "time is the formal ontological structure of the historicity of being" (Jüngel, *Tod*, 149; Jüngel, *Death*, 118).

47. Jüngel, *Tod*, 149; Jüngel, *Death*, 118.

48. Jüngel, *Tod*, 150; Jüngel, *Death*, 119.

49. Jüngel, *Tod*, 150–51; Jüngel, *Death*, 119.

hope in the resurrection "must be something different than hope in endless continuation."[50]

The truth of the resurrection is not an egotistical hope in *my* personal heavenly reward or the infinite extension of *my* life. Instead, following Paul, it is the hope that "God may be all in all" (1 Cor 15:28). Jüngel thus concludes:

> Hope in *God* is the essence of hope in the resurrection. This hope is hope in salvation only to the extent that it is directed toward the God who saves. And salvation can then mean nothing other than that *this lived* life is saved, not that one is saved *from* this life. Salvation is therefore the rescue by God of the lived life, the participation of earthly, bounded life in God's life, the participation of the limited time of life in God's eternity, the participation of existence that has incurred guilt in God's glory. . . . Finite life will be *eternalized* [*verewigt*] as finite. But not through endless extension—there is no immortality of the soul—but rather through participation in God's own life. Our life is *hidden* in God's life. In this sense the briefest form of resurrection hope is the statement: "God is my beyond."[51]

Jüngel thus follows Barth in understanding resurrection as the *eternalizing* of our lived history. Our resurrection is found in our participation in God, not in the infinite extension of our consciousness. In a sense we can say that we are resurrected in that God remembers us for eternity. But this does not mean that God's life is like "a museum collection" of past artifacts. "The redeemed past is more than past. The redeemed past is past in the present of God, [and] is made present by God." To participate in God is thus to be fully *known* by God (1 Cor 13:12; Gal 4:9), and this act of eternal knowing is the "gathering, eternalizing, and revealing of lived life" and as such is the resurrection of the dead.[52]

For those in North America, but also for many around the world, we live in a time of apocalyptic fervor, of great anxiety about the future of the world, and with an ever-increasing proliferation of religious fanaticism and evangelical zeal, particularly with respect to views about a future rescue by God that will bring the chosen people into an endless utopia. The history of religious views about the afterlife suggests that these developments are part of a long sociocultural evolution, but the biblical and theological reflections of Barth and Jüngel show that these views do not have the support within

50. Jüngel, *Tod*, 151; Jüngel, *Death*, 120.
51. Jüngel, *Tod*, 151–52; Jüngel, *Death*, 120.
52. Jüngel, *Tod*, 153; Jüngel, *Death*, 121.

the Jewish and Christian traditions that many believers today think they have. Theologians frequently shy away from the topic of eternal life, abandoning the subject to ministers who seek to address the existential questions of believers. For the sake of the future of the church, if not the wider society, it is time that theologians directly and honestly address these matters.[53]

The question of the afterlife is a vexing one for many believers. People want assurance that their lives have meaning and worth. They want to know that loved ones are in a "better place." While theology should never dictate in advance how one should respond to the exigencies of pastoral care, ministers of the gospel should avoid claiming that we will see our loved ones in heaven. They should preach instead that our lives are held securely by God: "My times are in your hand" (Ps 31:15). We may not have a firm grasp on ourselves, much less on God, but *God* has a firm grasp on us. This is the hope and promise of the gospel.

---

53. I am encouraged by the recent publication of Ziegler, *Eternal God.*

Bibliography

Agamben, Giorgio. *The Time That Remains: A Commentary on the Letter to the Romans.* Translated by Patricia Dailey. Stanford, CA: Stanford University Press, 2005.

Anderson, Clifford Blake. "The Crisis of Theological Science: A Contextual Study of the Development of Karl Barth's Concept of Theology as Science from 1901–1923." Ph.D. diss., Princeton Theological Seminary, 2005.

Anderson, Jeff S. *The Internal Diversification of Second Temple Judaism: An Introduction to the Second Temple Period.* Lanham, MD: University Press of America, 2002.

Aquilina, Mike, and James L. Papandrea. *Seven Revolutions: How Christianity Changed the World and Can Change It Again.* New York: Image, 2015.

Aring, Paul Gerhard. *Kirche als Ereignis: Ein Beitrag zur Neuorientierung der Missionstheologie.* Neukirchen-Vluyn: Neukirchener, 1971.

Aristotle. *The Complete Works of Aristotle: The Revised Oxford Translation.* Edited by Jonathan Barnes. 2 vols. Princeton, NJ: Princeton University Press, 1984.

Augustine. *Confessions.* Translated by F. J. Sheed. Rev. ed. Indianapolis: Hackett, 1993.

———. *The Trinity.* Translated by Edmund Hill. The Works of Saint Augustine I/5. Hyde Park, NY: New City, 1991.

Avery-Peck, Alan J., Jacob Neusner, and Bruce Chilton, eds. *Judaism in Late Antiquity.* 5 vols. Leiden: Brill, 1995.

Badiou, Alain. *Logics of Worlds: Being and Event 2.* Translated by Alberto Toscano. London: Continuum, 2009.

———. *Theory of the Subject.* Translated by Bruno Bosteels. London: Continuum, 2009.

Baeumker, Clemens. "Das pseudo-hermetische 'Buch der vierundzwanzig Meister' (*Liber XXIV philosophorum*) Ein Beitrag zur Geschichte des Neupythagoreismus und Neuplatonismus im Mittelalter." *Beiträge zur Geschichte der Philosophie des Mittelalters* 25, no. 1–2 (1927) 194–214.

Bainton, Roland H. *Here I Stand: A Life of Martin Luther.* Nashville: Abingdon, 1978.

Baker, Mark D., and Joel B. Green. *Recovering the Scandal of the Cross: Atonement in New Testament and Contemporary Contexts.* 2nd ed. Downers Grove, IL: IVP Academic, 2011.

Balthasar, Hans Urs von. *Dare We Hope "That All Men Be Saved"? With a Short Discourse on Hell.* Translated by David Kipp and Lothar Krauth. San Francisco: Ignatius, 1988.

Balz, Heinrich. "Hermeneutik und Mission." *Zeitschrift für Mission* 14, no. 4 (1988) 206–20.

Barth, Karl. "Die Autorität und Bedeutung der Bibel." In *Die Schrift und die Kirche*, 3–20. Zollikon-Zürich: Evangelischer Verlag A.G., 1947.

———. *Christ and Adam: Man and Humanity in Romans 5*. Translated by Thomas Allan Smail. New York: Harper, 1957.

———. "The Christian Proclamation Here and Now." In *God Here and Now*, 1–10. New York: Harper & Row, 1964.

———. *Church Dogmatics*. Edited by G. W. Bromiley and T. F. Torrance. 4 vols. Edinburgh: T. & T. Clark, 1956–75.

———. *Einführung in die evangelische Theologie*. Zürich: EVZ, 1962.

———. *The Epistle to the Romans*. Translated by Edwyn C. Hoskyns. 1933. Reprint. London: Oxford University Press, 1968.

———. *Erklärung des Johannes-Evangeliums (Kapitel 1–8)*. Edited by Walther Fürst. Gesamtausgabe 2.9. Zürich: TVZ, 1976.

———. "Evangelical Theology in the 19th Century." 1957. In *The Humanity of God*, 11–33. Richmond, VA: John Knox, 1960.

———. *Evangelical Theology: An Introduction*. New York: Holt, 1963.

———. "Fate and Idea in Theology." 1929. In *The Way of Theology in Karl Barth: Essays and Comments*, edited by Martin Rumscheidt, 25–61. Allison Park, PA: Pickwick, 1986.

———. *Gespräche 1959–1962*. Edited by Eberhard Busch. Gesamtausgabe 4. Zürich: TVZ, 1995.

———. *The Göttingen Dogmatics: Instruction in the Christian Religion*. Vol. 1. Edited by Hannelotte Reiffen. Translated by Geoffrey W. Bromiley. Grand Rapids: Eerdmans, 1991.

———. *The Humanity of God*. Translated by John Newton Thomas and Thomas Wieser. Richmond, VA: John Knox, 1960.

———. "The Humanity of God." 1956. In *The Humanity of God*, 37–65. Richmond, VA: John Knox, 1960.

———. *Karl Barth's Table Talk*. Edited by John D. Godsey. Richmond, VA: John Knox, 1963.

———. *Die kirchliche Dogmatik*. 4 vols. Zollikon-Zürich: Evangelischer Verlag A.G., 1932–70.

———. *Letters, 1961–1968*. Edited by Jürgen Fangmeier and Hinrich Stoevesandt. Translated by Geoffrey W. Bromiley. Edinburgh: T. & T. Clark, 1981.

———. *Nein! Antwort an Emil Brunner*. Munich: Kaiser, 1934.

———. *Der Römerbrief (Zweite Fassung) 1922*. Edited by Cornelis van der Kooi and Katja Tolstaja. Gesamtausgabe 2. Zürich: TVZ, 2010.

———. "Die Theologie und die Mission in der Gegenwart." *Zwischen den Zeiten* 10, no. 3 (1932) 189–215.

———. *Unterricht in der christlichen Religion, Teil 1: Prolegomena 1924*. Edited by Hannelotte Reiffen. Gesamtausgabe 2. Zürich: TVZ, 1985.

———. *Witness to the Word: A Commentary on John 1*. Edited by Walther Fürst. Translated by Geoffrey W. Bromiley. Grand Rapids: Eerdmans, 1986.

———. *Zwei theologische Studien: Rudolf Bultmann, ein Versuch ihn zu verstehen; Christus und Adam nach Rom. 5*. Zürich: EVZ-Verlag, 1964.

Barth, Karl, and Rudolf Bultmann. *Barth–Bultmann Letters, 1922–1966*. Edited by Bernd Jaspert. Translated by Geoffrey W. Bromiley. Grand Rapids: Eerdmans, 1981.

————. *Briefwechsel 1911–1966*. Edited by Bernd Jaspert. 2nd ed. Gesamtausgabe 5. Zürich: TVZ, 1994.

Bauckham, Richard. *Jesus and the God of Israel: God Crucified and Other Studies on the New Testament's Christology of Divine Identity*. Milton Keynes, UK: Paternoster, 2008.

Bayer, Oswald. *Gott als Autor: Zu einer poietologischen Theologie*. Tübingen: Mohr Siebeck, 1999.

————. "The Modern Narcissus." Translated by Christine Helmer. *Lutheran Quarterly* 9, no. 3 (1995) 301–13.

Beach, Lee. *The Church in Exile: Living in Hope after Christendom*. Downers Grove, IL: IVP Academic, 2015.

Bebbington, D. W. *Evangelicalism in Modern Britain: A History from the 1730s to the 1980s*. London: Unwin Hyman, 1989.

Becker, Eve-Marie, Troels Engberg-Pedersen, and Mogens Müller, eds. *Mark and Paul: Comparative Essays Part II. For and Against Pauline Influence on Mark*. Beihefte zur Zeitschrift für die neutestamentliche Wissenschaft 199. Berlin: de Gruyter, 2014.

Bell, David. "Queernaturecultures." In *Queer Ecologies: Sex, Nature, Politics, Desire*, edited by Catriona Mortimer-Sandilands and Bruce Erickson, 134–45. Bloomington, IN: Indiana University Press, 2010.

Bellah, Robert N. *Religion in Human Evolution: From the Paleolithic to the Axial Age*. Cambridge: Belknap Press of Harvard University Press, 2011.

Bender, Kimlyn J. *Confessing Christ for Church and World: Studies in Modern Theology*. Downers Grove, IL: IVP Academic, 2014.

Benjamin, Walter. "On the Concept of History." In *Selected Writings, Volume 4: 1938–1940*, edited by Howard Eiland and Michael W. Jennings, 389–400. Cambridge: The Belknap Press of Harvard University Press, 2003.

Berger, Peter L. *The Heretical Imperative: Contemporary Possibilities of Religious Affirmation*. Garden City, NY: Anchor, 1979.

Bernstein, Alan E. *The Formation of Hell: Death and Retribution in the Ancient and Early Christian Worlds*. Ithaca, NY: Cornell University Press, 1993.

Beuttler, Ulrich. *Gott und Raum: Theologie der Weltgegenwart Gottes*. Göttingen: Vandenhoeck & Ruprecht, 2010.

Bevans, Stephen B., and Roger P. Schroeder. *Constants in Context: A Theology of Mission for Today*. Maryknoll, NY: Orbis, 2004.

Biel, Gabriel. *Sacri canonis Missae expositio*. Tübingen: Johann Otmar and Friedrich Meynberger, 1499.

Boccaccini, Gabriele. "Inner-Jewish Debate on the Tension between Divine and Human Agency in Second Temple Judaism." In *Divine and Human Agency in Paul and His Cultural Environment*, edited by John M. G. Barclay and Simon J. Gathercole, 9–26. London: T. & T. Clark, 2006.

Boer, Martinus C. de. *Galatians: A Commentary*. Louisville, KY: Westminster John Knox, 2011.

Bonhoeffer, Dietrich. *Act and Being: Transcendental Philosophy and Ontology in Systematic Theology*. Edited by Hans-Richard Reuter and Wayne W. Floyd. Translated by Martin Rumscheidt. Dietrich Bonhoeffer Works 2. Minneapolis: Fortress, 1996.

———. *Berlin: 1932–1933*. Edited by Larry L. Rasmussen. Translated by Isabel Best and David Higgins. Dietrich Bonhoeffer Works 12. Minneapolis: Fortress, 2009.

———. *Conspiracy and Imprisonment: 1940–1945*. Edited by Mark S. Brocker. Dietrich Bonhoeffer Works 16. Minneapolis: Fortress, 2006.

———. *Creation and Fall: A Theological Exposition of Genesis 1–3*. Edited by John W. De Gruchy. Translated by Douglas S. Bax. Dietrich Bonhoeffer Works 3. Minneapolis: Fortress, 1997.

———. *Dietrich Bonhoeffer Werke*. Edited by Eberhard Bethge et al. 17 vols. Munich: Kaiser, 1986–2005.

———. *Ethics*. Edited by Clifford J. Green. Translated by Reinhard Krauss, Charles C. West, and Douglas W. Stott. Dietrich Bonhoeffer Works 6. Minneapolis: Fortress, 2005.

———. *Letters and Papers from Prison*. Edited by John W. De Gruchy. Translated by Isabel Best, Lisa E. Dahill, Reinhard Krauss, et al. Dietrich Bonhoeffer Works 8. Minneapolis: Fortress, 2010.

Bruce, Alexander Balmain. *The Kingdom of God, or, Christ's Teaching according to the Synoptical Gospels*. New York: Scribner & Welford, 1889.

Brunner, Emil, and Karl Barth. *Natural Theology: Comprising "Nature and Grace" by Professor Dr. Emil Brunner and the Reply "No!" by Dr. Karl Barth*. Translated by Peter Fraenkel. 1946. Reprint. Eugene, OR: Wipf and Stock, 2002.

Bultmann, Rudolf. "Adam and Christ according to Romans 5." In *Current Issues in New Testament Interpretation: Essays in Honor of Otto A. Piper*, edited by William Klassen and Graydon F. Snyder, 143–65. New York: Harper & Brothers, 1962.

———. "Das Befremdliche des christlichen Glaubens." 1958. In *Glauben und Verstehen: Gesammelte Aufsätze*, 4 vols., 3:197–212. Tübingen: Mohr, 1933–65.

———. "The Christological Confession of the World Council of Churches." 1951–52. In *Essays, Philosophical and Theological*, 273–90. New York: Macmillan, 1955.

———. *Exegetica: Aufsätze zur Erforschung des Neuen Testaments*. Edited by Erich Dinkler. Tübingen: Mohr, 1967.

———. "Faith in God the Creator." 1934. In *Existence and Faith: Shorter Writings of Rudolf Bultmann*, 171–82. New York: Meridian, 1960.

———. *Geschichte und Eschatologie*. Tübingen: Mohr, 1958.

———. *Glauben und Verstehen: Gesammelte Aufsätze*. 4 vols. Tübingen: Mohr, 1933–65.

———. *The Gospel of John: A Commentary*. Translated by G. R. Beasley-Murray, R. W. N. Hoare, and J. K. Riches. Philadelphia: Westminster, 1971.

———. *History and Eschatology: The Gifford Lectures 1955*. Edinburgh: Edinburgh University Press, 1957.

———. "Humanism and Christianity." *The Journal of Religion* 32, no. 2 (1952) 77–86.

———. *Jesus*. UTB für Wissenschaft. Tübingen: Mohr, 1983.

———. *Jesus and the Word*. Translated by Louise Pettibone Smith and Erminie Huntress Lantero. New York: Scribner, 1934.

———. *Jesus Christ and Mythology*. New York: Scribner, 1958.

———. "Liberal Theology and the Latest Theological Movement." 1924. In *Faith and Understanding*, edited by Robert W. Funk, 28–52. Philadelphia: Fortress, 1987.

———. "New Testament and Mythology: The Problem of Demythologizing the New Testament Proclamation." 1941. In *New Testament and Mythology and Other Basic Writings*, edited by Schubert M. Ogden, 1–43. Philadelphia: Fortress, 1984.

———. "On Behalf of Christian Freedom." *The Journal of Religion* 40, no. 2 (1960) 95–99.

———. "On the Problem of Demythologizing." 1952. In *New Testament and Mythology and Other Basic Writings*, edited by Schubert M. Ogden, 95–130. Philadelphia: Fortress, 1984.

———. "The Primitive Christian Kerygma and the Historical Jesus." In *The Historical Jesus and the Kerygmatic Christ: Essays on the New Quest of the Historical Jesus*, edited by Carl E. Braaten and Roy A. Harrisville, 15–42. New York: Abingdon, 1964.

———. *Primitive Christianity in Its Contemporary Setting*. Translated by R. H. Fuller. Cleveland, OH: World, 1956.

———. "The Problem of a Theological Exegesis of the New Testament." In *The Beginnings of Dialectic Theology*, edited by James M. Robinson, 236–56. Richmond, VA: John Knox, 1968.

———. "Science and Existence." 1955. In *New Testament and Mythology and Other Basic Writings*, edited by Schubert M. Ogden, 131–44. Philadelphia: Fortress, 1984.

———. "Sermon: Hendricks Chapel, Syracuse, NY, 26. April 1959." In *Hören und Handeln: Festschrift für Ernst Wolf zum 60. Geburtstag*, edited by Helmut Gollwitzer and Hellmut Traub, 47–51. Munich: Kaiser, 1962.

———. "The Significance of the Historical Jesus for the Theology of Paul." 1929. In *Faith and Understanding*, edited by Robert W. Funk, 220–46. Philadelphia: Fortress, 1987.

———. *Theologie des Neuen Testaments*. 2nd ed. Tübingen: Mohr, 1954.

———. *Theologische Enzyklopädie*. Edited by Eberhard Jüngel and Klaus W. Müller. Tübingen: Mohr, 1984.

———. "Theology as Science." 1941. In *New Testament and Mythology and Other Basic Writings*, edited by Schubert M. Ogden, 45–67. Philadelphia: Fortress, 1984.

———. *Theology of the New Testament*. Translated by Kendrick Grobel. 2 vols. New York: Scribner's Sons, 1951–55.

———. "Transformation of the Idea of the Church in the History of Early Christianity." Translated by S. M. Gilmour. *Canadian Journal of Theology* 1, no. 2 (1955) 73–81.

———. "Truth and Certainty." 1929. In *What Is Theology?* 167–89. Minneapolis: Fortress, 1997.

———. *Das Urchristentum im Rahmen der antiken Religionen*. Zürich: Artemis, 1949.

———. *Das Verhältnis der urchristlichen Christusbotschaft zum historischen Jesus*. Heidelberg: Winter, 1960.

———. *Das verkündigte Wort: Predigten, Andachten, Ansprachen 1906–1941*. Edited by Erich Grässer and Martin Evang. Tübingen: Mohr, 1984.

———. *What Is Theology?* Translated by Roy A. Harrisville. Minneapolis: Fortress, 1997.

———. "Zum Problem der Entmythologisierung." In *Kerygma und Mythos, Band II: Diskussion und Stimmen zum Problem der Entmythologisierung*, edited by Hans-Werner Bartsch, 179–208. Hamburg-Volksdorf: Reich, 1952.

Bultmann, Rudolf, and Friedrich Gogarten. *Briefwechsel 1921–1967*. Edited by Hermann Götz Göckeritz. Tübingen: Mohr Siebeck, 2002.

Butler, Judith. *Gender Trouble: Feminism and the Subversion of Identity*. New York: Routledge, 2006.

Calvin, John. *Institutes of the Christian Religion.* Edited by John T. McNeill. Translated by Ford Lewis Battles. 2 vols. Library of Christian Classics. Louisville, KY: Westminster John Knox, 2006.

Campbell, Douglas A. *The Deliverance of God: An Apocalyptic Rereading of Justification in Paul.* Grand Rapids: Eerdmans, 2009.

———. "Natural Theology in Paul? Reading Romans 1.19–20." *International Journal of Systematic Theology* 1, no. 3 (1999) 231–52.

Charles, J. Daryl. "Burying the Wrong Corpse: Evangelicals and Natural Law." In *Natural Law and Evangelical Political Thought,* edited by Bryan McGraw, Jesse Covington, and Micah Watson, 3–34. Lanham, MD: Lexington, 2013.

Clough, David. *On Animals, Volume One: Systematic Theology.* London: T. & T. Clark, 2012.

Colijn, Brenda B. *Images of Salvation in the New Testament.* Downers Grove, IL: IVP Academic, 2010.

Collier, Mary Jane. "Critical Community Engagement and Dancing with Cultural Difference: Analytical Framework and Research Itinerary." In *Community Engagement and Intercultural Praxis: Dancing with Difference in Diverse Contexts,* edited by Mary Jane Collier, 1–30. New York: Lang, 2014.

Collins Winn, Christian T., and Amos Yong. "The Apocalypse of Colonialism: Notes toward a Postcolonial Eschatology." In *Evangelical Postcolonial Conversations: Global Awakenings in Theology and Praxis,* edited by Kay Higuera Smith, Jayachitra Lalitha, and L. Daniel Hawk, 139–51. Downers Grove, IL: IVP Academic, 2014.

Cone, James H. *God of the Oppressed.* New York: Seabury, 1975.

Congdon, David W. "*Apokatastasis* and Apostolicity: A Response to Oliver Crisp on the Question of Barth's Universalism." *Scottish Journal of Theology* 67, no. 4 (2014) 464–80.

———. "Emancipatory Intercultural Hermeneutics: Interpreting Theo Sundermeier's *Differenzhermeneutik.*" *Mission Studies* 33 (2016) 127–46.

———. "Eschatologizing Apocalyptic: An Assessment of the Present Conversation on Pauline Apocalyptic." In *Apocalyptic and the Future of Theology: With and beyond J. Louis Martyn,* edited by Joshua B. Davis and Douglas K. Harink, 118–36. Eugene, OR: Cascade, 2012.

———. *The Mission of Demythologizing: Rudolf Bultmann's Dialectical Theology.* Minneapolis: Fortress, 2015.

———. *Rudolf Bultmann: A Companion to His Theology.* Eugene, OR: Cascade, 2015.

———. "The Spirit of Freedom: Eberhard Jüngel's Theology of the Third Article." In *Indicative of Grace—Imperative of Freedom: Essays in Honour of Eberhard Jüngel in His 80th Year,* edited by R. David Nelson, 13–27. London: Bloomsbury T. & T. Clark, 2014.

———. "Theology as Theanthropology: Barth's Theology of Existence in Its Existentialist Context." In *Karl Barth and the Making of Evangelical Theology: A Fifty-Year Perspective,* edited by Clifford B. Anderson and Bruce L. McCormack, 30–66. Grand Rapids: Eerdmans, 2015.

———. "The Trinitarian Shape of πίστις: A Theological Exegesis of Galatians." *Journal of Theological Interpretation* 2, no. 2 (2008) 231–58.

Covington, Jesse. "The Grammar of Virtue: Augustine and the Natural Law." In *Natural Law and Evangelical Political Thought,* edited by Bryan McGraw, Jesse Covington, and Micah Watson, 167–93. Lanham, MD: Lexington, 2013.

Dalferth, Ingolf U. *Crucified and Resurrected: Restructuring the Grammar of Christology.* Grand Rapids: Baker Academic, 2015.

Davies, W. D., and Dale C. Allison. *A Critical and Exegetical Commentary on the Gospel according to Saint Matthew.* 3 vols. Edinburgh: T. & T. Clark, 1988–97.

Deacon, Terrence, and Tyrone Cashman. "The Role of Symbolic Capacity in the Origins of Religion." *Journal for the Study of Religion, Nature and Culture* 3, no. 4 (2009) 490–517.

DeHart, Paul J. *The Trial of the Witnesses: The Rise and Decline of Postliberal Theology.* Oxford: Blackwell, 2006.

Deleuze, Gilles. *Difference and Repetition.* Translated by Paul Patton. New York: Columbia University Press, 1994.

Dempsey, Michael T., ed. *Trinity and Election in Contemporary Theology.* Grand Rapids: Eerdmans, 2011.

Descola, Philippe. *Beyond Nature and Culture.* Translated by Janet Lloyd. Chicago: University of Chicago Press, 2013.

Deutscher Evangelischer Kirchenausschuss. *Die Bekenntnisschriften der evangelisch-lutherischen Kirche.* Göttingen: Vandenhoeck & Ruprecht, 1930.

Dieter, Theodor. *Der junge Luther und Aristoteles: Eine historisch-systematische Untersuchung zum Verhältnis von Theologie und Philosophie.* Berlin: De Gruyter, 2001.

Dupré, John. *Humans and Other Animals.* Oxford: Clarendon, 2002.

Eagleton, Terry. *Reason, Faith, & Revolution: Reflections on the God Debate.* New Haven: Yale University Press, 2009.

Ebeling, Gerhard. *Dogmatik des christlichen Glaubens.* 3 vols. Tübingen: Mohr, 1979.

———. "Erwägungen zur Eschatologie." 1964. In *Wort und Glaube, Dritter Band: Beiträge zur Fundamentaltheologie, Soteriologie und Ekklesiologie,* 428–47. Tübingen: Mohr, 1975.

———. "Existenz zwischen Gott und Gott: Ein Beitrag zur Frage nach der Existenz Gottes." 1965. In *Wort und Glaube, Zweiter Band: Beiträge zur Fundamentaltheologie und zur Lehre von Gott,* 257–86. Tübingen: Mohr, 1969.

———. *The Problem of Historicity in the Church and Its Proclamation.* Translated by Grover Foley. Philadelphia: Fortress, 1967.

———. "The Significance of the Critical Historical Method for Church and Theology in Protestantism." 1950. In *Word and Faith,* 17–61. Philadelphia: Fortress, 1963.

———. "Theologische Erwägungen über das Gewissen." In *Wort und Glaube,* 429–46. Tübingen: Mohr, 1960.

———. *Theology and Proclamation: Dialogue with Bultmann.* Translated by John Riches. Philadelphia: Fortress, 1966.

Erickson, Millard J. *Introducing Christian Doctrine.* Edited by L. Arnold Hustad. 2nd ed. Grand Rapids: Baker Academic, 2001.

Fatum, Lone. "Image of God and Glory of Man: Women in the Pauline Congregations." In *The Image of God: Gender Models in Judaeo-Christian Tradition,* edited by Kari Elisabeth Børresen, 50–133. Minneapolis: Fortress, 1995.

Ferguson, Everett. *The Church of Christ: A Biblical Ecclesiology for Today.* Grand Rapids: Eerdmans, 1996.

Feuerbach, Ludwig. *The Essence of Christianity.* Translated by George Eliot. London: Chapman, 1854.

———. *Das Wesen des Christentums.* 2nd ed. Leipzig: Wigand, 1843.

Finney, Charles G. *Lectures on Revivals of Religion*. 2nd ed. New York: Leavitt, Lord & Co., 1835.

Flett, John G. *Apostolicity: The Ecumenical Question in World Christian Perspective*. Downers Grove, IL: IVP Academic, 2016.

———. "Communion as Propaganda: Reinhard Hütter and the Missionary Witness of the 'Church as Public.'" *Scottish Journal of Theology* 62, no. 4 (2009) 457–76.

Flusser, David. *Judaism of the Second Temple Period*. Translated by Azzan Yadin. 2 vols. Grand Rapids: Eerdmans, 2007.

Ford, David. *Self and Salvation: Being Transformed*. Cambridge: Cambridge University Press, 1999.

Forde, Gerhard O. *A More Radical Gospel: Essays on Eschatology, Authority, Atonement, and Ecumenism*. Edited by Mark C. Mattes and Steven D. Paulson. Grand Rapids: Eerdmans, 2004.

France, R. T. *The Gospel of Matthew*. The New International Commentary on the New Testament. Grand Rapids: Eerdmans, 2007.

Frei, Hans W. *The Identity of Jesus Christ: The Hermeneutical Bases of Dogmatic Theology*. Eugene, OR: Wipf and Stock, 1997.

———. *Theology and Narrative: Selected Essays*. Edited by George Hunsinger and William C. Placher. New York: Oxford University Press, 1993.

Frost, Michael. *Exiles: Living Missionally in a Post-Christian Culture*. Peabody, MA: Hendrickson, 2006.

Fuchs, Ernst. "Christus das Ende der Geschichte." 1949. In *Zur Frage nach dem historischen Jesus*, 79–99. Tübingen: Mohr, 1960.

———. "Jesus Christus in Person: Zum Problem der Geschichtlichkeit der Offenbarung." 1944. In *Zur Frage nach dem historischen Jesus*, 21–54. Tübingen: Mohr, 1960.

Gerhard, Johann. *Loci theologici*. 12 vols. Berlin: Schlawitz, 1863–85.

Gibbs, Raymond W. *Embodiment and Cognitive Science*. Cambridge: Cambridge University Press, 2006.

Gillespie, Thomas W. *The First Theologians: A Study in Early Christian Prophecy*. Grand Rapids: Eerdmans, 1994.

Gockel, Matthias. *Barth and Schleiermacher on the Doctrine of Election: A Systematic-Theological Comparison*. Oxford: Oxford University Press, 2006.

Gogarten, Friedrich. *Christ the Crisis*. Translated by R. A. Wilson. Richmond, VA: John Knox, 1970.

———. *Demythologizing and History*. London: SCM, 1955.

———. *Despair and Hope for Our Time*. Translated by Thomas Wieser. Philadelphia: Pilgrim, 1970.

———. *Politische Ethik: Versuch einer Grundlegung*. Jena, Germany: Diederichs, 1932.

Goodman, Lenn E. *Religious Pluralism and Values in the Public Sphere*. New York: Cambridge University Press, 2014.

Gorman, Michael J. *Inhabiting the Cruciform God: Kenosis, Justification, and Theosis in Paul's Narrative Soteriology*. Grand Rapids: Eerdmans, 2009.

Gosine, Andil. "Non-white Reproduction and Same-Sex Eroticism: Queer Acts against Nature." In *Queer Ecologies: Sex, Nature, Politics, Desire*, edited by Catriona Mortimer-Sandilands and Bruce Erickson, 149–72. Bloomington, IN: Indiana University Press, 2010.

Grant, Edward. *Much Ado about Nothing: Theories of Space and Vacuum from the Middle Ages to the Scientific Revolution.* Cambridge: Cambridge University Press, 1981.

Green, Joel B. "Kaleidoscopic View." In *The Nature of the Atonement: Four Views*, edited by James K. Beilby and Paul R. Eddy, 157–85. Downers Grove, IL: IVP Academic, 2006.

Greggs, Tom. *Barth, Origen, and Universal Salvation: Restoring Particularity.* Oxford: Oxford University Press, 2009.

———. "Church and Sacraments." In *Sanctified by Grace: A Theology of the Christian Life*, edited by Kent Eilers and Kyle Strobel, 157–69. London: Bloomsbury T. & T. Clark, 2014.

———. "'Jesus is Victor': Passing the Impasse of Barth on Universalism." *Scottish Journal of Theology* 60, no. 2 (2007) 196–212.

———. "Religionless Christianity and the Political Implications of Theological Speech: What Bonhoeffer's Theology Yields to a World of Fundamentalisms." *International Journal of Systematic Theology* 11, no. 3 (2009) 293–308.

Gregorii Nysseni. *De Vita Moysis.* Edited by Herbert Musurillo. Gregorii Nysseni Opera 7.1. Leiden: Brill, 1964.

Gregory of Nyssa. *The Life of Moses.* Translated by Abraham J. Malherbe and Everett Ferguson. The Classics of Western Spirituality. New York: Paulist, 1978.

Griffiths, Paul J. *Decreation: The Last Things of All Creatures.* Waco, TX: Baylor University Press, 2014.

Gundry, Robert H. *Mark: A Commentary on His Apology for the Cross.* Grand Rapids: Eerdmans, 1993.

Gunton, Colin E. *Act and Being: Towards a Theology of the Divine Attributes.* London: SCM, 2002.

———. *The Barth Lectures.* Edited by Paul Brazier. London: T. & T. Clark, 2007.

Haraway, Donna Jeanne. *When Species Meet.* Minneapolis: University of Minnesota Press, 2008.

Harrison, Peter. *The Bible, Protestantism, and the Rise of Natural Science.* Cambridge: Cambridge University Press, 1998.

Hart, David Bentley. *Atheist Delusions: The Christian Revolution and Its Fashionable Enemies.* New Haven: Yale University Press, 2009.

———. *The Experience of God: Being, Consciousness, Bliss.* New Haven, CT: Yale University Press, 2013.

Hays, Richard B. *The Faith of Jesus Christ: The Narrative Substructure of Galatians 3:1—4:11.* 2nd ed. Grand Rapids: Eerdmans, 2002.

Heaney, Robert S. "Prospects and Problems for Evangelical Postcolonialisms." In *Evangelical Postcolonial Conversations: Global Awakenings in Theology and Praxis*, edited by Kay Higuera Smith, Jayachitra Lalitha, and L. Daniel Hawk, 29–42. Downers Grove, IL: IVP Academic, 2014.

Hector, Kevin W. *The Theological Project of Modernism: Faith and the Conditions of Mineness.* Oxford: Oxford University Press, 2015.

———. *Theology without Metaphysics: God, Language, and the Spirit of Recognition.* Cambridge: Cambridge University Press, 2011.

Herrmann, Wilhelm. "Die Busse des evangelischen Christen." *Zeitschrift für Theologie und Kirche* 1 (1891) 28–81.

Hick, John. *Death and Eternal Life.* Louisville, KY: Westminster John Knox, 1994.

———. *Evil and the God of Love.* 2nd ed. Basingstoke, UK: Palgrave Macmillan, 2007.

————. *God Has Many Names*. Philadelphia: Westminster, 1982.

————. *The Metaphor of God Incarnate: Christology in a Pluralistic Age*. 2nd ed. Louisville, KY: Westminster John Knox, 2006.

Hodge, Charles. *Systematic Theology*. 3 vols. New York: Scribner, 1872.

Hoekendijk, Johannes Christiaan. *The Church Inside Out*. Translated by Isaac C. Rottenberg. Philadelphia: Westminster, 1966.

————. *Kirche und Volk in der deutschen Missionswissenschaft*. Edited by Erich-Walter Pollmann. Munich: Kaiser, 1967.

Hunsinger, George. *How to Read Karl Barth: The Shape of His Theology*. New York: Oxford University Press, 1991.

————. "What Karl Barth Learned from Martin Luther." 1998. In *Disruptive Grace: Studies in the Theology of Karl Barth*, 279–304. Grand Rapids: Eerdmans, 2000.

Hütter, Reinhard. "Karl Barth's 'Dialectical Catholicity': Sic et non." *Modern Theology* 16, no. 2 (2000) 137–57.

————. *Suffering Divine Things: Theology as Church Practice*. Grand Rapids: Eerdmans, 2000.

Jefford, Clayton N. *The Epistle to Diognetus (with the Fragment of Quadratus). Introduction, Text, and Commentary*. Oxford: Oxford Univiversity Press, 2013.

Jenson, Robert W. "Christ as Culture 1: Christ as Polity." *International Journal of Systematic Theology* 5, no. 3 (2003) 323–29.

————. "On the Doctrine of Atonement." *Princeton Seminary Bulletin* 27, no. 2 (2006) 100–108.

————. *Systematic Theology*. 2 vols. New York: Oxford University Press, 1997–99.

————. "You Wonder Where the Spirit Went." *Pro Ecclesia* 2, no. 3 (1993) 296–304.

Johnson, Keith L. "A Reappraisal of Karl Barth's Theological Development and His Dialogue with Catholicism." *International Journal of Systematic Theology* 14, no. 1 (2012) 3–25.

Johnston, Sarah Iles. *Religions of the Ancient World: A Guide*. Cambridge: Belknap Press of Harvard University Press, 2004.

Jüngel, Eberhard. "Anfechtung und Gewißheit des Glaubens." 1976. In *Ganz werden*, 89–114. Tübingen: Mohr Siebeck, 2003.

————. "'Auch das Schöne muß sterben'—Schönheit im Lichte der Wahrheit: Theologische Bemerkungen zum ästhetischen Verhältnis." 1984. In *Wertlose Wahrheit: Zur Identität und Relevanz des christlichen Glaubens—Theologische Erörterungen III*, 378–96. Munich: Kaiser, 1990.

————. *Death: The Riddle and the Mystery*. Translated by Iain and Ute Nicol. Philadelphia: Westminster, 1975.

————. "The Dogmatic Significance of the Question of the Historical Jesus." In *Theological Essays II*, edited by J. B. Webster, 82–119. Edinburgh: T. & T. Clark, 1995.

————. "Der Geist der Hoffnung und des Trostes: Thesen zur Begründung des eschatologischen Lehrstücks vom Reich der Freiheit." 2000. In *Ganz werden*, 306–22. Tübingen: Mohr Siebeck, 2003.

————. "Das Gesetz zwischen Adam und Christus: Eine theologische Studie zu Röm 5,12–21." 1963. In *Unterwegs zur Sache: Theologische Bemerkungen*, 145–72. Munich: Kaiser, 1972.

————. *God as the Mystery of the World: On the Foundation of the Theology of the Crucified One in the Dispute between Theism and Atheism.* Translated by Darrell L. Guder. Grand Rapids: Eerdmans, 1983.

————. *God's Being Is in Becoming: The Trinitarian Being of God in the Theology of Karl Barth. A Paraphrase.* Translated by John Webster. Grand Rapids: Eerdmans, 2001.

————. *Gott als Geheimnis der Welt: Zur Begründung der Theologie des Gekreuzigten im Streit zwischen Theismus und Atheismus.* Tübingen: Mohr, 1977.

————. *Gottes Sein ist im Werden: Verantwortliche Rede vom Sein Gottes bei Karl Barth: Eine Paraphrase.* 4th ed. Tübingen: Mohr, 1986.

————. "Humanity in Correspondence to God." In *Theological Essays I,* edited by J. B. Webster, 124–53. Edinburgh: T. & T. Clark, 1989.

————. *Justification: The Heart of the Christian Faith.* Translated by Jeffrey F. Cayzer. Edinburgh: T. & T. Clark, 2001.

————. "Mission und Evangelisation." 1999. In *Ganz werden,* 115–36. Tübingen: Mohr Siebeck, 2003.

————. "Nemo contra deum nisi deus ipse: Zum Verhältnis von theologia crucis und Trinitätslehre." In *Ganz werden,* 231–52. Tübingen: Mohr Siebeck, 2003.

————. "On Becoming Truly Human." In *Theological Essays II,* edited by J. B. Webster, 216–40. Edinburgh: T. & T. Clark, 1995.

————. *Paulus und Jesus: Eine Untersuchung zur Präzisierung der Frage nach dem Ursprung der Christologie.* Tübingen: Mohr, 1962.

————. "Säkularisierung—Theologische Anmerkungen zum Begriff einer weltlichen Welt." 1972. In *Entsprechungen: Gott, Wahrheit, Mensch. Theologische Erörterungen,* 285–89. Munich: Kaiser, 1980.

————. "Das Sein Jesu Christi als Ereignis der Versöhnung Gottes mit einer gottlosen Welt: Die Hingabe des Gekreuzigten." 1978. In *Entsprechungen: Gott, Wahrheit, Mensch. Theologische Erörterungen,* 276–84. Munich: Kaiser, 1980.

————. "Thesen zur Grundlegung der Christologie." 1969–70. In *Unterwegs zur Sache: Theologische Bemerkungen,* 274–95. Munich: Kaiser, 1972.

————. *Tod.* Stuttgart: Kreuz-Verlag, 1971.

————. "Der Tod als Geheimnis des Lebens." 1976. In *Entsprechungen: Gott, Wahrheit, Mensch. Theologische Erörterungen,* 327–54. Munich: Kaiser, 1980.

————. "Das Verhältnis von 'ökonomischer' und 'immanenter' Trinität." 1975. In *Entsprechungen: Gott, Wahrheit, Mensch. Theologische Erörterungen,* 265–75. Munich: Kaiser, 1980.

————. "Die Wahrheit des Mythos und die Notwendigkeit der Entmythologisierung." 1990. In *Indikative der Gnade—Imperative der Freiheit: Theologische Erörterungen* 4, 40–57. Tübingen: Mohr Siebeck, 2000.

————. "Zur Lehre vom heiligen Geist: Thesen." In *Die Mitte des Neuen Testaments: Einheit und Vielfalt neutestamentlicher Theologie,* edited by Ulrich Luz and Hans Weder, 97–118. Göttingen: Vandenhoeck & Ruprecht, 1983.

Kangas, David J. *Kierkegaard's Instant: On Beginnings.* Bloomington, IN: Indiana University Press, 2007.

Käsemann, Ernst. *Commentary on Romans.* Translated by Geoffrey W. Bromiley. Grand Rapids: Eerdmans, 1980.

————. *Essays on New Testament Themes.* Studies in Biblical Theology no 41. Translated by W. J. Montague. London: SCM, 1964.

———. *New Testament Questions of Today.* Translated by W. J. Montague. London: SCM, 1969.

———. *On Being a Disciple of the Crucified Nazarene: Unpublished Lectures and Sermons.* Edited by Rudolf Landau and Wolfgang Kraus. Translated by Roy A. Harrisville. Grand Rapids: Eerdmans, 2010.

———. *Paulinische Perspektiven.* Tübingen: Mohr, 1969.

———. *Perspectives on Paul.* Philadelphia: Fortress, 1971.

Kay, James F. *Christus Praesens: A Reconsideration of Rudolf Bultmann's Christology.* Grand Rapids: Eerdmans, 1994.

Keller, Catherine. *Apocalypse Now and Then: A Feminist Guide to the End of the World.* Boston: Beacon, 1996.

Kelly, Geffrey B. "'Unconscious Christianity' and the 'Anonymous Christian' in the Theology of Dietrich Bonhoeffer and Karl Rahner." *Philosophy & Theology* 9, no. 1–2 (1995) 117–49.

Kelsey, David H. *Eccentric Existence: A Theological Anthropology.* Louisville: Westminster John Knox, 2009.

Kierkegaard, Søren. *Repetition and Philosophical Crumbs.* Translated by M. G. Piety. Oxford: Oxford University Press, 2009.

Kim, Sung-Sup. *Deus Providebit: Calvin, Schleiermacher, and Barth on the Providence of God.* Minneapolis: Fortress, 2014.

Knitter, Paul F. *One Earth Many Religions: Multifaith Dialogue and Global Responsibility.* Maryknoll, NY: Orbis, 1995.

Kolb, Robert. "God Kills to Make Alive: Romans 6 and Luther's Understanding of Justification (1535)." *Lutheran Quarterly* 12, no. 1 (1998) 33–56.

Kolb, Robert, and Timothy J. Wengert, eds. *The Book of Concord: The Confessions of the Evangelical Lutheran Church.* Minneapolis: Fortress, 2000.

Kraidy, Marwan M. *Hybridity, or the Cultural Logic of Globalization.* Philadelphia: Temple University Press, 2005.

Kreck, Walter. *Die Zukunft des Gekommenen: Grundprobleme der Eschatologie.* Munich: Kaiser, 1961.

Kuck, David W. *Judgment and Community Conflict: Paul's Use of Apocalyptic Judgment Language in 1 Corinthians 3:5—4:5.* Leiden: Brill, 1992.

Lacoste, Jean-Yves. *Experience and the Absolute: Disputed Questions on the Humanity of Man.* New York: Fordham University Press, 2004.

Lakoff, George, and Mark Johnson. *Philosophy in the Flesh: The Embodied Mind and Its Challenge to Western Thought.* New York: Basic, 1999.

Larchet, Jean-Claude. "Ancestral Guilt according to St. Maximus the Confessor: A Bridge between Eastern and Western Conceptions." *Sobornost* 20 (1998) 26–48.

Lehmann, Paul L. "Karl Barth, Theologian of Permanent Revolution." *Union Seminary Quarterly Review* 28, no. 1 (1972) 67–81.

Leithart, Peter J. *Delivered from the Elements of the World: Atonement, Justification, Mission.* Downers Grove, IL: IVP Academic, 2016.

Lindbeck, George A. "Atonement and the Hermeneutics of Social Embodiment." *Pro Ecclesia* 5, no. 2 (1996) 144–60.

———. "Confession and Community: An Israel-like View of the Church." *Christian Century* 107, no. 16 (1990) 492–96.

———. "The Gospel's Uniqueness: Election and Untranslatability." *Modern Theology* 13, no. 4 (1997) 423–50.

————. *The Nature of Doctrine: Religion and Theology in a Postliberal Age*. 25th Anniversary ed. Louisville, KY: Westminster John Knox, 2009.

————. "The Sectarian Future of the Church." In *The God Experience: Essays in Hope*, edited by Joseph P. Whelan, 226–43. New York: Newman, 1971.

Lohse, Bernhard. *Martin Luther's Theology: Its Historical and Systematic Development*. Translated by Roy A. Harrisville. Minneapolis: Fortress, 1999.

Loon, Hans van. *The Dyophysite Christology of Cyril of Alexandria*. Leiden: Brill, 2009.

Lubac, Henri de. *Corpus Mysticum: The Eucharist and the Church in the Middle Ages*. Edited by Laurence Paul Hemming and Susan Frank Parsons. Translated by Gemma Simmonds, Richard Price, and Christopher Stephens. London: SCM, 2006.

Luther, Martin. *Briefwechsel*. 18 vols. Weimar: Böhlaus Nachfolger, 1930.

————. *D. Martin Luthers Werke: Kritische Gesamtausgabe*. Weimar: Böhlau, 1883-.

————. *Luther's Works*. Edited by Jaroslav Pelikan and Helmut T. Lehman. American ed. 55 vols. Philadelphia: Fortress, 1955–72.

Luz, Ulrich. *Das Geschichtsverständnis des Paulus*. Munich: Kaiser, 1968.

MacDonald, Gregory, ed. *"All Shall Be Well": Explorations in Universalism and Christian Theology from Origen to Moltmann*. Eugene, OR: Cascade, 2011.

————. *The Evangelical Universalist*. 1st ed. Eugene, OR: Cascade Books, 2006.

————. "Introduction: Between Heresy and Dogma." In *"All Shall Be Well": Explorations in Universalism and Christian Theology from Origen to Moltmann*, edited by Gregory MacDonald, 1–25. Eugene, OR: Cascade, 2011.

Mackintosh, H. R. *The Doctrine of the Person of Jesus Christ*. New York: Scribner's Sons, 1912.

Marcus, Joel. *Mark 8–16: A New Translation with Introduction and Commentary*. The Anchor Yale Bible 27A. New Haven, CT: Yale University Press, 2009.

————. *The Way of the Lord: Christological Exegesis of the Old Testament in the Gospel of Mark*. Louisville, KY: Westminster John Knox, 1992.

Martyn, J. Louis. "The Apocalyptic Gospel in Galatians." *Interpretation* 54, no. 3 (2000) 246–66.

————. *Galatians: A New Translation with Introduction and Commentary*. New York: Doubleday, 1997.

————. *Theological Issues in the Letters of Paul*. Nashville: Abingdon, 1997.

Maximus the Confessor. *Maximus Confessor: Selected Writings*. Translated by George Berthold. Classics of Western Spirituality. Mahwah, NJ: Paulist, 1985.

————. *On the Cosmic Mystery of Jesus Christ: Selected Writings*. Translated by Paul M. Blowers and Robert Louis Wilken. Crestwood, NY: St. Vladimir's Seminary Press, 2003.

McCall, Thomas H. *Forsaken: The Trinity and the Cross, and Why It Matters*. Downers Grove, IL: IVP Academic, 2012.

McCormack, Bruce L. "The Doctrine of the Trinity after Barth: An Attempt to Reconstruct Barth's Doctrine in the Light of His Later Christology." In *Trinitarian Theology after Barth*, edited by Myk Habets and Phillip Tolliday, 87–118. Eugene, OR: Pickwick, 2011.

————. "Historical-Criticism and Dogmatic Interest in Karl Barth's Theological Exegesis of the New Testament." *Lutheran Quarterly* 5, no. 2 (1991) 211–25.

————. *Karl Barth's Critically Realistic Dialectical Theology: Its Genesis and Development, 1909–1936*. New York: Oxford University Press, 1995.

————. "The Ontological Presuppositions of Barth's Doctrine of the Atonement." In *The Glory of the Atonement: Biblical, Historical, and Practical Perspectives*, edited by Charles E. Hill and Frank A. James III, 346–66. Downers Grove, IL: IVP Academic, 2004.

————. *Orthodox and Modern: Studies in the Theology of Karl Barth*. Grand Rapids: Baker Academic, 2008.

————. "Processions and Missions: A Point of Convergence between Thomas Aquinas and Karl Barth." In *Thomas Aquinas and Karl Barth: An Unofficial Catholic-Protestant Dialogue*, edited by Bruce L. McCormack and Thomas Joseph White, 99–126. Grand Rapids: Eerdmans, 2013.

————. "So That He May Be Merciful to All: Karl Barth and the Problem of Universalism." In *Karl Barth and American Evangelicalism*, edited by Bruce L. McCormack and Clifford B. Anderson, 227–49. Grand Rapids: Eerdmans, 2011.

————. "Witness to the Word: A Barthian Engagement with Reinhard Hütter's Ontology of the Church." *Zeitschrift für Dialektische Theologie* Supplement Series 5 (2011) 59–77.

McDonald, Suzanne. "Barth's 'Other' Doctrine of Election in the *Church Dogmatics*." *International Journal of Systematic Theology* 9, no. 2 (2007) 134–47.

McGinn, Bernard. *The Foundations of Mysticism*. The Presence of God 1. New York: Crossroad, 1991.

McGrath, Alister E. *Christian Theology: An Introduction*. 5th ed. Malden, MA: Wiley-Blackwell, 2011.

————. *A Scientific Theology*. 3 vols. Grand Rapids: Eerdmans, 2001–3.

McGuckin, John A. *Saint Cyril of Alexandria and the Christological Controversy*. Crestwood, NY: St. Vladimir's Seminary Press, 2004.

McMaken, W. Travis. "Definitive, Defective or Deft? Reassessing Barth's Doctrine of Baptism in *Church Dogmatics* IV/4." *International Journal of Systematic Theology* 17, no. 1 (2015) 89–114.

————. *The Sign of the Gospel: Toward an Evangelical Doctrine of Infant Baptism After Karl Barth*. Minneapolis: Fortress, 2013.

Melanchthon, Philipp, and Martin Bucer. *Melanchthon and Bucer*. Edited by Wilhelm Pauck. Library of Christian Classics 19. Louisville: Westminster John Knox, 2006.

Migne, J.-P., ed. *Patrologia Latina*. 221 vols. Paris, 1844–65.

Mikalson, Jon D. *Ancient Greek Religion*. 2nd ed. Malden, MA: Wiley-Blackwell, 2010.

Milbank, John. *Theology and Social Theory: Beyond Secular Reason*. Oxford: Blackwell, 1991.

————. *The Word Made Strange: Theology, Language, Culture*. Oxford: Blackwell, 1997.

Milbank, John, and Catherine Pickstock. *Truth in Aquinas*. London: Routledge, 2001.

Miller, Patrick D. *The Religion of Ancient Israel*. Louisville: Westminster John Knox, 2000.

Mills, Antonia, and Richard Slobodin, eds. *Amerindian Rebirth: Reincarnation Belief among North American Indians and Inuit*. Toronto: University of Toronto Press, 1994.

Moltmann, Jürgen. *The Crucified God: The Cross of Christ as the Foundation and Criticism of Christian Theology*. Translated by R. A. Wilson and John Bowden. New York: Harper & Row, 1974.

————. *God for a Secular Society: The Public Relevance of Theology*. Minneapolis: Fortress, 1999.

———. *The Trinity and the Kingdom: The Doctrine of God.* Translated by Margaret Kohl. San Francisco: Harper & Row, 1981.

Mortimer-Sandilands, Catriona, and Bruce Erickson, eds. *Queer Ecologies: Sex, Nature, Politics, Desire.* Bloomington, IN: Indiana University Press, 2010.

Moss, Candida R. *The Myth of Persecution: How Early Christians Invented a Story of Martyrdom.* New York: HarperOne, 2013.

Mostert, Walter. *Glaube und Hermeneutik: Gesammelte Aufsätze.* Edited by Pierre Bühler and Gerhard Ebeling. Tübingen: Mohr Siebeck, 1998.

Myers, David G. "A Levels-of-Explanation View." In *Psychology & Christianity: Five Views*, edited by Eric L. Johnson, 49–78. Downers Grove, IL: IVP Academic, 2010.

Nagel, Norman E. "'Heresy, Doctor Luther, Heresy!': The Person and Work of Christ." In *Seven-Headed Luther: Essays in Commemoration of a Quincentenary, 1483–1983*, edited by Peter Newman Brooks, 25–49. Oxford: Clarendon, 1983.

Neill, Stephen. *Creative Tension.* London: Edinburgh House, 1959.

Nelson, R. David. *The Interruptive Word: Eberhard Jüngel on the Sacramental Structure of God's Relation to the World.* London: Bloomsbury T. & T. Clark, 2013.

Nicholas of Cusa. *Selected Spiritual Writings.* Translated by H. Lawrence Bond. New York: Paulist, 1997.

Noll, Mark A. *America's God: From Jonathan Edwards to Abraham Lincoln.* New York: Oxford University Press, 2002.

Novakovic, Lidija. *Raised from the Dead according to Scripture: The Role of Israel's Scripture in the Early Christian Interpretations of Jesus' Resurrection.* London: Bloomsbury T. & T. Clark, 2012.

Obeyesekere, Gananath. *Imagining Karma: Ethical Transformation in Amerindian, Buddhist, and Greek Rebirth.* Berkeley: University of California Press, 2002.

Ochs, Peter. *Another Reformation: Postliberal Christianity and the Jews.* Grand Rapids: Baker Academic, 2011.

Ogden, Schubert M. *Christ without Myth: A Study Based on the Theology of Rudolf Bultmann.* New York: Harper, 1961.

Ott, Heinrich. "What Is Systematic Theology?" In *The Later Heidegger and Theology: New Frontiers in Theology, Volume 1*, edited by James M. Robinson and John B. Cobb, 77–111. New York: Harper and Row, 1963.

Padgett, Alan G. *As Christ Submits to the Church: A Biblical Understanding of Leadership and Mutual Submission.* Grand Rapids: Baker Academic, 2011.

Pannenberg, Wolfhart. *Jesus: God and Man.* Translated by Lewis L. Wilkins and Duane A. Priebe. Philadelphia: Westminster, 1968.

———. *Systematic Theology.* Translated by Geoffrey W. Bromiley. 3 vols. Grand Rapids: Eerdmans, 1991–98.

———. *Theology and the Kingdom of God.* Philadelphia: Westminster, 1969.

———. *Toward a Theology of Nature: Essays on Science and Faith.* Edited by Ted Peters. Louisville: Westminster/John Knox, 1993.

Papandrea, James L. *The Earliest Christologies: Five Images of Christ in the Postapostolic Age.* Downers Grove, IL: IVP Academic, 2016.

Parry, Robin A., and Christopher H. Partridge. "Introduction." In *Universal Salvation?: The Current Debate*, edited by Robin A. Parry and Christopher H. Partridge, xv–xxvii. Grand Rapids: Eerdmans, 2003.

Peirce, Charles S. *The Essential Peirce: Selected Philosophical Writings, Volume 2 (1893–1913)*. Edited by Peirce Edition Project. Bloomington, IN: Indiana University Press, 1998.

Pelikan, Jaroslav. *The Christian Tradition: A History of the Development of Doctrine*. 5 vols. Chicago: University of Chicago Press, 1971–89.

Pickard, Stephen K. *Seeking the Church: An Introduction to Ecclesiology*. London: SCM, 2012.

Pickstock, Catherine. *After Writing: On the Liturgical Consummation of Philosophy*. Oxford: Blackwell, 1998.

———. *Repetition and Identity*. Oxford: Oxford University Press, 2013.

Polanyi, Michael. *Personal Knowledge: Towards a Post-Critical Philosophy*. London: Routledge, 1958.

Porter, Jean. *Nature as Reason: A Thomistic Theory of the Natural Law*. Grand Rapids: Eerdmans, 2004.

Portier-Young, Anathea. *Apocalypse against Empire: Theologies of Resistance in Early Judaism*. Grand Rapids: Eerdmans, 2011.

Powell, Samuel M. *The Trinity in German Thought*. Cambridge: Cambridge University Press, 2001.

Przywara, Erich. *Analogia Entis: Metaphysics. Original Structure and Universal Rhythm*. Translated by John R. Betz and David Bentley Hart. Grand Rapids: Eerdmans, 2014.

Pseudo-Dionysius the Areopagite. *Pseudo-Dionysius: The Complete Works*. Edited by Colm Luibhéid and Paul Rorem. New York: Paulist, 1987.

Pullman, Philip. *The Good Man Jesus and the Scoundrel Christ*. Edinburgh: Canongate, 2010.

Putnam, Hilary. *Realism and Reason: Philosophical Papers, Volume 3*. Cambridge: Cambridge University Press, 1983.

Rade, Martin. *Unbewußtes Christentum*. Tübingen: Mohr, 1905.

Ramelli, Ilaria. *The Christian Doctrine of Apokatastasis: A Critical Assessment from the New Testament to Eriugena*. Leiden: Brill, 2013.

Robinson, John A. T. *In the End, God: A Study of the Christian Doctrine and the Last Things—Special Edition*. Edited by Robin Parry. Eugene, OR: Cascade, 2011.

Rogers, Eugene F., Jr. "The Eclipse of the Spirit in Karl Barth." In *Conversing with Barth*, edited by Mike Higton and John C. McDowell, 173–90. Aldershot, UK: Ashgate, 2004.

Rutledge, Fleming. *The Crucifixion: Understanding the Death of Jesus Christ*. Grand Rapids: Eerdmans, 2015.

Sanneh, Lamin. *Translating the Message: The Missionary Impact on Culture*. 2nd ed. Maryknoll, NY: Orbis, 2008.

Schleiermacher, Friedrich. *Brief Outline of Theology as a Field of Study*. Translated by Terrence N. Tice. Lewiston, NY: Mellen, 1990.

Schmidt, Axel. *Die Christologie in Martin Luthers späten Disputationen*. St. Ottilien, Germany: EOS, 1990.

Schüssler Fiorenza, Elisabeth. *Bread Not Stone: The Challenge of Feminist Biblical Interpretation*. Rev. ed. Boston: Beacon, 1995.

———. *But She Said: Feminist Practices of Biblical Interpretation*. Boston: Beacon, 1992.

———. *In Memory of Her: A Feminist Theological Reconstruction of Christian Origins*. 10th Anniversary ed. New York: Crossroad, 1994.

Schuon, Frithjof. *The Transcendent Unity of Religions*. Wheaton, IL: Quest, 1984.

Schwarz, Reinhard. "Gott ist Mensch: Zur Lehre von der Person Christi bei den Ockhamisten und bei Luther." *Zeitschrift für Theologie und Kirche* 63, no. 3 (1966) 289–351.

Segal, Alan F. *Life after Death: A History of the Afterlife in the Religions of the West*. New York: Doubleday, 2004.

Seow, C. L. *Job 1–21: Interpretation and Commentary*. Grand Rapids: Eerdmans, 2013.

Sepúlveda, Juan. "Born Again: Baptism of the Spirit. A Pentecostal Perspective." In *Pentecostal Movements as an Ecumenical Challenge*, edited by Jürgen Moltmann and Karl-Josef Kuschel, 104–9. London: SCM, 1996.

Seymour, Nicole. *Strange Natures: Futurity, Empathy, and the Queer Ecological Imagination*. Urbana, IL: University of Illinois Press, 2013.

Sloterdijk, Peter. *Globes: Macrospherology*. Translated by Wieland Hoban. Spheres 2. South Pasadena, CA: Semiotext(e) 2014.

Smith, James K. A. *The Fall of Interpretation: Philosophical Foundations for a Creational Hermeneutic*. 2nd ed. Grand Rapids: Baker Academic, 2012.

Smith, Ronald Gregor. *Secular Christianity*. New York: Harper & Row, 1966.

Smith, Ted A. *The New Measures: A Theological History of Democratic Practice*. New York: Cambridge University Press, 2007.

Snyder, Timothy. *Black Earth: The Holocaust as History and Warning*. New York: Duggan, 2015.

Sölle, Dorothee. *Christ the Representative: An Essay in Theology after the 'Death of God'*. Translated by David Lewis. London: SCM, 1967.

———. *Political Theology*. Translated by John Shelley. Philadelphia: Fortress, 1974.

Solomon, Miriam. "Situated Cognition." In *Philosophy of Psychology and Cognitive Science*, edited by Paul Thagard, 413–28. Amsterdam: North-Holland, 2007.

Sorrells, Kathryn. *Intercultural Communication: Globalization and Social Justice*. Thousand Oaks, CA: SAGE, 2013.

Soskice, Janet. "Trinity and Feminism." In *The Cambridge Companion to Feminist Theology*, edited by Susan Frank Parsons, 135–50. Cambridge: Cambridge University Press, 2002.

Soulen, R. Kendall. "YHWH the Triune God." *Modern Theology* 15, no. 1 (1999) 25–54.

Stoevesandt, Hinrich. "Basel—Marburg: Ein (un)erledigter Konflikt?" In *Bibel und Mythos: Fünfzig Jahre nach Rudolf Bultmanns Entmythologisierungsprogramm*, edited by Bernd Jaspert, 91–113. Göttingen: Vandenhoeck & Ruprecht, 1991.

Sumner, Darren O. *Karl Barth and the Incarnation: Christology and the Humility of God*. London: Bloomsbury T. & T. Clark, 2014.

Sundermeier, Theo. *Den Fremden verstehen: Eine praktische Hermeneutik*. Göttingen: Vandenhoeck & Ruprecht, 1996.

———. "Erwägungen zu einer Hermeneutik interkulturellen Verstehens." 1991. In *Konvivenz und Differenz: Studien zu einer verstehenden Missionswissenschaft*, edited by Volker Küster, 87–101. Erlangen: Verlag der Ev.-Luth. Mission, 1995.

———. *Mission—Geschenk der Freiheit: Bausteine für eine Theologie der Mission*. Frankfurt am Main: Lembeck, 2005.

Tanner, Kathryn. *Christ the Key*. Cambridge: Cambridge University Press, 2010.

Taubes, Jacob. *Occidental Eschatology*. Translated by David Ratmoko. Stanford: Stanford University Press, 2009.

Teel, Karen. *Racism and the Image of God*. New York: Palgrave Macmillan, 2010.

Theodore of Mopsuestia. *Commentary on the Twelve Prophets*. Translated by Robert C. Hill. Washington, DC: The Catholic University of America Press, 2004.

Thielicke, Helmut. *The Silence of God*. Translated by Geoffrey W. Bromiley. Grand Rapids: Eerdmans, 1962.

Thiemann, Ronald F. *Revelation and Theology: The Gospel as Narrated Promise*. Notre Dame, IN: University of Notre Dame Press, 1985.

Thomas Aquinas. *Summa Theologica*. Translated by Fathers of the English Dominican Province. Complete English ed. 5 vols. Notre Dame, IN: Christian Classics, 1981.

Thompson, James. *The Church in Exile: God's Counter Culture in a Non-Christian World*. Abilene, TX: ACU, 1990.

Thunberg, Lars. *Microcosm and Mediator: The Theological Anthropology of Maximus the Confessor*. 2nd ed. Chicago: Open Court, 1995.

Tillich, Paul. *The Protestant Era*. Translated by James Luther Adams. Chicago: University of Chicago Press, 1948.

———. *Systematic Theology*. 3 vols. Chicago: University of Chicago Press, 1951–63.

Torrance, T. F. "Universalism or Election?" *Scottish Journal of Theology* 2 (1949) 310–18.

van Buren, Paul M. *The Secular Meaning of the Gospel: Based on an Analysis of its Language*. New York: Macmillan, 1963.

van Driel, Edwin Chr. *Incarnation Anyway: Arguments for Supralapsarian Christology*. New York: Oxford University Press, 2008.

———. "The Logic of Assumption." In *Exploring Kenotic Christology: The Self-Emptying of God*, edited by C. Stephen Evans, 265–90. New York: Oxford University Press, 2006.

Vanhoozer, Kevin J. "Atonement." In *Mapping Modern Theology: A Thematic and Historical Introduction*, edited by Kelly M. Kapic and Bruce L. McCormack, 175–202. Grand Rapids: Baker Academic, 2012.

———. *Remythologizing Theology: Divine Action, Passion, and Authorship*. Cambridge: Cambridge University Press, 2010.

Walls, Andrew F. *The Missionary Movement in Christian History: Studies in the Transmission of Faith*. Maryknoll, NY: Orbis, 1996.

Walton, John H. *The Lost World of Genesis One: Ancient Cosmology and the Origins Debate*. Downers Grove, IL: IVP Academic, 2009.

Wenham, Gordon J. "Sanctuary Symbolism in the Garden of Eden Story." In *Proceedings of the Ninth World Congress of Jewish Studies, Division A: The Period of the Bible*, 19–25. Jerusalem: World Union of Jewish Studies, 1986.

White, Graham. *Luther as Nominalist: A Study of the Logical Methods Used in Martin Luther's Disputations in the Light of Their Medieval Background*. Helsinki: Luther-Agricola-Society, 1994.

Wilken, Robert L. "The Church as Culture." *First Things* 142 (2004) 31–36.

———. "The Church's Way of Speaking." *First Things* 155 (2005) 27–31.

Williamson, Clark M. *A Guest in the House of Israel: Post-Holocaust Church Theology*. Louisville, KY: Westminster John Knox, 1993.

Wissenschaftliche Gesellschaft für Theologie and Deutsche Gesellschaft für Missionswissenschaft. "Mission Studies as Intercultural Theology and Its Relationship to Religious Studies." *Mission Studies* 25, no. 1 (2008) 103–8.

Wittgenstein, Ludwig. *Philosophical Investigations: The German Text, with a Revised English Translation*. Translated by G. E. M. Anscombe. 3rd ed. Malden, MA: Blackwell, 2001.

Wolters, Albert M. "Nature and Grace in the Interpretation of Proverbs 31:10–31." *Calvin Theological Journal* 19, no. 2 (1984) 153–66.

Yeago, David S. "The Bread of Life: Patristic Christology and Evangelical Soteriology in Martin Luther's Sermons on John 6." *St Vladimir's Theological Quarterly* 39, no. 3 (1995) 257–79.

———. "The New Testament and the Nicene Dogma: A Contribution to the Recovery of Theological Exegesis." In *The Theological Interpretation of Scripture: Classic and Contemporary Readings*, edited by Stephen E. Fowl, 87–100. Malden, MA: Blackwell, 1997.

Ziegler, Philip G., ed. *Eternal God, Eternal Life: Theological Investigations into the Concept of Immortality*. London: Bloomsbury T. & T. Clark, 2016.

Zoloth, Laurie. "Interrupting Your Life: An Ethics for the Coming Storm." *Journal of the American Academy of Religion* 84, no. 1 (2016) 3–24.

General Index

actualism, xvii

actus directus, 90–93, 93n110, 97, 100

actus reflexus, 90–91, 93n110, 100

afterlife, 263–74

    Barth on, 74n45, 265n9, 268–71, 273

    Jüngel on, 271–73

    See also eternal life; heaven; hell; resurrection

Agamben, Giorgio, 145, 180

agency, divine and human, 16–17

analogy, 219, 235

anarchy, 187

ancient Near East (ANE), 15n22, 52, 64, 235, 265

Anderson, Clifford, 26n7

anhypostasis, 135–38

    as interruption, 158

Anselm, 64

anthropocentrism, 204, 207–11

anthropology, 30, 131, 134–37, 211–20, 223–25, 228–30, 233, 235–39, 266

    actualistic, 229

    and the body, 219n73, 238

    canonical, 212

    eccentric, 211–13

    patristic, 109–10

    of Paul, 216–18

    queer, 230

    and suffering, 213

    and unconsciousness, 215–17

    See also human person; image of God; soul; theanthropology

apocalypse, xvii, 18, 64–72, 77, 79–83, 85, 96–97, 102, 145, 234, 267n20

    as cocrucifixion, 81–83, 85, 187

    constitutes the apostolate/church, 189, 193

    as existential interruption, 181

    of faith, 79, 151, 243

    future of, 253–54

    ground of, 250–54

    imminent, 67–69, 85, 101, 124

    inbreaking in Christ of, 244–46

    as justification, 82–83, 192

    logically prior to triunity, 255

    makes the church, 189

    paradoxical, 256

    past, 81, 85, 248

    power of, 246–51

    as retroapocalypse, 85

    of salvation, 77, 79–80, 124, 129, 138, 156, 192, 238

    unconscious, 97, 99, 121, 189, 192

    visible and invisible, 192

    See also bifocal vision; eschatology; faith: existential apocalypse of; imminent expectation; salvation

apocalyptic language and literature, 66, 68n31, 75, 115, 225n92, 267–68

apokatastasis, 3n5, 13–14, 16, 93, 155n177

Apollinaris of Laodicea, 110

apologetics, 28, 100

apostolate, 68n29, 149, 158, 182–89, 247–48

    eschatological moment of, 186–87

Ancient Documents Index

2 Corinthians

1 Corinthians

Galatians